Schooling the Movement

Schooling the Movement

The Activism of Southern Black Educators from Reconstruction through the Civil Rights Era

Edited by

DERRICK P. ALRIDGE, JON N. HALE, &
TONDRA L. LODER-JACKSON

THE UNIVERSITY OF
SOUTH CAROLINA PRESS

© 2023 University of South Carolina

Published by the University of South Carolina Press
Columbia, South Carolina 29208

www.uscpress.com

Manufactured in the United States of America

32 31 30 29 28 27 26 25 24 23
10 9 8 7 6 5 4 3 2 1

Library of Congress Cataloging-in-Publication Data
can be found at http://catalog.loc.gov/.

ISBN 978-1-64336-374-5 (hardcover)
ISBN 978-1-64336-375-2 (paperback)
ISBN 978-1-64336-376-9 (ebook)

CONTENTS

List of Illustrations *vii*

Acknowledgments *ix*

Introduction *1*

DERRICK P. ALRIDGE, JON N. HALE,
& TONDRA L. LODER-JACKSON

Part I: The Spectrum of Teacher Activism

Teaching to "Undo Their Narratively Condemned Status":
Black Educators and the Problem of Curricular Violence *15*

JARVIS R. GIVENS

Cynthia Plair Roddey: *Carolina Activist and Teacher in the Movement* *39*

ALEXIS M. JOHNSON, DANIELLE WINGFIELD,
& DERRICK P. ALRIDGE

"It Only Takes a Spark to Get a Fire Going": *Lois A. Simms and
Pedagogical Activism during the Black Freedom Struggle, 1920–2015* *57*

JON N. HALE

"We Experienced Our Freedom": *The Impact of Valued
Segregated Spaces on Teacher Practice and Activism* *76*

KRISTAN L. MCCULLUM & HUNTER HOLT

"In the Face of Her Splendid Record": *Willa Cofield Johnson and
Teacher Dismissal in the Civil Rights Era* *91*

CRYSTAL R. SANDERS

Part II: Activism Across the South and Beyond

Planning, Persistence, and Pedagogy: *How Elizabeth City State
Colored Normal School Survived North Carolina's
White Supremacy Campaign, 1898–1905* *111*

GLEN BOWMAN

"They Were Very Low Key, But They Spoke from Wisdom and Experience": *How Black Teachers Taught Self-Determination at Carver Senior High School in New Orleans* 126

KRISTEN L. BURAS

"Dedication to the Highest of Callings": *Florence Coleman Bryant, School Desegregation, and the Black Freedom Struggle in Postwar Virginia, 1946–2004* 148

ALEXANDER HYRES

Hidden in Plain Sight: *Black Educators in the "Militant Middle" of Alabama's Municipal Civil Rights Battlegrounds* 166

TONDRA L. LODER-JACKSON

From Jim Crow to the Civil Rights Movement: *The University of Missouri's Black Faculty, Staff, and Student Organizations Fight Back!* 187

VANESSA GARRY & E. PAULETTE ISAAC-SAVAGE

W. E. B. Du Bois and the University of Berlin: *The Transnational Path to Educational Activism* 205

BRYAN GANAWAY

Afterword 219

DERRICK P. ALRIDGE, JON N. HALE, & TONDRA L. LODER-JACKSON

Notes 223

Selected Bibliography 271

Contributors 277

Index 281

ILLUSTRATIONS

Cynthia Plair Roddey *49*

Hugh Cale *113*

Peter W. Moore in the classroom, 1890s *114*

Peter W. Moore with students, ca. 1899 *116*

A Curriculum Council at Carver High School *137*

Yvonne Busch with Band Students in 1973 Yearbook *141*

Lenora Condoll in 1982 Yearbook *145*

Soil Collection Jar of Elizabeth Lawrence, National
Memorial for Peace and Justice *169*

ACKNOWLEDGMENTS

The idea of a volume exploring Black educators' activism during the Black Freedom Struggle emerged from conversations between Derrick Alridge and Jon Hale during a Teachers in the Movement summer institute for teachers at the University of Virginia in 2018. The attendees at the institute were racially and ethnically diverse and inspired by the institute's workshops about teachers' involvement in the civil rights movement. Participants were inspired by civil rights–era teachers' "pedagogical activism" and the notion of teachers as activists. Our conversations were cogent at the time because the country was in the midst of a new culture war about what teachers should teach about American history and issues of race and how they should go about teaching these topics. During the institute, Jon suggested writing an edited volume about the role of Black teachers in the movement. Shortly thereafter, we began to identify scholars we hoped would contribute chapters. One of those scholars we invited was education historian Tondra Loder-Jackson. Both Jon and I were admirers of her book *Schoolhouse Activists: African American Educators and the Long Birmingham Civil Rights Movement*, so we asked her to join us as a coeditor. To our delight, Tondra accepted our invitation and was critically instrumental in bringing the volume into fruition. Since 2019, we have worked together swimmingly—so much so, it often has seemed as if we had previously edited a volume together. It has been a joy working together over the past three years.

Collectively, we are thankful to our respective institutions, University of Virginia, University of Illinois, and University of Alabama at Birmingham, for their support throughout the process. We also thank the following individuals: Lori Alridge, Terrance Alridge, Larry Rowley, Stephanie Rowley, Ronald Chennault, Jerome Morris, Herb Jackson, the Loders, Lois Simms, Carmen Gaston, Bertis English, renowned civil rights–movement photographer Cecil Williams, graduate student assistants including Nathan Tanner, and the many educators interviewed for the Teachers in the Movement project and other oral history projects led by us and our contributors.

Last, but not least, we extend our sincerest thanks to the University of South Carolina Press. Our collaboration and relationship with the press was excellent. Thanks to Ehren Foley, acquisitions editor at the Press, for his enthusiasm about the volume from the very beginning and throughout the process. Thanks also to Kerri Tolan, production editor, for shepherding the volume toward the end of the process. We would also like to thank the Spencer Foundation for helping bring this book project to fruition. The Spencer Foundation's generous support and encouragement of Teachers in the Movement were foundational in the development of this volume.

We dedicate this book to the many Black educators across the United States who have inspired generations.

Introduction

DERRICK P. ALRIDGE, JON N. HALE,
& TONDRA L. LODER-JACKSON

Teaching has always been a political endeavor in the United States. From educating citizens in a new republic to building and reconstructing schools after the Civil War, teachers have undertaken the deep and serious work of forging notions of citizenship throughout US history. The political nature of teaching is readily apparent in the struggle to attain a quality education for full citizenship in a highly unequal nation. Particularly in connection with the Black freedom struggle, teaching has always been deeply contested work. Since the era when educators and scholars acquired literacy in clandestine locations, the Black freedom struggle has proffered an ideology that literacy is a pathway to liberation. The politicization of teaching and the curriculum today is a part of a much longer historical trajectory, but it often is overlooked or misunderstood.

Education did not escape the myriad controversies spawned under the US White House administration of Donald J. Trump. Controversy over how and what we taught reached deeply into nearly every classroom across the nation. In a reckoning of how we teach about slavery—documented in publications such as the *1619 Project*, which resituated America's founding around its first documented enslavement of Africans rather than the signing of the Declaration of Independence in 1776—educators and the larger public became embroiled in national discourse about what should be taught and how.[1] At least thirty-six states have passed legislation that took aim at teaching "controversial" history while banning any semblance of critical race theory (CRT).[2] In response to the overwhelming number of states in the United States that have introduced legislation banning the teaching and discussion of topics deemed controversial, the American Association of University Professors, the American Historical Association, the Association of American Colleges and Universities, and other professional organizations issued a stern rebuke.[3] Teachers and historians occupied professions that were once again marred in conflict and opposition.

Legislation that bans histories of Black and marginalized communities illuminates a well-known and long racist history of the school curriculum and the precarious position of educators who are in the political milieu. Banning discussions of race and the teaching of our racist past is but the most recent manifestation of this history. Although less recognized, teachers have been on the front lines of determining what is taught, how it is taught, and the extent to which educators positioned themselves in the long struggle to teach this history.

Schooling the Movement: The Activism of Southern Black Educators from Reconstruction through the Civil Rights Era explores the activism of teachers in the US South from Reconstruction through the desegregation era of the 1970s. Since Reconstruction, Black educators and school administrators in the US South organized for equal educational opportunity, demanded a right to teach in all-Black schools, and instilled notions of civic engagement that challenged the logic behind southern segregation. The work of teaching in Black schools connected to inherently political and deeper philosophical questions that challenged an anti-Black social, political, and economic order and reimagined new forms of citizenship and relationships to the nation that centered Black experiences, culture, and history.

As part of this larger project that originated from the schoolhouse, Black teachers engaged in *intellectual and pedagogical activism* in their classrooms and communities, promulgating ideals of freedom and liberation prevalent in the civil rights movement through teaching, leading, researching, and mentoring. Contributors in *Schooling the Movement* expound on this notion of intellectual and pedagogical activism to recenter the contributions of Black teachers and analyze the unique contribution they made to a long struggle for Black freedom, decisively refuting prevailing misinterpretations that teachers were absent or, worse, impediments to racial and social progress by comprehensively demonstrating that educators played an integral role in the civil rights movement.

In telling the stories of Black teachers, the authors in our volume draw extensively on oral histories. Reflecting the African—particularly, the Akan—oral tradition of the storyteller, or *griot*, the volume forthrightly acknowledges the validity of oral history as a means of hearing and preserving Black teachers' memories and testimonies of their pedagogy. Further, we recognize that Black teachers are, in most cases, the best firsthand sources of their intellectual and pedagogical activism during the civil rights era. Like the griots' stories passed down from generation to generation, Black teachers' stories, we contend, live across space and time and will resonate with all teachers today teaching in the midst of contemporary turbulent social movements—most notably, Black Lives Matter. Some interviews of teachers were conducted by the authors themselves, whereas other interviews were found in oral history collections. Collectively, oral histories were used liberally throughout the volume not only for the valuable insights on teaching but also to give voice to a group that has gone largely unheard.[4]

Historians and the general public typically revere brazen college students or defiant ministers, resourceful independent business owners, or strategic National Association for the Advancement of Colored People (NAACP) lawyers as *the* activists behind the movement. By historicizing a notion of activism from the vantage point of Black teachers, scholars, and administrators, the chapters in this volume purport that educators were central contributors and legitimate "activists" of the civil rights movement. As such, we maintain that educators' work constitutes a largely overlooked form of activism that denies the public an accurate view of teachers' contributions to the movement in their classrooms, schools, universities, and communities. By illuminating teachers' activism during the long civil rights movement, we intentionally connect the past with the present and contextualize how teachers play an active role in social justice issues today.

Schooling the Movement builds on the histories of education that have documented the struggle to obtain literacy when it was prohibited from the antebellum period through the establishment of Black schools after the Civil War, when Black legislators eradicated antiliteracy laws and established a system of schools for recently freed communities. It follows the work of historians James Anderson, V. P. Franklin, Vanessa Siddle Walker, Patrice Preston-Grimes, Sonya Ramsey, Michael Fultz, David Cecelksi, Joy Ann Williamson-Lott, R. Scott Baker, Karen Johnson, Adah Ward Randolph, Hilton Kelly, Dionne Danns, Michelle A. Purdy, Christopher Span, the authors featured in this volume, and others who have documented the integral role of Black secondary and postsecondary public schools during and since Reconstruction.[5] These histories have documented the academic excellence, high expectations, and shared notions of community "institutional care."[6] This volume extends the scholarship of historians who have begun to lay important groundwork in documenting the individual lives of instrumental Black educators. For example, Randal Jelks examined the work, life, and legacy of Benjamin Elijah Mays. Katherine Charron and Karen Johnson articulated the legacy of Septima Clark and her role in a long civil rights movement. Derrick Alridge has traced the intellectual genesis of W. E. B. Du Bois and leading Black educators and philosophers. R. Scott Baker has demonstrated that teachers often practiced "pedagogies of protest" in segregated schools during the era of Jim Crow to inculcate a notion of participatory democracy.[7] As these scholars have documented, Black communities labored to support secondary and postsecondary institutions of education to provide social and politically autonomous spaces that met the collective needs of communities oppressed during the nadir of racialization in the US South. The traditions espoused by these institutions inspired the notable actions of individual educators such as Septima Clark, Mary McLeod Bethune, Benjamin Elijah Mays, W. E. B. Du Bois, and others who understood the nexus of education and civil rights-based activism.

Our volume builds on the historiography of educator activism in the southern civil rights movement and the histories of education that encompass the long traditions of education as liberation by exploring in more detail how activism functioned among those educators who were not visibly engaged in protest. Teacher activism most often begins with traditional understandings of activism embedded in the work of educators such as Septima Clark, Aline Elizabeth Black, or Gladys Noel Bates, who served as plaintiffs in salary equalization litigation or maintained enrollment in the NAACP despite policies against it.[8] It also includes the work of notable educators who willingly joined direct-action nonviolent protests at the expense of their career.[9]

Following the activism of educators, no matter how nuanced, does not suggest that teaching or working in the field of education was inherently civil rights work, nor does it suggest activism without conflict. Not all Black educators supported the changes of this era or embraced modes of intellectual or pedagogical activism. This ground has been covered in the extant civil rights historiography. Many did, however, and they provided nuanced and varied levels of support and, at times, were directly involved on the front lines. Furthermore, Black teachers shared the experiences of racial exclusion, discrimination, and violence based in a society undergirded by white supremacy.

The teachers examined in this volume also illustrate the complex ways in which class, gender, religious, and regional identities affected teachers who participated in the freedom struggle. Lois Simms, for instance, enjoyed privileges connected to attending local Presbyterian churches and attending the private Avery Normal Institute in Charleston, South Carolina. Cynthia Roddey had familial connections that helped earn her admission into Winthrop University over other Black applicants who did not have the same social or political capital. Black women experienced participation differently than men, often serving in less visible roles and relegated to secondary or marginal positions in the movement defined by one's gender as opposed to ability.[10] Gendered notions shaped the field of teaching itself, practically the only profession open to women in a society underpinned by sexual violence and discrimination. Moreover, the focus on southern activism does not intend to dismiss the activism of teachers outside the South. The southern emphasis, rather, is intended to build on and provide more nuance to our understandings of a "Black New South" to deepen our understanding of teacher activism writ large and of the civil rights movement.[11]

Intellectual and pedagogical activism, as delineated in this volume, was manifest in various forms, some subtler than others. This volume identifies and elaborates on a form of intellectual and pedagogical activism predicated on professional and progressive networks built across the South since Reconstruction, which included teacher associations and private support networks. Although barred from the white national and state teacher associations, Black teachers organized autonomously and forged ideological alliances with Black laborers, including steelworkers, longshoremen, and women engaged in domestic work throughout the South.[12] This volume also considers the activism behind Black communities that developed social and political networks built on donated time, labor, and private resources committed to the development of public schools and pressuring local governments to provide financial support for schools their children attended. Yet another critical tenet of the intellectual and pedagogical activism that teachers practiced included the curriculum, extracurricular courses, culturally relevant education, and community engagement opportunities fashioned by educators in Black schools during the era of segregation. This included developing a curriculum that featured the work of Carter G. Woodson, Negro History Week, and other acts of pedagogical activism that included teaching and singing the Black national anthem, "Lift Ev'ry Voice and Sing."[13] Another way Black educators contributed to the larger freedom struggle, as education historian Tondra Loder-Jackson and her co-authors argued, was through educational research. Skilled researchers such as Marion Thompson Wright, Mamie and Kenneth Clark, Charles Hamilton Houston, and John Hope Franklin demonstrated how their professional work constituted a form of intellectual activism that contributed directly to the movement by providing the evidence, sources, and findings required by the *Brown* decision.[14] As the authors in this volume contend, teaching behind closed doors, developing their profession, and committing their careers to the improvement of education inculcated a sense of resistance throughout segregated Black schools across the South that resonated deeply with the principles of the civil rights movement.

In building on a historiography that has documented the role of Black teachers and administrators, this volume proffers a notion of intellectual and pedagogical activism that broadens our conceptions of what it meant to actively participate in or contribute to the civil rights movement. The intellectual and pedagogical activism regularly practiced by educators delineates a spectrum of activism that essentially redefines activism during the civil rights movement.[15] As such, the educators discussed in this volume challenge a predominant trope in the civil rights historiography that often portrays teachers as marginal to the movement; neutral bystanders who refused to engage in the movement; or, at times, obstructionists to the movement.[16] Educators who engaged in intellectual and pedagogical activism shared characteristics that included designing a curriculum, teaching critical thinking in the classroom, shaping local education policy, and engaging the community—the nuances of which are addressed by each of the chapters in this volume. Historically repositioning educators on a broader spectrum of activism that includes a range of commitment to the struggle challenges the prevailing narrative that teachers were not a part of the struggle or, worse, staunch defenders of the status quo. Educators' work did not often place them in the headlines or spotlight of the movement. Yet the intellectual and pedagogical work they practiced facilitated an understanding that imbued a segregated society with the groundwork to challenge structural discrimination in earnest by the 1950s.[17]

Schooling the Movement moves beyond a prevailing notion in the civil rights historiography that activism was defined solely by litigation and direct-action forms of protest. In doing so, the volume closely examines pedagogy, curriculum development, research, and particular administrative initiatives as forms of activism. The broader notion of activism articulated in this edited volume, which includes the deliberative and patient work of daily instruction and education for participatory citizenship, reveals what some might consider a radical notion of teachers during the civil rights movement: teachers as activists. Our view of teachers as activists complicates and revises the historical narrative of the teacher as a nonentity, and in some cases, as obstructionists to the civil rights movement. Further, the volume moves civil rights and education historiography beyond the predominant interpretation that desegregation, a notion advocated by the NAACP (but not the only plan for a quality education), was the barometer by which to measure the integrity of activism in the 1950s and 1960s.

After a large and unprecedented dismissal and demotion of a Black teaching force after the *Brown v. Board of Education* (1954) decision, teachers were hesitant, to say the least, to embrace desegregation.[18] Yet the narrow definition of civil rights as desegregation, and the attempt to prohibit racial discrimination and exclusion in accessing public spaces including spaces from schools to lunch counters, has shaped our perceptions of teachers as conservative and passive actors in American history. Adam Fairclough, for instance, illustrated how teachers in Louisiana engaged in civil rights activity by equalizing salaries, a move that was replicated across the South. Yet in his overview of southern Black teachers, he suggested that "black teachers' support for integration may have been widespread, but it was shallow."[19] John Dittmer noted in his examination of the Mississippi movement from the local perspective that "as a group black teachers in the 1950s refused to take a stand and the movement of the early 1960s passed them by."[20] However, situating the history of teacher organizations in a broader spectrum of civil rights activism disrupts a narrative of passivity to widen the spectrum of civil rights activists to include educators. Moreover, it posits that educators organized themselves by following a consistent and coherent agenda of civil rights. Many educators in the South saw their work as political and inherently connected to civil rights, and their subsequent articulation of a right to a quality education contributed significantly to the civil rights movement.

This volume examines how educators and administrators at all levels of education from elementary schools to the college classroom practiced forms of intellectual and pedagogical activism from Reconstruction through the civil rights movement. It utilizes oral history and archival research to historicize the role of educators and the institutions they developed in establishing the intellectual foundation of the civil rights movement. The chapters in this volume draw from dozens of oral histories with Black educators, many of which are part of a large-scale oral history project that documents the role of Black educators across the South. One such project is Teachers in the Movement, at the University of Virginia, which conducts and catalogs hundreds of interviews of teachers during the civil rights era throughout the South.[21] Research is also drawn from numerous archives across the southern United States, including, but not limited to, the Departments of Archives and History both in Alabama and in Mississippi; the Library of Virginia; Small Special Collections at the University of Virginia; the Louisiana State University Archives; the Caroliniana at the University of South Carolina; the Louise Pettus Archives and Special Collections at Winthrop University; the Margaret Alexander Walker Research Library; and the Martin Luther King, Jr. Library and Archives. Some authors also draw on archival collections at historically Black colleges and universities (HBCUs), for example, Miles College in Birmingham, Alabama, and Paine College in Augusta, Georgia.

This volume is organized into two parts. *Part I: The Spectrum of Teacher Activism* elucidates the dynamic spectrum of teacher activism to illustrate the range of civic engagement from less-or-more overt activist commitments among teachers. This included direct-action protests such as desegregating white colleges to teaching Black history in high school. It also entailed activism on the campuses of HBCUs where administrators, faculty, and students fought to preserve and commemorate their revered institutional traditions in spite of desegregation. This part also explores the range of intellectual and pedagogical activism among Black teachers across the South. This activism included the ways teachers taught and the curriculum they developed, which were less visible than other forms of direct-action protest but still grounded in the larger freedom struggle. This section also explores some teachers who engaged in more direct action, including desegregating white institutions and participating in legal strategies to ensure fair treatment during desegregation.

Jarvis R. Givens examines the intellectual and pedagogical work of educators in "Teaching to 'Undo Their Narratively Condemned Status': Black Educators and the Problem of Curricular Violence," detailing how the pervasiveness of anti-Blackness in curriculum placed unique ethical, intellectual, and pedagogical demands on the work of Black teachers. Working against a "narratively condemned status," Black teachers carried forth critical work in their classrooms. As Givens demonstrates, in addition to the dynamic and loving relationships that Black teachers cultivated with Black students, and their political activity beyond their classrooms, Black teachers often embraced the need to think against the grain of the dominant curriculum. Black teachers did this to cultivate a positive self-image among their students but also to assert their own human dignity, having long recognized their vulnerability (and freedom) to be bound up with that of their students.

Drawing on their Teachers in the Movement oral history archive, Alexis M. Johnson, Danielle Wingfield, and Derrick P. Alridge's chapter, "Cynthia Plair Roddey: Carolina Activist and Teacher in the Movement," examines the life and work of Rock Hill, South Carolina, educator Cynthia Plair Roddey. Roddey was the first Black student admitted to Winthrop College in Rock Hill in 1964, and she taught in Rock Hill and Charlotte, North Carolina, for several decades after the movement. Using Tondra L. Loder-Jackson's conceptualization of a "schoolhouse activist," the authors advance our understanding of activism beyond protest activism of picketing, marching, and sit-ins to a more subtle, but important form of activism that occurs in classrooms. Similarly, in "'It Only Takes a Spark to Get a Fire Going': Lois A. Simms and Pedagogical Activism during the Black Freedom Struggle, 1920–2015" Jon N. Hale provides a biographical analysis of the educational experiences of Lois A. Simms, an English teacher in Charleston, South Carolina, from 1941 to 1971. As an educator who was always critical of unequal opportunity, her career spanned the era of segregation and the first phase of widescale desegregation of public schools, providing insights into the work of education during these tumultuous years of the Black freedom struggle.

In "'We Experienced Our Freedom': The Impact of Valued Segregated Spaces on Teacher Practice and Activism," Kristan L. McCullum and Hunter Holt trace the lives of Genevieve Farmer, Delores Revis, and Dorothy Thompson, three Black women who taught in Raleigh, North Carolina, from 1959 to 2000. Each of these women grew up in segregated communities and attended segregated schools and HBCUs before starting their careers. By examining their trajectories, the chapter highlights how teachers, parents, community members, and activists influenced their teaching and conceptualization of activism. These relationships and their lived experiences during their formative years enabled them to cultivate education as a "practice of freedom" in their own classrooms and confront forms of racism within their schools during and after the civil rights movement. The chapter builds on previous scholarship to demonstrate the ways valued segregated schooling informed the philosophy and practice of students who became teachers before and after desegregation.

Crystal R. Sanders investigates the resistance that Black teachers faced in her chapter, "'In the Face of Her Splendid Record': Willa Cofield Johnson and Teacher Dismissal in the Civil Rights Era." Sanders examines in close detail Willa Johnson, a twelve-year veteran Black teacher in North Carolina, who—like thousands of other teachers—was fired after the 1963–1964 school year because of her civil rights activity. She sued for wrongful termination and secured victory in 1967 in federal court. Sanders uses Johnson's story as the lens to examine the reprisals that Black teachers endured for participating in the freedom struggle and explores how they fought back through lawsuits and mobilizations for teacher tenure.

Part II: Activism Across the South and Beyond explores teacher activism across the US South with one connection abroad, elucidating the geographic diversity of the movement and challenging the notion of a monolithic region. From Virginia to Alabama, Black educators across the South engaged in the freedom struggle in a myriad of ways and in a multitude of settings that included small towns and southern cities. Activism permeated local levels across the South, which constituted a widespread movement that affected the lives of people of the entire region. An examination of the geographic diversity of teacher activism across the South includes small South Carolina towns; midsized towns such as Charlottesville, Virginia; and large urban systems such as that found in New Orleans, Louisiana, all of which present nuance and depth to our understanding of Southern history. It also examines activism in the realm of higher education, underscoring that intellectual and pedagogical activism includes the work of Black educators in the K–12 public school system as well as that of administrators and faculty at postsecondary educational institutions inclusive of HBCUs.

In "Planning, Persistence, and Pedagogy: How Elizabeth City State Colored Normal School Survived North Carolina's White Supremacy Campaign, 1898–1905," Glen Bowman examines the work of educators in Elizabeth City, North Carolina, and the politics of teacher organization and activism in the segregated South through Elizabeth City State Colored Normal School. As Bowman underscores, survival during the violent suppression of Black freedoms would require not only planning, cunning, and luck but also a public espousal of "industrial education," which reflected a significant shift in institutional mission and reflected a particularly destructive political landscape for Black Americans in turn-of-the-century North Carolina. This chapter foregrounds the importance of commemorating the significance and relevance of HBCUs that fought to retain their independence and identities in the midst of desegregation.

Kristen L. Buras, in "'They Were Very Low Key, But They Spoke from Wisdom and Experience': How Black Teachers Taught Self-Determination at Carver Senior High School in New Orleans," similarly provides an institutional history, examining the history and evolution of George Washington Carver Senior High School in New Orleans. Carver, an all-Black school built in the face of white resistance to desegregation and as part of the Desire Public Housing community, was a thriving center of critical race pedagogy. Buras chronicles the everyday activism of teachers and the culture and climate they created in the Crescent City to nurture a generation of youths for academic excellence and civic engagement in the city they called home, illustrating the nuance of intellectual and pedagogical activism in the city.

Alexander Hyres, in his chapter, "'Dedication to the Highest of Callings': Florence Coleman Bryant, School Desegregation, and the Black Freedom Struggle in Postwar Virginia, 1946–2004," also analyzes the activism at the high school level during the civil rights era in Charlottesville, Virginia. Specifically, Hyres reveals how Florence Coleman Bryant, in her various roles as an educator across various school settings, sought justice for Black students, including her own children, in a city situated in the shadow of Thomas Jefferson's university, during a career spanning several decades of the twentieth century.

Black educators also practiced intellectual and pedagogical activism across Alabama in the state's larger towns and cities, as evidenced in Tondra L. Loder-Jackson's chapter, "Hidden in Plain Sight: Black Educators in the 'Militant Middle' of Alabama's Municipal Civil Rights Battlegrounds." In this chapter, Loder-Jackson investigates the role that Black educators played in Tuskegee, Montgomery, Birmingham, and Selma, Alabama, in the early- to mid-twentieth century, framing her analysis around Dr. Martin Luther King's call for social scientists in 1967 to reconsider their role in the civil rights movement. This chapter amplifies Black educators' involvement in the movement statewide by coalescing narratives of their contributions, which included: researching and documenting racial inequities in educational, social, economic, and political life; acknowledging and addressing intraracial hindrances to coalition building; negotiating civil rights reforms with the white power structure behind the scenes; and mentoring younger generations of student activists, among other contributions. Often, Black educators and their contributions to the Alabama movement were hidden in plain sight through their unassuming participation in civic, religious, political, and educational organizations.

Pushing past the traditional geographic boundaries of the Deep South and mid-Atlantic "southern" states, Vanessa Garry and E. Paulette Isaac-Savage, in "From Jim Crow to the Civil Rights Movement: The University of Missouri's Black Faculty, Staff, and Student Organizations Fight Back!" examine how Black faculty and staff organizations (BFSOs) developed during the late 1960s and 1970s as support systems for Black students, faculty, and staff new to predominantly white institutions (PWIs). This chapter explores how Black faculty created the inaugural BFSO in 1970 at the University of Missouri, the site of the *Gaines v. Canada* (1938) school desegregation case, and how Black-led organizations at PWIs were critical to the well-being of Black students and faculty.

In "W. E. B. Du Bois and the University of Berlin: The Transnational Path to Educational Activism," Bryan Ganaway analyzes the doctoral work of W. E. B. Du Bois at the University of Berlin in Germany and its influence on his dissertation; his first years of teaching at Fisk University in Nashville, Tennessee; and a developing sense of activism within a segregated society. Examining Du Bois's education in Germany in the 1890s illuminates several factors: how he decided to embrace sociology as a public intellectual; why he joined the NAACP at its founding; and his burgeoning notions of education as an activist endeavor.

As the contributing authors in this volume illustrate, nuance and variance underpin this underappreciated history of teacher activism and that of other educators. The essence of teacher activism in the South transcends political, social, economic, and geographic lines, illustrating a depth and breadth of intellectual and pedagogical activism during the long civil rights movement that underscores the conceptualization of the profession in the United States.[22] Rather than standing on the sidelines of the movement, Black educators instead shaped and advanced it in substantial ways. In doing so, they deployed forms of activism often overlooked. This volume also elucidates how the nature of Black education was, and remains, inherently political. The educators discussed in this volume, along with countless others, helped their students and their communities to articulate and reconfigure how they thought about citizenship and belonging. The contributors to this volume not only bring long-deserved attention to the activist legacy of Black educators but also provide critical historical context to the ongoing debates and tensions in the field of education today.

PART I

The Spectrum of
Teacher Activism

Teaching to "Undo Their Narratively Condemned Status"

Black Educators and the Problem of Curricular Violence

JARVIS R. GIVENS

To handicap a student by teaching him that his black face is a curse and that his struggle to change his condition is hopeless is the worst sort of lynching. It kills one's aspirations and dooms him to vagabondage and crime. It is strange, then, that the friends of truth and the promoters of freedom have not risen up against the present propaganda in the schools and crushed it.

—*Carter G. Woodson,* The Mis-Education of the Negro *(1933)*

The issue here was that of deconstructing the curriculum mechanisms which expelled the Black Conceptual Other outside the "universe of obligation;" . . . .

We must now undo their narratively condemned status.

—*Sylvia Wynter, "No Humans Involved" (1992)*

Anti-Blackness is endemic to the American curriculum. The knowledge base serving as the foundation of education in the United States positioned Black people as a group who had no history and culture, or at least none worthy of respect. If culture and history are, in fact, ordinary to human experience, then the denial of such elements in Black life effectively positioned Black teachers, students, and their communities as part of a subgenre of the human species. This idea, as foundational to the United States as the precept that "all men are created equal," and having been legitimized by various religious and "scientific" myths, proved (in the white imagination) that Blacks were destined to be enslaved or subjected to the will of a race more intellectually capable and socially accomplished. Such distortion in knowledge, and rupture in human kinship, was—and continues to be—a fundamental antagonism for African-descendant people.[1]

The degraded position of Black teachers in the system of knowledge, as individual members of a collective persecuted group, made their vocation distinct in kind. An affirmation of their own human dignity required their refusal of dominant scripts of knowledge. Such movement in thought is the focus of this chapter. I argue that the pervasiveness of anti-Blackness in curriculum placed unique ethical, intellectual, and pedagogical demands on the work of Black teachers through the period of Jim Crow. In addition to the dynamic and loving relationships Black teachers cultivated with Black students and their political activity beyond classrooms, these educators often embraced the need to think against the grain of dominant curriculum. They did this to cultivate a positive self-image among their students but also to assert their own human dignity, having long recognized their vulnerability—and freedom—as bound up with that of their students.[2]

How these educators responded to such trouble in curriculum amounts to an epic tale of intellectual and spiritual striving in American education. They inherited and sustained a countervailing educational tradition. Black teachers reimagined what constituted knowledge; who could be producers and repositories of knowledge; and, ultimately, how students were to conceive of human life and their place within it. Generation after generation of Black teachers arrived at this conclusion, compelling them to build on liberatory curricular visions that can be traced from the antebellum era through the twentieth century.[3]

BLACK NARRATIVE CONDEMNATION
AS CURRICULAR VIOLENCE

Black people occupied a "narratively condemned status" in the American curriculum and Western thought, to borrow from Black studies theorist Sylvia Wynter. Reflecting on the writings of Jim Crow–era teacher and historian Carter G. Woodson, Wynter named how distortions in textbooks and curriculum sought "to induce Black students to believe that their ancestors had done nothing worth doing, whether in the human or in the American past." What's more, the American curriculum's distorted representation of Black life played a central role, she argued, in shaping "psycho-social responses" in society. This knowledge system represented "the rules governing our human modes of perception and the behaviors to which they lead." To this point, Wynter observed that the degraded image of Blacks in curriculum performed "extra-cognitive functions." It did more than cast aspersions on Blackness in the minds of students; it motivated and compelled human behavior in the social world.[4] Both Woodson, writing in 1933, and Wynter, in 1992, insisted that Black suffering in the material world was narratively constituted. The physical violence circumscribing Black life had been structured by, and was an expression of, their narratively condemned status in the symbolic order.

"Why not exploit, enslave, or exterminate a class that everybody is taught to regard as inferior?" inquired Woodson. He insisted, "There would be no lynching if it did not start in the schoolroom."[5] By Woodson's assessment, the injustice in American education was not only about access and opportunity; most important was the content and substance of education and what it was intended to do in the world. Deeply embedded in the struggle of Black people for education was a battle against their misrecognition in official knowledge, which was the primary frame of reference used to order human sociality. The classroom and the textbook were the battleground for how we were to know the world and, therefore, how we could be in the world. This philosophical perspective on anti-Blackness and education, Wynter insisted, was "Woodson's conceptual breakthrough."[6]

This phenomenon, named by Woodson and expanded by Wynter, constitutes what we might call *anti-Black curricular violence*. Disparaging representations of specific groups in the dominant symbolic order, otherwise known as curriculum, have motivated, legitimized, and been inextricably linked to the harm physically and socially inflicted on members of symbolically violated groups. Such harm manifested in various forms of violence: exclusion from social opportunities, lynchings and mob violence, resource deprivation, and civic alienation within the national polity. Race is but one mode through which curricular violence is expressed, although it was the primary classification used to stratify human life in the United States through the Jim Crow era. Curricular violence, as structured by race, is experienced through other categories of identity, especially as we consider that class and gender are key modalities through which race is lived.[7]

Furthermore, all nonwhite groups were stigmatized through the American curriculum, even if not on equal terms. "Whilst the past of all other groups was stigmatized," explained Wynter, "they were nevertheless left with certain shreds of human dignity." Yet, reflecting on Woodson's theorization, she wrote that "this was not so with respect to the 1933 [Jim Crow] curriculum's misrepresentation of the Afro-American past and [. . .] present." Anti-Blackness formed a kind of molten core of racial animus in the new world. It was reflected in a color line expressed in curriculum, the social policies that segregated Black people from the rest of American society, and by the immutable fact that "Black Americans are the only population of the post-1492 Americans who have been legitimately owned, i.e., enslaved, over several centuries."[8] Their status as people who could be property by virtue of their race, which was legitimized through laws and official knowledge, had residual implications for how Blacks were perceived and treated, even in the afterlife of racial chattel slavery.

The scripts of official knowledge legitimized slavery and, subsequently, Black people's disenfranchisement, legal segregation, and social policies were premised on the idea that Black people were inherently more prone to crime and vice than any other group.[9] Recognizing this relationship between the symbolic and the material world, Black people committed themselves to thinking against the grain of dominant epistemology. Writing new scripts of human experience amounted to a matter of life and death.

Beginning in slavery and continuing beyond emancipation, Black people engaged in the work of countering such distortions in the system of knowledge.[10] Given the political desires of Black educators to uplift their race and challenge injustice through education, it was inevitable that the curriculum would be of direct and immediate concern. Black teachers became key leaders in the Black intellectual tradition, insisting that the lived experiences of Black people had no shortage of human struggle, culture, and achievement. Leading educators across time named such intellectual work as essential to their vocation. Black teachers' writings and actions in the historical record present great evidence of this intellectual tradition and expression of critical pedagogy.

What follows is a chronicling of Black teachers' writings and practices that disrupted anti-Black curricular violence in American education from the nineteenth century through Jim Crow. The narratives reveal that Black teachers long understood their work as a professional group to be set apart from dominant curricular protocols and concerned with more than the procedural and utilitarian elements of schooling. The demands on their work were always about more than access to physical school buildings or challenging inequitable distribution of resources. Pressing intellectual tasks also required their attention. They repeatedly returned to this question: How might knowledge and the substance of education be accountable to Black life? African American educators insisted on recognizing the human struggles and achievements of Black people while also allowing their suffering to speak. This problem of curricular violence constituted a perennial challenge in the professional lives of Black teachers.

SLAVERY AND THE EMERGENCE OF ANTI-BLACK CURRICULAR VIOLENCE

This intellectual task inherited by Black teachers developed in the time of slavery. Challenging the narrative condemnation of Black people was linked to intellectual work begun by enslaved people who challenged "the chattel principle," or the laws and logics that deemed Blacks a race of people who could be property, traded, and purchased in the marketplace. Fugitive slave and teacher James W. C. Pennington insisted that this idea, the chattel principle, was the true violence of slavery. It was the foundational idea that legitimatized and called on the whipping post, disrupted Black family ties, and imposed illiteracy and ignorance, producing the life of labor under the lash. Writing as a fugitive slave, Pennington insisted that the material world was structured by the symbolic world of ideas, and this political clarity led him to consider the representation of Black life in knowledge as having posed important tasks for the very work of abolishing the chattel principle.[11]

In 1841, Pennington wrote the first Black-authored textbook, titled *A Text Book on the Origins and History of the Colored People*, while living in Hartford, Connecticut, where he also taught at the African Free School. He inaugurated and formalized a distinct intellectual practice, one in which Black people strived to rewrite the epistemological order by upending the anti-Black foundations of knowledge and curriculum. Having observed that "we suffer from the want of a collection of facts so arranged as to present a just view of our historical origin," Pennington assembled a Black counternarrative rooted in biblical genealogy and history of ancient Ethiopia and Egypt. He refused the master narrative, such as the one posed by Noah Webster, architect of America's chosen orthography, who insisted in 1843 that, as for "the woolly haired Africans, who constitute the principal part of the inhabitants of Africa, there is no history and there can be none"[12] Pennington's fugitive textbook reflects a history of Black people appropriating technology and the literary arts as an authoritative form and turning them on their heads.[13] This was part and parcel of an expansive tradition in Black intellectual and political life.

Pennington's textbook resonates with the freedom narratives of escaped slaves such as Frederick Douglass and Harriet Jacobs.[14] Black people set out to know the world and themselves on new terms in anticipation of, and as a means of bringing about, slavery's demise. This intellectual tradition continued once Emancipation arrived, because the condemnation of Black life persisted, in both the narrative and material realms. There continued to be a need for new scripts of knowledge. Black teachers carried this tradition forward.

But Pennington was not the only Black person teaching against the grain of dominant knowledge before emancipation. Abolitionist and teacher Charlotte Forten Grimké also embodied this tradition. Although born free in Philadelphia to a wealthy abolitionist family and having been educated in mixed schools outside of Boston, Grimké always understood her alienation in the world as a young Black woman to be bound up with the suffering of enslaved members of her race. Because of this political orientation and sense of racial kinship, she jumped at the opportunity to go south and teach during the Civil War.

Grimké arrived at St. Helena's Island of the coast of South Carolina in October of 1862. In addition to lessons in reading and writing, Grimké noted in her diary that she also taught her students things not found in the curricular resources provided for the freedpeople by white missionaries. On Monday, November 10, she recorded, "We taught—or rather commenced teaching the children 'John Brown,' which they entered into eagerly." Grimké continued, "I felt the full significance of that song being sung here in S.C. by the little negro children, by those whom he—the glorious old man—died to save." As many historians noted, the radical white abolitionist John Brown was widely thought to be demented in dominant historical narratives and by the broader white public, but he was held up as a hero to Black people for his heroic efforts at Harper's Ferry to lead an insurrection against the slave system. Twentieth-century historian Benjamin Quarles observed that, contrary to dominant portrayals of Brown, African Americans carried "a single-minded negative attitude to the charge that he was mostly mentally imbalanced [. . . .] Blacks held that society, rather than John Brown was deranged."[15]

However, Grimké went further than teaching students about the radical white abolitionist. Three days after teaching students about John Brown, Grimké described that she "talked to the children a little while to-day about the noble Toussaint," and the students "listened very attentively." Pleased with her actions, she wrote assertively, "It is well that they sh'ld know what one of their own color c'ld do for his race." Grimké believed that the legacy of Toussaint Louverture would "inspire them with courage and ambitions (of a noble sort) and high purpose."[16] These sentiments were common among Black abolitionists who were teachers. Maria Stewart, for instance, who worked as a teacher in New England and Washington DC, once expressed: "When I cast my eyes on the long list of illustrious names that are enrolled in the bright annals of fame among whites, I turn my eyes within, and ask my thoughts, 'Where are the names of our illustrious ones?'"[17]

Grimké's curricular imagination was shaped by her own experiences as a student, when she herself became sensitive to distortions about Black history and culture in dominant knowledge. Nearly a decade earlier, while attending school in Salem, Massachusetts, Grimké expressed her delight when reading poems by Phillis Wheatley in her spare time. She took comfort in the eighteenth-century poems of this enslaved girl while witnessing the daily insults made on Black people, even in Massachusetts. She wrote the following in her diary on July 28, 1854: "This evening read 'Poems of Phillis Wheatley,' an African slave, who lived in Boston at the time of the Revolution. She was a wonderfully gifted woman, and many of her poems are very beautiful. *Her character and genius afford a striking proof* of the falseness of the assertion made by some that hers is an inferior race."[18] Grimké recognized that, like Wheatley, the condition of her color meant she was always on trial in the eyes of the dominant society. Yet, Wheatley's poetry represented proof of concept in Grimké's mind that the races were equal as far as intellectual capacity was concerned.

The same observation Grimké made as a student, refuting ideas about Black intellectual inferiority, she would make again as a teacher. Writing of her formerly enslaved students during the Civil War, she explained, "I never before saw children so eager to learn, although I had several years' experience in New-England schools."[19] Grimké continued, "Coming to school is a constant delight and recreation to them. They come here as other children go to play [. . .] as bright and as anxious to learn as ever." Having observed that these formerly enslaved children were just as capable of learning as her students, Black and white, in New England, Grimké expressed her discontent with dominant representations of Black people as intellectually inferior. "One cannot believe that the haughty Anglo-Saxon race, after centuries of such an experience as these people have had, would be very much superior to them. And one's indignation increases against those who, North as well as South, taunt the colored race with inferiority while they themselves use every means in their power to crush and degrade them, denying them every right and privilege, closing against them every avenue of elevation and improvement."[20]

As demonstrated by Grimké's witness as a teenage student and later as an in-service teacher during the Civil War, anti-Black curricular violence was a factor in the life of Black teachers and Black students. Black teachers would have to assume the intellectual task of challenging such dominant ideas by offering counterhistorical perspectives and ideological orientations to schooling. However, such affirming representations of Black history and achievement desired by Grimké, and surely others, were not offered in the formal curricular resources provided by supporters of the Union or the Confederacy.

Historian Heather Williams described how textbooks "with competing ideologies floated around the South" during and after the Civil War. There were "those that supporters of the Confederacy designed to inculcate values such as the morality of slavery and the inferiority of African Americans," and there were "those that white abolitionists produced to advise Black people how to carry out their new roles as free people." Although the latter were pro-abolition, they were also overdetermined by white paternalism and plagued by studious omission of Black life. According to the book offered to the freedpeople by white abolitionists, white soldiers died to free Blacks, yet these texts "neglected any mention that Black men had also fought for their freedom."[21] Such context is essential to fully appreciate why Grimké taught students on the South Carolina Sea Islands about Toussaint Louverture and Haiti but also to grasp the deeper conceptual meaning of her insistence that the freed children "should know what one of their own color had done for his race."[22]

African American educators took on a key role in working to undo the narratively condemned status of Black people post-emancipation, carrying forward an intellectual tradition with deep antebellum roots. There continued to be those like the formerly enslaved Edward A. Johnson, who wrote *A School History of the Negro Race in America from 1619 to 1890* while working as a school principal in 1890. Like Frederick Douglass's use of photography and literature,

Black educators insisted that the very mediums and technologies used "to read the Negro out of the human family" could be used "to read him back in" through subversive means.[23]

Educators worked to expand this intellectual tradition. By the late nineteenth century, there were hopes for making this practice more than the work of individual teachers. Educators needed new resources for their practice. The very practice of publishing school textbooks in the Black intellectual tradition embodied a desire to develop systemic curricular programs that might have greater impact in the lives of students and the world. An 1894 essay by formerly enslaved educator Richard Robert Wright, also the first valedictorian of Atlanta University and a founder of the American Negro Academy (ANA), illuminates this point.

In "The Possibilities of the Negro Teacher," Wright explained that the time had arrived to move beyond curriculum materials that took white experiences as the educational norm. The Black teacher—whom he conceptualizes as a distinguishable category of professional—must take up the work of developing new educational models. Observing that white teachers played an important role in supporting Black people in the earliest years of freedom, Wright explained, "I think the Negro is on the eve of graduating from their tutorage. [. . .] The next stage of our development is to be under the Negro teachers and by Negro methods and not without text books written by Negroes."[24]

"While totally and disdainfully rejecting the theories and conclusions" made about the Black race by mental and physical scientists and theologians of the nineteenth century, Wright acknowledged that it was important to recognize the existence of such ideas and that they were operative in the world, including through schools. Nineteenth-century race science led Wright to believe that Black scholars and educators had a charge to develop new educational models grounded in the experiences of Black life. Such ingenuity was necessary if they were to build an educational program set apart from the anti-Black perspectives embedded in the dominant culture and academy. He was attentive to the fact that ideas about race and the experiences of different racial groups played important roles in shaping the dynamics of education.[25]

Wright asked, "Is it a fact that not only the teachers and the books, but the methods patterned and cut for the white man are the only ones fitted for the development of the Negro mind? There has not been a school book written nor a school method formulated from the Negro standpoint. I think it is time we should do a little tailoring for ourselves." He proposed the following curricular vision for the future: "In this approaching era the Negro is going to write school text books for himself. He is going to adorn them with pictures of his own thoughtful men and virtuous women, with likenesses of his own bright boys and pretty girls. The Negro youth of the land are going to be taught to catch inspiration and hope from the virtue, goodness and intellectual endeavors of their own race."[26]

Writing during the final decade of the nineteenth century, a period of violent retrenchment when advances made by Black Americans following the Civil War were undermined, Wright projected a future where the former slaves and their descendants might craft an educational program suited to their distinct needs as America's emancipated people. This vision included school textbooks and models of teaching that were accountable to Black life and culture, informed by political visions suited to their material and spiritual needs. He asserted, "it is the duty of the Negro teacher to make the necessary investigation and to formulate the methods by which our youth may be enabled to enjoy their superior advantages and to assert their undisputed claims."[27]

Post-emancipation, the spiritual strivings of Black people continued to be met by violent white backlash, and this carried over into the twentieth century. In this context, not only was Black life a problem in the physical realm, where the former planters and white southern elites relied on Blacks as an exploitable group of laborers, but it was also a problem as it pertained to school knowledge, as one generation after another of Black children entered a world persistently structured by the anti-Black color line. Blacks' efforts to challenge curricular distortions became increasingly important in the twentieth century, especially as the relative equality gained during Reconstruction was stripped away almost entirely during the period of "the Nadir."[28] In fact, the very topic of Reconstruction would itself emerge as a curricular problem.

STRIVING TO KNOW THEMSELVES OTHERWISE

Black inferiority and poor leadership resulted in a failed period of Reconstruction, according to the dominant curriculum. Prominent Columbia University historian William A. Dunning argued that Reconstruction was corrupted by the Radical Republicans and unqualified freedmen in leadership. The Dunning school of thought fundamentally justified Black disenfranchisement and informed much of the historical writing on the subject during the first few decades of the twentieth century.[29] Yet, many African American teachers provided counternarratives of the era as a source of pride and inspiration for continued Black political struggle. Just as Black Americans during the pre-emancipation era celebrated figures such as Nat Turner and John Brown—despite mainstream white Americans and even white abolitionists viewing such figures as demented and deluded—this trend persisted into the twentieth century. Black leaders from the period of Reconstruction were jettisoned in mainstream school textbooks but reclaimed in the Black curricular imagination.

Oliver Pope taught in Templeton, Virginia, for three years when his lesson on Reconstruction cost him his job in 1908. The white superintendent, who was a former Confederate soldier, walked into the classroom as Pope was in the middle of a lesson with his back turned to the door. He recalled the following details: "We were discussing the reconstruction period when he entered without my knowledge, as I was defending, contrary to our text, the Congressional plan: 'If the Negro had not been given the vote at that time—' A sharp 'Then what?' interrupted, and I turned, startled and confused." Having been caught off guard, it was too late to change course after the voice behind him disrupted the lesson. Recognizing the superintendent, Pope invited him to address the class. Then "the red-faced old soldier turned on his heels," Pope explained, "and walked out with military dignity. And then I knew my name was Ichabod." Pope's teaching contract was terminated shortly after the incident.[30]

Black educators continued to teach against the grain of the dominant curriculum, despite such violent oversight. Benjamin E. Mays, born in Greenwood County, South Carolina, in 1894, recalled how his teachers in the early twentieth century exposed students to historical figures who challenged dominant ideas of Black inferiority. The recent period of Reconstruction became essential to this work. Although African Americans were a majority in Greenwood, school curriculum and policies were set by white officials. Black schools were open four months out of the year to accommodate the crop calendar, whereas white schools were open for six months. Despite this context, Mays recalled his teachers and community members striving to offer students a positive self-image and a new conception of human history.

Mays explained, "We never felt sorry for ourselves because we were dark, and we accepted Africa as the home of our ancestors." And Black leaders during Reconstruction were presented to students as heroes: "The Negroes in the South Carolina Legislation during the Reconstruction and post-Reconstruction years were the men held up to us in high school history class as being great men, and not the Negro-hating Benjamin Ryan Tillman and his kind, who strove so long and hard to deprive the Black man of his vote." Simply put, Mays asserted, "I had identity."[31] Black Reconstruction leaders were part of a long lineage of Black intellectual and political history. Mays emphasized how his Black identity was intentionally cultivated by his teachers. This required exposing students to thinkers and leaders that fell outside the margins of the official curriculum. Mays recalled, "My heroes were black. Every once in a while, some Negro came along selling pictures of, or pamphlets about, a few Negro Leaders. Pictures of Frederick Douglass, Booker T. Washington, and Paul Laurence Dunbar hung on our walls. In my high school days, Booker T. Washington meant more to me than George Washington; Frederick Douglass was more of a hero than William Lloyd Garrison; Dunbar inspired me more than Longfellow. I heard about Crispus Attucks and was thrilled. The Negro preachers and teachers in my county, I worshipped."[32]

Black teachers' challenge to dominant curricula had to do with protecting the dignity of their students—but their own self-respect was also on the line. This was the case with Oliver Pope in 1908, as he offered students a counternarrative about the history of Black political leadership and the importance of the Black vote. This was also the case for teachers who taught Mays in South Carolina, from the time he attended the one-room Brickhouse School in Greenwood to the time he enrolled in the high school program at South Carolina State College.[33] His teachers revised the dominant curriculum, allowing Mays to see himself as situated in a continuum of consciousness, where Black people pushed for social transformation and cultivated a political and cultural heritage worthy of study and admiration.

The dignity of Black teachers, as a professional group, was on the line. The narratively condemned status of Black people was a position shared by educators and students. Both groups experienced violence in the American school and society as Black people, and such shared vulnerability in the world was inextricably linked to distortions about Black life in curriculum. Challenging dominant scripts of knowledge amounted to a professional and personal obligation for these educators. The human dignity of Black teachers was always already bound up with that of their students, both in the symbolic and materials realms of human experience.

Roscoe C. Bruce, Assistant Superintendent of Colored Schools in Washington, DC, appealed to officials above him in July 1915, about the omission of Black life in curriculum. He posed the following question in his report: "Can it be that all the generals, all the statesmen, all the men of letters were white men?" Bruce's question was motivated by a professional concern, where the needs of Black students needed to be taken into consideration. However, it was also personal for him, as the overrepresentation of whiteness in school curriculum undermined his own position in the world, and also his family history. Bruce's formerly enslaved father became the second Black American elected to the U.S. Senate during Reconstruction, and his mother had been a teacher and a leader in the National Association of Colored Women. Bruce was intimately aware that all the statesmen and men of letters were not white men. He continued, "Is there not danger that our colored children and youth will be overwhelmed with what I may call the prestige of the white man?"[34] Like educators before him, Bruce understood disrupting anti-Black curricular violence to be an essential part of the work of Black teachers.

Offering students intellectual resources to think about Black life beyond the frames offered in a Jim Crow society amounted to more than an intellectual project. It was not just about teaching a different school of thought. Black teachers partnered with their students to combat the violence and precarious position they shared in society, a position of subjection that manifested in the unequal distribution of resources and power as dictated by racial logics, but one that was legitimated, motivated, and reinforced by the official system of knowledge. When Black teachers developed alternative scripts of knowledge and disrupted dominant portrayals of human history and ideas of Black inferiority, they were fundamentally striving to undo their narratively condemned status. Black teachers continued their efforts to meet resistance in mainstream education, and they continued to develop strategies to contest such curricular violence.

COORDINATED EFFORTS TO CHALLENGE CURRICULAR VIOLENCE

As the professional world of Black educators expanded in the first decade of the twentieth century, both in the number of teachers and institutions, questions about curriculum and its system of representation became a permanent agenda item. Across time and space, groups of educators critiqued the dominant curriculum, particularly as it pertained to race and white supremacist ideology. Beyond expressing their discontent, they worked to develop curricular alternatives. As the previous examples demonstrate, individual teachers made efforts to introduce students to important events and figures from the Black past, but there were also coordinated efforts to address the problem of curricular violence. The issue was taken up in teachers' associations, summer school classes, and groups of educators who organized themselves in their local communities to take action.

Leila Amos Pendleton, a teacher in DC public schools, published *A Narrative of the Negro* in 1912, and the textbook was reviewed in *The Crisis* magazine as recommended reading for nearly a decade. Jessie Fauset, also a teacher in DC (and later the literary editor for the magazine), offered to following review after the book's initial release:

> **A Narrative of the Negro.** By Mrs. Leila Amos Pendleton. Published by the author, Washington, D. C., 1912.
>
> Now, at last, it would seem, we have an historian of no mean ability who has arisen in answer to our need. Too much credit cannot be given Mrs. Pendleton for the interest and effort manifested in the conception and execution of her book.
>
> The modest title and the slenderness of the volume hardly lead the reader to suspect the comprehensiveness of treatment which actually awaits him. For this book treats not only of the Negro in the United States, but considers his condition here only as an important phase of his general history. This last is surveyed from his earliest days in Africa. Viewed in this light one gains a new idea of the immense historical value of the Negro and of the persistence with which he plays his part in the drama of nations. Despised, hated,

debased, exploited in every imaginable way by every nation on every continent, the Negro still is. And so out of the blackness of despair springs eternal hope.

The colored American would do well to put this book in the hands of his children, to let them know that they, too, have great men and splendid women. In these pages is told the story of Toussaint L'Ouverture, of Denmark Vesey, Nat Turner, Sojourner Truth, Harriet Tubman. We know too little of the cause for the fame of these characters—if, indeed, we know of them at all. Whereas, these are names to conjure with—to inspire in all people of color high purpose, unflinching courage, great persistence. When one thinks of the fearful odds in slavery times against the black man who dared to try to lift his head, and then remembers that these people dared—there is nothing finer in all history. And these people are ours, not the borrowed types of a hostile race whose members hold us persistently aloof.

The style is simple, concise and very readable—the general presentation as a whole is very commendable.[35]

Pendleton's textbook offered students a story of persistent persecution of Black life and, simultaneously, one of Black people's ongoing resistance in their quest for freedom and justice. Pendleton situated her writing within this tradition of Black people's spiritual striving, and she hoped that students might also see themselves situated within this continuum of consciousness. In the preface for the textbook, Pendleton explained, "There are some of us who feel that, pitifully small though it be, we have given the very best and done the very most it is possible for us to give and to do for the race, and we are looking to you, dear children, to perform the things which we, in our youth had hoped and planned."[36]

Important here is not only the extraordinary accomplishment of Pendleton writing a textbook but also that it was reviewed in such a thoughtful manner in one of the most widely circulated Black publications in the country. Fauset's review of the book authored by her fellow Washington, DC, teacher reflects Black educators' organized efforts to challenge curricular violence. Such coordination reflects an integral part of the political and intellectual history of Black educators. Their organizing expanded and their strategies became increasingly sophisticated.

Afro–Puerto Rican bibliophile and Black Renaissance thinker Arturo Schomburg gave a lecture titled, "Racial Integrity: A Plea for the Establishment of a Chair of Negro History in Our Schools and Colleges" in July 1913, before a teachers' summer school at Cheyney Institute in Pennsylvania, a normal school and the oldest historically Black college in the United States. Schomburg declared that the textbooks used in schools were created to inspire white students, "but when applied or measured up to the black people, they lack the substantial and inspiring." He continued, "They are like meat without salt, they bear no analogy to our own; for this reason it would be a wise plan for us to law down a course of study in Negro History and achievements, before or after men and women have left certain schools." Because traditional departments and disciplines failed to account for the experiences of Black people, particularly the field of history, there needed to be a "chair in Negro History" at Black schools and colleges. Schomburg insisted, "We have chairs of almost everything, and believe we lack nothing, but we sadly need a chair of Negro history."[37] Schomburg continued, "The white institutions have their chair of history; it is the history of their people, and whenever the Negro is mentioned in the text-books it dwindles down to a footnote. The white scholar's mind and heart are fired because in the temple of learning he is told how on March 5, 1770, the Americans were able to beat the English; but to find Crispus Attucks it is necessary to go deep into special books."[38]

Schomburg urged teachers to assume responsibility for writing and developing new scripts of knowledge. He acknowledged that there would be trial and error, but coordinated effort on their part was necessary. Schomburg declared, "It is the season for us to devote our time in kindling the torches that will inspire us to racial integrity. We need a collection or list of books written by our men and women. If they lack style, let the children of tomorrow correct the omissions of their sires. Let them build upon the crude work. Let them, because of the opportunities that colleges and universitas grant, crystallize the crude work and bring it out flawless."[39] He appealed to Black educators to lay the groundwork for new curriculum orientations, foundations that their students could build on and improve in years to come.[40]

"Racial Integrity" was printed and circulated among the Black intellectual elite, especially among other members of the American Negro Academy (ANA; an organization referenced in Schomburg's speech). At the time, W. E. B. Du Bois was the president of the ANA and editor of *The Crisis* magazine, Richard Robert Wright was a member of the ANA, and Carter G. Woodson and Schomburg were ANA co-initiates. Thus, the ideas expressed by Schomburg were thoughts that resonated with some of the most influential Black thinkers of the period, and they circulated through the networked world to which they belonged. These same intellectual circuits connected Black teachers around the country.

Schomburg called for some leader to help move this work forward. "We need in the coming dawn the man who will give us the background for our future; it matters not whether he comes from the cloisters of the university or from the rank and file of the fields," he declared.[41] Perhaps Carter G. Woodson, a teacher representing a kind of hybrid of the two, was just the man to answer this call. Woodson was a man of the university, but his roots were in Buckingham County,

Virginia, where he grew up poor and working on his family's farm. From these humble beginnings, Woodson began high school at the age of twenty in West Virginia, and eventually became the second Black PhD recipient from Harvard University in 1912. While teaching high school in Washington, DC, Woodson founded the Association for the Study of Negro Life and History (ASNLH) in 1915 and, subsequently, Negro History Week in 1926. It is also worth noting that Woodson preserved a copy of Schomburg's address in his personal library.[42]

Although "Racial Integrity" was addressed to the teachers assembled at Cheyney Institute, Black educators in other parts of the country wrestled with similar ideas, before and after 1913. This is evident by the stories of Roscoe C. Bruce, Leila Amos Pendleton, and Jessie Fauset recalled earlier. Across time and space, Black teachers found themselves confronting and working to transcend curricular violence in their classrooms.

Bruce wrote to the DC school board about the need to look beyond "the prestige of the white man" when developing curriculum. However, he also noted the long efforts of Black teachers to include smatterings of Black life and culture in school whenever possible—how they commemorated the birthdays of Phillis Wheatley and Frederick Douglass, for instance. Black teachers in the nation's capital, however, desired more for their students and for themselves. Bruce explained, "In the teaching of American history in the elementary schools and in the high schools reference is more and more made by our teachers to the place of the American Negro in that history, to the part which he has played in American life."[43]

Bruce cited Black educators in DC schools who published books to support this work. "Two of our teachers—Principal John W. Cromwell, of Crummell School, and Dr. C. G. Woodson, of M Street High School—have written important volumes that in their fields should constitute sources for the use of our teachers." He emphasized that such expanded views of history and Black culture were essential for the developmental needs of African American students. "It gives our children and youth a sense of pride in the stock from which they sprang, an honorable self-confidence, a faith in the future and its possibilities, to know what men and woman of Negro blood have actually done, whether in the fields or in the schoolroom or in the war for the building of America."[44] Bruce alerted the school board that he would support the teachers in organizing a series of professional development seminars during the next academic year to explore possibilities for curriculum adjustments.

The year 1915 was the fiftieth anniversary of Black emancipation. Thus, Bruce was appealing to the local school board at a time of deep introspection for Black Americans and the entire country. How far had Black people come since the abolition of slavery, and in what position did they find themselves in twentieth-century America? What's more, national awareness of the film *The Birth of a*

Nation, which was released earlier that year, made Black educators particularly concerned about the relationships between curricular violence and the brutality Black people experienced in the material world. The film drew on popular tropes of Black people as inadequate leaders and inherently violent while presenting a militant white nationalist vision of the nation. Black Americans across the country protested the film.[45] Thus, before the time of the New Negro and the Black Renaissance on the horizon, Black teachers raised questions about Black heritage and identity. In this context, Woodson published his first book in spring 1915, *The Education of the Negro Prior to 1861*, and while conducting research in Chicago, he assembled four other men and founded the ASNLH. This organization set out to study and disseminate scholarship on Black life and culture. Its aim was to correct distortions, to describe Black life and history in a rigorous academic fashion, and to circulate this work that it might disrupt dominant portrayals of Black people in schools and public discourse. This work had wide-reaching political implications. In setting the record straight, champions of "the early Black history movement" hoped that the Negro would "not become a negligible factor in the thought of the world," as Woodson often professed.[46] This fight against curricular violence was understood to be part and parcel of the fight against anti-Black violence in earthly places.

In November 1915, Woodson was back in DC, and the city's Black educators kicked off their self-initiated seminars. W. E. B. Du Bois gave a keynote address on "Outlines of Negro History." He also led a workshop just for high school teachers on "Sources and Methods in Negro History."[47] Woodson participated in these workshops while producing the inaugural issue of the *Journal of Negro History*, published in January of 1916. Black schoolteachers were critical to getting this publication of the ground, successfully making it the first academic publication committed to the study of race, particularly of Black life and history. Not only was the journal published by Woodson from his post as an M Street schoolteacher, but his colleagues Jessie Fauset and Mary Church Terrell contributed book reviews; William Hartgrove, DC teacher and co-founder of the ASNLH, contributed a historical essay about a Black mother and daughter's struggle for education and their lives as teachers; the issue also featured a review of *The Negro in American History*, written by John Cromwell, a DC principal and member of the ANA.[48] Woodson's Association and its publications were the product of the intellectual and political culture at the center of Black teachers' professional worlds.

Teachers in DC planned professional development seminars during the spring semester as well. In March 1916, Woodson facilitated a workshop on "History and Civics."[49] Around this same time, the M Street faculty changed the school's name to Dunbar High School, honoring the memory of poet and ANA founder Paul Laurence Dunbar, exactly ten years after his death. Such naming practices became distinguishable phenomena, Dunbar having effectively been elevated as the bard of Black school life. His poetry became widely cited and studied by African Americans, and many communities named schools after him, making Dunbar one of the most popular names for Black schools across the country.

The grassroots organizing among Black teachers in Washington, DC, was not an isolated event; it reflected an ongoing struggle in the professional world of Black teachers. Black educators organized to challenge curricular violence in their classrooms, and it was not sporadic. It reflected persistent struggle and a blossoming intellectual culture nurtured in networks created and sustained by Black teachers.

COMBATING CURRICULAR VIOLENCE AS AN ENDURING STRUGGLE

As the decades progressed, Black Americans continued to struggle for influence and control over education in their communities, and curricular violence persisted as a major issue. In 1927, Woodson observed, "In practically all the schoolhouses of Europe and America there is not a picture on the wall or a book on the shelf to show that a Negro has ever achieved anything."[50] To challenge this erasure of Black life, Woodson published textbooks beginning in 1922, founded Negro History Week in 1926, and produced supplementary curricular materials through his Association.

Black educators across the country partnered with Woodson's Association in this work, many setting up local committees to review curricula and create supplementary units. In the late 1930s the Louisiana Colored Teachers Association "formulated a committee to review the textbooks used in the public schools to assure that unfair statements dealing with Black people were not included," and that more expansive representations of Black life were featured in school lessons.[51] This work was ongoing. A decade after this committee was formed, George Longe, a prominent New Orleans educator, wrote to school board officials notifying them that a book circulating in the schools described Blacks to be "ugly as monkeys and stupid as owls."[52]

However, Black educators did not limit their work to responding to anti-Black curriculum. They also developed new learning material and units of study that teachers could incorporate into their classes. Between the 1930s and 1940s, Black educators in cities such as Chicago, Houston, and New Orleans developed supplementary units of study focused on Black history and literature in the United States and beyond.[53] Many of these teachers took up this work in partnership with some larger Black organization, whether it was their state teachers' association or Woodson's ANSLH. These efforts would overlap and intersect with the campaigns waged by the NAACP to remove racist curricula from schools, particularly in the post-World War II era. Black teachers had long supported the NAACP and were central to this work.[54]

Black educators engaged emerging scholarship published by the Black intellectual elite in their efforts to challenge curricular violence. Sustained study of new narratives about history and social issues of the day allowed Black educators to challenge dominant curricular scripts. For instance, in February 1934, W. E. B. Du Bois lectured before more than four hundred teachers and students affiliated with the New Orleans Teachers Association. His talk focused on the impact of fugitive slaves on the abolitionist movement and how their political efforts laid the groundwork for many of the campaigns waged by Black leaders and their allies during Reconstruction. Du Bois based his lecture on his forthcoming book, *Black Reconstruction*, published the following year. Teachers sat spellbound in the historic Central Congregationalist Church for nearly an hour while Du Bois presented his "conclusive facts and figures on 'The Negro and Reconstruction.'" The substance of his talk was enough to hold the audience on the edge of their seats, even while rendered in a subdued manner. The esteemed scholar presented his case without moving "from a chosen spot, without any mannerisms, without any oratorical flights of fancy, without any play upon the emotions of his listeners."[55]

In the coming months, Du Bois would implore Black educators to break loose from worn curricular frameworks in the American school that continued to distort Black life and culture. He insisted, "Negroes must know the history of the Negro race in America, and this they will seldom get in white institutions." He pointed to the work of contemporary Black intellectuals as a foundation on which educators might develop new programs of study. Black children "ought to study textbooks like Brawley's 'Short History,' the first edition of Woodson's 'Negro in Our History' [. . .]. They ought to study intelligently and from their own point of view, the slave trade, slavery, emancipation, Reconstruction and present economic development."[56] Indeed, this was the very impression Du Bois left on Black teachers in New Orleans after his 1934 Negro History Week lecture.

By November 1934, the city's teachers were still discussing the topic of Reconstruction, plotting how they might incorporate these new insights into their academic program for the new school year. At the annual ASNLH meeting in Houston, a delegation of New Orleans teachers shared with Woodson that "the public schools of New Orleans were preparing to arrange a float for the Mardi Gras Carnival which depicts the outstanding Negroes in the reconstruction history of Louisiana."[57] These conversations continued among the city's educators once Du Bois's *Black Reconstruction* was published. For instance, in 1937—two years after the book's release—Vivian Robinson, a senior at the Valena C. Jones Normal and Practice School of New Orleans, reviewed the book in her school's publication. Robinson appealed to her readers, likely other preservice teachers at the normal school, to "Read the book, 'Black Reconstruction' and make all of this information part of your own!"[58]

In 1934, Miss Tamah Richardson, a veteran elementary school teacher at the George P. Phenix School in Hampton, Virginia, decided to build a ten-week unit on Black history and culture. Her decision was sparked by a question posed by a third grader. Midway through a social studies lesson about the diversity of people around the world, where students used their "Let's Go Traveling Map," Calvin worked up the nerve to ask, in a rather assertive manner, "May we study ourselves, too?" Intrigued by the boy's query, Richardson embraced the opportunity to demonstrate her pedagogical agility. She called a vote among the thirty-seven students: "How many would like to study the Negro?" Seeing every hand shoot up caused Richardson to smile, as she looked at Miss Annie Rivers, a preservice teacher assigned to her class for the year. They were "happy to have the children show an interest in a study about their own people," and at such a young age. They would not wait until Negro History Week to respond to Calvin's question. According to their article in the *Virginia Teachers Bulletin*, Richardson and Rivers used an essay from the *Journal of Negro History* on "What We Should Teach the Negro Child" to develop their ten-week unit of work, which ran from late fall 1934 through February 1935.[59]

During the ten-week unit, students interviewed formerly enslaved members of their community, read about important Black historical figures, used social studies lessons to create travel plans to African countries of their choice, studied the Negro national anthem, and wrote songs of their own. The students also mailed handwritten letters to Black students at the J. C. Training School in North Carolina, who responded with properly formatted letters detailing their own studies of Black life. Richardson and Rivers emphasized that they developed their lessons while still adhering to established learning objectives for their grade level.

However, although Richardson and Rivers were attentive to core learning objectives based on official educational standards, they also adhered to key political convictions that exceeded such requirements. They declared, "In our schools we are trying to prepare our boys and girls to meet the problems they will have to face as a Negro." To face these problems, or to even recognize that such challenges existed, students needed to study those men and women "who have risen above [. . .] discrimination, prejudice, and even active opposition, to accomplish great things." When Negro History Week arrived in February, students dramatized what they learned in a formal program, expressing a shared vision for their collective futures.[60]

At their 1936 annual meeting, members of Woodson's ASNLH elected Mary McLeod Bethune their president.[61] Bethune was an educator, political figure, and school founder, and she was a giant in the world of Black teachers.

She was also a familiar face to the Association's membership, having been the first woman to present a major paper at its annual meeting in 1923.[62] Bethune was also a past president of the National Association of Teachers in Colored Schools. In short, her leadership in the ASNLH embodied the convergence between Woodson's mission of challenging distortions about Black life in dominant scripts of knowledge and the professional work taken up by Black educators.

In 1935, as a new member of the ASNLH's executive council, Bethune delivered an address demanding greater focus on "interpreting" the findings produced by trained scholars for lay readers, especially students in schools. Bethune asserted, "Already we have an ample supply of investigators, but it appears to me that there is a shortage of readable and responsible interpreters, men and women who can effectively play the role of mediator between the trained investigator and the masses."[63] Bethune's appeal informed the theme for the 1936 meeting, "The Teaching of Negro History, Literature, and Art." Key sessions focused on using emerging scholarship on Black life and history to transform the learning experiences of students at the elementary through collegiate levels.[64]

Heeding Bethune's call for more emphasis on translating academic writing for grade school students, Woodson began publishing the *Negro History Bulletin* in 1937, as the Association's director of research. Many of the articles, stories, lesson plans, and class assignments published in this magazine were written by schoolteachers. As historian John Hope Franklin observed years later, the *Negro History Bulletin* became the "most vigorous extension of the work of Dr. Woodson" into the lives of Black students. He continued, "Teachers were to find in it materials for use in classes in secondary and elementary schools, while students themselves were to discover in its pages stimulating and inspirational materials that would be valuable to their studies."[65]

According to Woodson, the magazine's singular objective was "the stimulation of the study of the Negro in the public schools." The publication was written at a fifth-grade reading level to make it accessible to the widest range of students possible. The Association published nine issues per year, from October to June, thus aligning with the school year calendar.[66]

Woodson utilized the infrastructure of colored teachers' associations to popularize the *Negro History Bulletin*. Miss Pearl Schwartz, chair of the Missouri State Association of Negro Teachers, wrote to Woodson ordering three hundred copies of the publication after the inaugural issue in October 1937. She circulated and publicized the magazine at their state meeting the following month. Woodson's friend and protégé Lorenzo Johnson Greene also helped promote the *Bulletin* at this meeting. Greene assured Woodson that it was his "intention to personally present the matter of the *Negro History Bulletin* to this group." Woodson often relied on close associates and members of the ASNLH, many of whom were schoolteachers or faculty members at Black colleges, to advance the cause of the Association when he himself could not be physically present.[67]

As a professor at Lincoln University, Greene taught summer school courses for teachers. In 1938, he requested that Woodson send literature about the ASNLH to share with teachers enrolled in his summer courses, along with copies of books that could be purchased from the Association to stock their classrooms and school libraries. Woodson subsequently requested teachers' mailing addresses to include them in the Association's national outreach campaign.[68] Black educators were highly networked as a professional group, and such communication channels helped fortify their work to challenge curricular violence in their classrooms, alongside other advocacy campaigns they waged in response to other social and political issues.[69]

Hilda Grayson was a South Carolina field agent for the ASNLH and a leader within South Carolina's black teachers' association. In 1941, Grayson traveled to summer schools across the state, educating Black teachers about publications by the ASNLH and the organization's larger mission.[70] Woodson described Grayson as a "field representative of the Association." She worked "with the teachers through their conferences, associations, and conventions to demonstrate how the work of the Association may be correlated with what they are doing from day to day," and Grayson "conducted a number of demonstrations with exhibits set up according to suggested themes, with pictures, newspapers, magazines, and books appropriate for school work."[71] Because of dedicated teachers like Grayson, the original scholarship produced by scholars such as Woodson was able to reach ordinary teachers across the country, often even in the most remote and rural contexts.

Dwight O. W. Holmes, president of Morgan State University, described encountering the curricular materials produced and circulated by the ASNLH being "displayed in large urban high schools and in small schools in towns and rural areas for use at special exercises for pupils in classes in history." Across these variety of schools, pictures of Black leaders and thinkers such as Frederick Douglass and Harriet Tubman could be found "hung so that they could constantly be seen." Holmes observed that these decorations were "a minor, but none-the-less important project [...] instilling in the minds of school children, respect for and familiarity with successful colored persons."[72]

In her history of the American Teachers Association (formerly the National Association of Teachers in Colored Schools), Thelma Perry insisted that Woodson's partnership with teachers represented a movement in Black educational thought. Woodson and Black teachers collectively strived "for a new perspective" as it pertained to educating black children. Such movement required an intentional "shift away from acceptance of black people as inferior, even sub-human by so-called scholars."[73] Like Richard Robert Wright in the late nineteenth century, Black educators during the first half of the twentieth century recognized their work to be in direct conflict with "so-called scholars" who perpetuated ideas of Black inferiority within the academy. African American teachers assumed the intellectual task of challenging dominant curricular scripts, which were based on histories and cultural ideas that continued to legitimize white supremacy and, therefore, too, the violence that Black people experienced in the social world.

— ✺ —

One Friday evening in April 1942, more than two thousand five hundred delegates of the Georgia Teachers and Education Association (GT&EA) walked up the steps and through the six pillars of Sisters Chapel at Spelman College. They filled the pews inside of the red brick structure. When the sanctuary reached capacity, the remaining educators stood on chairs outside the building while looking in through the windows. Carter G. Woodson gave the opening address for the annual meeting of the GT&EA. "Do not hang your heads in shame because your face is black for yours is a great heritage," he said to them. Do not teach students "away from their environment and leave them suspended in the air, but teach them with a more realistic approach." He declared, "The whole educational system as applied to the Negro is wrong."[74] Woodson then criticized popular geography books and representations of Africa in school curricula, likely offering the same critique raised in his iconic treatise, *The Mis-education of the Negro*, published nearly ten years prior.

> In geography the races were described in conformity with the program of the usual propaganda to engender in whites a race hate of the Negro, and in the Negroes contempt for themselves. A poet of distinction was selected to illustrate the physical features of the white race, a bedecked chief of a tribe those of the red, a proud warrior the brown, a prince the yellow, and a savage with a ring in his nose the black. The Negro, of course, stood at the foot of the social ladder.
>
> The description of the various parts of the world was worked out according to the same plan. The parts inhabited by the Caucasian were treated in detail. Less attention was given to the yellow people, still less to the red, very little to the brown, and practically none to the black race. Those people who are far removed from the physical characteristics of the Caucasians or who do not materially assist them in the domination or exploitation of others were not mentioned except to be belittled or decried.[75]

For these reasons, Woodson cautioned the teachers against "imitating whites" in their curricular orientations and educational standards.[76] Woodson regularly attended meetings convened by colored teachers' associations. He recognized how critical these spaces were to the political and intellectual work necessary to improve the experiences and impact of Black teachers. Woodson learned this lesson early in life, given that his own family members were early members of West Virginia's association, founded in 1891.[77]

Such organizations created a professional public for Black educators to strategize in their efforts to combat the proliferation of curricular violence in American schools. Washington, DC, educator Albert N. D. Brooks emphasized this point in 1945. "It is certain," wrote Brooks, "that boards of education generally cannot be relied upon to furnish satisfactory educational programs for the Negro." To achieve meaningful education for African American students, Brooks declared that Black teachers and communities must work around white school boards. He encouraged those reading the *Negro History Bulletin* to organize "Negro Planning Committees" in their communities to develop collective local strategies.[78]

Black teachers recognized the condemnation of Blackness—as manifested through physical violence, racist social policy, and the unequal allocation of resources and opportunity—to be narratively constituted.[79] It was prefigured, legitimized, and reinforced through dominant curricula, a system of representation that structured and reflected the national consciousness. Such violence and injustice in the world rested on ideas engrained in official knowledge. This curricular violence persisted over time. Likewise, Black educators (and students) continued to challenge knowledge systems that helped sustain their suffering. This violent conflict in knowledge amounted to one of the primary assaults against African-descendant people in the modern world, and it represents an ongoing struggle, even to this day. The problem evolved over time but, nonetheless, remains a central antagonism in Black educational life.

As demonstrated by Brooks's comments and the event hosted by the GT&EA, Black teachers used intellectual and organizing strategies to combat curricular violence. Such strategies appear to have been quite consistent from the Civil War era through Jim Crow. Black educators took the initiative to conduct research and develop new perspectives about curriculum, especially as it pertained to history and ideas about race. They organized learning communities for themselves to explore and encounter ideas that challenged hegemonic discourse in school curriculum. They taught students to be suspicious of ideas in the official knowledge system that diminished Black history and culture or that insisted that one race was superior to another.

Black teachers cultivated a distinct professional disposition, whereby their vocational commitments were intentionally set apart from the dominant ideology of American schooling. Many Black educators strived to be more than conduits for dominant scripts of knowledge to pass through, having recognized the dominant symbolic order—the realm of ideas, stories, and human history—to be the same frames of reference that legitimized and structured their suffering. Greatest among them were those who assumed the responsibility of being producers of knowledge, educators who chose to actively teach against the grain and think otherwise, to refuse their narratively condemned status. They were educators who chose to know the world and themselves on new terms, requiring sustained resistance in both thought and deed.

Combating curricular violence was part and parcel of Black teachers' tradition of "fugitive pedagogy," whereby various intellectual and political strategies were used to subvert anti-Black domination in school and society. This work took place in organized and often clandestine fashion. It was a countervailing educational project with roots in the time of slavery, persisting into the post-emancipation era when Black education continued to be met by violent white resistance.[80] The word "tradition" is used here to characterize this intellectual history of Black teachers' critical pedagogy because, as demonstrated in this essay, the strategies they used were passed down in both formal and informal ways. These strategies were inherited and reconfigured by new generations of teachers, some having been students themselves whose lives were enhanced by this tradition. Such repetition grounded Black pedagogical practices, allowing them to be traced back. Black teachers' traditions were set apart from official protocols of the American school, because for so long the mainstream curriculum and policies of this institution helped fortify the condemnation of Blackness in the known world.

Cynthia Plair Roddey

Carolina Activist and Teacher in the Movement

ALEXIS M. JOHNSON, DANIELLE WINGFIELD,
& DERRICK P. ALRIDGE

At 7:15 in the morning of July 20, 1964, Black student Cynthia Plair Roddey arrived at the campus of the all-women's Winthrop College in Rock Hill, South Carolina, to begin her graduate education. Roddey passed through Winthrop's guarded gate and sat in the administration building waiting for school officials to orchestrate her day. At around 7:30 that morning, the officials arrived and assisted Roddey in locating her classes and navigating the campus, a process that proceeded without incident.[1]

Like many of her fellow teachers, Roddey pursued her graduate studies during the summer months. Roddey had graduated from Johnson C. Smith University in Charlotte, North Carolina, several years earlier, and after a few years of teaching, she had decided to attend Winthrop to obtain a master's degree in library science. Rock Hill was considered by some to be more progressive than many other South Carolina towns. However, it was still a Jim Crow town with a history of hostility toward civil rights activism. Thus, Roddey and her family were well aware of the dangers of desegregating a Southern women's college.[2]

Although many in the Carolinas know Roddey as Winthrop's first Black enrollee and Black graduate student, she is also a highly respected educator and activist. Her work as a teacher and librarian in Rock Hill and Charlotte spans six decades and has influenced the lives of countless students from preschool through college.[3] Moreover, Roddey's career as an educator activist mirrors the work of thousands of Black teachers throughout the South and across the country who began their teaching careers during the civil rights movement and taught for several decades thereafter.

For many Black teachers in the South, their pedagogical activism was influenced both by growing up in a Jim Crow society and by the civil rights movement, which shaped the context in which they were educated and in which they taught.[4] Roddey engaged the civil rights movement in multiple ways. As a student, she was part of a contingency of youth activists whom historian V. P. Franklin called "the young crusaders" and historian Martha Jones characterized more specifically as "the vanguard of Black women" who broke through barriers during the Black freedom struggle. As a teacher, Roddey also represents a group whom historian Tondra L. Loder-Jackson described as "schoolhouse activists,"[5] who used teaching to advance the cause of civil rights.[6]

Our chapter builds on the work of historians who have written extensively about the activism of Black teachers—Black women teachers, in particular— in the civil rights movement. In telling Roddey's story, this chapter will further illuminate the vital contributions of Black women educators. Drawing primarily on interviews with Roddey, in addition to other primary and secondary sources, we seek to answer the following questions: (1) What experiences influenced Dr. Roddey's activism? (2) How did she engage in activism in her teaching? (3) What is Dr. Roddey's legacy for contemporary educators?

HISTORIOGRAPHY AND APPROACH

Some scholars of the civil rights movement have claimed that teachers were not fully engaged in activism during the movement. Teachers, they have argued, often stayed silent because they feared repercussions from their all-white school boards, being branded as radical by their school communities, or both. However, other historians have provided a different portrayal of teachers' engagement based on an exploration of their roles before, during, and after the civil rights movement.[7]

Historian James Anderson examined the role of Black teachers from Reconstruction through the first decades of the twentieth century. His work is foundational in demonstrating how, several decades before the civil rights movement of the 1960s, teachers engaged in pedagogical activism and offered culturally relevant curricula to ground the education of Black students in the history and realities of Black life. Vanessa Siddle Walker provides further documentation of Black educators' activism in her scholarship on the years before and during the civil rights movement, which encompasses teachers and administrators in Caswell County, North Carolina, and in Gainesville and Atlanta, Georgia. Jarvis Given argues that, during the first half of the twentieth century, teachers utilized the scholarship of Black historian Carter G. Woodson to teach Black history and thus used a "fugitive pedagogy" to counter the information about Blacks found in many southern textbooks.[8]

South Carolina was a hotbed of teacher activism in the 1950s and 1960s. For instance, R. Scott Baker tells the story of Black teachers and students in Charleston, South Carolina, arguing that the teachers used Deweyan educational strategies to teach students. Likewise, Candace Cunningham has explored the activism of teachers at the Elloree Training School in Orangeburg County, South Carolina, who engaged in frontline activism in their push for school desegregation. Jon Hale has examined Black teachers' activism through their involvement in Black teachers' associations. These studies are instrumental in providing context for Cynthia Plair Roddey's activism and educational work in upstate South Carolina and Charlotte, North Carolina.[9]

In *Reading, Writing, and Segregation: A Century of Black Women Teachers in Nashville*, historian Sonya Ramsey chronicles the lives and pedagogy of Nashville teachers. In illuminating the importance of teaching reading and writing as liberatory acts, Ramsey has helped shape our conceptualization of pedagogical activism. We see the work of Roddey, a Black woman teacher, reflected in Ramsey's narratives of Black women teachers.[10]

This chapter extends the literature on desegregation in higher education. Works such as Maurice Daniels's *Horace T. Ward: Desegregation of the University of Georgia, Civil Rights Advocacy, and Jurisprudence*; Robert Pratt's *We Shall Not Be Moved: The Desegregation of the University of Georgia*; Robert Greene and Tyler Parry's *Invisible No More: The African American Experience at the University of South Carolina*; and B. J. Hollars's *Opening the Doors: The Desegregation of the University of Alabama and the Fight for Civil Rights in Tuscaloosa* are just a few of the books that explore desegregation at Southern universities. The story of Roddey's admission to Winthrop College extends existing scholarship on the desegregation of higher education and adds to the rather sparse literature on graduate students' desegregation.

This chapter builds on the previous scholarship on Black teachers and draws extensively from the oral history collection called the Teachers in the Movement (TIM) project at the University of Virginia. TIM conducts interviews with teachers who taught between 1950 and 1980 to discern what, how, and why they taught during the civil rights and post–civil rights eras. In collecting Black teachers' oral histories, TIM seeks to learn about their pedagogy and activism both inside and outside the classroom through their own words and voices.[11]

The three interviews with Roddey housed in the TIM project collection were conducted in 2005, 2015, and 2021.[12] Derrick Alridge, director of the TIM project and a coauthor of this chapter, has known Roddey since childhood through his friendship with Roddey's two sons and daughter. During his youth, Alridge also attended Liberty Hill Missionary Baptist Church in Catawba, South Carolina, where Roddey was a member and served as the church pianist.

The interviews with Roddey, like most in the TIM collection, were secured through personal relationships between TIM team members and Black communities in the South. Alridge and Alexis M. Johnson, an associate director of the TIM project and a native of Cheraw, South Carolina, who also has expertise on South Carolina history, conducted the 2021 interview. Johnson and Alridge drew on their local knowledge of South Carolina in conducting the interview. Our third coauthor, Danielle Wingfield, is also an associate director of the TIM project. A native of Lynchburg, Virginia, and a professor of law at the University of Richmond, she has expertise on Southern history and oral history research.

ROCK HILL, SOUTH CAROLINA, AND CIVIL RIGHTS

Like other Southern towns during the first half of the twentieth century, Rock Hill, South Carolina, was a Jim Crow town. Blacks and whites attended separate schools, ate in different restaurants, and socialized in different areas of town. Located in York County, South Carolina, Rock Hill is located about fifty miles south of Charlotte, North Carolina, in the Piedmont region of the Carolinas. The town was established in 1852, at a time when slavery was legal throughout the South and talk of an impending conflict between the states was in the air. Its name came from a rocky hill in the area where workers were building a rail line from Charlotte to Columbia, South Carolina.[13]

After the Civil War, Rock Hill's population was a mere two hundred fifty residents, including formerly enslaved Blacks. Blacks organized the Union League, which also comprised Black Republicans, to help educate Blacks about the government, political platforms, Reconstruction bills, and elections. Such Black political activism was met with resistance from the Ku Klux Klan and other groups that wanted to preserve the tradition of Black servitude. Yorkville—later York—South Carolina, which was adjacent to Rock Hill, would become home to the first Klan unit in South Carolina. From Reconstruction through the first decades of the twentieth century, the Black citizens of York County endured Klan terrorism. As a result, Rock Hill was ripe for civil rights activism to emerge.[14]

Rock Hill, South Carolina was a pivotal site in the civil rights movement of the 1960s. During the 1950s and 1960s, several legendary Rock Hill leaders were at the forefront of making the town more equitable as it pertained to Blacks. One of those leaders was Reverend Cecil Ivory, pastor of the Hermon United Presbyterian Church and president of the National Association for the Advancement of Colored People (NAACP) during the 1950s. A large man confined to a wheelchair, Ivory helped organize a boycott of the buses in Rock Hill to protest racial segregation on buses in 1957. Eventually, the bus system was desegregated and Ivory's stature as a civil rights leader was further solidified as he would play a central role in civil rights battles in Rock Hill until his death in 1961.[15]

In 1961, students at the local all-Black Friendship Junior College sat in at McCrory's lunch counter in Rock Hill to protest segregated lunch counters and other segregated businesses in town. After being refused service, the students, who became known as the Friendship Nine, were arrested and, instead of paying bail, chose to serve thirty days in the York County jail. The "Jail, No Bail" campaign, as it was called, was legendary in Alridge's youth and marked an important moment in the civil rights movement. One of the students who served jail time was William "Dub" Massey, who later became a sixth-grade teacher at Jefferson Elementary in York, South Carolina, and an influential community leader in Rock Hill.[16]

In 1961, the Congress of Racial Equality and its leader, James Farmer Jr., decided to send buses of youths throughout the South to test states' compliance with the desegregation of buses. Members of the Student Nonviolent Coordinating Committee and other organizations joined the Freedom Rides, which consisted of approximately 1000 riders. In May 1961, Freedom Riders arrived in Rock Hill. John Lewis was one of the youths attacked. The stories of the Friendship Nine and the Freedom Riders are just two of many that constitute Rock Hill's rich civil rights history, which provided fertile ground for the activism of Roddey.[17]

THE PLAIRS OF ROCK HILL, SOUTH CAROLINA

Cynthia Plair Roddey was born in 1940 into a family of educators. She recalls that her grandmother was a classmate of Mary McCleod Bethune. Roddey's father, Isaiah Plair, was a graduate of South Carolina State College and served as principal of Liberty Hill School, a Rosenwald School in Catawba, South Carolina. Her mother, Ruth Jordan Plair, taught at Fairfield Elementary—also a Rosenwald School—in Winnsboro, South Carolina.[18]

It was rare for any Black child born in the Jim Crow South to have two college-educated parents. With such parents, Roddey grew up surrounded by role models, books, music, and intellectual stimulation. Roddey recalls participating as a child in a program at Johnson C. Smith University called Let's Pretend, which encouraged Black youths to imagine themselves in positions of leadership and helped them envision possibilities for their future.[19] Roddey also grew up with talented siblings. Her oldest brother, Bobby Plair, was a talented musician who played many different instruments. He became well known in South Carolina as a music teacher and also as the leader of various bands, including a band called Plair. Roddey's youngest brother, Isaiah Plair, was an athlete, well known in Rock Hill for scoring fifty points in a basketball game at Emmett Scott High School. He would later become a local businessman.[20]

Like other Blacks of her generation, Roddey did not see herself as deprived or perceive her segregated Black community as inferior to white society. Roddey viewed her community as a village and remembers it as loving, tight knit, and self-sufficient, a model for other segregated Black communities throughout the South. She recalls, "We were pretty much self-contained, with doctors and ministers and grave diggers and cooks and laundry people, but it was a very, very close community."[21] Her description of the Rock Hill in which she grew up is not unlike descriptions of other Black communities throughout the South and is reminiscent of the segregated, self-sufficient communities that the scholar W. E. B. Du Bois studied in Farmville, Virginia, and Durham, North Carolina.[22] The social capital that Roddey developed through her childhood experiences with her family and community would go a long way in preparing her for the challenges she would face as an educator.

The Plairs had a long history of civil rights activism and education in South Carolina. Roddey recalled:

> Growing up with my parents, they owned a store, so I learned a lot about business. My grandfather was a Realtor, so I learned a lot about how to collect rent and maintenance of properties, [those] kinds of things, growing up. So they were businesspeople and tradespeople.[23]

Church was an integral part of life for most Black families in the Jim Crow South. At eight years old, Roddey thought she might follow in the footsteps of her grandmother, who established several churches and served as a bishop in the Holiness Pentecostal Church. To discern whether the ministry might be young Roddey's calling, her grandmother asked her to give a trial sermon. The sermon evidently did not go well, as Roddey recalled her grandmother telling her she would need to "find another vocation."[24]

Throughout Roddey's childhood, she was constantly surrounded by music. Her father played guitar, drums, and piano, and her mother played piano at church. An avid pianist, Roddey could play anything she heard by ear. In addition to music, Roddey's parents surrounded her with art and literature while she was growing up, although she noted that most Black children did not have such advantages.[25] Roddey was also surrounded by Black history. "As a child, I never got toys at Christmas; I always got books, and I remember among them being Black history books, because Black history was not taught in the schools, but our parents made sure that we knew our history."[26]

Roddey's tight-knit family provided a haven in which she could grow intellectually and develop the confidence she would need later in life. Recognizing Roddey's academic abilities, her family sent her to a private school in Greensboro, North Carolina. Greensboro, a college town that was home to two historically Black colleges, Bennett College and North Carolina A&T State University, offered a vibrant intellectual environment. While in Greensboro, Roddey also traveled to nearby Davidson College for interracial meetings to discuss the country's transition to a new world of harmony between the races.[27]

Roddey's experiences growing up in a loving and supportive Black community, her exposure to a larger world in Greensboro, and the pedagogical influences she encountered in high school and college would prepare her for direct involvement in the civil rights movement.[28] As a librarian and, later, as a teacher in the 1960s and beyond, Roddey exposed her students, both Black and white, to literature that would broaden their horizons far beyond their local communities. She also introduced them to Black history, believing, as W. E. B. Du Bois and Carter G. Woodson did, that a knowledge of Black history was essential to the healthy psychological development of Black children.

COLLEGE YEARS

Roddey's first choice for college was Purdue University, but as was the case for most Black teachers who came of age during Jim Crow, Roddey attained her undergraduate education at a historically Black college. Although South Carolina had several prominent historically Black colleges and universities (HBCUs) that Roddey could have attended, including South Carolina State College (University), Claflin College (University), Morris College, Benedict College, and Allen University, she instead chose to cross the state line to North Carolina to attend Johnson C. Smith University.[29]

Located in Charlotte, Smith was only a stone's throw from Rock Hill, and Roddey had close family ties to the institution. She explained:

> My father attended school there when it was Biddle, when it was a boarding high school, so he was there. I had uncles and cousins who had graduated from there. My great-grandmother was a laundress there. We lived down the street from there, so I was on that campus as a five-year-old going to a program called "Let's Pretend," and really just kind of grew up on Smith's campus. And so that was just a logical progression. . . . This was a great historical Black college with a lot of family history.[30]

Despite being born into a family of educators, Roddey did not plan to become a teacher. Initially pursuing her dream of becoming a religious social worker, she majored in religion and English and minored in psychology.[31] As in Greensboro, Roddey's experience at Smith was exhilarating, and her professors influenced her future teaching philosophy and pedagogy. "I had one teacher . . . who said that students' minds are like a blackboard . . . you can write on it, you can make changes."[32] Her professor's Lockean perspective of a *tabula rasa* would guide Roddey's pedagogy throughout her career, reminding her always of the teacher's power to mold young minds.

During the civil rights era, seemingly wherever a Black college or university existed, student activism blossomed. As historian Jelani Favors wrote in *Shelter in a Time of Storm: How Black Colleges Fostered Generations of Leadership and Activism*, not only were HBCUs "seedbeds of activism," but they were also "an essential, and noncollapsible, space that oriented and trained Black youths to serve as agents of justice."[33] Therefore, it seemed predestined that North Carolina, with its twelve HBCUs,[34] would be the site of a prolific student movement.

As historian Tom Hanchett has claimed, it was the network of HBCUs in North Carolina that distinguished the movement in the Tar Heel State from those of its Southern counterparts:

> North Carolina has at times prided itself on being "progressive." One of the things that it has that a lot of other Southern states don't have is a very strong HBCU tradition, going back to the years right after the Civil War when Johnson C. Smith University in Charlotte was launched.[35]

Indeed, a prolific student movement based in the state's HBCUs flourished. The Black student movement, and the direct-action phase[36] of the classical period of the civil rights movement, had its roots in North Carolina with the sit-ins launched by the Greensboro Four (Joseph McNeil, Franklin McCain, Ezell Blair Jr., and David Richmond) at a Woolworth's lunch counter in Greensboro on February 1, 1960. However, Roddey's participation in the movement during her years at Smith (1957–1960) suggests that the Black student movement in North Carolina began years earlier. As was the case for students at North Carolina A&T State University at this time, Johnson C. Smith students, including Roddey, were involved in various efforts to eradicate white supremacy in the Queen City and across the Tar Heel State.

That same year, students across the United States converged on the campus of Shaw University in Raleigh, North Carolina, to establish the Student Nonviolent Coordinating Committee (SNCC). The group's advisors included civil rights activist and Southern Christian Leadership Conference acting executive director Ella Baker and historian Howard Zinn, but the students were the backbone of the group. Attendees included Marion Barry, John Lewis, Diane Nash, and others who would later become key figures in the civil rights movement.[37]

Roddey was active in the student chapter of the NAACP[38] and also participated in a series of dialogues between Johnson C. Smith and Davidson College,[39] a predominantly white private liberal arts college in Davidson, North Carolina, a suburb of Charlotte. Roddey described the dialogues as "conversations between Black and White students who were trying to talk about how we can bring about some positive changes."[40] Such interracial academic partnerships were common during the civil rights era. They included the Brown–Tougaloo Partnership between Brown University and the historically Black Tougaloo College in Jackson, Mississippi,[41] as well as a series of programs developed by the American Friends Service Committee to address the five-year closure of public schools in Prince Edward County, Virginia.[42]

Roddey's involvement also extended beyond such quieter acts of resistance. Although she claims that she "would not have made a very good nonviolent protestor,"[43] she joined other Smith students in participating in a sit-in to desegregate the lunchroom at Ivey's department store.[44] Nevertheless, Roddey did not allow her activism to detract from her studies, successfully balancing the rigors of both to graduate in just three years.[45]

Upon graduation, Roddey remained at Smith, working as a library assistant under the auspices of Mr. Gunn, a longtime family friend.[46]

It was during this transition period that Roddey's entry into teaching began, at the behest of her mother. She recalled:

> Back in that age, your mama still told you what to do if you were still in her house. So my mother told me that I was going to get a teaching certificate. I had planned to work in the area of social work and wanted to get my master's in social work, and she said, "Oh no, you're going to get a teaching certificate." So I stayed an extra year at Smith to do practice teaching; that was the only thing that I had not done. The librarian was a family friend, so I spent a lot of time in the library when I was at Smith, and so it just worked out. He hired me as an assistant because I wanted to finish and get the teaching certificate.[47]

Black parents often insisted that their children in college obtain coursework or certification to teach. Before the civil rights era, Blacks often identified teaching or preaching as stable jobs that offered means of moving into or maintaining middle-class status.

After serving as a library assistant at Johnson C. Smith from June 1960 to May 1961, Roddey took a teaching job at Emmett Scott High School in Rock Hill School District 3. At Emmett Scott High School, named after Booker T. Washington's trusted aide at Tuskegee University, Roddey worked with William Witherspoon, who served as principal for schools throughout York County in the 1950s and 1960s. Roddey remained in this role for a year before taking a position as a librarian and elementary school teacher in the York County School District.[48]

WINTHROP DESEGREGATION

When applying to a master's program, Roddey had a choice between two HBCUs: Atlanta University (now Clark Atlanta) and Benedict College in Columbia, South Carolina. However, practical considerations prevented her from applying to either. "I looked at the school in Atlanta; the closest school with a library certification was Benedict—that's 70 miles one way. I had two toddlers in diapers, and this was going to be quite a task to do that."[49]

A fateful conversation with a fellow teacher about her options would propel Roddey to make history:

I was talking to Mrs. [Louise] Rhinehart, who was an English teacher. And she mentioned to me, "Well, why don't you go to Winthrop?" And I said, "Winthrop?" She said, "Yes. You know Harvey Gantt has gotten into Clemson. And now all of the state universities are integrated."[50]

Located in Rock Hill, Winthrop College (later University) is a public institution founded in 1886 to train white women to become teachers.[51] If Roddey were accepted, she would break the institution's color barrier. On the advice of Mrs. Rhinehart, Roddey sent a postcard to Winthrop requesting an application. After receiving and completing the application, Roddey received notice within a matter of months that she had been accepted to Winthrop.[52]

Although Roddey knew of at least ten other Black teachers who had applied to Winthrop,[53] she was the only one accepted. She was taken aback on learning of her admission. "I was really, really shocked, and I guess dismayed, when I found out that I was the [only] one selected."[54]

Roddey's history-making acceptance was likely due to a combination of factors, including Roddey's own merit, the sociopolitical context of higher education desegregation, and Southern politicking. First, Roddey was accepted because she was an exceptional student. She stated:

On paper I am the ideal student. [I] graduated from a SACS-accredited college, had already taken the Graduate Record Exam, had a National Teacher's Certificate, belonged to two national honor societies, [and] was a member of a national service organization. Straight A average in [my] majors, just really ideal.[55]

In Roddey's estimation, the other teachers who applied were equally qualified, and she felt certain that, had they not indicated their race on the application, Winthrop would also have accepted them. In 1964, three other African American women enrolled as undergraduates at Winthrop. They were Delores Johnson Hurt, Arnetta Gladden Mackey, and Sue Frances Meriwether Steed.[56]

However, because Roddey had also identified her race on the application, she posited another theory to account for her acceptance. "I also know that one of the trustees was John T. Roddey, who has a family connection to us, and I know that he was inquiring about me in the community and among other family members."[57] John T. Roddey was a white attorney who served as legal counsel to the Roddey family. Roddey explained that the relationship between John T. Roddey and her husband's family extended beyond the traditional attorney–client relationship. "In the South, there are Black families and white families from the plantation that have the same grandfathers and that kind of thing. So, John T. Roddey always called my husband's family cousins."[58]

Cynthia Plair Roddey,
Winthrop College, 1964.

John T. Roddey was not the only white power player who was involved in Roddey's admission. According to Roddey, her transcript was sent to then-governor of South Carolina Ernest F. (Fritz) Hollings for review and approval.[59] Why was the governor involved in reviewing Roddey's application to Winthrop? Because higher education desegregation elsewhere across the South was happening violently, and South Carolina hoped to avoid the precedent set at the University of Georgia in 1961 and the University of Mississippi in 1962.

When Charlayne Hunter and Hamilton Holmes attempted to desegregate the University of Georgia in 1961 after a lengthy legal battle, they were confronted by mobs of white students, Ku Klux Klan members, and local white Athenians. The violence to which Hunter and Holmes were subjected—including the mob throwing bricks at Hunter's dorm room—led to Holmes's and Hunter's suspension and a police escort of the two students back to their hometown of Atlanta. A federal judge subsequently ordered the readmission of both students.[60]

Similarly, after another legal battle, James Meredith's effort to desegregate the University of Mississippi in 1963, not only was met with mob violence but also led to a showdown between Mississippi Governor Ross Barnett and President John F. Kennedy. Despite being compelled by the state's Board of Trustees to desegregate the state's flagship institution, Barnett closed the entrance to the registration office on the day Meredith was scheduled to register for classes. Ten days after Meredith's attempted registration and eight days after Barnett was found guilty of civil contempt, Meredith tried to desegregate the institution.[61] Despite being escorted by federal marshals, Meredith's presence on campus led to a violent insurrection involving around three thousand rioters. Lasting some fifteen hours, the rioting resulted in two deaths. The following day, Meredith officially desegregated the institution.[62]

Witnessing these public acts of terror, South Carolina hoped to accomplish desegregation differently. Their test came in 1963 when Harvey Gantt desegregated Clemson University, the state's historically white land-grant institution.[63] As with his predecessors in Georgia and Mississippi, Gantt's admission to Clemson followed a legal battle; Gantt had filed a lawsuit on July 7, 1962, challenging the institution's policy of segregation.[64]

Unlike the politicians in Mississippi and Georgia, South Carolina's power players were determined to ensure a peaceful desegregation rather than doing everything in their power to prevent it. The desegregation process involved a collaborative effort between Clemson President Robert C. Edwards, State Senators Edgar Brown and Marion Gressette, and Governor Fritz Hollings. Senator Brown, who also served as chairman of Clemson's Board of Trustees, declared at the outset of the process that Clemson would not tolerate any violence.[65]

Governor Hollings, who later became a US senator, "ordered state law enforcement officials to develop a foolproof plan to ensure that Gantt's enrollment would be orderly, and later convinced U.S. Attorney General Robert F. Kennedy not to send federal marshals to the Palmetto State."[66] Gressette, who chaired the Gressette Commission, which "recommended actions on racial issues" for the state, surprised many by supporting rather than opposing desegregation.[67] Although Gantt was escorted by state troopers and police aircraft, he peacefully desegregated Clemson on January 28, 1963.[68] That fall, the University of South Carolina followed Clemson when Henrie Monteith, niece of South Carolina civil rights activist Modjeska Monteith Simkins; James Solomon; and Robert Anderson peacefully desegregated the state's flagship institution.[69]

Desegregation of the state's historically white land-grant institution and flagship institution laid the groundwork for Roddey to eradicate the color line at Winthrop. Although the state had committed to ensuring that the desegregation of Winthrop would also be peaceful, Roddey nevertheless recognized the dangers she confronted in her historic act. Despite the peaceful desegregation of Clemson and the University of South Carolina, Roddey was acutely aware of the violence that had transpired in Mississippi, Georgia, and then Alabama, where Governor George Wallace Jr. infamously stood in the doorway at the University of Alabama to prevent James Hood and Vivian Malone from desegregating the university in 1963.

Roddey recalled that her concerns at the time were primarily for her young sons. "I was watching what was happening in Mississippi, what was happening in Alabama, and I thought, 'these two little boys—I can't expose them to this.'"[70] Roddey's unease was warranted not only by what had already occurred in the Deep South but also by the conversations occurring about her own act of desegregating Winthrop. She stated, "I know that there were people saying, 'Please don't let this Black girl go. . . . Don't let her integrate the schools; [it would] be the ruin of Winthrop if you do this.'"[71]

Roddey's family and community helped her navigate her historic act, at times using covert means to protect her. For example, she related:

> When I got accepted, they didn't get the name right. My maiden name was Plair. They knew it was a schoolteacher. And they knew it was a Plair. They thought it was my mother. So my mother let them think it was her. Because we said, with all of this stuff going on. Right up until the day that I went a lot of people did not know who was coming.[72]

Approaching the actual day of desegregating Winthrop, Roddey also received support from two Black policemen from the Rock Hill Police Department who would help escort her onto campus in relative obscurity.[73]

Roddey's time at Winthrop was marked by invisibility. She was not particularly close to any of her classmates but instead established friendships with Black staff members at Winthrop with whom she had attended elementary school.

> Nobody invited me to lunch with them. I didn't do study groups. I was not integrated into the school social fabric. I spent my time with the workers, the people who were doing the grounds and in the kitchen, because these were my classmates from elementary school. So, when I took a break, I would go over to the dormitory and find them where they were someplace and sit down and have lunch with them when I did eat on campus. I could walk home, so a lot of times I would walk home. I never felt a part of Winthrop.[74]

Although relationships with her peers were virtually nonexistent, Roddey did have strong relationships with the Winthrop administration and the faculty in her program. She noted, "The relationship with the administration I would say was excellent. They really tried to make sure that there was no harassment; that I got everything that I needed when I needed it."[75]

Roddey established camaraderie with the faculty, even helping to dismantle stereotypes about Blacks. She stated:

In one class I had, every time I started to say something, somebody would interrupt me. And at the end of the class, the instructor called me out in the hall and said, "This was the first time I've taught an African American student, and I was anxious about the problems." She said, "But I'm not going to have problems with African American students. I'm going to have problems with rednecks."[76]

Roddey also fondly recalled making an "A" in a course on John Milton, noting the significance of evolving from attending "a historically Black elementary school where they had outdoor bathrooms to get[ting] an A in John Milton."[77]

During her time at Winthrop, Roddey recalled spending her time the with the Black custodians, groundskeepers, and cooks, many of whom, she knew since elementary school. During her breaks, she remembers visiting with them and eating with them during lunch time. These interactions with members of the Black community were instrumental in helping Roddey navigate Winthrop during this tumultuous time, and it alleviated some of her loneliness.[78]

In the fall of 1964, Black students Arnetta Gladden (later Mackey) and Delores Johnson (later Hurt) were admitted to Winthrop as undergraduates. Like Roddey, they also experienced alienation from their white peers. However, the two had single rooms with a connecting bathroom, which gave them a means of supporting one another as young crusaders in the movement.[79] Sue Frances Meriwether (later Steed) enrolled at Winthrop College in 1965 and would graduate in May 1967, making her Winthrop's first Black graduate.

POST-WINTHROP CAREER AND PEDAGOGICAL LESSONS

When Roddey completed her master's degree in August 1967, becoming the first Black graduate student and the second Black graduate of Winthrop, she joined the Charlotte-Mecklenburg Schools as a traveling librarian, working in schools in downtown Charlotte as well as Matthews, a smaller suburb of Charlotte.[80] During this time, the Charlotte-Mecklenburg Schools were still largely segregated, despite the *Brown v. Board of Education* decision in 1954. Eleven years after the passage of *Brown*, sixty-six of Charlotte's one hundred nine schools remained completely segregated.[81]

The glacial pace at which desegregation took place in the Queen City prompted the Supreme Court's ruling in *Swann v. the Charlotte-Mecklenburg Board of Education* (1971), a case that begin in 1965. The Black American Swann family asked the Board of Education to allow their son James to attend a deseg-regated school close to their home. However, the Board refused, insisting that he enroll in an all-Black school.

In response, on January 19, 1965, attorney Julius Chambers filed a lawsuit in which the Swanns were joined as plaintiffs by nine other Black families. Seven months later, a judge ruled against the Black families, stating that the Board of Education was, indeed, making progress towards desegregating Charlotte's schools. Although Chambers appealed the decision, the Fourth Circuit Court of Appeals upheld the ruling.[82]

The Swann case might have died had it not been for the Supreme Court decision in *Green v. County School Board of New Kent County* (1968), a case that emanated from Virginia. The nation's highest court ruled that "freedom of choice," an approach used by Virginia to avoid complying with *Brown*, was not sufficient to desegregate schools. This case produced the "Green factors" used to determine whether a school district's desegregation plans were satisfactory.

The Green factors included transportation, facilities, extracurricular activities, and the ratio of Black and white students and faculty in schools.[83] Chambers capitalized on the New Kent County ruling and refiled the Swann case in 1969. Just a month after refiling, a federal judge ruled in favor of the Swanns and ordered Charlotte's Board of Education to submit a plan to desegregate the district's schools. It was due to *Swann v. Charlotte-Mecklenburg* that court-ordered busing as a remedy was born.[84]

Roddey's position as a teacher in Lancaster, South Carolina, was followed by her long tenure as a teacher, media coordinator, and librarian at Olympic High School in Charlotte from 1968 to 1994. At Olympic, Roddey had the opportunity to teach grammar, which she viewed as an essential skill. She notes that she often began her writing lessons by asking students to give her a verb, then a subject, then to add adjectives and adverbs. Her hope was, "If you can write one good sentence, then you can write a paragraph, and from the paragraph you can go on to the essay."[85] Throughout her career, she stressed the importance of such incremental steps as an essential component of good pedagogy.

The construction of sentences, Roddey believed, was critical in teaching students to communicate effectively, and she recalled her mother telling her that people will hear you better if you communicate effectively. This lesson stayed with Roddey throughout her teaching career. Roddey believed writing was a liberatory tool for students in both the liberal arts and the trades, as it was critical in helping students express themselves and build confidence in their ability to present information to others. In her courses, Roddey encouraged practical education by asking students to write about their own interests.[86]

Roddey was proud of the trade curriculum at Olympic. Students could focus on learning skills such as brick masonry, electronics, or cosmetology. Although she grew up around books, and her parents encouraged a classical education, they also emphasized the practicality of the trades. It was, therefore, not surprising that Roddey embraced a philosophy that encompassed both the liberal arts and vocational education. Roddey was so committed to the trades that she and a colleague started an honor society for students studying the trades at Olympic High School.

Although the Swann case entails a top-down narrative in which compliance with *Brown* was imposed on the Queen City, Roddey's story, especially her experience at Olympic High School, provides insight into what was imposed inside Charlotte's classrooms during the nascent years of court-ordered desegregation. Olympic High, located in the Steele Creek neighborhood of Charlotte, opened in 1966, just as the Swann case was underway. As Roddey noted, the school "brought together students from the Black high school there and the neighborhood, Steele Creek, brought in quite a diverse population."[87]

Although it might seem that Olympic was created on the basis of good-faith efforts to comply with *Brown*, Roddey suggests that the decision was more sinister. "They actually built Olympic, which is out near the airport, to prevent White students from going to Kennedy, which was over on South Tryon Street—which is in a Black community—so [as] to prevent the White children having to go to the Black community."[88] Although Olympic High may have been desegregated, like many other schools across the nation, it was far from integrated. As at other desegregated schools, tensions were high. Roddey recalls that Olympic was the site of a race riot "caused by conflicts in culture or just things that were happening in the community—Blacks and Whites trying to learn how to get along with each other."[89]

The process of learning to coexist introduced some opportunities to teach tolerance. Roddey recalls changing the mindset of one of her students, whose uncle was a member of the Klan. "One of the young men I had, [his] uncle was a Klansman, and he took the African American history class because he wanted to know about these Black folks. He had a change of attitude once he took the class because he learned some things and realized there was some worth to Black people."[90]

Roddey's ability to teach Black history to her students can be attributed to the emergence of the Black studies movement across the nation. A submovement of the Black Power movement (1966–1975), the Black studies movement, also known as the Black campus movement,[91] saw Black students working to implement courses in Black history and culture, establish Black student unions and cultural centers, and increase the number of Black faculty and administrators. Although the Black studies movement occurred primarily in colleges and universities, many secondary schools also experienced a robust movement.[92] Although scholars typically focus on the role of students in the Black studies movement, Roddey's work at Olympic reveals the extent to which teachers were also at the forefront of Black studies. As was common across both secondary and postsecondary institutions, Roddey and other Black faculty and students worked to implement Black history and literature courses, which were not previously offered at Olympic.

Additionally, Roddey notes that Black students accounted for a higher population of students enrolled in vocational courses such as brick masonry, electronics, and cosmetology. Rather than viewing this "tracking" through a deficit lens, Roddey and others chose to turn tracking into an asset. She explained:

> A coworker and I founded a national honor society for those trade courses, a vocational honor society, so that those Black students could be recognized for their academic achievements, even though they didn't want to call it academic. But you know, if you get an "A" in electronics, why would that not be equivalent to an "A" in English?[93]

Roddey helped expand extracurricular opportunities for Black students as well. Observing the lack of representation of Black students on the prom court, she and others "started an Ebony Forum so that we could elect our own Black queens and kings."[94]

Roddey provided many pedagogical lessons over her long career. A core component of Roddey's teaching style has always been to meet students where they are and expose them to new ideas through books, arts, music, and cultural activities. Roddey recognized that children came to school with different interests and believed in individualized lessons when necessary. She recalled, for instance, how she reached students of different racial and class backgrounds by exposing them to a variety of music and literature. In teaching history, she stressed the importance of viewing events in their historical context. However, she also emphasized the relevancy of history to the present, especially in the area of economics and religion. Roddey also recalled watching the news with her students to teach about current events and the contemporary world. Through the news, Roddey believed students would see history taking place around them and in their lives. Although Roddey did not use the term *culturally relevant pedagogy*,[95] she practiced it throughout her long career of teaching.[96]

Roddey herself received a liberal arts education, but she emphasized basic life skills in her pedagogy. She believed that it was important for students to learn how to make a personal budget, write legibly and in cursive, and speak properly. Although modern technology has its benefits, she believes that texting and spell-check on smartphones and computers have stifled students' learning of writing and spelling, which are skills needed by all students.[97]

Roddey also asked philosophical questions of her students, a practice that undoubtedly emerged from her interests and academic background in philosophy and religion. She encouraged her students to look beyond the current moment, which encouraged Black youths to imagine themselves in positions of leadership and helped them envision possibilities for their future. She asked them, "How would you have made your community better? Did you make anyone happy? . . . Do you do artwork? Do you do gardening?"[98] These life questions, she noted, encouraged students to be less self-centered and to focus more on helping others. Roddey's reading of literature and philosophy influenced her pedagogy as it pertained to life's big questions.

CONCLUSION

Cynthia Plair Roddey's activism and teaching career provides a window into the world of Black teachers' work during the civil rights and post–civil rights eras. During her career of over sixty years, she desegregated Winthrop College, taught in segregated and desegregated schools in North and South Carolina, and would later become a college professor at Clinton College in her hometown of Rock Hill. Roddey is one of many Black educators who worked both publicly and behind the scenes during the civil rights and post–civil rights eras to provide an excellent education for their students.

Throughout her career, Roddey has been recognized for her contributions as an educator and activist. In 1990, she earned a Doctor of Ministry degree from the Mid-Atlantic Theological Seminary; in 2017, Winthrop University recognized her with its Alumni Distinguished Service Award; and in 2021, the South Carolina House of Representatives honored her with <u>resolution</u> (H. 3912, 2021–2022). Roddey remains an active member of the Delta Sigma Theta sorority, works with a nonprofit that she co-founded serving special-needs children, and teaches courses at Clinton College in Rock Hill.[99]

In the midst of the current curriculum culture wars about how and what teachers should teach, Roddey's reflections on her inspirations, classroom pedagogy, and curricula can inform the current generation of teachers seeking to become effective activist educators. Her emphasis on teaching history to inform the present, using literature and music to expand student knowledge about the world, providing basic skills for living life, and encouraging students to think about the meaning of life and what they will contribute to the world are teaching attributes that Roddey developed growing up, living, and teaching during one of the most transformative movements of the twentieth century. Roddey has much to teach us today and for generations to come.

"It Only Takes a Spark to Get a Fire Going"

Lois A. Simms and Pedagogical Activism during the Black Freedom Struggle, 1920–2015

JON N. HALE

Lois Averetta Simms held interviews in her home, surrounded by books, newspapers, and handwritten notes. A member of the Association for the Study of African American Life and History, she had a stack of the latest issues of the *Journal of African American History* that rested on her staircase. The house—her family home where she was born and raised—was a museum in its own right and a testament to her lifelong learning. Outside reflected little of the original Black neighborhood, part of an urban and social network that defined the city of Charleston, South Carolina. The city, historically, was predominantly Black. Before the Civil War, the number of enslaved persons outnumbered whites at least two to one and, at times, four to one.[1] The space was also a critical site of resistance in the larger freedom struggle, from efforts to acquire an education during slavery to the struggle for desegregated schools one century later. Local activists from Denmark Vesey to Septima Clark labored in Charleston as part of the movement for liberation. One would not guess the shift of historical magnitude that unfolded outside their doors when gazing at the preserved newspapers, books, mementos, and other artifacts or ephemera that reflected the tenure of her life and long career as an educator. However, at the time of our interview, families of color in the city experienced rollbacks of civil rights gains, including the privatization of schools and gentrification. Simms's narrative preserves a fleeting account of the city's civil rights past, as it presents a counternarrative of Black teaching during and after state-sanctioned segregation in the South. Simms's career and life challenge us to consider how teaching shaped the storied past of teaching during Jim Crow and the first years of desegregation. Simms also illustrates how a Black counternarrative persists during an erasure of the past from the city's landscape and the system of education.

As the city in which Simms lived and taught became a platform for larger social, political, and historical narratives, so too did Simms's illustrious career, particularly regarding civil rights. Lois Simms's teaching career bespoke a narrative that paralleled and, in meaningful moments, intersected with the Black freedom struggle. Her career spanned the most tumultuous times of public education. Her teaching began in the era of segregation and Jim Crow in 1941. She retired in 1976 after thirty-five years of teaching in the city of Charleston. While teaching at the historic Burke High School, Simms experienced the teacher equalization case, *Duvall v. J. F. Seignous et al.* (1944), in which Judge Julius W. Waring ordered that school salaries must be equal regardless of race.[2] She earned her master's degree from Howard University in 1954, the year the Supreme Court passed the monumental *Brown v. Board of Education* decision. She later taught as one of the first Black teachers in the formerly all-white Charleston High School from 1973 until her retirement in 1976.[3] The life and illustrious career of Lois Simms provide a lens through which to understand the nuanced and integral role of education in Charleston and the history of the civil rights movement.

Simms's career also illuminates the function of gender in the teaching careers of Black teachers in the South. Her position as a teacher was deeply shaped by the feminization of teaching that defined the origins of public education in the United States during the mid-nineteenth century. Hiring women to teach for salaries negligently lower than those for men structured an integral, though marginal, space for women in the teaching profession. At the intersection of race and gender within a segregated system that largely disenfranchised women, women of color faced layered obstacles that largely prohibited their entrée into the administrative level. Barred from leadership positions, Simms and other Black women were situated closer to the community, and they helped negotiate educational institutions with students, parents, and families. Serving as the "bridge" between local movement and national civil rights organizations, women were integral to their community from the early phases of the freedom struggle through desegregation.[4] Women constituted their own movement— a movement both a part of and distinct from the larger freedom struggle. As the educator activist Septima Clark of Charleston, South Carolina, noted, "Many people think the women's liberation movement came out of the civil rights movement, but the women's movement started quite a number of years before the civil rights movement."[5] Indeed, South Carolina women such as the activist educators and stalwart advocates of education such as Septima Clark, Mary McLeod Bethune, Ruby Forsythe, Fannie Phelps Adams, and Millicent Brown galvanized and shaped the movement from the local level to the national level during the freedom struggle. Although Simms did not necessarily define herself in activist-oriented terms, by her very position as a woman teaching in Charleston, she occupied a position of influence and political engagement throughout her life.

Simms's five-foot stature communicated a quiet presence compared with the oft-recognized leaders of the movement, often larger than life figures who themselves had to fight, and continue to fight, for recognition. Simms exuded a profound pedagogy that remained behind closed doors and never carried into the street or the public forum directly. As such, her story could have been easily swept into one of the multitude of teachers who remained, on the surface of things, behind the scenes as the field of education was transformed by the larger freedom struggle. However, a closer analysis and contextualization suggest otherwise. Her slight frame belied a woman whom her niece, Carmen Gaston, identified as "stern and strong in her convictions . . . [a woman] who spoke and did not care if someone was hurt by it."[6] Simms's steadfast commitment to students and education in general constituted one of the foundational pillars of the long freedom struggle that reverberated loudly across the nation.

Lois Simms's career and profession constituted a "chalk and chalkboard career," a phrase she selected to title her memoir that she published in 1996. Her chalk spelled out, and her chalkboard conveyed, the lessons of a protracted political struggle and the inculcation of skills for survival in a segregated society. As the most defining moments of the long freedom struggle cascaded outside her classroom door, her chalk and chalkboard instilled lessons that did not directly lead to the movement but, nonetheless, imbued her classrooms with the integrity and wisdom that the movement sought to cultivate in all scholars. Although she kept a calculated distance from the front lines of the freedom struggle, Lois Simms and other teachers of color practiced a form of intellectual and pedagogical activism that defined the contributions of teachers to the larger movement. This form of educational activism included implementing curricula, extracurricular courses, and culturally relevant education in historically Black elementary, middle, and high schools during the era of segregation. Teaching behind closed doors and developing the profession of teaching inculcated an overlooked modicum of resistance throughout segregated Black schools across the South that resonated deeply with the principles of the Black freedom struggle. This line of work delineates a spectrum of activism that expanded a notion of teacher-based activism during the civil rights movement. Her work, along with that of other teachers of color, challenges the prevailing narrative that teachers were not a part of the struggle or, worse, staunch defenders of the status quo. Lois Simms's pedagogy did not place her in the headlines or spotlight of the movement; yet her intellectual and pedagogical work facilitated an understanding that instilled in her scholars a groundwork to challenge structural discrimination in earnest by the 1950s.[7] Simms, like thousands of other Black educators and administrators, enacted standards for academic excellence, high expectations, a sense of community, and notions of "institutional care," which in many ways betray a notion of inherent inferiority that underlined the *Brown* decision.[8] Although not a self-defined activist, Simms operated within and shaped a baseline of excellence that was itself a platform of the larger freedom struggle.

⚬∞⚬

Necessity, circumstance, and exclusion drove the education of Ms. Simms. She was born in Charleston in 1920; her father died at a young age, but she recollected that he received up to an eighth-grade education. White administrators typically did not provide more than that and anything beyond necessitated a private education, dependent upon wealth that most did not possess.[9] By the time Simms was born, Burke High School was the only public option for high school in the city and surrounding area, and it was the only public school for less than ten years. The Avery Normal Institute, a private school that exacted a tuition often beyond the reach of the working class, was open since 1865. For Simms and so many others, the home was the first encounter with education and schooling that presaged formal instruction. In Simms's words, her mother was her "first teacher." As in many homes across the nation, "My mother took the lead in disciplining," she recalled.[10] "She spanked us with a leather strap cut so there were two or three 'tails.' . . . I hated the 'feel' of the leather strap, hence I seldom did anything to merit a whipping."[11] Simms was raised to follow her mother, who graduated from Avery Normal Institute in 1912 and began teaching in Charleston at the Wallingford Academy. With the encouragement from her supervisor, she continued her pursuit of a higher education. She enrolled at the closest school open to Black youth living in Charleston, the all-Black South Carolina State College.[12] The College of Charleston, just blocks away, remained segregated until 1963.

As in many families in the American South, religion played a defining role for Simms and her family. Her parents attended the Presbyterian Church, and Simms continued to do so throughout her life. Claiming to be more religious than her mother, before she finished high school, Simms was teaching the beginners class in Sunday school and regularly attended youth organization meetings. She attended both the Wallingford Presbyterian Church, where she served as an organist, as well as the Zion Presbyterian Church (which later burned and merged with Zion-Olivet Presbyterian), which was her parents' church, and served in the choir there.[13] She played the piano, and her brother played the violin.[14] Simms remained devoted throughout her life, committing her time after retirement to the service of the Presbyterian community and her congregation. Her religious zeal led to one of her three books, *Growing Up Presbyterian: Life in Presbyterian Colleges and Churches*, which she published in 1992.

Simms's mother and the role of education played a similarly influential role that effected a lasting influence. In particular, the Avery Normal Institute played a pivotal role in the lives of the Simms family, as it had for most Black families who enrolled in the institution. Even before the ratification of South Carolina's 1868 constitution, the Freedmen's Bureau, northern philanthropic and missionary associations, and local Black leaders established the state's first private schools for Black youths. In 1865, the American Missionary Association established the Avery Normal Institute as the first secondary private school for Black families in Charleston. The Avery Normal Institute required tuition and focused on training professionals and leaders of the local upper-class Black community through a classical education curriculum. It emerged as a premier private institution and remained one of the only secondary schools for Black youth in the Lowcountry until the end of the nineteenth century.

Simms attended Avery and thrived. She took a liking to English and history. Admittedly, Simms later professed that her "admiration for my English teacher accounts in part for my great liking for English, and the 'crush' that I had on my history teacher probably increased my liking for it as I wanted to excel in his class."[15] She enjoyed the Avery Dramatic Club and the annual junior and senior proms. Simms took second prize in a tuberculosis essay contest in her junior year and was chosen to receive from the outgoing seniors the Avery Shield, the "symbol of all that Avery stood for."[16] Simms graduated from Avery in 1937 as valedictorian.[17] This promised Simms access and opportunity in one of the few professional options afforded to Black graduates in the South.

Simms continued her education, becoming a product of the "talented tenth" supported by W. E. B. Du Bois and following the professional routes available to women of color during segregation. She enrolled in college, first attending Barber-Scotia Junior College. She was a member of the choir, the dramatic club, the newspaper staff, and the Young Women's Christian Association, or YWCA. Her work at Johnson C. Smith University was similar. Later in her career, she enrolled at Howard University and Syracuse University to enroll in and complete graduate school with master's degrees.[18] Her mother introduced her to the field, but Simms's time in institutions of higher education, particularly at Howard, left an indelible impact on how Simms understood the art and theory of teaching.

Teacher training and continuing professional education were salient features of teacher professionalization in the American South. Teacher education programs of the 1920s and 1930s, often referred to as the progressive era of education, facilitated an intellectual climate inspired in part by northern urban educators; most notably, the philosopher and pedagogue John Dewey but other contemporaries, including William Kilpatrick, Harold Rugg, and George Counts. The "progressive" educators and theorists revamped traditional methods of teaching, incorporating social methods of learning and experience geared at the whole child. In addition to a new pedagogy, many viewed teachers as key actors in political and social change and their schools as a democratic space. For one faction of progressive educators, schools were the logical place to facilitate a redistribution of resources to reconstruct a broken society along radically democratic principles. As Counts noted in *Dare the School Build a New Social Order?* all "resources must be dedicated to the promotion of the welfare of the great masses of the people."[19] Teacher education programs were often rooted in a mode of social critique, critical thinking, and an ardent commitment to democracy that defined progressive education.

Some Black educators studied directly under this vanguard of progressive educational thought in the North. Many others from the South earned degrees in higher education from premier universities across the nation. As Vanessa Siddle Walker noted, educators studied under professors who attended the University of Chicago, Columbia University, Harvard University, Cornell University, New York University, and others. They also studied at high-caliber historically Black colleges and universities (HBCUs) such as Morehouse College, Fisk University, and Howard University. Majoring in biology, chemistry, mathematics, or physics from high-quality institutions across the country, Black teachers went through college at a time when just over half of all Americans attended high schools. As high schools and secondary education developed, teachers constituted a highly educated segment of the Black professional class.[20]

Most teachers did not enroll in the programs at Howard, Fisk, the University of Chicago, or Columbia University, nor did every teacher read the works of radical progressive thinkers in their teacher education programs. Still, all teachers were exposed to progressive discourse in one form or another through ongoing education and professional development. Most Black teachers received the lessons of progressive education through Black colleges and even more examined progressive ideals as they continued their education after they began teaching through summer programs or memberships in professional teaching associations, which, in Simms's case, was the all-Black Palmetto Education Association that affiliated with the National Education Association. Additionally, most teachers—historian Adam Fairclough estimated that, by 1928, this would be over twenty-three thousand educators, which was over one-half of all teachers in Black schools—enrolled in courses during summer sessions held at local colleges, northern universities, or training schools to earn college credit, study and pass licensure examinations, or to increase their pay.[21]

White progressive educators theorists often dismissed race, but Black public intellectuals, scholars, and educators such as W. E. B. Du Bois, Benjamin Mays, Septima Clark, Carter G. Woodson, and Mary McLeod Bethune placed race at the center of teacher education and professional discourse.[22] Through ongoing education and publications stemming from the networks cultivated by the

Association for the Study of Negro Life and History (ASNLH), Black teachers studied their craft in professional spaces that addressed race directly.[23] Teacher education during the era of Jim Crow provided an opportunity to apply progressivism in a uniquely Black and segregated context.

Simms entered the profession in the wake of the progressive era of education, which left an indelible impact on her and her cohort's professional careers. Her journey to Howard for graduate study was instrumental in shaping her embrace of a curriculum that shared desires and history for uplift. She was immersed in the progressive tradition of teacher education. Part of this education offered a whole-child approach, focusing on addressing the numerous social and emotional aspects of children. Philosopher John Dewey put forth one of the most pervasive notions of "progressive education" that was ubiquitous in teacher education programs across the country. One of Dewey's core principles is the belief that "the only true education comes through the stimulation of the child's powers by the demands of the social situations in which he finds himself."[24] This formed a core body of knowledge for his theories of education informed by pragmaticism, which he expounded on later in his career. "The fundamental unity of the newer philosophy," Dewey wrote in 1938 in reference to the thriving paradigm of progressive education "is found in the idea that there is an intimate and necessary relations between the processes of actual experience and education."[25] Dewey inspired a pedagogical movement that identified a social realm necessary to address whether one was going to effectively teach. The social realm of the student and the experience therein constitutes an important aspect of this philosophy that is central to common practices in today's classrooms that focuses on recognizing the totality of students' experiences and the necessity of building on it in the school.[26] Simms's notes from the course "Principles of Guidance" reflect the progressive whole-child approach that defined this era of training. "The individual is not only an intellectual being," she wrote in a report for the class, "but a social and emotional being as well, and the emotional and social nature of the learner enter very strongly in the process of getting an education."[27]

Simms was also introduced to a curriculum that focused on Black history through her studies at Howard University. One of the courses she took was a "History of Negro Education," which plugged Simms into the history that shaped her career and trajectory in Charleston and signifying a critical consciousness that emerged from her studies at Howard University. She wrote a paper on "An Analysis of the Biological Factors in Race Relations." "The one group emigrating to America against their will for whom Americanization has been slow and incomplete is the Negro," Simms wrote.[28] Pointing toward the emerging canon of social scientists critical of biological conceptions of race, Simms reported that "some scientists are of the opinion that there is no conclusive evidence of inferiority due to the difficulty of disentangling heredity and environment factors." This led to her conclusion that "in a biological sense, then, the Negro is not inferior to other racial groups." In fact, she pointed out, "in some respects their achievement on tests have been superior to whites."[29] There was also the climate of Howard and its status as an intellectual hub for a growing freedom movement. The Graduate School of Education, led by Charles H. Thompson, editor of the *Journal of Negro Education*, organized a panel, "The Courts and Racial Integration in Education."[30] It was an ideal location to learn of the movement for education justice, as Charles Hamilton Houston served as vice dean of the Law School and was the architect behind the National Association for the Advancement of Colored People's (NAACP's) legal strategy to dismantle Jim Crow.[31] Simms took this course as part of her education. The status of thinkers at Howard, an intellectual pillar of the movement, ensured that Simms and other scholars at the institution were introduced to the most progressive thinking of the time.

Even more telling is her capstone thesis project, submitted as part of her work for a master's degree in the Department of Education at Howard University. As part of her coursework Simms argued that "a change in Southern educational policy will be necessary if the schools of South Carolina are to provide equality of education in terms of the democratic ideal for Negro and white youth alike."[32] Her base assumption was stated clearly: "Equality of opportunity in education is the right of every individual in a democracy."[33] Across the board, Simms found that expenditures and capital investment in Black education increased, precipitated by Governor James F. (Jimmy) Byrnes's sales tax, the first sales tax in the Palmetto State, to be distributed by the Education Finance Commission.[34] Between 1945 and 1951, for instance, expenditures for Black students in elementary and high school increased from thirty-three dollars per capita to eighty dollars per capita. The expenditures for transportation of Black students increased from $11.03 to $19.31. Notably, the salaries of Black female high school teachers increased from eight hundred seven dollars to two thousand sixty-six dollars during the same six-year period.[35]

The inspiration and motivation behind her thesis provide a lens through which to understand Charleston in a critical context. Simms wrote her thesis after reading an article, "The Education of Negroes in South Carolina," in *The Journal of Negro Education*, in an issue devoted to studying the provision of education to students of color in separate schools, by Dr. Frank A. DeCosta, the former principal of the Avery Normal Institute, under whom Simms graduated. In this piece, DeCosta carefully outlined the provision of education with statistical information provided by the state and clearly demonstrated the disparities in provision to Black students and schools when compared to whites.[36]

The assessment proffered in this piece inspired Simms to successfully complete her master's thesis on the funding discrepancies between Black and white schools in South Carolina—a move that connected to educator activists and their work with the NAACP since the 1930s.[37] Teachers who worked with Black teacher associations and the NAACP for teacher salary equalization pressured Southern states to live up to the premise of *Plessy v. Ferguson*'s (1896) "separate but equal" doctrine. Higher and equal wages were not an end goal in and of itself but, instead, a means to equalize a segregated system of education. As upstanding professionals and recognized community leaders acting within the larger context of teacher organization and progressive pedagogy, Black educators fueled the momentum of the civil rights movement through a less visible but nonetheless direct affront to social injustices. Beyond engaging educators in the process of litigation, Simms and other researchers provided the objective evidence, carefully compiled, that fueled the quest for equal opportunities in Black education during the 1940s. As historian Tondra Loder-Jackson argued, researchers who focused on the field of education, such as Marion Thompson Wright, Mamie and Kenneth Clark, Charles Hamilton Houston, and John Hope Franklin, provided the data needed in court. This research constituted a form of intellectual activism that contributed directly to the burgeoning movement by providing the evidence, sources, and findings required by litigation surrounding the *Brown* cases.[38]

The movement toward salary equalization took place in South Carolina, too, as it had across the South, and Simms was familiar with the case in South Carolina for teacher equalization. Two of her colleagues at Burke High School—Malissa Theresa Smith, a history teacher, and Viola Louise Duvall, a science teacher—were the first to push for equal salaries in South Carolina. Smith worked with NAACP State President James Hinton and Charleston Branch member J. Arthur Brown. When she was dismissed, the NAACP, under the direction of Thurgood Marshall and the Columbia-based attorney, Harold Boulware, worked with Duvall and brought the case to court, where Judge Julius Waring ruled in favor of the plaintiffs, "from discriminating in the payment of salaries . . . on account of race or color."[39] Moreover, Simms was teaching in Charleston, just miles from Clarendon County, which was the site of the *Briggs v. Elliott* (1952) case.[40] This was a context in which educational activism could ferment into raised political consciousness that came to define the civil rights movement.

This educational background prepared Simms and thousands of other teachers for a politicized profession. Although equalization and protracted legal battles determined the nature of the regional assault on Jim Crow, implementing a curriculum in Black schools was a politically potent weapon in the fight to combat segregation in the classroom, particularly as many of Jim Crow's harmful effects were perpetuated through stereotypes, misinformation, and a complete dismissal of Black history and culture in public schools. Southern teachers' associations combated this ignorance directly. The teachers' association in North Carolina formally opposed the use of textbooks written from a pro-Confederacy vantage point.[41] Other Black teacher associations actively sought to incorporate the achievement of Black history and culture into the curriculum by emulating the work of Carter G. Woodson and incorporating into the curriculum the literature published through his organization, the ASNLH.[42] A findings committee of the National Association of Teachers in Colored Schools released a report in 1925 in which they wrote, "We earnestly recommend the increased study of Negro History in our schools." The teachers' association in North Carolina wrote in 1928 to the state department of education "to call again to your attention the rather general desire among the Negro school people of the state that there shall be courses in Negro Life and History."[43] Other Southern states followed a similar pattern. "If the South wishes to avoid amalgamation of the races, to maintain separate races, it can profitably stock the shelves of its public schools with books designed to bring respect to the Negro," the *Mississippi Educational Advance* published in 1940, "the wealth of contributions from individuals makes rich the society which is democratic."[44] W. A. Walters, faculty member in the Department of Social Sciences at Rust College in Mississippi, wrote to his peers, "we educators should start a campaign to have . . . a course in Negro History as a partial requirement for graduation."[45]

In close proximity to the defining struggles of the Black freedom struggle and engrossed in a progressive teaching tradition, even those who consciously distanced themselves from the movement acted in a context of civil rights. Regardless of the distance she maintained, Simms served at the front lines of community engagement. As an educator, she negotiated the politics of education for the families she served, serving as a conduit between the prevailing winds of civil rights—and the forces of segregation they challenged—and the local community. It was a position she committed herself fully. Simms never married and never had children. Her students, in many ways, became her children and her family. They were her *raison d'être* and her students recognized this in compassionate ways. As one note from her students read: "We know that we have a very vague way of showing our appreciation but when it all boils down we love you deeply and dearly. Thanks again for the wonderful job that you have done in guiding us for the past five years. [signed] *Your Children*."[46]

———— ∞∞∞ ————

With her education and relationship to the community, Simms stood poised to enact change by way of her students in the classroom. As historian Valinda

Littlefield wrote, teachers instilled world views to look beyond the narrow color line drawn by a racist society, to inculcate a sense of pride and history in Black culture, and to recognize the values of uplift and service. Black teachers, specifically women, established a foundation for activism, or at least the potential for it, "by pointing out unequal power structures within the Jim Crow system, teachers both directly and indirectly motivated students to challenge an oppressive system."[47] Not directly on the front lines, Simms and other women were positioned in a secondary line of defense, preparing their students for future struggles if they chose to enter the fray. However, civil rights teaching did not define her curriculum or teaching philosophy, nor did she reveal many personal connections or clandestine support for the movement. The larger context influenced her teaching, however, and generally affected her teaching.

In addition to her teacher training and background that inherently connected to the civil rights movement, Simms, and other Black teachers in the South, entered the politicized spaces of Black schools during the era of Jim Crow. Although Simms taught in the private schools of Charleston, including Avery, she spent the bulk of her career teaching in public schools; namely, Burke High School on the peninsula of Charleston. Burke High School emerged from the organizational efforts of the Black community to acquire an education after universal public education was written into the state constitution in 1868. Reverend John L. Dart, an ordained Baptist minister and graduate of Atlanta University, opened the Charleston Industrial Institute in 1894, which eventually become known as the Charleston Colored Industrial School. In reference to the origins of the school, Dart penned "Established in 1894 by the Colored People on the basis of self help. [The School] Trains Teaches, Christian and Industrial Workers for the Colored Race."[48] As the original prospectus of the school read:

> In view of the startling fact that there are more than 5,000 colored children in Charleston without free public school advantages, and knowing that the many boys and girls who are now growing up in ignorance, idleness and crime must become, in future, a large criminal and dependent class, a number of the leading and progressive colored men of this city . . . undertook the work of establishing a school for colored children, where they could be taught not only reading and writing, but the lessons of morals, temperance, sewing, cooking, nursing, housework, carpentering, etc.[49]

Reverend Dart built the school on his own property before a new building was constructed and opened in 1911. The school district changed the name to Burke High School, in honor of city board member James E. Burke, who passed away in 1921.[50] Established through the initiatives of Black Charlestonians, the school pushed back against the desires of a white community that wished to see a subservient Black community trained to fill positions of manual labor. Still, the intended curriculum at Burke mirrored the vocational or industrial paradigm that whites utilized in attempts to shape Black educational policy during Reconstruction and into the early twentieth century.[51] Under the purview of the local school board as a public institution, the school served the community as the largest public high school in the city of Charleston. Although the city did not provide for transportation downtown, students from the surrounding sea islands and low country flocked to the school as circumstances permitted.

Simms's courses introduced students to the classics, an attribute to her classical training at Avery. In February of 1957, Simms's students studied *Julius Caesar*. She executed lesson plans that enforced the rigorous study of canonical literature, including Charles Dickens, Ralph Waldo Emerson, and Mark Twain.[52] Simms further developed the classical curriculum that she learned herself at Avery. In her lesson plans from March of 1960, for instance, Ms. Simms introduced students to Black poets, including, but not limited to, Langston Hughes, Arna Bontemps, Countee Cullen, and Paul Laurence Dunbar.[53] In her collection is a copy of "Negroes and the War," with a critical foreword that stated, "There is still a long way to go before equality is attained, but the pace is faster, and never faster than now."[54]

Simms balanced her lesson plans with a vocational emphasis that traditionally defined schools such as Burke High School. Students in her classes wrote job application letters and critiqued samples that she provided. She shared information about part-time jobs, summer jobs, and afternoon jobs. She analyzed the roles of the applicant and the employer and devoted part of her instruction to building interview skills.[55] She also taught organization skills. Quite notably, she taught lessons on "conducting a class, club meetings, making motions, discussing motions."[56]

The application and interviewing process touches more directly on the essence of her teaching philosophy as she explained it than that of Black history, literature, or culture. When asked specifically about her teaching philosophy, she responded, "I wanted [my students] to be able to compete when they left high school. So, I gave them all I knew to prepare them for the competition that they would run into after leaving high school." She elaborated, noting that "if you're going further then you have to be prepared to do, to say, or to continue and that's the way I think of it and, of course, if they could do that, yes, they could get the better jobs."[57] Simms saw education and her teaching philosophy as a way to prepare students for jobs at a base level, but she wanted them to be able to compete for the higher-level positions and academically in college as well.

Burke High School, particularly after Avery closed, accommodated both vocational and academic pursuits. Although Burke has origins as an industrial training school fashioned in an accommodationist and vocational philosophy, by 1960 Burke graduated far more students on the academic track than the vocational track. Students graduating in the academic and other nonvocational tracks tripled those in the vocational track.[58] The academic emphasis is also reflected in the college emphasis evidenced in Burke's extracurricular activities. In 1962, for instance, Burke supported a "Choose Your College" event organized by guidance counselors. Simms's alma mater was represented (Barber-Scotia and Johnson C. Smith), alongside Spelman, Lincoln, and Howard universities, as well as South Carolina State College, in addition to private historically Black schools in the state, including Allen University and Claflin College (University).[59]

Extracurricular activities flourished at Burke. Students at Burke were exposed to a host of activities; the student council sent representatives to state conventions, and the newspaper staff regularly attended state annual meetings for the Palmetto Scholastic Press Association, for instance.[60] The student council emphasized particular values and convictions that resonated with the movement that would soon engulf students in the 1960s. As students wrote in the school newspaper, the *Parvenue,* the purpose of the council is "to maintain the principles and ideals of character training of the students; also to give training in more effective procedures and practices of school affairs and to train the student to be a loyal citizen."[61] Burke also organized a Future Teachers of America club (originally known as the Mary McLeod Bethune Future Teachers of America Club), the Senior Honor Society, the Criterion Club, the senior dramatic guild, and the Science Club.[62] Students at Burke were exposed to ideas of participatory citizenship, democratic organization, and commitment to larger social and political contexts that teachers intentionally integrated into the curriculum. With this level of political socialization, student activists were not unfamiliar with the principles of the civil rights movement.

These activities, contained within the safety and auspices of a friendly environment governed by a Black administration and a sympathetic Black faculty, created a space in which students articulated developing viewpoints in strong social and political terms. Teachers instituted a "This I Believe" essay series in which students articulated their desires as free citizens. "I believe something can be done about segregation if we would accept the idea that all men are brothers," Larry Talbot wrote in his essay. "I believe that problems can be settled in an orderly manner, then there wouldn't be any wars, poverty, or crime . . . only in this way can we get rid of the ills of mankind and brink about the world of peace as God intended it to be."[63] Another student echoed similar sentiments. "I think that Burke is the best school in this community," the student wrote. "I believe that as a student at Burke School, it is my responsibility to do what I can to improve it. . . . As a Charlestonian, I believe that I have a responsibility to do what I can to bring about these improvements."[64]

The *Parvenue* served as a conduit for the activist voice among the student population. It long served as a place for students to publish their ideas, and many authors used the *Parvenue* pages to debate issues of race and citizenship. Students took their role in schools very seriously, and they were conscious of the positions of their institutions in the larger society. "Education is the freedom of knowledge to everyone, in every field and in every aspect of life," Dolly Louise Bonneau wrote from Burke in 1952. "Education today . . . means a happier life, higher standards for recognition, and better security."[65] The *Parvenue* also debated the merits of various curricular initiatives. Lewalter Dilligard discussed the advantages of including Black history as early as 1956. Noting the achievements of George Washington Carver, Mary McLeod Bethune, and Paul Laurence Dunbar, Dilligard suggested the collective benefits of studying history, which the social science department at the school provided.[66] Students at Burke actively discussed issues connected to the "race problem." As Ernest Thompson wrote in the *Parvenue* just before the *Brown v. Board of Education* (1954) decision, "the main causes of our racial problems are our ignorance and misunderstanding. We the patriotic Americans must eliminate these two stumbling blocks on the road to a better America."[67]

Other teachers were active at Burke, prompting Simms to reflect on what the struggle meant for her students. Her colleague, Eugene Hunt, was an English teacher at Burke. Hunt worked with the NAACP, identifying plaintiffs for the equalization suit. He introduced his students to notions of democratic equality and the avenues to substantive change in American government.[68] From the vantage point of teachers who organized the curriculum in the high schools, the right to an education included receiving the same quality of education as that of their white counterparts. Simms reflected about the latter years of her career on the impact of Hunt's teaching and presence at Burke High School, writing "from the homeroom students of Eugene C. Hunt, I learned how bitter some of them were about the events of slavery."[69] James Blake, a Burke High School student and member of the NAACP Youth Council in the early 1960s, recalled of teacher influence at the school, noting that "right in E.C. Hunt's class, and J. Michael Grave's class was the insurrection movement in the City of Charleston."[70]

It would be easy to overlook Simms's career in the context of the long freedom struggle. For instance, in her memoir, *A Chalk and Chalkboard Career*, Simms makes only passing reference to the monumental *Brown v. Board of Education* (1954) decision, "A Supreme Court decision altering the educational and social pattern of the South changed the status quo."[71] It is easy to overlook, given the student activism that engulfed the state since the 1940s, but gained momentum in Charleston in 1960 after the sit-ins in Greensboro, which sparked sit-ins across the former Confederacy. Students acted in Charleston, two months after those in North Carolina and in the midst of ongoing protests in Columbia and Orangeburg. Twenty-four Burke High School students marched to S. H. Kress & Co., a segregated five-and-dime store on King Street in downtown Charleston, South Carolina. They sat in on the lunch counters and were arrested.[72] It galvanized a local movement, one of the precursors to the "Charleston movement" of 1963. Organizing gained momentum after the sit-in, and within three years, the number of activists in Charleston had proliferated. Students joined the mass meetings in local churches such as Morris Brown African Methodist Episcopal, Morris Street Baptist, and Emmanuel African Methodist Episcopal, where they joined thousands of other Charlestonians determined to end legal segregation in their city. Young people at Burke remained committed to the cause of civil rights subsequent to the sit-in, picketing downtown businesses and involving incoming students in the NAACP Youth Council. The NAACP and local community activists persisted in pushing for reform, and in the fall of 1963, the school board at last desegregated Charleston County's public K–12 system.[73] While students joined the front lines of the movement, Simms remained quietly committed to her career, and the pages of her memoir mention little of these historical events that unfolded in her city.

Through interviews and her written memoirs, Simms indicated why she distanced herself from the movement. "I was too busy with my career to really concentrate on a feeling for Dr. King's mission, as such," Simms recalled. "But, everybody knew bits about that thing and we saw pictures in the newspaper and that kind of thing. But, I didn't really have strong feeling, cause I was too busy trying to follow a career."[74] However, in 1969, closer to the end of her career, Simms took to the streets and marched in support of her students and their families. She recalled:

> We have students whose parents, parents were on that strike, that hospital strike and we wanted our students to realize that we were concerned about them. We marched with our students to let them know that we were concerned about their moms and theirs, too.[75]

Simms's positioning as a woman and an educator placed her near the front lines of the movement in Charleston during the hospital strike of 1969, which gained national attention. Her commitment to her students, families, and the community motivated her to cross into the front lines. Although Simms marched and went through the actions of protest and classic civil rights demonstrations, she never embraced the identity of an activist as defined then or by contemporary standards. However, she identified, locally and immediately, with her students and their parents; specifically, their mothers, because "mom was the one that was working most of the time."[76]

During her last year at Burke High School, Simms created more units on Black history that connected directly to her students' interest in the program. Her students demonstrated how "bitter some of them were about the events of slavery."[77] One of her students, Michael Whack, "was so incensed by the books he read on the subject that I began to feel afraid that he would not make a wholesome adjustment to the establishment."[78] She interviewed Whack later as she was completing her memoirs, reporting that he "became a part of mainstream America at Syracuse University," where he was working with local governments "on behalf of Black America as a civil rights proponent."[79] Framed in this way, Simms resolved her concern about her former student, and she also took away valuable lessons in the moment. "To teach is to learn," she wrote to her readers in her professional autobiography, in a chapter titled, "Black is Beautiful."[80]

Although never identified as one of the teachers behind the protests—nor did she directly identify with them—Simms shared a compassion and understanding of the struggles of Black students during the civil rights era. The movement and the politics of the schools in Charleston, as in schools across the South, were so immersed in a movement and politics that one could not escape its influence. One could only mediate its pressure and presence behind closed doors. Although not sharing the overtly political stance that many activists preferred, her commitment, compassion, and shared experience and common bond with students constituted a critical component of Black education; as Simms noted in her memoirs, "a strong desire to awaken teachers to the need to prepare themselves to do their best for African American students."[81]

———— ❧ ————

The final phase of Simms's teaching career in the 1970s intersected with full-scale desegregation after the *Green v. County School Board* (1968) and *Alexander v. Holmes County Board of Education* (1969) decisions. It was an era that did not treat kindly the tens of thousands of Black educators who were dismissed from their teaching positions. They not only constituted a significant section of a vibrant middle class, but they also supported Black institutions and intimately knew and cared for the families that depended on them. Within the first decade after the *Brown* decision, thirty-eight thousand teachers lost their jobs in the seventeen southern and border states. Opportunities for leadership diminished as well. In North Carolina, for instance, over two hundred Black principals led high schools, but only three remained in the leadership position by 1970. In Alabama, the number of principals dropped from two hundred fifty to forty.[82] Black teachers regularly voiced concerns about the prospect of dismissal in the wake of widescale desegregation. In South Carolina, Black teachers noted the "increasing deprivation of the rights of Black teachers as school desegregation proceeds." They predicted Black educators "will have to go to court in order to retain or secure positions which are commensurate with their qualifications."[83]

Simms fared well in the transition to desegregated schools. Having faithfully served since 1941, with distinction and without formal affiliation or connection to the movement, Simms was safe from dismissal or demotion as schools desegregated in the South. Having also volunteered to take the National Teacher Examination, an assessment that was used to "objectively" hire teachers regardless of race but also achieved its intended effect of eliminating teachers of color from the classroom, Simms was in a small class of Black teachers unscathed by the changing tide of education.[84] In fact, she earned a promotion of sorts. She began teaching at Charleston High School in 1973, a previously all-white school that she and many others held in high regard. It was claimed to be the third oldest high school in the country and the oldest in the South, what Simms described with "illustrious facts," noting that it produced some of "America's influential citizens."[85] To teach at such an illustrious school was a career achievement for Simms. Not only did Simms survive, thrive, and achieve in the era of segregation, but Simms also transferred to what was, according to some standards, one of the best public schools in Charleston. In their student newspaper, *The Bantam*, Simms described teaching at the new high school "as being a challenge which thus far has aroused here enthusiasm for work will remain alive."[86] As Simms noted about the transfer to Charleston High School, "I followed my heart. I'm glad I did. This was because I had such a short time left and a number of years that I intended to give the community as a teacher. And so, I left. But, I enjoyed it. I enjoyed it, because I saw competent students, my race and the other race, competent students. And they accepted one another so fully. They really adjusted themselves well and could express themselves well."[87] She maintained the integrity of teaching. She covered the "classics," including, but not limited to, *Beowulf, The Canterbury Tales*, John Milton, Thomas Becket, and Shakespeare.[88]

A lifelong learner, Simms developed a racially conscious curriculum in the twilight of her career. As in her teaching during the era of segregation, Simms remained committed to teaching Black history and the values of Black culture in her classroom. During the academic year of 1972–1973, Simms continued to incorporate Black literature and history into her curriculum. She assigned Maya Angelou, James Weldon Johnson, and others. "I gave them a unit on Black History, Black poetry in particular," she recalled of teaching at the school, "and I required everybody to learn at least one poem and recite it before the class."[89] She taught the poems "Black Power" and "The Emancipation of George Hector." In history, she spent nearly a month on slavery. She examined the Fugitive Slave Law, the *Dred Scott* case, "King Cotton," John Brown, and abolitionism. She assigned excerpts from *Uncle Tom's Cabin*, too.[90] It was a robust curriculum

that facilitated a deep understanding of Black history at the moment of desegregation.

One lesson in which she assigned a poem stuck out in particular. Simms
taught the "Black Finger" by Angelina Weld Grimké. As Simms recalled:

> I gave them a unit on Black History, Black poetry in particular and I re-
> quired everybody to learn at least one poem and recite it before the class.
> And, one of the boys whose skin was similar to mine in texture and he had
> a big Afro. He chose a poem [and] you know what he did? He colored his
> fingers and put it up like that and recited his poem "The Black Finger." I have
> never forgotten that. You see how unique folk can be. And he was in a class
> with a whole lot of Caucasian students, that particular division of English. I
> know they have never forgotten that, because that was unique.[91]

The poem, first published in 1923 by Grimké in *Opportunity: A Negro Life*, is
profound:

> I have just seen a most beautiful thing
> Slim and still
> Against a gold, gold sky,
> A straight Black cypress,
> Sensitive,
> Exquisite,
> A Black finger
> Pointing upwards.
> Why, beautiful still finger, are you Black?
> And why are you pointing upwards?[92]

This was a vital moment in a southern classroom. In a recently desegregated
school, with a Black teacher and a handful of Black students, students read and
studied Grimké's poem, which bespoke of Black pride and an essential struggle
that defined the country. It encouraged deep reflection and rumination among
students in a turbulent time. A student of color, donning an Afro and coloring
his finger to dramatize the aesthetics of the poem, emboldened by the historic
moment and Grimké's words, acting out the poetic lines in an integrated classroom set the stage for lively discourse and debate—the very elements that advocates for integration envisioned for classrooms and students across the United
States.

Simms carried the knowledge and importance of Black history and culture,
developed within a segregated system and society, into the era of desegregation.
As tens of thousands of teachers were dismissed and demoted, Simms illustrates
that her deep understanding of Black history and culture became increasingly
rare during the era of desegregation. At the juncture of political and social

vicissitude in public education, Simms simultaneously demonstrates the integral value that she brought with her into desegregated classroom spaces.

———— ∞∞∞ ————

Simms achieved a strong sense of actualization and purpose in retirement, devoting herself selflessly to her church, community, and ongoing educational pursuits. This was also a generative period of tremendous growth and production. She remained the consummate educator as a lifelong learner and scholar, dutifully serving the field of education in retirement. She authored no fewer than three books: *Profiles of African-American Females in the Low Country of South Carolina* (1992), *Growing Up Presbyterian: Life in Presbyterian Colleges and Churches* (1992), and *A Chalk and Chalkboard Career in Carolina* (1996).[93] She also regularly donated to Howard University as a lifelong financial supporter. Simms maintained connections with the Avery Research Center for African American History and Culture, formerly the Avery Normal Institute, where she graduated in 1937. She maintained connections and contributed to the Association for the Study of African American Life and History, Johnson C. Smith University, and Barber-Scotia College. She remained devotedly committed to Zion Olive Presbyterian Church as well.

Simms passed away in 2015, amidst the Black Lives Matter movement that continued the struggle she observed during her career. The schools she taught in were still segregated, and the teaching force was largely white. Looking back on Simms's life and career provides a counternarrative as a consummate educator and devoted lifelong learner, an exemplar for all teachers. At first glance, her teaching and career may not stand out as an illustration of teacher activism during the civil rights movement, as popularly imagined. However, her career inspires a deeper understanding of the civil rights movement and its legacies, as it illustrates how deeply it penetrated Black institutions. Simms practiced the principles inherent to the civil rights movement without outwardly identifying as an activist. Still, movement principles were part of her professional labor, from examining inequitable resource allocation to teaching Black history when it was not part of the mainstream curriculum. In short, teaching during Jim Crow through desegregation was a political act. Her career also demonstrates how Black educators continued to participate in and shape desegregated schools after the *Brown* decision. As these voices have begun to be re-centered in our historical analysis, her story, the contributions she made, and how she made them are instructive in assessing the intersection of civil rights and education.

"We Experienced Our Freedom"

The Impact of Valued Segregated Spaces on Teacher Practice and Activism

KRISTAN L. MCCULLUM & HUNTER HOLT

On February 1, 1960, four students from North Carolina Agricultural and Technical (A&T) College sat down at the Woolworth's lunch counter in downtown Greensboro, North Carolina, to protest racial discrimination in public spaces. Their carefully planned demonstration would spark the student sit-in movement across the South.[1] Soon after, Ella Baker, acting executive director of the Southern Christian Leadership Conference (SCLC), planned a conference for young activists at Shaw University in Raleigh. It was out of this meeting that the Student Nonviolent Coordinating Committee (SNCC) was born.[2]

In the early to mid-1960s, students from Shaw and other historically Black universities such as St. Augustine's and North Carolina A&T were marching and protesting for civil rights.[3] Some high school students, including Dorothy Thompson, were inspired to join the demonstrations. Others, such as Genevieve Farmer, were protesting more quietly or offering their support to those in the streets. Delores Revis, a teacher at the time, would watch the youths lead the movement, having helped shape Black students' sense of self and identity within a Jim Crow society. Many of these students, including Thompson and Farmer, would also become teachers who espoused lessons on Black history within their various subjects and affirmed the humanity of their students.

This chapter uses oral history to trace the lives of three Black women educators—Delores Revis, Genevieve Farmer, and Dorothy Thompson—who worked in North Carolina, mainly in Raleigh, from 1959 to 2000. Each of these women grew up in segregated communities and attended all-Black schools. Farmer was born and raised in Kingstree, South Carolina, and Revis and Thompson lived their formative years in Raleigh. The intersections of home, family, school, and church in these towns provided a safe and nurturing environment, where parents and teachers held high expectations that enabled the women's self-determination in pursuing higher education and careers as educators. Revis, Farmer, and Thompson attended historically Black colleges and universities (HBCUs) where they encountered civil rights activists and other college students demanding social change. Farmer studied music at Hampton Institute (now Hampton University), Revis studied English at Saint Augustine's College, and Thompson studied art and education at North Carolina Central College at Durham (now North Carolina Central University). It was at their colleges that they also received the further training that they would take with them into their classrooms and into their pedagogies and philosophies about educating students.

They each began working in education after graduating from their respective institutions. In 1959, Revis started teaching English at W. B. Wicker High School in Sanford, North Carolina. From 1960 to the late 1970s, she taught at J. W. Ligon Jr.-Sr. High School and Needham B. Broughton High School in Raleigh. Before officially retiring in 2000, she worked as an administrator at Crosby Sixth Grade Center, J. W. York Elementary School, Kingswood Middle School, M. E. Phillips High School, and Brentwood Elementary School. She earned her administrative certification from Duke University. Farmer taught music in Raleigh public schools from 1962 to 1976, working at Washington School, Carnage Junior High School, and Daniels Junior High School during this time. After earning a master's degree in school counseling from North Carolina Central College, she worked as a counselor in Wake County at Carroll Junior High School and Garner Senior High School from 1976 to 1993. Thompson began teaching art in 1968. Throughout her career as a teacher, she worked at Atkins Senior High School in Winston-Salem and Enloe Senior High School and J. W. Ligon Jr.-Sr. High School in Raleigh.

This narrative of their careers in Raleigh extends the scholarship on "valued segregated schooling" that Vanessa Siddle Walker introduced in her important study of Caswell County Training School in North Carolina. In *Their Highest Potential*, Walker challenges the myth that segregated Black schools were inherently inferior to white schools. Instead, she argues that, despite being underfunded and deprived of adequate resources, the all-Black school served as a site of excellence during its years of operation between 1933 and 1969. The principal and teachers were caring, were well educated, and held high expectations for their students, and the parents were also actively involved in providing better opportunities for their children. This counternarrative demonstrates that Black educators, administrators, and parents created an environment in which students could realize their "highest potential" despite the ugly realities of Jim Crow.[4]

In this chapter, we use the concept of *valued segregated spaces*, defined as both formal and informal educational contexts that exhibited these attributes that have characterized the relationships between all-Black schools, communal organizations, and community advocacy within the historiography of segregated education.[5] The trajectories of Revis, Farmer, and Thompson highlight how these valued segregated spaces influenced their teaching and conceptualization of activism during the civil rights movement and the longer Black freedom struggle. Their relationships with parents, teachers, and community members, as well as their lived experiences and their encounters and participation in activism during their formative years, informed the philosophy and practice of students who became teachers before and after desegregation. These valued segregated spaces within the context of Jim Crow were educative—they helped to cultivate the women's self-determination and agency that allowed them to reach their full potential through what bell hooks called "education as the practice of freedom."[6] This practice, which Revis, Farmer, and Thompson exemplified in their own teaching, consisted of (1) care, high expectations, and the affirmation of Black identity; and (2) strategies to navigate and confront racism both inside and outside the classroom. The chapter concludes with the women's reflections on the movement and the ways in which educators can learn from it to help their students reach their full potential. By examining the culminating influence of these spaces and experiences on their teaching, we can better understand the ways in which valued segregated education shaped subsequent generations of Black educators and students within the broader Black struggle for freedom. The multigenerational impact of education as the practice of freedom offers considerations for teaching during this historical moment.[7]

"TEACHING THE WHOLE CHILD": CARE, HIGH EXPECTATIONS, AND AFFIRMING BLACK IDENTITY

These three women were educated and nurtured within valued segregated schools and communities, and these experiences shaped their own ideals and philosophies about teaching and providing quality educational opportunities to their students. Their teachers set high expectations within the walls of their classrooms; meanwhile, their parents and the church also played a significant role in raising and protecting them under Jim Crow: "So we had the home, the community, and the church, and the school to help rear us and comfort us."[8] These intersections of family, home, church, and school enabled children to feel safe and secure within their segregated neighborhood and encompassed what Dolores Revis refers to as the "rearing community":[9]

> Everybody in my community knew everybody because these were segregated times. And so, it meant that the community was part of the rearing of all the children in the neighborhood. . . . We all felt safe and secure and felt loved. Of course, the fact that everybody was part of that training and

rearing meant that your parents knew everything that you did good or bad. When I was in school, elementary school was grades one through eight. So that meant I stayed in the same school for eight years. And I knew all the teachers. All the teachers knew me. They knew all the students, they knew their families, and so forth.[10]

Because these communities were small and close-knit, the lives of students and teachers were interconnected in several ways. While at St. Augustine's, Revis returned to her former high school to complete her student teaching along-side her former teachers. Genevieve Farmer, who grew up in the small town of Kingstree, South Carolina, remembers that her teachers often boarded with families in the community. Therefore, in many cases, students and teachers were neighbors.[11] It was also common for teachers to attend the same churches as their students. The school was only two blocks away from Farmer's house. It was within these segregated spaces in the community that Black students found a sense of freedom:[12]

Well, in little Kingstree, life was quiet . . . I would say African Americans knew their place. We went to school and we went to church. There, we found, or experienced, our freedom.[13]

Farmer attended Tomlinson School, an all-Black school that served grades one through twelve. She describes her teachers as being encouraging and caring yet stern—they set high expectations for students to "do our very best."[14] Her educators were also strict disciplinarians—they felt responsible for student learning and would not allow "students to sit back and not learn."[15] Dorothy Thompson, who attended school in Raleigh from second through twelfth grade, echoes the sentiment that teachers demanded students' best efforts and encouraged them to pursue higher education:

Many people were very poor at the school I went to, but the education was excellent. It was excellent. My high school education, too. I had wonderful teachers. School was challenging. Teachers didn't let you get by with much, you know, in terms of not doing your best. They encouraged you always to be your best. And it was no question that I was going to graduate and I was going to go to college.[16]

Revis notes that her teachers were concerned with "teaching the whole child," extending care and excellence beyond the classroom to emphasize the importance of good hygiene and dressing well as constructions and reflections of pride and self-respect.[17] Even though they did not explicitly address issues of racism and discrimination, teachers encouraged students to respect themselves and to realize their full potential in a white-dominated society that tried to diminish their humanity. Thompson reflects on how she carried these high expectations into her own teaching:

> We basically were encouraged that we could be anything we wanted to be. [Teachers] insisted that we write well, that we speak well. Even today, if somebody splits a verb, I correct them automatically because that's what happened [to us]. You know, when I was a kid, if somebody split a verb, the teacher corrected you. So, they were very efficient, I thought, in sending the message to us, that we could be anything and anybody that we wanted to be without reference to race. They never said, "Now, because you're Black there are people who are going think"—well, at that time they said "colored" and "Negro"—"there are people who will think such and such." I never heard a message like that. It was that I, as a person, could be and do whatever I want to do.[18]

Their teachers demonstrated respect toward them as not only students but human beings and, in turn, earned their students' admiration. Their influence continued to mold the trajectories of Revis, Thompson, and Farmer. Although occupations and careers were still often restricted for Black women during the 1940s and 1950s, Revis credits the admiration she had for her own English teacher in her choosing the profession of teaching English. When these three educators entered their own classrooms, they translated their former teachers' pedagogical approaches into their own practice. For instance, Farmer did not talk openly about civil rights issues. Instead, she actively prepared students to become the best versions of themselves so that they may compete in a changing society. This often meant dedicating additional hours outside the classroom:

> I can't say that I would use the word civil rights to teach something, but in talking with the students, that's the way I got them to realize the importance—and all of the teachers did likewise, I'm sure—the importance of preparing themselves for the future. So, we talked about the need for them to study and to do well, kept them after school to work with them. We didn't call it tutoring at that time. We just kept them after school to work with them.[19]

Similarly to Farmer, Revis taught her students informally about impending integration and motivated them to prepare for these changes. She helped them conceptualize what freedom may look like beyond the walls of their all-Black school:

> We always did teach, though, that one day, schools are going to be integrated. One day, we will be free in society, and you need to be prepared for that. And you need to get something in your head because nobody else can take that from you if it's in your head. They can take other things from you, but

not what's in your head. And I think that was a common theme in the Black community.[20]

Revis, Farmer, and Thompson continued to seek spaces of freedom once they graduated from their all-Black schools and enrolled in Black colleges. For Farmer, this meant leaving the small and rural town of Kingstree to enroll at Hampton Institute in Virginia: "Hampton was a dream for me. I enjoyed being away from Kingstree. And even though I had a stuttering problem, a very serious stuttering problem . . . I just enjoyed being away."[21] Farmer credits her English professor for her dedication and diligence in helping her overcome this impediment:

> and in my English class, we had to write an essay. And luckily, I knew what an essay was because my sisters had gone to college and they had talked about their college life, which included writing essays. And so, in my essay— the essay was to be about me—and I told the teacher that I was a stutterer, and as a result, do not call on me in class. . . . Well, she kept me after class and asked who my speech teacher was. I told her, and so she contacted him, and he called me in and I had speech lessons with him, which by Christmas, believe it or not, most of my stuttering had left. So that was a wonderful, wonderful experience for me. . . .[22]

Farmer's teachers in her previous all-Black school had shown the same dedication to their students in helping them become the best version of themselves. Her professors at Hampton were no different—they continued to take the time to prepare their students for fulfilling futures.

Parents also shaped these educators' career paths and classroom practices. Revis's parents—and her mother, in particular—strongly believed in the power of education. To encourage learning, she purchased her only child a dictionary, desk, and an easel with a dual chalkboard-corkboard. She encouraged her daughter to become a teacher, and Revis did go on to teach—only it was high school rather than elementary school, as her mother had envisioned.[23] Revis's mother did not teach, but she was actively involved in helping to provide quality educational opportunities at the all-Black school. She served in the role as a "great parent" who assisted the teacher with performing tasks, fundraising, and community relations.[24] Farmer's parents had obtained degrees and were educators themselves—her mother taught third grade, and her father was both the principal of the school as well as the physics and chemistry teacher.[25] Thompson's mother was a sixth-grade teacher who believed in the importance in recognizing the potential of all children, regardless of background, and working with them to help them fulfill that potential:

So, I would like every teacher to enter the classroom looking at their human beings as potential, and not at what they look like or where they come from. And I will tell you, I know it can be done, because that's what happened for us when I was in elementary school and in high school, and in college, and my mother taught this way. My mother preferred to teach the kids who were having the most trouble in school. She preferred as the sixth-grade teacher to get a child who was reading on a third-grade level because she loved bringing them up to the sixth grade. She loved that . . . because my mother didn't believe that there was a child on the planet that couldn't learn and she saw herself as the person who was supposed to decode that. And I'm not just talking about my mother. There were many, many, many teachers like that. And so far, as I'm concerned, one of the problems with integration is that that was not recognized.[26]

Later on, when Thompson became a parent, she advocated for not only her students but also her children and grandchildren. She recalls that her son entered kindergarten reading on a third-grade level, which was not recognized by his teachers:

That's just the brain he had. Very, very bright, gifted kid. I had to say this to people. I had to tell the teachers that he was gifted, and my husband's mouth would fall out. You know, they would say, "Well, you know, he finishes his work too soon." And I'd say, "Well, did he get it right?" "Well, yes, but then he's sitting there, and he doesn't know what to do with himself. And then when we start on something else, he has to ask another kid, 'Well, what are we doing now?'" And I said, "At least he's still asking."[27]

Thompson challenged her son's teachers to ensure that they saw him as a child with potential. She laments on the fact that, years later, little had changed:

I had to do the same thing with my grandson. That was devastating to me–that nothing had changed. . . . I had the same experience with my son when he was five, and the same experience with my grandson when he was five. Because what that then let me know is that we have not done enough to understand this problem. We have not done enough to correct it. Thirty years should have been enough time."[28]

This advocacy she demonstrated for her son and grandson reflected similar work that she performed on behalf of other Black parents in Raleigh. After she finished teaching, Thompson and other parents formed a parent advocacy group called the Black Parents Association that later became Concerned Citizens for Education Advocacy. Through this group, Thompson would accompany guardians to parent conference meetings at school. She recalls one story in which the parents did not show up for a meeting with their son's principal and teachers:

> After I left the conference, I went to the home. These people were really poor, and I went to their home. And I said, "Where were you?" [The father] said, "I couldn't go." I said, "Why couldn't you go?" He said, "Miss Thompson, they will respect you. . . . But they will make me feel bad. . . . My wife already said she wouldn't go." See, we have to have an atmosphere that is welcoming. . . . My theory is you don't go where you hear bad news. So, to me, if all we've got [for] the parents is bad news, if all we can see is what the children are not doing, then we are not ever going to be able to get out of this.[29]

Along with influencing how they advocated for children, the three women's parents also played a role in promoting Black history and identity in the home, which manifested into the women's future teaching practices. For instance, Thompson's mother regularly took her to the library to get books on influential Black civil rights leaders such as Dr. Martin Luther King, Jr. and Malcolm X.[30] Thompson went on to emphasize Black history and the contributions of Black people in her own classroom and school, even after schools had integrated. Because she taught art, she was responsible for constructing bulletin boards in the school. Thompson made an intentional effort to highlight the accomplishments and contributions of Black people:

> And during Black History Week, I had a lot of pictures of historically well-known Black people. But, I also had people who many of the kids didn't know. You know, people like the guy that did the design of D.C. And I would have Stokely Carmichael up there and I might have something that said, "This is Black power."

Thompson's commitment to teaching histories of Black excellence offered a counternarrative to dominant historical narratives and ensured that Black students could feel affirmed in their identities even after they had lost the sacred space of the all-Black school and now found themselves sitting and learning next to white students in the classroom.

Meanwhile, Dolores Revis also emphasized the importance of including narratives about Black accomplishments within school. She recalls that, where she taught, the school infused "Black history into lots of things" to instill Black pride within their students: "We had plays. We had drama class. In our subject fields, we included contributions of Blacks."[31] Farmer used the music classroom as a space for lessons on Black history and civil rights. As a college student at Hampton, she had encountered prominent Black musicians who came to perform on campus. As a music major, she would be assigned to these artists backstage, providing them flowers, water, or anything else they needed.[32] Farmer highlighted the brilliance of these Black musicians to reflect that her students were also brilliant and could achieve their own personal goals:

> I would emphasize the musicians and music about African Americans, how it all began, the words, and the meaning of the words and that equals spiritual. I would play [Louis] Armstrong and Duke Ellington, so that they would know that we are musicians. We can be musicians. And just look what they have done, and what can you do maybe in something that you really like . . . so that was the way of getting across the importance of doing things for civil rights purposes.[33]

When Thompson taught advanced art, she remembers struggling to reach a student who was hesitant to draw because of her lack of confidence in being the only Black student in class. Thompson had known this student since the student was a small child, so she called her mother to express her concern; the mother encouraged her to talk with her child:

> I told [the student] we needed to talk. So, what I found out was, she wasn't sure of how good she was. She didn't have the confidence. I had some really good students. I mean, these kids, she was the only Black person in that advanced art class. And she was as good as the rest of them. And I had some really good students. But she wasn't confident of her own work. So, I just made her draw. And I put her work up. And when the other students, you know, saw her work and they complimented her, you know, she became more involved with it enough to pass the class. Because I was determined I was not going to let her get away with not doing work and getting good grades.[34]

The student went on to college, where she majored in art. She then became an art teacher herself, while also earning her master's degree. Just as Thompson had grown up and been nurtured by her community, she transferred these ideals of care into practice with her own students. This student manifested this care into her own growth, in turn influencing her own trajectory.

The formal and informal lessons that teachers and parents imparted to Revis, Farmer, and Thompson through care and high expectations molded the women into caring educators who also believed in rigor and excellence. They were protected and nurtured within these segregated spaces and were allowed to envision and actively work toward their futures during Jim Crow and beyond. These lessons enabled them to articulate a sense of freedom in which they could realize their full potential, and they carried this practice of freedom into their own classrooms. The affirmation of their identity and humanity would continue to inform them as they navigated and challenged racism throughout their lives.

"I BELIEVE IN ACTION": CONFRONTING
RACISM AND SUPPORTING THE MOVEMENT

Revis, Farmer, and Thompson's formative years prepared them to confront racist and discriminatory actions within their future schools and find different ways to support the movement for civil rights in Raleigh. Their actions reflect an activist mindset that resonates with how other scholars have documented forms of teacher activism throughout the Black struggle for freedom.[35] Growing up in segregated communities and then attending HBCUs, each teacher was exposed to or participated in civil rights activities and protests—acts of resistance that would manifest later in their classroom practice. For example, Thompson's family influenced her at an early age to participate in marches:

> My sister, who is three years older than I, went to North Carolina A&T where the sit-ins started. And I remember when I was in high school, we got this letter from my sister. It was written in pencil. And when my mother saw it written in pencil, she immediately said, "That girl has gone and got herself in jail." And that was right. She was writing from jail. And I think because of that, you know, being that close and personal to that situation, I would, after school as a high school student, we would go downtown and march. So, I was a marcher. I was a protester.[36]

After school and on weekends, Thompson would participate in marches with other high school and college students throughout Raleigh. Thompson's mother worried for her and her older sister, feeling that their activities might place them in danger. "My mother and one of my best friend's mothers would stand on the other side of the street and watch us," Thompson recalls, "I think they thought they were keeping us safe."[37] Within this protective community, Thompson cultivated a sense for activism, even through small acts of resistance such as drinking from the white-designated water fountain.

Upon graduating high school, Thompson went to North Carolina College at Durham, now North Carolina Central University, and she continued to attend marches, rallies, and speeches. In Durham, she heard speeches from prominent activists such as Dr. Martin Luther King Jr., Malcolm X, and Angela Davis. Thompson describes one memorable speech from Stokely Carmichael:

> I will tell you one experience I had with Stokely Carmichael that made a difference in my life. He was, of course, educating us about how we bought into the "system" without even realizing it. . . . He went into telling us that we worked so hard to be accepted by, as he called it, the white power structure that we'd change the way we look. We'd lighten our skins. We straightened

our hair. We dyed our hair. And that none of that was the real you. That stuck with me. And that's why, since then, I have always worn my hair naturally.[38]

This example, along with her earlier experiences in Raleigh, highlight how Thompson's environment prompted her to continually question and challenge racial injustice. "I was incredulous. And I continue to be incredulous about this insanity called racism," she states.[39]

Thompson went on to share how her civil rights activism translated into her approach to teaching and how she would confront forms of racism and what she refers to as "subtle things that have been going on in the school system for some children."[40] Although these were not in the same vein as the protests or marches she participated in during her formative years, she was an activist for her students. For instance, in one of her first years teaching art at Atkins Senior High School in Winston-Salem, North Carolina, Thompson was responsible for decorating bulletin boards throughout the school, as previously mentioned. She would decorate bulletin boards with well-known and less recognized Black people, including many of the activists she saw speak in college, such as Stokely Carmichael. She recalls an incident that occurred one year in which a white male teacher at the school confronted the principal about the bulletin board, asking for it to be taken down:

> I said, "I would not do it . . . I'm willing to talk to these guys about it." And they said that if we made the statement, "Black is beautiful" or "I'm Black and I'm proud" that we were saying that white was not beautiful. And that, you know, that maybe white people shouldn't be proud. . . . I said, "that's just not meant to help us think that way . . . if you see a rose and you say, oh, that's a beautiful red rose. Are you then saying that a daisy isn't beautiful?" . . . We would go back and forth. I don't know if we ever resolved it. But, I didn't take my bulletin board down. Thank you very much.[41]

Thompson's refusal to remove her Black history bulletin boards demonstrates her conviction in making sure that all students learned about Black history, even in a newly integrated environment where she may have been expected to conform to white expectations.

In another case, Thompson confronted a white teacher she worked with who had made racist comments to an advanced class of students. After school one day, two Black students shared with her how this teacher had stated that "Black people would never reach, you know, the achievement of white people in our society. We would never do well on tests."[42] In school the next day, Thompson went into the teacher's class in front of the students and confronted the teacher about her remarks, requesting that each of them bring in their National Teacher Examination and Scholastic Aptitude Test scores to see if what she had told the students was true. The day after this incident, Thompson was called into the principal's office to see him and the other teacher. The principal could not believe that Thompson had interrupted a class, and she responded:

> "Well, I did. But see, she [the teacher] said this in front of all the students, so I had to respond to it in front of all the students. . . . And interestingly enough she didn't bring her grades, her test scores in . . . so something made her doubt that she was going to be able to prove her point. . . ." I told her, "This was racist . . . you know, you told these boys that they were not good enough. Not only did you tell them, you told the other students in the class . . . I couldn't let you get away with that."[43]

The teacher would apologize to Thompson, writing her a letter claiming she was unaware of the impact of what she had said and believed. These stories convey how Thompson challenged injustice in the schools she taught in, carrying on a tradition of activism that was cultivated in her Raleigh upbringing; as she emphasizes, "I believe in action."[44]

Similar to Thompson, Farmer also engaged in civil rights activities when she was a college student. She reflects on how sit-ins and marches organized by college students began to occur at Hampton:

> I shall always remember 1960, and everything was planned for our protest, and I participated in it. I was a little nervous about it, because if people in Kingstree found out that I had participated in something like that, maybe my parents would have lost their jobs. But I did, and made it a purpose to be in the group so that if anything was taped I would not be a part of it.[45]

Farmer shared how the protest in which she participated happened in Norfolk, Virginia, in which police dogs were present though there were no attacks or violent incidents.[46] Her cautiousness toward her parents' employment is something that she was mindful of when she was teaching in Raleigh.[47] Meanwhile, Revis also acknowledges how "during that time, teachers could be fired for being involved in politics, and lose their jobs and that sort of thing. So, it was not something that we could be heavily involved in."[48] Although Farmer did not continue to protest directly, she recalls other ways in which people contributed to local activism that was organized by college students in Raleigh:

> Those of us who did not participate in the actual marching, supported them, you know, by having water for them and giving money to them, so that was, I guess, my way of participating, through funds and just support in general.[49]

Revis describes how these protests were mostly peaceful in which college students would march quietly downtown on Fayetteville Street: "No speaking, no talking, no yelling, no anything. Nobody bothered them."[50] She demonstrated

her support of the movement through observance of some of these first demonstrations in Raleigh and staying up to date on what students were planning at
nearby Shaw University.

During this period, Revis's local church also exposed her to prominent leaders of the movement, including Coretta Scott King and Jesse Jackson. She could
not remember exactly what King spoke about during her visit, but she shares her
memory of the event and how the church would structure these events:

> We always had a theme . . . I am thinking that a lot of what she had to say
> was kind of general and sharing what her husband believed and that kind of
> thing. And, following the theme . . . I know that she was an attractive woman
> and commanding. You know, you respected her.[51]

Revis and Farmer both commented on how this type of exposure to speakers
and local activism influenced how they would talk to students and ensure that
they were prepared for the realities of the country in which they lived. Revis
especially sees this type of engagement as its own form of activism:

> I believe change sometimes has to be pushed. We don't just do things, usu-
> ally, so quickly, unless somebody motivates us to do it . . . I think that when
> teachers teach students to think they are doing one of the greatest things to
> help civil rights in all other areas. When you can analyze for yourself, when
> you can synthesize, when you can extrapolate, when you can evaluate, when
> you've been taught how to do that, I think it leads to the best kind of citizen
> possible.[52]

In line with what scholars have identified as "intellectual activism" and "intellectual resistance," all three teachers cultivated this approach to teaching through
their own lived experiences.[53] Their time growing up in segregated communities, attending HBCUs, and participating in or witnessing protests had an impact on how they interacted with and inspired their own students, challenging
subtle forms of injustice and contributing to the movement in ways that they
could.

"A MOVEMENT FOR THE BETTERMENT OF THIS WORLD": LESSONS FOR TODAY'S MOMENT

Farmer, Revis, and Thompson's reflections on growing up, attending school, and
teaching during the civil rights movement offer important lessons for educators
to consider today. We see their stories as a continuation of bell hooks's notion of
"education as the practice of freedom":

> But learning is a place where paradise can be created. The classroom, with all
> its limitations, remains a location of possibility. In that field of possibility, we

have the opportunity to labor for freedom, to demand of ourselves and our comrades, an openness of mind and heart that allows us to face reality even as we collectively imagine ways to move beyond boundaries, to transgress.[54]

Their advice speaks to the ongoing movement for Black freedom and the importance of teaching students to their full potential. Their intellect had been nurtured by their own teachers within all-Black schools where they "experienced learning as a revolution."[55] Their teachers had taught them that learning itself was what bell hooks called a "counter-hegemonic act" against racism.[56] Their teachers' mission was for students to succeed, regardless of background, and Thompson, Farmer, and Revis maintained this philosophy in their own practice. For example, with regard to issues she still sees in schools, Thompson expresses a desire for more teachers to focus on "what is [a] child able to do?":

> Why do we not look at the difference in those people's experiences and always focus on what children don't have in their houses or whether their parents can read or not or if their parents are on drugs or not? Why do we take the negative to change the narrative? Why don't we go to the positive?[57]

bell hooks also argues that an additional element of education as the practice of freedom includes making the classroom a site where students experience joy and care. Those who had taught Thompson, Farmer, and Revis had known them as human beings and were part of their community. Farmer and Revis echo the importance of demonstrating this type of care toward students, as well as seeing teachers and students alike as lifelong learners. When Revis was a principal, for example, she had the opportunity to travel overseas and observe schools abroad. She reflects on how her experience studying different schools could provide insight for teachers today:

> When you get beyond your own little area, you begin to see that people are more alike than they are different. We all seem to have some of the same desires. And everybody kind of is the same. And so, I think that if teachers encourage students to think and encourage students to go beyond their little area of comfort, that is the kind of advice that I think would be helpful to everybody.[58]

In this sense, we can see how Revis's view on teaching continues a tradition that was instilled in her at a young age—challenging students and opening their eyes to the world . She also describes how the uniqueness of the profession lends itself to continued empowerment: "[Y]ou're teaching other people, but you're also learning and you're developing yourself. And that is one of the wonderful things about being an educator. You are developing yourself, along with helping other people to develop themselves."[59]

Farmer, Revis, and Thompson's early valued segregated spaces affirmed their identity and humanity, which provided the foundation for them to navigate discrimination later on. In college, they continued to learn about the importance of asserting their voices in demanding first-class citizenship through activism and encountering others who sought change. Commenting on the role of teachers in developing citizens, Revis expresses concern about our current historical moment:

> Today, I find that a lot of people do not understand some of the basic principles of living in America. I find a lot of people don't know what fascism is. And so, when somebody dangles the word fascism in their face, they act the way they were told to act. There are some people who believe that democracy means you can do anything you want to do. Liberty means doing anything. I can do whatever I want to do.[60]

Each of the teachers acknowledge the importance of teachers in advancing not only the life of a community, as was central to them in their formative years, but also the health of democracy and the nation itself. Speaking about what she would want teachers and students to know about the civil rights movement, Thompson shares:

> I really want them to understand that it is a movement for the betterment of this world that we live in. That it is not about people getting rights because we already have them. It's about people actualizing those rights . . . we are all equal. And we are endowed by our Creator with that kind of equality that allows us to have, you know, the right to pursue happiness, the right to stand and be a human being in this world. And we're still struggling with this in 2021. And so, I would want them to know that at a point in time, people stood up and said, "No more." People stood up and said, "I would die before I will succumb to this attitude towards us."[61]

All three teachers draw similar connections between struggles from the past and issues they see confronting students and teachers today, emphasizing the importance of learning about past movements for justice to recognize and achieve a truer democracy. The impact of valued segregated spaces on their trajectories as career educators cannot be underestimated. These spaces and experiences significantly shaped their conceptualizations of activism and their teaching philosophies and practice. In turn, Revis, Farmer, and Thompson provided their own students a space in which they could practice freedom. This historical legacy continues to inform and shape this moment in which "the classroom remains the most radical site of possibility."[62]

"In the Face of Her Splendid Record"

Willa Cofield Johnson and Teacher
Dismissal in the Civil Rights Era

CRYSTAL R. SANDERS

By all accounts, Willa Cofield Johnson was the consummate educator. The Black woman high school English teacher at the all-Black T. S. Inborden High School in Enfield, North Carolina, went the extra mile for her students. She started the school's newspaper to give Black youths an outlet to express their ideas and demonstrate their creativity. She established the school's chapter of the National Honor Society to reinforce the importance of scholarship, service, and character. She also incorporated current events into her curriculum, ensuring that her pupils knew that individuals not much older than they were challenging segregation at lunch counters and bus terminals throughout the South. During the 1962–1963 school year, Luther Williams, Inborden's principal, rated Johnson as excellent and above average in all fields because of her exemplary work.[1]

Given her contributions to the school community and her outstanding teaching evaluation, Willa Johnson's job termination in June of 1964 was clearly an act of retaliation for her and her family members' involvement in the local Black freedom struggle. Johnson's extensive civil rights work to dismantle white supremacy threatened the community's racially segregated way of life. Rather than condemn Johnson's political work outright, Inborden High School Principal Luther Williams cooperated with white school authorities to frame charges against her, and at the end of the school year, he informed her that the Halifax County School System declined to renew her teaching contract because of insubordination. In reality, Johnson was one in a long line of teachers who lost their jobs because of their connection to the Black freedom struggle.[2]

Job security for Black educators in the South became especially fraught in the wake of the 1954 *Brown v. Board of Education of Topeka* decision.[3] From the mid-1950s until the mid-1970s, Black school staff—including teachers, principals, counselors, and coaches—faced termination, demotion, and harassment as southern communities implemented court-ordered desegregation.[4] Many white officials and parents believed that Black educators were only qualified to teach Black students, but this racist philosophy was not the only reason for the mass exodus of Black educators during the civil rights era. Another reason for the displacement of Black school personnel was abolishment of state teacher tenure laws in the South. Most southern states gave their public school teachers continuing contracts that would be renewed unless the teacher was notified by a certain date and the employer showed just cause for nonrenewal. Massive resistance to the *Brown* decision led southern states to repeal continuing contract laws and put teachers on a year-to-year basis. Such a move allowed racist school boards to fire Black teachers who were no longer wanted or who transgressed the racial status quo.[5]

Teacher tenure in US public education began in 1909 in New Jersey as a way to end politically influenced teacher appointments. Tenure provided teachers with protection from persecution for their activities both inside and outside the classroom. Tenure was never meant to prevent justified termination but, rather, to ensure that the grounds under which teachers were fired were reasonable and justified. It protected teachers' freedom of association (e.g., union membership, membership in the National Association for the Advancement of Colored People [NAACP]) and academic freedom.[6]

In spite of its progressive reputation, North Carolina repealed its teachers' tenure law in 1955. Before the change, a teacher was hired for a one-year contract in the first year of employment. Thereafter, retained teachers received a continuing contract, and the teacher retained employment without renewal unless terminated.[7] In making the case for the elimination of the continuing contract provisions, the North Carolina Attorney General's office released a statement that asserted it was "impractical to continue to employ" the nearly nine thousand Black public school teachers in the state if the US Supreme Court enforced the *Brown* decision.[8] Thus, Black educators in North Carolina bore the brunt of displacement with the end of teacher tenure. For example, the number of Black high school principals in the state dropped from two hundred twenty-seven to eight between 1963 and 1970, as school districts moved from dual school systems to unitary ones.[9]

Desegregation was not the only factor that made repeal of teacher tenure laws so consequential. Yearly employment contracts made Black educators who openly resisted white supremacy vulnerable to harassment and termination. Even before *Brown*, activist educators faced job termination for challenging the white supremacist order. When Reverend Joseph DeLaine, a public school teacher, advocated for better Black schools in Clarendon County, South Carolina, in a 1948 struggle that became the landmark case *Briggs v. Elliott*, the school board fired DeLaine and his wife in retaliation for their activism. Black educators did not even have to be at the center of the protests to lose their jobs. When the principal of a Black high school in Prince Edward County, Virginia, failed to quell a strike by Black students protesting the school's dilapidated conditions in 1951, the school board terminated him. Across the South, all-white school boards were on high alert to squelch Black dissent, and the repeal of teacher tenure laws made it easier to do so.[10]

Willa Johnson was a public school teacher who dared to engage in civil rights activity without the protection of teacher tenure in a rural, materially impoverished northeastern North Carolina county, and her activism led segregationists to fire her in 1964. Her story is significant, not only because it debunks the myth that Black schoolteachers remained politically neutral during the civil rights era, but also because it testifies to the existence, vitality, and importance of grassroots Black freedom struggles in rural North Carolina. Most accounts of civil rights activity in the South dismiss North Carolina as a racially moderate area free of the racial violence and Black disfranchisement endemic to places such as Alabama and Mississippi. When civil rights activism in the Tar Heel State is considered, the focus is usually on activity in cities such as Greensboro at the beginning of the student sit-in movement in 1960.[11] Political scientists Jack Bass and Walter De Vries went so far as to claim that the civil rights movement "bypassed" the rural eastern region of North Carolina.[12] Willa Johnson's work, alongside other Black activists in Halifax County, blows this assertation out of the water. These local insurgents organized sit-ins, marches, picket lines, boycotts, and voter registration campaigns. They dared to remake their world anew in the face of strong white resistance.

Moreover, Willa Johnson's story brings into focus an understudied aspect of educational history: teacher dismissal. She waged a groundbreaking battle to challenge unfair teacher termination, and her efforts made it harder for school boards across the United States to subjectively fire teachers for their activism. Thus, her efforts paved the way for untold numbers of public school teachers to more freely participate in freedom struggles without fear of jeopardizing their jobs, even if they did not have tenure.

Finally, Willa Johnson's pedagogical activism should be understood as the rule and not the exception among Black educators. In a covert manner, Black teachers taught their students lessons and histories that countered narratives of anti-Blackness and prepared them to challenge white supremacy. Their actions were part of a much larger "history of fugitive educational practices that began in the time of slavery."[13] What was different about Johnson's work, however, was that she did not keep her political activity outside of the classroom and underground, as many of her fellow Black educators did. By choosing not to do so, she became a target for economic reprisals.

Willa Cofield (Johnson's maiden name) was born one year before the start of the Great Depression, into a large family known and respected for its entrepreneurship, fidelity to the Christian faith, and commitment to racial uplift. The oldest of four children, Cofield was raised in the rural northeastern North Carolina town of Enfield in the Black-majority Halifax County.[14] The town's claim to fame was being the world's largest peanut market in the first half of the twentieth century. Halifax County itself had significance as part of North Carolina's Black Belt, one of eleven counties in eastern North Carolina with a majority-Black population.[15] After white supremacists amended North Carolina's state constitution in 1900 and added a subjective literacy test, the overwhelming majority of Blacks in the Black Belt lost their right to vote.[16]

With determination and hard work, Willa's grandfather, Henry Cofield, who was born seven years after the end of the Civil War, established several businesses, including a grocery store and a funeral home, to insulate his family financially from the violence, fraud, and other injustices that came with Black disfranchisement. After his death, Willa's father, Thomas, and her uncles and aunt continued and expanded the family businesses. Catering to a Black clientele who routinely needed food, shelter, and sundry items and who desired dignified homegoing services meant that the Cofields always had steady business.

Young Willa often accompanied her father to work, where she witnessed his concern for his people and his commitment to uplifting the race. Owning his own businesses made him a confidant to many and a leader in the region. It also provided him with a relatively greater degree of independence than many other Black residents had, because his livelihood came from the Black community. Thomas Cofield used that independence in the 1930s to invite a speaker to his church to discuss Black voting rights. White men broke in, stopped the meeting, and ran the speaker out of town. This kind of racial intimidation during the 1930s was common, but Cofield remained undeterred and kept his ear to the ground, determined to learn about other initiatives that promoted Black progress. Years later, the Cofield family businesses played pivotal roles in the Halifax County civil rights movement, providing everything from mimeograph services to meeting locations outside of the white gaze.[17]

Willa Cofield's mother, Mae, also served the community and engaged in Black consciousness. She and Willa started a garden club to promote the improvement of Black areas through flower cultivation. Mae Cofield was an ardent support of Black newspapers, which provided an alternative to the stereotypical and false depictions of Blacks that white newspapers often published. In 1934, she won second place in a subscription contest sponsored by the Black *Norfolk Journal and Guide* newspaper, which was founded in 1900. She visited Black churches, schools, and homes, soliciting subscriptions to help that media outlet remain financially solvent. Mae Cofield and her husband were devoted members of the Wayman-Enfield Branch of the NAACP. They exposed their children to the NAACP's *Crisis* magazine, the civil rights organization's political and news publication that also showcased Black literature, art, and education.[18]

Thomas and Mae Cofield's relative financial freedom, independent minds, and race work made them strong leaders in the community. They searched for independent ways to make a living, worked hard, and spent money carefully. Notwithstanding competition from white businesses, the Cofields kept their businesses afloat and their interest in race matters alive. A young Willa Cofield was closely watching her parents' example.[19]

Willa Cofield's formal schooling began in 1933 at the Enfield Colored Graded School. She excelled academically and developed a love of learning, despite the bare-bones education offered to her and her classmates because of the gross underfunding of Black education. Historian Vanessa Siddle Walker documented positive "unintended consequences" of intentional white school board neglect in Black education and the kinds of affirmative learning environments that, as Walker discovered, were also present at the Enfield Colored Graded School. What the school lacked in amenities, the teachers made up for by embracing their young charges with tough love and by offering a curriculum that negated notions of Black inferiority. For example, Cofield's teachers introduced her to Black figures such as singer and composer Roland Hayes and Revolutionary War hero Crispus Attucks, who were not covered in the standard textbooks but were held up as models of Black leadership and excellence. Years later, Cofield would implement some of these same pedagogical tools in her own classroom to build students' self-esteem, foster racial pride, and increase student aspiration.[20]

White students in Enfield attended Enfield High, but Black students had no in-town option. Thus, Cofield received her secondary education at the Brick Tri-County High School that served Black students from Halifax, Nash, and Edgecombe Counties. The school was located on the grounds of the former Joseph Keasby Brick Agricultural, Industrial, and Normal School (later named Brick Junior College), a private boarding school that was founded by the American Missionary Association in 1895 and closed in 1933. Black communities in the three counties served by the school double-taxed themselves and raised money for the school's operation and upkeep to supplement the meager amount that white public officials provided. Although students did not have access to the latest lab equipment or the newest edition of textbooks, the school was a source of pride, as it was a Black institution that celebrated Blackness. Unlike most schools during the 1940s, the Brick Tri-County High School offered students a course solely dedicated to Black history, and Willa Cofield enrolled.[21]

Even though Black parents and teachers went out of their way to make up for the racial inequality in the education offered to Black students, they could not hide the inequity. By Cofield's senior year, she and her classmates were fed up with the used textbooks, outdated equipment, and shoddy buildings. They expressed their discontent in a series of three skits performed in lieu of a traditional commencement speaker.[22] Little did Cofield know that the high school production was preparing her to speak out against racial discrimination on a larger stage.

After graduating as valedictorian of her senior class, Willa Cofield matriculated at Hampton Institute in the fall of 1944.[23] She came of age at the Black college where she was on her own and far from home for the first time. During her tenure at Hampton, student activism was vibrant at the institution, with students threatening to strike if the board of trustees did not fire the white president, who had spoken about Hampton students in a condescending manner to a white audience.[24] In the end, the president resigned, unable to overcome the widespread dissatisfaction of faculty, staff, and students.[25] The experience exposed Cofield to the power of collective action.

Hampton also exposed an impressionable Cofield to some of the most prominent members of the Black intelligentsia. The English major took classes from literary critic J. Saunders Redding and drama professor Esther Merle Jackson. She dreamed of returning to her hometown after graduation in 1948 and securing employment as a high school English teacher, where she could emulate her Hampton professors; only, Enfield did not have a high school for Black students, and the Brick Tri-County High School was destroyed in a fire years earlier.[26]

Blacks in Enfield mobilized to secure better educational opportunities for their children. In 1948, a group of parents addressed the Halifax County Board of Education and demanded that the board establish a Black high school on the grounds of the T. S. Inborden School, which served elementary students. The parents expressed dissatisfaction with the fact that, despite being taxpayers, their children were forced to travel long distances outside of Enfield for secondary education. The board took no immediate action on the parents' request, and students continued attending Eastman High School, a rural school in the county, or Phillips High School, a Black institution in a neighboring county. Both schools were a significant distance from Enfield.[27]

Willa Cofield began her teaching career at Eastman High School the same year when Black parents demanded a high school in Enfield. Eastman's poor facilities were a tangible reminder of the substandard conditions that Black educators and students often endured. The rural school lacked an auditorium, gymnasium, and cafeteria. Student attendance was spotty, as many stayed out of school to work on farms during planting and harvesting seasons. Despite the difficult circumstances, Cofield took seriously her responsibility to offer her students a first-rate education. The twenty-year-old novice educator taught English and typing. Never mind that basic grammar rules were often ignored by students or that some of the students might have never seen a typewriter before: Cofield maintained high expectations for all of her pupils and encouraged them to study hard and be successful. Their personal circumstances did not dictate their futures.[28]

Although a first-year teacher, Cofield maintained some semblance of a social life outside of the classroom. She maintained her deep friendship with Reed Johnson, a World War II veteran who had attended Hampton with her and who taught at Tuskegee Institute. At the end of the school year, the couple married. Years later, they opened a flower shop together and worked in the movement as a couple committed to Black freedom.[29]

In fall of 1952, Halifax County officials finally built a Black high school in Enfield. The secondary school was an addition to the Inborden Elementary School and its opening gave Willa Cofield Johnson the opportunity to pursue her dream of teaching in her hometown. She had spent one year in graduate school; almost two years as bookkeeper/secretary at the Brick Rural Life School, a farm school on the campus of the former Brick Junior College; and two years teaching in Halifax County, but not in Enfield. When the high school opened, she became one of the inaugural faculty members there, where she taught language arts and literature. Just as had been the case at Eastman High, Johnson had high expectations of her students, letting them know that they were capable of learning, no matter their personal circumstances or background. She left the school after six years to give birth to her daughter.[30]

After a year home with the new baby, Johnson returned to Inborden High School. When she reclaimed her job in 1959, the school had a new principal, Luther Williams. Williams and Johnson were familiar with one another, both having worked at Eastman High School and owning homes on the same street. Additionally, the two were part of the same pinochle card game group. Their social connections fostered a positive working relationship, with Williams supporting Johnson's efforts to establish new student organizations at the school.[31]

In the classroom, Willa Johnson regularly discussed civil rights with her students. She brought in newspaper articles about the Freedom Rides and filled her bulletin boards with photographs of college students sitting in at lunch counters throughout the South. She believed that it was imperative to expose her students to current events challenging segregation and the role of young people in those events, so that they knew one could never be too young to make a difference.[32]

Despite her efforts to incorporate the national Black freedom struggle into her classroom curriculum, Black protests were not unheard of in that part of the state. Black activists in Halifax and surrounding counties, including some of Willa Johnson's family members, had been engaged in a struggle for voting rights throughout the 1950s. In fact, in 1957, Louise Lassiter, a Black woman in neighboring Northampton County, filed suit in federal district court challenging the constitutionality of literacy tests as a criterion for voter registration, because racist registrars discriminated against Blacks. In the Tar Heel State, the fairness of literacy test administration was inversely proportional to the percentage of Blacks in a county's population. As the population of Blacks increased, the number of registered Black voters decreased. A three-judge federal court panel found that the literacy test Lassiter took violated the Fourteenth and Fifteenth Amendments, but because North Carolina lawmakers had recently revised the test, the judges ordered her to attempt to register again and, if unsatisfied, to seek relief with the North Carolina Supreme Court. Lassiter exhausted all new state-level remedies and lost her appeal at the US Supreme Court.[33] Thus, Black political activity was not new to Halifax County. What was new was a Black public school teacher so openly making news of Black political activity part of the daily instruction.

The growing civil rights movement to which Willa Johnson had exposed her students throughout the 1950s and early 1960s came to her classroom in April 1963, when her husband, Reed Johnson, ran for a seat on the Enfield Board of Commissioners. He was one of twelve candidates on the ballot for the board of commissioners in the May election.[34] Johnson ran because he knew that his candidacy would encourage Black residents of the town to register to vote. He desired to see the town hire a Black police officer and install sidewalks, lights, and proper drainage in Black neighborhoods. In short, he wanted to empower the Black community, as well as enjoy the benefits of his tax dollars. White officials had disenfranchised the majority of Black residents in Enfield, so Reed Johnson's decision to participate in electoral politics was not well received in white circles. The white power structure had not expected Black residents to control anything beyond their churches.[35]

Reed Johnson's candidacy galvanized Enfield's Black population and mobilized white resistance. Black residents intensified their efforts to register to vote, and students in Willa Johnson's classes volunteered to help with registration drives before the April 26 registration deadline.[36] The students finally had the opportunity to engage in some of the Black freedom struggle work that they had learned about from their teacher.[37]

Although Reed Johnson did not win, his campaign ignited a spark in Inborden High students to become more involved in civic affairs, and Willa Johnson's classroom became the safe space for them to discuss their newfound interests. Two students in her English class reported that they had recently traveled to the all-Black North Carolina College in Durham, where they saw students protesting outside of a segregated Howard Johnson's restaurant. Their recollections precipitated discussions about challenging segregation in Enfield, and later in the week, several of the students decided to attempt to use the all-white Enfield Public Library, because their parents were taxpayers whose hard-earned dollars financed the library. Twelve students walked from Inborden to the library after school, where the librarian summarily denied them service on account of their race. They decided to appeal the policy to the mayor, but he was unavailable, so they made an appointment for a later date.[38]

When word of the students' library challenge reached Inborden Principal Luther Williams, he was incensed. He met with the students and chastised them for challenging the racial status quo. Furthermore, he advised them to cancel their scheduled meeting with the mayor. Williams's actions were not surprising, given the fact that he was a Black man who reported to a white superintendent and an all-white school board. To protect his job and prevent any sort of funding retaliation against his school, he strongly condemned Black activism. Willa Johnson, however, saw the situation differently. She had taught her students about young people who risked their educations and their very lives to secure first-class citizenship for Blacks, and she believed that the Inborden students should have been celebrated rather than rebuked for their efforts. She shared her thoughts with Williams and questioned why he told the students to cancel their meeting with the mayor. He denied doing any such thing. What could not be denied was that there was now tension between Principal Luther Williams and Willa Johnson, because the two had very different ideas about appropriate behavior for Inborden students and neither planned to back down.[39]

In the coming weeks and months, Willa Johnson became even more committed to supporting Black student activism. She drove students to a Roanoke Rapids civil rights movement rally to hear Floyd McKissick, who had been one of the first Black students to desegregate the University of North Carolina Law School in 1951. The history-making attorney urged his Black audience to resist anything less than first-class citizenship, comparing their struggle to the biblical story of Israelites in the Battle of Jericho. The day after the McKissick rally, students gathered in Willa Johnson's home. Inspired by McKissick, the youths planned a challenge to the segregated seating policy at the Levon Movie Theater, which was the only cinema in Enfield. Levon's owners required Black customers to sit in the balcony, whereas white customers could sit on the main floor. In the Johnson home, students made picket signs and practiced walking around in a circle as they planned to do on the sidewalk in front of the theater.[40]

The fact that students met at Willa Johnson's house to plan their direct-action protest demonstrated the strong teacher–student relationship that existed. The students saw Johnson as someone who cared about their education and their right to dignity and respect. Johnson saw her students as capable young adults who had leadership potential and the ability to make their own decisions independently of adult leaders. In short, Johnson empowered her students and encouraged them to articulate their demands and carry out their own efforts to bring those demands to fruition.

For several weeks beginning in late May, Inborden students picketed the Levon theater to get the theater's management to end its segregation policy.[41] After marching up and down the street for hours, the students usually assembled at Cofield Funeral Home, where they sang freedom songs and planned for the next day's protest. Willa Johnson served in an advisory capacity and provided support and advice when necessary. The students' consistent demonstrations led the theater's owner to close the business rather than integrate in late June 1963.[42]

The student demonstrations energized adults who petitioned the Enfield commissioners for municipal services in Black communities and an end to segregation in public places. Several hundred Black residents signed onto the demands that Reed Johnson presented before the town board.[43] Elected officials took no action in response to the demands other than appointing a biracial committee to study the demands. In support of the petition, Inborden students once again began demonstrating downtown. They picketed local businesses that practiced segregation.

The students' protests led Enfield's commissioners to pass an ordinance regulating demonstrations. The ordinance required demonstrators to give the police at least five hours advance notice of demonstrations, limited the number of picketers to five, and stipulated that picketing had to be done in silence and that picketers had to be fifteen feet apart. Most important, no person under the age of eighteen could picket in Enfield. The latter requirement was supposed to be the death knell of demonstrations, because all of the picketing had been done by students, almost all of them under the age of eighteen.[44]

The fact that segregationist white men had found a way to limit the moral, peaceful, and innocent actions of Black youths shamed adults into action. Meeting at the Cofield Funeral Home, Enfield's Black residents strategized about their next steps. Rather than end the Enfield movement in response to the ordinance severely limiting demonstrations, adults decided to take over the picket lines. The first protest held after the ordinance went into effect occurred at a restaurant on US Highway 301 that refused to serve Black patrons. Among the twelve Black picketers were Reed and Willa Johnson. The public school teacher had masterminded many pickets from behind the scenes, but she now engaged in resistance from the front. It was rare for teachers to engage in public protests.[45]

Enfield demonstrations continued throughout the remainder of 1963. Weary protestors were reinvigorated after attending the March on Washington. Willa Johnson had hoped to join the Enfield delegation traveling to Washington, DC, for the historic event but had to change her plans at the last minute and remain home after her daughter had a health emergency hours before the bus left for the nation's capital.[46]

Inspired by the historic March on Washington, the protestors returned to Enfield and defied the town's picketing ordinance in a mass protest on the last day in August. Having missed the trip to Washington, Johnson eagerly joined the protest, driving young picketers from the funeral home to downtown streets and taking them back once they were released from jail. After picketers were denied bail and held in the Enfield jail, a crowd of one thousand to twelve hundred Blacks protesting segregation did not go home as ordered by the police, and town officials brought out the fire truck and trained high-powered hoses of water on unarmed Black people of all ages. The force of the water sent many protestors to the hospital and rightly angered Black residents who saw the extent of the injuries and who knew that nothing they had done made the town's response acceptable.[47] For their part, law enforcement saw nothing wrong with their actions. The Enfield police chief, F. C. Sykes, boldly asserted that "if it becomes necessary, we'll use anything we've got to stop them."[48] The Black community responded by boycotting downtown stores for over three months. Willa Johnson's husband, Reed, organized the boycotts, making sure there were picketers outside of downtown stores every Saturday, which had been the busiest shopping day for local merchants. Under his guidance, the boycotts lasted until a few weeks before Christmas.[49]

By challenging the local white power structure and encouraging students to do the same, Willa Johnson put herself at odds with Inborden High School Principal Luther Williams, who had to go before that same white power structure and ask for money to outfit his school. When Johnson and Williams met for a routine conference in the fall of 1963, she first realized that her job was in jeopardy. In the course of their meeting, Williams casually told her that he would "protect any teacher up to a point." In other words, the principal was warning Johnson to tread carefully, because her political activities could lead to reprisals, including job termination.[50]

Shortly after Johnson's ominous meeting with her principal, she learned that the Halifax County superintendent had visited her close friend and fellow teacher Lillie Cousins Smith at the Eastman school where she worked. Smith was also the only other public school teacher involved in the Enfield protests. During the surprise meeting, the superintendent revealed that he knew Smith had participated in public demonstrations, and he intimated that her participation could result in job termination. Unmoved by the intimation, Smith told the administrator that she had already discussed her political work with a representative from North Carolina Governor Terry Sanford's office and learned that there was no law prohibiting public school teachers from picketing. Once Smith recounted the meeting to Johnson, she knew that the superintendent would visit Inborden soon.[51]

Sure enough, Halifax Superintendent William Overman visited Inborden days after his Eastman School visit. Johnson braced herself for a meeting with him but was never called into the office. The superintendent only met with Luther Williams. Johnson overhead the superintendent tell Williams, "I just don't want the school involved." His words were a tell-tell sign that county school officials knew that Johnson mentored and encouraged many of the young activists who had been essential to the Enfield movement. Another sign that Johnson was considered to be an agitator was that, beginning the very next day after the superintendent's visit, Williams began treating her with suspicion and derision.[52]

Throughout the 1963–1964 school year, Principal Luther Williams found ways to belittle and discipline Willa Johnson. He monitored what time she arrived at school daily. He denied her request to bring in community members as guest speakers in her English class. He wrote her up for writing some attendance entries in pencil when she was supposed to use ink. He reminded her that she had to stand in the hall between classes rather than remain in her classroom to prepare for the next class. In the past, none of these things had bothered Williams, but now, they were major issues that he took pleasure in bringing to Johnson's attention.[53]

It was no coincidence that Principal Williams's "polite" harassment of Willa Johnson occurred in tandem with the formation of the Halifax Voters Movement, of which Johnson was a founding member. In February 1964, Black Halifax residents of all economic classes founded the countywide organization to demand more equitable distribution of county resources and to increase the number of registered Black voters. The county had a total population of fifty-nine thousand. Of the thirty-three thousand Black residents, only thirty-six hundred of them were registered to vote.[54] Despite their population majority, Blacks received inferior and segregated care at the county hospital. Black residents held no positions above menial jobs in county or municipal government. The Halifax Voters Movement challenged these injustices by encouraging its members to pack county commissioner meetings and other public gatherings to put undemocratically elected white officials on notice that Black residents would no longer accept second-class citizenship.

The Halifax Voters Movement frequently operated out of the Johnson home and the flower shop that the Johnsons operated. The organization received invaluable financial assistance and personnel support from the Southern Conference Educational Fund (SCEF) in the form of John Salter Jr., a white and Native American civil rights activist native of Arizona by way of Mississippi. The SCEF's mission was dismantling racial segregation in the South. James

Dombrowski was its executive director, and, in addition to Salter, its field secretaries included Anne and Carl Braden and Ella Baker.[55] Salter's civil rights bona fides included community-organizing work in Mississippi from 1961 to 1963, where he was a strategist for the Jackson movement, whose most intense crisis was the murder of Medgar Evers.[56] Salter relocated to North Carolina during the 1963 summer with his wife, Eldri. He traveled throughout Halifax County, speaking at community meetings and organizing grassroots activists. He and the Johnsons became close friends and colleagues, with the three trampling racial mores by dining together in the Johnsons' home. Whenever the Halifax Voters Movement faced harassment and reprisals from white authorities, Salter secured legal counsel, often contracting attorneys from outside of the South.[57]

The Halifax Voters Movement also received some funding from the Voter Education Project (VEP), an umbrella organization that coordinated voter registration funds donated by nonprofit foundations.[58] The Kennedy Administration supported the work of the VEP in the hopes of curtailing direct action protests that created foreign policy embarrassments throughout the sixties.[59] Although the Halifax Voters Movement welcomed every dollar contributed to the fight, whether from individuals or foundations such as VEP, it was SCEF whose support was most instrumental to the cause.

⁂

One month after Willa Johnson and others established the Halifax Voters Movement, she began to have serious concerns about her job security. Principal Williams had given Johnson a memo outlining seven issues that he had with her job performance. She shared the memo with John Salter and other activists, who decided to attend Inborden's April Parent–Teacher Association (PTA) meeting en masse. During the meeting, Salter went on record, warning school officials that if any teacher lost his or her employment because of political work, then a federal lawsuit would follow. The very next day, Principal Williams assured Johnson that he was recommending her for contract renewal. She felt satisfied that the threat of a lawsuit had settled the issue, and she continued to be an active participant in Halifax's Black insurgency.[60]

The registration books in Halifax County were opened on three Saturdays leading up to the June primary election. The Halifax Voters Movement designated every Saturday in the month as "Freedom Day" and encouraged Blacks to attempt to register to vote. As a way to foster excitement about registration, the organization sponsored the candidacies of eleven Blacks for elected office in the upcoming Democratic primary. The eight men and three women on the ballot included Reed Johnson, who ran for state senator; Thomas Cofield, who ran for state representative; and Augustus Cofield, who ran for a seat in the US House of Representatives.[61] The men were Willa Johnson's husband, father, and uncle, respectively. She made countless telephone calls to spread the word about Freedom Days and encourage potential Black registrants to show up. On each Saturday, she joined other movement workers to canvass for prospective registrants, support student volunteers, and encourage people who waited in line, often for hours.[62]

Halifax Voters Movement Chairperson Augustus Cofield alleged that, as increasingly more potential Black voters attempted to register, Halifax County registrars deliberately slowed down the registration process. On the first Freedom Day in May, fifteen hundred Black adults traveled to registration locations throughout the county to register, but only five hundred were added to the voter rolls. Adding insult to injury, election officials moved the polling place from its regular location to the police station, assuming that the station was a location that Blacks would not want to frequent. In other parts of the county, a registrar took thirty minutes to register one applicant, and another registrar took a three-hour lunch. Black citizens resisted the delaying tactics by sending telegrams to a host of public officials, including the county election board chairperson, the governor, and Justice Department representatives.[63]

The Halifax Voters Movement, with Reed Johnson, Thomas Cofield, and Augustus Cofield listed among the plaintiffs, filed suit in federal court, asserting that registration officials engaged in a deliberate slowdown to limit the number of Black voter registrants. The organization was represented by an impressive team of attorneys, including Morton Stavis of Newark, New Jersey; William Kunstler of New York City; and T. T. Clayton of Warrenton, North Carolina. In a hearing held in US District Court for the Eastern District of North Carolina, Judge John D. Larkins Jr. agreed with Halifax Voters Movement officers that white registrars in the county had deliberately slowed down the registration process. He decreed that registration officials could not spend more time qualifying Black applicants than qualifying white applicants. Larkins stipulated a time limit of five minutes for qualifying any applicant and instructed registrars to process three registration applications at the same time.[64] Larkins's ruling affirmed Black citizenship rights, including the right to participate in the electoral process.

Despite the Halifax Voters Movement's impressive voter registration campaign, no Black candidates could overcome the wide gap in the numbers of registered white and Black voters. Even though not a single Black person held elected office in a Black-majority county, white supremacists set out to punish Blacks who had dared to challenge the racial status quo. At the top of their list was Willa Cofield Johnson. On June 2, 1964, Inborden High School Principal Luther Williams notified her that her teaching contract for the coming year would not be renewed. The stated cause of her termination was insubordination. Johnson was shocked by the news because, two months earlier, Williams had told her that he was recommending that her teaching contract be renewed for the coming school year. The only thing that had changed between the promise of renewal in April 1964 and job termination in June 1964 was the intensive voter registration campaign conducted by the Halifax Voters Movement.[65]

If segregationists wanted to make an example out of a civil rights leader to curtail future activism, Willa Johnson was the perfect choice. As a public school teacher, Johnson taught at the pleasure of an all-white school board and super-intendent. She had no job security, as North Carolina had done away with its semblance of teacher tenure in response to *Brown*, and any action that school officials found unbecoming of a teacher could be used against her. Johnson had co-founded the Halifax Voters Movement, and she had been quite vocal and visible in the effort to desegregate Enfield businesses and register Black voters. She had engaged in picketing, speaking, poll watching, and helping Blacks to register to vote for more than a year. She had also encouraged her students to get active in the movement and supported their activity. As if her actions alone were not enough to trouble segregationists, she was also related to three of the most well-known Black men involved the county's Black freedom struggle.

Willa Johnson refused to be silenced or sidelined by job termination. The day after Johnson's termination, SCEF organizer John Salter called attorney William Kunstler on her behalf and asked him to represent her. The lawyer who would later found the Center for Constitutional Rights agreed, and in late June 1964, he and fellow attorney Phillip Hirschkop filed suit in federal court, alleg-ing that Johnson's firing was "arbitrary, capricious, malicious and without legal cause and was designed to intimidate and harass her and members of the class she represents in the exercise of their rights under the federal constitution."[66] Johnson sought two hundred fifty thousand dollars in damages, reinstatement as a teacher, and an order preventing Halifax County School Board officials from similar acts against other employees. The lead defendant in the lawsuit was Joseph Branch, attorney for the Halifax County Board of Education, who was also managing the campaign of soon to be governor, Dan Moore.[67] When North Carolina's attorney general, Wade Bruton, got word of the pending lawsuit, he filed a motion asking for permission to appear as a friend of the court. Bruton argued that Cofield's challenge raised questions about the authority and power that boards of education had to enter into contracts for teaching services. In other words, the state's top attorney understood the precedent-setting nature of the case and hoped to protect the state's unfair and discriminatory contractual policies.[68]

As the educator activist prepared for her day in court, local racists upped the ante. Armed members of the Ku Klux Klan began to drive through Black neigh-borhoods at night to instill fear and terror, and white supremacists made several anonymous phone calls to the Johnson home. On July 4, Klansmen burned a cross in front of Willa Johnson's house.[69] Johnson was not moved by the acts of intimidation and spent her days continuing to work in the Halifax County Voters Movement. She volunteered to become an SCLC Citizenship School teacher, offering Black residents literacy skills in advance of voter registration and making plain for her students the connection between the ballot and community empowerment.[70]

Willa Johnson attempted to secure employment with other school districts, but none would hire her, because she had been labeled as a troublemaker. Unlike many persecuted activists, Johnson's family was a bit more insulated from economic reprisals, because her husband was employed by Cofield Funeral Home rather than by a white employer who could punish him for his wife's activities. Nevertheless, Willa Johnson's financial contribution to the household expenses was missed. Thus, she appealed to the National Education Association (NEA), the largest union of education professionals, for support and assistance. The group summoned her to Washington, DC, and interviewed her before agreeing to support her legal case. The NEA's support came with a monthly stipend from their DuShane Defense Fund and access to their organizational attorneys. The group also agreed to have an NEA member testify on Johnson's behalf during her trial.

Judge John D. Larkins, the same judge who had heard arguments in the Halifax Voters Movement's voter suppression case a year earlier, presided in Willa Johnson's case. During the trial, Luther Williams testified that Johnson had committed more infractions than any other teacher under his jurisdiction during his twelve years at Inborden. He maintained that it was her poor job performance rather than her outside activities that resulted in her termination. Along those same lines, Macon Moore, chairman of the school board, testified that the board acted at the recommendation of the principal and had no knowledge of Johnson's civil rights activities, a claim that was hard to believe, given her visibility in Enfield demonstrations. The only witness who testified on Johnson's behalf was a white school principal from Florida who represented the NEA and maintained that Johnson's actions did not warrant loss of her job.[71] Judge Larkins ruled against Johnson, finding that "there are no vested rights in regard to re-employment of public school teachers." He stated that Johnson had "tended to minimize her professional transgressions while maximizing her notoriety as a known participant in the civil rights movement."[72]

Despite losing in federal district court, Willa Johnson refused to give up, because there was too much at stake for educators everywhere. If she did not appeal her case and advocate for teachers' rights to engage in political activity outside of the classroom, then no teacher was safe from political persecution. She instructed her attorney to appeal to the Fourth Circuit Court of Appeals, knowing that it might be years before judges ruled on her suit. Family businesses that were patronized by Black clientele helped sustain her during the long legal fight.[73]

In June 1966, two years after Willa Johnson lost her job teaching high school English, the Fourth Circuit Court of Appeals ruled in her favor. A panel of five appellate justices sitting in Richmond, Virginia, noted that Halifax school officials cited as evidence of insubordination Johnson's being late to school but not to class, Johnson's failure to give a written explanation for missing one PTA meeting, and Johnson's failure to stand at her classroom door in between classes. The justices asserted that the only reasonable inference that could be made "from the failure to renew Mrs. Johnson's contract in the face of her splendid record of twelve years on such trivial charges was the board members' objections to her racial activity."[74] The court directed the Halifax County School Board to renew Johnson's contract and determine her damages.[75]

The US Supreme Court upheld Willa Johnson's constitutional right to protest when it made no comment and declined to hear an appeal by Halifax school officials in 1967.[76] Her fight cleared the way for other Black public school teachers in North Carolina to regain jobs lost because of civil rights activity. In a settlement that gave her ten thousand dollars in damages after deducting her attorney's fees, she agreed to never to seek employment with Halifax County Schools again. She had already secured employment working for the North Carolina Fund, a precursor to the War on Poverty's community action program.[77]

Although racism took her out of the traditional classroom, Willa Johnson has never stopped learning and teaching. She earned a doctorate degree in urban planning from Rutgers University in 1977 and then returned to Enfield, where she organized for affordable and decent housing for all. She also took part in the effort to elect the first Black person to the Enfield Board of Commissioners since Reconstruction, a feat that was achieved in 1980. She spent seventeen years in the equity office of the New Jersey Department of Education and worked summers for National SEED (Seeking Educational Equity and Diversity), the largest teacher professional development agency in the nation. As an active member of her New Jersey community, she co-founded the Black Women's History Conference and Women in Conversation, a reading and discussion group. Always a student of history, she produced two video documentaries: *The Brick School Legacy* in 2004 and *The Nine O'clock Whistle* in 2021. A book by the same name as the latter documentary, written with two of her former Inborden High School students, is forthcoming.[78]

Willa Johnson's decision to risk her career and livelihood for the sake of the movement was not in vain, as North Carolina's Black Belt sent Eva Clayton to the US House of Representatives in 1992. Clayton was the first Black North

Carolinian to serve in Congress since 1901 and the first Black woman ever to represent North Carolina. Clayton's district included Halifax County, and there was a direct line between her historic election and the groundwork done by Johnson and others in the Halifax Voters Movement to increase Black electoral participation.

In addition to the historic election of Eva Clayton, Willa Johnson's courageous fight against unfair teacher dismissal is reflected in the present-day activist work of educators. In 2018 and again in 2019, thousands of North Carolina public school teachers took to the streets of downtown Raleigh marching in support of higher pay and more school funding. These educators participated freely and openly because of the trail that Willa Johnson had blazed so courageously decades earlier. Her stand protected teacher activism and wielded a significant blow to segregationists who hoped to control educators' political activity to preserve a racist order. In fighting back, Willa Cofield Johnson made it possible for future generations of educators everywhere to raise their voices and pursue justice.

PART II

Activism Across the South and Beyond

Planning, Persistence, and Pedagogy

How Elizabeth City State Colored Normal School Survived North Carolina's White Supremacy Campaign, 1898–1905

GLEN BOWMAN

Frederick Douglass said, "If there is no struggle, there is no progress." Although this great man never visited Elizabeth City, North Carolina, the rural home of the historically Black Elizabeth City State University, his words ring true as if he had had a firsthand experience of this school's history of resilience. Chartered as Elizabeth City State Colored Normal School in the late nineteenth century in Pasquotank County, Elizabeth City State University is now a constituent institution of the University of North Carolina system, offering twenty-eight baccalaureate and four master's programs, including signature programs in aviation science and unmanned aircraft systems (drones), with a strong reputation for economic mobility and a proud history of student activism.[1]

From its beginnings, this institution has had to overcome white supremacy, which can be defined as "a political, economic and cultural system in which whites overwhelmingly control power and material resources, conscious and unconscious ideas of white superiority and entitlement are widespread, and relations of white dominance and non-white subordination are daily reenacted across a broad array of institutions and social settings."[2] Examples of the pernicious effects of the resulting systemic racism are replete. Not a single person of color was appointed on the institution's board of trustees until 1949. Although the institution was founded over a decade before the traditionally white institution East Carolina University, Elizabeth City State did not confer its own graduate degrees until nearly eighty years after East Carolina already had. Black Elizabeth City State faculty who wanted to earn advanced degrees could not attend the University of North Carolina at Chapel Hill until 1951. It was not until March 1965 that the North Carolina governor's office acknowledged that the state needed to provide compensatory funds for its minority institutions for at least the next fifteen years to make up for the intentional neglect the school had endured from its inception.[3] The worst such crisis that directly involved white supremacy, however, took place between 1898 and 1905, when the institution's very existence was threatened. To survive would require not only planning and persistence, along with some cunning and luck, but also a public espousal of "industrial education," which reflected a significant shift in institutional mission and pedagogy and reflected a particularly destructive political landscape for Blacks in turn-of-the-century North Carolina.

EARLY OPTIMISM AND SUCCESS

Elizabeth City State Colored Normal School was founded on March 3, 1891, with the passage of a bill written by Hugh Cale, a Black man who represented Pasquotank County in the North Carolina General Assembly. Although normal schools were established primarily so prospective teachers could teach the "norms" of education, these institutions also offered a variety of advanced academic subjects constituting something akin to a liberal arts education. For example, Fayetteville State Colored Normal School, founded in 1877 as the first public normal school for Blacks in North Carolina, offered ancient history, moral and natural philosophy, and Latin.[4] Elizabeth City State Colored Normal School opened on January 4, 1892, in a rented building, with thirty-six students and two teachers, one of whom also served as the principal, Peter W. Moore. Born into slavery in 1858 in Sampson County, North Carolina, and raised by his mother after his father's apparent murder by the Ku Klux Klan, Moore earned an AB degree from Shaw University in 1887. A "modest, patient, scholarly man," he would become "remarkably courageous and bold" when needed, qualities that would serve the institution well in the coming crisis.[5] The school's objective was, as one state superintendent literally underscored it, to produce "well qualified and thoroughly equipped teachers for the public schools [underlines in original]."[6] During the first year, Moore was expected to do all this on barebones appropriations of nine hundred dollars.[7]

Despite such underfunding, the early years were filled with great success. By September 1893, ninety-five were enrolled, and by 1894, one hundred thirty-six were enrolled, convincing Moore that "the normal has never been so successful in every way. . . ."[8] Required reading for the preparatory class was *A School History of the Negro Race in America*, a textbook written by Edward Austin Johnson who, like Moore, was a Shaw University graduate. Originally an educator, Johnson later served as an assistant district attorney in the federal district of eastern North Carolina, an area that included Elizabeth City. Writing to "inspire" in his young Black readers a "new self-respect and confidence," he dedicated the textbook specifically to Black teachers so they could avoid other textbooks that teach "the inferiority of the Negro."[9] As historian Jarvis R. Givens has recently noted, Johnson seemingly wrote to "transform the educational experience of

While representing Pasquotank County in the North Carolina General Assembly, Hugh Cale (1835–1910) set forth the bill that led to the establishment of the Elizabeth City State Colored Normal School. To this day he is regarded as the founder of what is now named Elizabeth City State University.

Black pupils"; along with other contemporary Black authors of textbooks, Johnson demonstrated "a commitment to liberating the race on a discursive level."[10]

Although the normal school was founded to prepare Black teachers for North Carolina's Black public schools. Principal Moore had a higher purpose. He wanted his students to be articulate, informed citizens. This is why he mandated attendance and participation at weekly Lyceum, which consisted of debates, speeches, and orations, among other forms of creative expression.[11] Through such experience some students gained confidence to pursue professional careers outside of teaching, such as in law and medicine. In chapter eight of his 1933 classic, *The Mis-Education of the Negro*, Carter G. Woodson decried the lack of Black professionals. By requiring students to hone their critical thinking and speaking skills at Lyceum, Principal Moore recognized, from his first years as principal, that his students may well have careers outside of the classroom. Indeed, he sometimes brought outside speakers to further encourage his pupils. Delivering an address titled "Barriers" at the 1896 commencement was noted Black North Carolina congressman George Henry White.[12]

By the mid-1890s, a foundation of student success was being constructed, brick by brick. In 1896, Elizabeth City had just seven graduates, but that was seven more than Winston-Salem, Fayetteville, and Plymouth Normal Schools had, combined.[13] Promising to do his "very best to prepare, as thoroughly as possible, men and women to teach the children," by the end of the decade, Moore had become regarded well outside of Elizabeth City as an elite instructor.[14] Unlike many Black normal schools, Elizabeth City State enjoyed strong community support. A local paper proudly boasted that, because of the school,

The founding principal and first chief executive of the Elizabeth
City State Colored Normal School, Peter W. Moore (1859–1934)
produced outstanding teachers despite a lack of financial support.
Until fall 1912, classes were held in rented facilities.

Elizabeth City itself is "enjoying educational advantages and facilities that are
unsurpassed by any town of equal size in the State" and is "surely becoming the
'mecca' of Eastern North Carolina."[15]

Although other Southern states were becoming deeply hostile to Blacks by
the mid-1890s, North Carolina temporarily bucked that trend. The Populists—
farmers and others hurt by the 1893 depression—united with the Republican
Party in what was called Fusion. By 1896, the Fusionists controlled both the
executive and legislative branches. They increased appropriations at the state's
Black normal schools and passed "An act to establish a school for the training
of colored teachers."[16] Although somewhat receptive to greater Black leadership
in the educational hierarchy, the Fusionists had limits. In early February 1897,
local North Carolina General Assembly Representative W. G. Pool set forth
House Bill 691, "An Act in Relation to the Elizabeth City State Colored Normal
School," which would have made founder Hugh Cale the first Black person on
the Board of Managers.[17] Although he served on boards at both Livingstone
College and the Agricultural and Mechanical College for the Colored Race (now
North Carolina A&T State University), he would not serve as such at the school
he founded. Although the bill passed its readings, it died in the Senate.[18] Despite

this disappointment, Blacks were enjoying greater political status under Fusion. By 1896, almost one thousand held political office. By 1898, North Carolina had more Black postmasters than the rest of the South combined.[19] Such progress angered the out-of-power Democrats, who would be willing to stoop to hate speech, electoral fraud, and even murder to regain their power.

THE 1898 ELECTION AND THE WHITE SUPREMACY MOVEMENT

To regain power in the 1898 election, the Democratic Party in North Carolina focused on promulgating white supremacist propaganda, thereby turning the electorate against the most vulnerable part of the Fusionist coalition—Black people. Newspaper editors such as the Raleigh *News and Observer*'s Josephus Daniels published alarmist warnings about Black men, going as far as smearing James Young, a bona fide patriot who had commanded the Third North Carolina Regiment, composed of Black volunteers during the Spanish-American War.[20] The party's message was simple: Democrats represent whites, and only whites should rule. Elizabeth City's newspaper *Fisherman and Farmer* parroted Daniels's slanderous filth, warning about "black imps" attacking the "spotless chastity" of white women and calling for readers to support "the White Man's Party—the Democratic party." In Elizabeth City, an organization called the White Man's Union condemned what it saw as "the dominion of inferior men and an inferior race." This was politics at its dirtiest and most delusional, as Black domination existed only in the paranoid minds of those fearing a loss of white privilege. Such tactics succeeded nevertheless: On the day after the 1898 election, *Fisherman and Farmer* crowed that the "White Man's Party has swept the state" in "an unprecedented Landslide . . . No longer will she be under Negro domination."[21]

When the North Carolina General Assembly convened in January 1899, Black educators feared what legislators elected in the hateful, irrational, and destructive spirit of white supremacy would do to their schools. Principal Moore asked Superintendent Charles Mebane for updates, and the news from Raleigh was not reassuring: "Nothing has been done in regard to the Colored Normal School. I heard one member say he was ready to abolish all of them." One update was particularly disconcerting: "One thing seems very evident [sic] that your representative had very little interest in your welfare. . . ." Moore's colleague at the Slater School in Winston, S. G. Atkins, admitted to "have been somewhat frightened at times."[22] One can see such fear in Principal Moore's 1899 annual report, which differed from previous ones in that he emphasized values appealing to the new regime. Declaring students "honest, mannerly, respectful, studious, clearly obedient, peaceable and loyal to the school," he closed with the sadly sycophantic "Obediently yours."[23]

Faced with the threat of closure during and after the White
Supremacy movement in North Carolina, Principal Peter W. Moore
nevertheless continued to focus on student success, as he continually
encouraged students, as he put it, to "be somebody."

The General Assembly eventually decided not to abolish the Black normal
schools—at least for the moment—but, rather, to modify them. Over the coming years, these institutions were fundamentally and radically reshaped, largely
in ways reflecting the ideology of white supremacy. For instance, in fall 1899,
a new course was required: Civil Government.[24] Although such knowledge
can encourage effective citizenship, this class was likely required because of
the common stereotype that Blacks were politically naïve. If anyone needed a
course in civil government, however, it would be those whites who had ille-
gitimately taken over through voter intimidation and especially those who had
overthrown the elected Fusionist government in Wilmington. The offices of the
Daily Record, that city's local Black newspaper, were destroyed, and a still unde-
termined number of Blacks were murdered.[25]

Now firmly in control, the Democrats worked to build a one-party state by
disfranchising as many Blacks as possible. A referendum election that would
amend the state constitution by requiring literacy tests was held in summer
1900. To generate electoral enthusiasm, the Democratic Party encouraged town-
ships to establish white supremacy clubs, and in Elizabeth City, a "grand white
supremacy rally" and parade were held.[26] The actual voting was replete with
fraud.[27] In one Elizabeth City ward, less than half of Blacks present at the polls
were even allowed to vote, since the Democratic election board spent an average

of ten minutes challenging each Black voter. In another ward, only one Republican ballot made it in the box before polls closed.[28] On the surface, this amendment might not appear to have been racially discriminatory, because it required all voters—Black and white—to pay poll taxes and pass literacy tests. No written reference to skin color appeared. However, there was a loophole regarding literacy tests: Illiterates would be allowed to vote if they or their ancestors had been registered before 1867, as long as they registered before 1908. This meant that no whites were disfranchised and that no Black could be grandfathered in, as Blacks could not even vote until March 1867. By 1902, Blacks constituted less than 3 percent of all registered voters.[29]

In November 1900, Charles Aycock—a leading orator of the white supremacy and disfranchisement campaigns—was elected governor on a platform of "universal education."[30] During his term, education for Blacks, especially at normal schools, was transformed. Over the next several years, the Democratic Party established a dual-track system of "universal education": a well-funded white track designed to prepare literate, first-class citizens and an underfunded Black track designed under the guise of "industrial education" to create minimally literate second-class citizens loyal to the state.

During his May 1900 campaign visit to Elizabeth City, future governor Aycock confidently declared that "we will disfranchise no white child because we will teach them to read and write in the next eight years."[31] Once in office, he endeavored to fulfill that pledge by expanding educational opportunities for whites. The state took over existing white normal schools in Boone (now Appalachian State University) in 1903 and Cullowhee (now Western Carolina University) in 1905. In 1905, a delegation from Elizabeth City asked the General Assembly to charter a normal school for whites. In March 1907, the General Assembly established the East Carolina Teacher Training School (now East Carolina University), not in Elizabeth City but in Greenville.[32] Such schools would help ensure that young whites could eventually vote, as the grandfather clause in the disfranchisement amendment that protected white voting rights would expire in 1908. After that, whites would presumably have to demonstrate literacy.

As for the Elizabeth City State Colored Normal School, the successful white supremacy campaigns meant that the Board of Managers would consist of those supporting the new one-party regime. One member of the new board was a newspaper editor who defended lynching and who wrote in one editorial that the "white man was created to rule. The history of centuries is a history of white supremacy. The white man was created the superior of black and . . . will never submit to the dictation of an inferior race."[33]

Meanwhile, funding for the state's Black normal schools was at risk. By this point, seven existed, one each in Plymouth, Salisbury, Franklinton, Goldsboro, Fayetteville, Winston, and Elizabeth City. In 1901, the General Assembly passed

"An act for the consolidation and government of the colored normal schools,"
thereby giving the state board of education the authority to close or move Black
normal schools as it saw fit. Some Blacks supported this for pedagogical reasons,
believing that consolidation would improve educational quality. However, the
act was also motivated by finances. Since the 1898 white supremacy campaign,
money for Black schools had dried up.At one point, the state superintendent
recommended that the Elizabeth City treasurer borrow from a bank to meet
payroll.[34] This new 1901 law would put into motion a series of three separate
consolidation crises that would ultimately close the majority of the state's Black
normal schools over the next four years.

THE 1901 AND 1903 CONSOLIDATION CRISES

To their credit, many of the most prominent whites in northeastern North Carolina saw the coming danger and proactively obtained support for the school.
They petitioned their General Assembly representative and asked the local
Economist newspaper for positive publicity.That petition was delivered to the
General Assembly's Committee on Education in a matter of weeks, in January
1901.[35] The Board of Managers authorized members S. L. Sheep and E. F. Lamb
to attend North Carolina State Board of Education meetings in Raleigh to save
the school from consolidation. The Elizabeth City Board of Aldermen (now
City Council) resolved "to try to retain the colored Normal School at this place."
Pasquotank County's representative to the state house, J. B. Leigh, met with State
Superintendent Thomas Toon to advocate retaining the normal school in Elizabeth City. The board's heartfelt commitment to the school was duly noted by
the North Carolina State Board of Examiners, which criticized the boards
of several other Black normal schools—Plymouth, Goldsboro, Salisbury, and
Franklinton—for their indifference, but not Elizabeth City.[36] Despite such criti-
cisms, no Black normal school was closed during 1901.

Considering the strength of the white supremacy movement, such local support from whites might seem illogical. It was not. Because many whites frowned
on paying taxes to support Black schools, a state-funded normal school saved
them money and gave them a reason to cut local financing for Black primary
schools. After all, why build new schools for Black children when they could
be sent to state normal school instead? This happened, as the normal school in
Elizabeth City was used to teach schoolchildren to the point that a 1916 report
actually described it as a "small elementary school"! Indeed, some whites considered the notion of closing the school as an affront not to Black citizens but,
rather, to themselves.[37] Support of Black normal schools was sometimes even
seen by whites as promoting white supremacy. As one Elizabeth City educator
put it, Elizabeth City State Colored Normal School students "realize that the
white man is their best friend, and that they must not presume or expect to be

on an equal footing with the white man until they have attained their plane of culture and demonstrated their ability and fitness for such an elevation."[38]

In February 1902, James Yadkin Joyner, dean of State Normal and Industrial College (now University of North Carolina—Greensboro) became state superintendent of public instruction. His writings indicate support of the Aycock administration's white supremacist ideology. To him, "Anglo-Saxons" had the "strongest, cleanest blood on earth." North Carolina's Blacks must work in agriculture and industry so they can be "happier, more prosperous and useful." Higher education was only for a few, "perhaps for some generations to come." Joyner advocated lower wages for Black teachers, as in his view they "are more incompetent and deserve less salary . . . if quietly managed [they] will give no trouble about it." Joyner saw such intentional inequality as necessary prudence, as, in the past, "the great and generous Anglo-Saxon race . . . often flung [the Black] the part of the money that the Constitution required us to give, and then left him without direction to waste it at his will."[39]

Talk of closing down Elizabeth City State Colored Normal School remained just that—talk—but to his credit, Principal Moore realized, by 1902, that he needed to ingratiate himself with State Superintendent Joyner. Many times, he invited him to speak at commencement and summer school. Although Joyner usually declined, citing scheduling conflicts, he eventually accepted Moore's invitation to speak at a North Carolina Teachers Association meeting at Bennett College. Joyner thought highly enough of Moore to commend him to General Education Board President Wallace Buttrick.[40] More important, Moore told Joyner what he wanted to hear: Elizabeth City was interested in industrial education. In June, Moore wrote that "I firmly believe that an Industrial department, however limited, would greatly enhance the present usefulness of our school. This conclusion is drawn from my observation of student life." Not only that, it can be done "without much expense." Board members promised that this venture would not detract from teacher training, and the school successfully solicited funds, including one hundred dollars from a white family from York, Pennsylvania. The state chipped in five hundred fifteen dollars.[41] Moore himself provided clear evidence of his tacit support of industrial education, visiting Booker T. Washington's Tuskegee Institute. Ever creative, Moore made school stationery a marketing vehicle. By January 1903, even though the school's name had not changed, the principal's letterhead identified it as "State Normal and Industrial School."[42]

Was Principal Moore truly a supporter of industrial education, or was he only bluffing in order to please state officials and, therefore, save the school he loved from consolidation? It is hard to say. Back in 1896, he wrote that students must be "taught by precept and example that it is no disgrace for any person to work with his or her hands." In 1898, he asked Superintendent Charles Mebane about his thoughts on establishing a sewing department in Elizabeth City. Nevertheless, there is also evidence that Moore's professed faith in industrial education was a calculated ruse. Isabella Hollowell, a student in 1892, paraphrased Moore as saying "we don't want to start a school to go to work. Who cut the forests for present people to live in pomp and splendor!" Reverend Wells of Mt. Lebanon Church, a historic Black church in Elizabeth City, wrote that Moore "was once a staunch enemy to industrial training. . . . But he is right in changing with conditions altho [sic] he cannot use a pitch fork nor a hand saw."[43]

Although we can never know Moore's definite motives, by summer 1903, in Raleigh, serious discussion of closing down some Black normal schools began.[44] As in 1901, this threat too brought out supporters, including two petitions: one signed by Black female teachers in summer school and one by the area's most prominent white men, including former Fusionist-era congressman Harry Skinner. Fearing for their own institutional lives, other normal schools sent their own petitions. Salisbury State Colored Normal School even had a supporting letter from sitting US Senator Lee S. Overman.[45]

Knowing that his years of work could be undone in moments at the upcoming consolidation meetings at the State Board of Education, Moore wrote to Superintendent Joyner, not to beg but to inform him that he had given his all: "If the school here has not been successful, it is not because my best self has not been entirely put into the work. In fact, Prof. Joyner, it would be imprudent for me to work more faithfully and earnestly that I have endeavored to do." Moore's staff was concerned about their jobs and asked the Board what they should do.[46] Like everyone else, they would have to wait.

At the meeting on June 30, the State Board of Education—minus one—voted on the motion to close down three of North Carolina's seven Black normal schools. After a three-three tie, they met again on July 4, this time with a telegraph from the missing member. Consolidation passed four to three. Which three would now be closed? That question would be answered on July 13, when Treasurer Benjamin L. Lacy made a motion that the surviving schools be those at Winston, Salisbury, Fayetteville, and Franklinton and that the other three, including the one at Elizabeth City, be shuttered.

In many meetings held according to established protocol, by the time a motion is made, debate has already taken place, and the motion is merely a declarative statement expressing the collective thoughts of the attendees. In other words, motions are often quickly passed once made, voting being just a formality. The motion now being on the floor, the Elizabeth City State Colored Normal School was one vote away from elimination. Luckily, one person spoke up: Secretary of State J. Bryan Grimes. He moved to amend, recommending that "Elizabeth City" be substituted for "Salisbury" on the list of survivors. His motion was carried, and then Lacy's original motion as amended prevailed.[47]

Elizabeth City State Colored Normal School had just survived the greatest threat to its existence. The normal schools at Salisbury and Goldsboro did not. Also closing was the Plymouth State Normal, whose books, maps, charts, and sewing machine were ordered shipped to Elizabeth City. The consolidation meant that "Elizabeth City will be the center of education of the colored race for the large territory east of Raleigh." State officials praised Moore, one proclaiming that he was "easily winning the position of the Booker T. Washington of North Carolina."[48] This suggests that his staunch support of industrial education may well have saved the school. Women were now to be required to take "Sewing and Cooking for Females" and men were required to take "Farming and Carpentry for Males." Joyner wanted the normal schools to emphasize teacher training and industrial work.[49]

Additional pedagogical changes were expected. Principal Moore had taught Latin but was now told to stop.[50] This request might seem reasonable to modern observers, but in 1903, this was seen as a radical proposal, for two reasons. First, as James Anderson has suggested in his seminal work, *The Education of Blacks in the South, 1860–1935*, Blacks wanted their youths to have a classical liberal arts education not merely to imitate white schools but to provide students "access to the best intellectual traditions of their era and the best means to understanding their own historical development and sociological uniqueness."[51] By viewing Black normal schools strictly as industrial education and teacher training centers, and by intentionally eliminating the liberal arts, the state was arguably trying to redefine Black cultural identity. Second, Elizabeth City itself was the birth and final resting place of one of the greatest Black classical scholars of the nineteenth century, Wiley Lane (1852–1885). A "most distinguished" graduate of Howard University's preparatory school, he earned a bachelor's degree at Amherst College, becoming one of the first Blacks to become a Phi Beta Kappa. He then became Howard's first Black professor of Greek.[52] Tragically, he died at age 32; among those speaking at his funeral was Frederick Douglass, who called him "a man among men, and a scholar among scholars."[53] At the birthplace of this renowned Black scholar, classical languages were no longer to be taught. Such pedagogical changes were, nevertheless, the price of survival. Joyner saw such state micromanagement of Black normal schools as necessary, fearing what would happen if "others that do not understand our social structure, that are ignorant of the nature and needs of the negro and have false notions of his relation to the white race in the South" took control.[54]

THE CONSOLIDATION CRISIS OF 1905

If Moore believed that consolidation would ensure greater financial stability for Elizabeth City State Colored Normal School, he was mistaken. Desperate, Moore took on more, teaching six classes daily, in addition to administrating and fundraising.[55] The students raised money through cultural functions. Meanwhile, opponents of Black education were politically strong in 1903 and into 1904, many wanting to divide taxpayer funds by race, thereby crippling schools for a people who had been free less than forty years.

Now having survived the 1903 consolidation crisis, the normal school sought permanent facilities. Since 1893, it had been located at the Freedmen's Bureau School, which had been constructed in 1870, but that location had no room for future growth. In October 1903, the school received a major gift—five acres of land one mile outside of town, from the Reverend William and Mrs. Mary Yost of Cleveland, Ohio; their daughter Ella Yost Preyer; and their son-in-law Robert Preyer, an Elizabeth City lumber executive.[56] The Preyer family had a history of donating land to Blacks.[57]

Elizabeth City State Colored Normal School was not the first school to own this land. On October 2, 1896, the Yosts and Preyers had sold the land for the token sum of a dollar an acre to the trustees of George Mebane's Normal and Industrial Institute.[58] A Black man born in Bertie County, North Carolina, Mebane had served as a state senator and openly questioned the false assumptions that underlay white supremacy. His private school competed with Peter W. Moore's school and even received state appropriations.[59] There was but one condition that the school's trustees had to meet to keep the land: It had to be open at least three months a year. Mebane's school, however, burned down in 1901. With the condition unmet, the land reverted back to the Yosts and Preyers, who gave it to Elizabeth City State.[60]

Despite having closed down three Black normal schools, the state provided only a pittance of appropriations to the four survivors. State Superintendent Joyner, to his credit, tried to persuade the General Assembly to provide an additional five thousand dollars for them to share, but his request was denied.[61] On April 19, 1905, he told the State Board of Education that, because of this, drastic measures were necessary. He therefore recommended abolishing two of the four remaining Black normal schools. The existence of Elizabeth City once again was in jeopardy. Winston's Slater Industrial and State Normal School, already having permanent facilities, presumably was safe. That meant that if two were to be closed, Elizabeth City's chances of survival were only one in three. As in 1903, a state board member recommended modifying the motion. This time, it was State Auditor B. F. Dixon, who proposed keeping three schools and closing only one. Governor Robert Glenn agreed and moved; his motion was carried three to two.[62]

The Black normal school boards were then notified that, on June 19, the State Board of Education expected their representatives to appear to explain why their schools should survive. The school making the weakest case would be closed. The Elizabeth City Board determined that Principal Moore and Board

Chair E. F. Lamb would speak on the school's behalf. Lamb already had been working to influence Superintendent Joyner, asserting that "No amount of money can supplant the usefulness of this school at this point. . . . The removal of this school at this time will simply break up an institution of great usefullness [sic] and your people must stand by us."[63]

Representatives would have to show state bureaucrats evidence of strong local financial support. How could they do that? The Board agreed that Lamb would offer the state the deed to the five acres gifted in 1903, worth fifteen hundred dollars, plus pledges. Local citizens had been giving whatever they could— sometimes only a dime or a quarter. Alumni gave heavily. Little by little, the tiny capital campaign grew to around seventy-five hundred dollars in cash and assets.In addition, the Board said that Lamb "shall proffer a deed to the State for the town lot and building now occupied by this School worth $3,000."[64]

There was a problem with this plan. Back in early 1900, during the heights of the white supremacy movement, Moore suggested that the school property be transferred to the state, a suggestion that Superintendent Mebane rejected. This idea was now being resurrected, but the same problem remained: Elizabeth City State Colored Normal School was renting the building from its trustees and, arguably, had no legal authority to make this transaction. The individual appointed to do the dirty work of getting the property transferred from the building's trustees—the rightful owners—to the state was Principal Moore, who happened to be on this other board. He succeeded, and the transfer was signed on August 5, 1905. On June 19, the State Board of Education met to determine which normal would be abolished. The Elizabeth City entourage offered forty-five hundred dollars in property and $3,332.50 in pledges.[65] Would it be enough?

The victory won by Elizabeth City on that early summer day was by default. No one supporting Franklinton bothered to appear, so the decision was easy: That school—clearly lacking the necessary community support that had sustained Elizabeth City State Colored Normal School—was to be closed. A few days later, Joyner wrote to the surviving boards, telling them that as long as they met their pledges, their schools would survive. He gave them more good news: The State Board planned to establish permanent facilities at Elizabeth City and Fayetteville equal to those at Winston. Joyner found a way to secure five hundred dollars in state funds for this effort.[66] Consolidation helped attract donors, who could now send money in confidence. Moore traveled during summer to the Midwest and New England to solicit additional gifts. His salesmanship impressed one Elizabeth City board member, who remarked that "Prof. Moore with the time he has to put to this work is doing remarkably well."[67]

The principal also had an eye for real estate. In March 1905, he told Super-intendent Joyner that land next to their current five acres (the Preyer property) was on the market for two thousand dollars. After some delay, the Board of

Managers made an offer to purchase twenty acres. This land was once owned by George Mebane's Normal and Industrial Institute, which had borrowed twelve hundred dollars against it in January 1900. Apparently, because it failed to pay back the loan, the property was foreclosed upon in May 1900.[68] After negotiations, eighteen acres were bought for two thousand dollars, and the property was conveyed to the state. A total of $1,652.43 had been contributed by one hundred sixty Blacks, and the rest had been contributed by thirty-eight whites. With such property, the building campaign did well over the next year, attracting sizable gifts from Pennsylvania, from gospel music publisher Hall-Mack Company, and Quaker publisher Edwin Sallew.[69] It was on this land that the first classroom building and first women's residence hall were constructed. Although the classroom building was completed by fall 1909, classes were not held in there until fall 1912, because the school could not afford to equip the building.[70]

CONCLUSION: HOW ELIZABETH CITY STATE COLORED NORMAL SCHOOL SURVIVED WHITE SUPREMACY

To survive three separate threats to existence directly inspired by white supremacist ideology, the institution had changed its very identity from a teacher-training school that offered academic subjects consistent with a classical liberal arts education, to one that publicly espoused the ideals of "industrial education." Convinced of his own commitment, which may or may not have been little more than a tactical bluff used as a survival tactic, Principal Moore was proclaimed by whites as the "Booker T. Washington of North Carolina"—but did the state of North Carolina provide him with anything like a Tar Heel Tuskegee? By 1916, the school's twenty-fifth anniversary, one report described the school as "offering a very limited amount of industrial training." Not only that, among teacher-training institutions, it had the nation's second highest student–faculty ratio.[71] To borrow an adage from that time, the state was unwilling to provide the straw for State Colored Normal School to make the proverbial bricks that Blacks needed and deserved. Done right, "industrial education" required not lip service but cash, but little of that was forthcoming. In 1916, Principal Moore was still hoping to establish a bona fide, "character-building" industrial education program.[72] He even referred to the school in catalogs as the "North Carolina State Colored Normal and Industrial School," but such pretenses did not change the fact that North Carolina was failing to invest adequately in its Black citizens.

By 1917, the neglect was so blatant that even State Superintendent Joyner admitted that the three Black normal schools were living on "starvation appropriations." A particularly pernicious General Assembly law was the "Act to Issue Bonds of the State for the Permanent Enlargement and Improvement of the State's Educational and Charitable Institutions." "Separate but equal" had long been a cruel oxymoron, but few times crueler than this act. Of the bond money earmarked for higher education, white schools received 98 percent. East Carolina Teachers Training School alone was to receive two hundred thousand dollars, whereas the three Black normal schools were to share ten thousand dollars.[73] Such legislation helped cement the ever-widening chasm between the state's public white and Black institutions.

Principal Moore had no control over such particularly galling aspects of systemic racism, but he and his staff, nevertheless, rose above that to produce a bumper crop of outstanding educators. Among the graduates during the consolidation crisis included Annie Jones (class of 1901), who became a legendary Elizabeth City elementary school teacher; Thomas Settle Cooper (class of 1902), who became a supervising principal of Elizabeth City Black schools; and John Paige Law (class of 1902), who would have a remarkable fifty-six-year teaching career. All three would have their names grace an elementary school in northeastern North Carolina. David K. Cherry ('04) eventually became president of Kittrell College. One enterprising graduate, Alfred L. E. Weeks ('00), founded his own normal school—Newbern Collegiate and Industrial Institute.

Despite such successes, when it came to public higher education in the Tar Heel state, there existed two separate but quite unequal universes. Such systemic racism would largely remain unchallenged until Blacks realized that they needed more than faith in Booker T. Washington's idealism and demanded that the voting rights they lost in 1900 be restored. That way, they could finally hold political leaders accountable for their broken promises. These efforts toward greater access to the franchise would begin in earnest long before the 1960s, perhaps in the 1920s, as Black normal schools such as the one in Elizabeth City would honor a distinctly Black past by recognizing Negro History Week and by honoring alternatives to the Washington model, such as that proposed by W. E. B. Du Bois.[74] It was only then that they could force the state to provide a truly universal education, so Elizabeth City State and its peers could finally start reaching their potential as transformative academic institutions.

"They Were Very Low Key, But They Spoke from Wisdom and Experience"

How Black Teachers Taught Self-Determination at Carver Senior High School in New Orleans

KRISTEN L. BURAS

We did not know about Ms. Busch . . . Mr. Hatfield . . . [or] Coach Hicks. We didn't know anything about their histories. . . . They all had done amazing things in their youth [despite racial segregation]. . . . I remember one of the band members [said], "Ms. Busch [music teacher] told me, 'You better stop tryin' to chase them little nickel gigs and try and learn some music.'" He said, "What you know about nickel gigs?" Well, she knew about 'em. . . . It was one of those things that [teachers] were very low key, but you can tell when they spoke to you, they spoke from wisdom. They had experience. They didn't just come off the top of their head and say, "Oh, I read this." They had lived it.

—*Leonard Smith, 1973 Carver Senior High School graduate*

New Orleans' all-Black George Washington Carver Senior High School was founded in 1958, four years after *Brown v. Board of Education of Topeka*.[1] The Supreme Court had ruled racial segregation unconstitutional. Thus, it is no small irony that, in New Orleans, white segregationist policymakers scrambled to build more Black public schools during the *Brown* era. They hoped that additional schools and new facilities for Blacks might curtail integrationist demands.[2] Carver was part of the plan, and one of eight Black schools opened in New Orleans that year.[3]

If all-Black schools following *Brown* were consistent with segregationist desires, they might seem antithetical to the civil rights movement. For many African Americans, however, racial integration was not the primary aim; Black self-determination was the deeper goal.[4] There were other ways to advance this goal in the face of mass white resistance, and Carver teachers embraced them.

They built on a long-standing tradition of Black power teaching that reached back to enslaved African peoples in the swamps of Louisiana and teachers who taught amid racist violence in Jim Crow New Orleans.[5]

This chapter profiles five founding teachers from Carver—Black veteran educators who began work there in 1958 and taught for three-plus decades. These profiles provide a glimpse into the lives and teachings of men and women who built a culture of self-determination and achievement against incredible odds. Carver was constructed on the geographic margin of the city surrounded by train tracks, near a public dump, and adjacent to the Desire Housing Development. Although the facility was state-of-the-art in comparison with other Black schools of the period, once built, not much else was invested by the school board in maintaining or resourcing the Carver complex. As I show, teachers were the ones who supported and advocated for students, nurturing intergenerational ties and embracing a dual commitment to academic achievement and the development of civic consciousness in the context of racially oppressive conditions.

Although self-determination and civic consciousness were central to Carver's culture, these things were fostered organically as an outgrowth of who teachers were, what they experienced as Black people in New Orleans, what they desired for the students in their care, and how they taught. As Smith alluded, teachers' antiracism was "low key." In large part, it was woven into the microcosm of the science lab, social studies classroom, band room, and athletic field.

Although the day-to-day work of Carver teachers may seem distinct from the sit-ins and marches of the civil rights movement—and Black Power politics—it was squarely in the ambit of pro-Black activism. Each teacher's profile highlights the need for a more complex conception of activism, along a continuum from more obvious forms of protest, such as fighting in court and organizing teachers, to behind-the-scenes groundwork, such as mentoring students for Black excellence or ushering them into self- and political consciousness. Moreover, as I argue, the hard work of Black teachers, especially in systematically underresourced public schools, required more than "dedication." It required the tenacity associated with civil rights activism.

I open with a dash of history on Black public schools in New Orleans before *Brown* and the background on Carver's founding in the immediate post-*Brown* years. Next, I profile five founding teachers—language instructor and teacher unionist Charles Hatfield, science teacher Lamar Smith, athletic coach Enos Hicks, music teacher Yvonne Busch, and social studies educator Lenora Condoll Gray—by charting their early life histories and revealing how self-determination and consciousness were central to their educational advocacy.[6] In conclusion, I underscore the challenges of such pedagogy in the context of the systematic neglect of Black public schools and recognize the unwavering commitment of teachers to schooling for racial equity.

BLACK PUBLIC SCHOOLS IN NEW ORLEANS

For most of their history, New Orleans public schools were considered the property of southern whites, with perpetual state neglect of Black education. This neglect did not go unchallenged, as African Americans created educational spaces of their own and fought for support of Black public schools.[7]

In 1900, the New Orleans school board limited public education for Blacks to the first five grades. The city's first Black public high school, McDonogh No. 35, did not open until 1917 and was largely the result of the demands of African Americans. Booker T. Washington, the second high school, did not open until 1942 and followed on the heels of the Grace Report.[8] Headed by Alonzo Grace, the Citizens' Planning Committee completed a comprehensive study of New Orleans public schools during 1938–1939. Funded by the board and local citizens, the report was issued in 1940.[9]

Regarding Black elementary schools—twenty-three out of twenty-five were visited—the Grace Report concluded that most required complete replacement. It also noted that the schools were provided only "a minimum supply of educational materials" by the state.[10] Only four schools had a separate room for a library, and six reported having no library books; only seven had facilities for hot lunches. In terms of Black secondary schools, McDonogh No. 35 was the city's only senior high school, with two additional junior high schools in existence.

With *Brown* in 1954, the Supreme Court deemed "separate but equal" unconstitutional in public education. This led to massive resistance by local and state authorities, as well as white citizens. By May 1960, Federal Judge Skelly Wright had yet to receive desegregation plans from the Orleans Parish School Board and therefore issued a proposal. In November 1960, two all-white elementary schools—William Frantz and McDonogh No. 19—were set to be desegregated. White parents harassed Black children on the front lines and quickly withdrew their children.[11]

FOUNDING OF CARVER SENIOR HIGH SCHOOL

Designated a "Negro school," Carver opened in 1958 in Brown's shadow. There was a pressing need for housing and schooling in New Orleans' Black community. Central City had become a densely populated, all-Black tract, with scant land for additional housing, inadequate school capacity, and woefully dilapidated school buildings. The little land that remained was expensive, and white neighborhoods were off limits.[12]

In the early 1950s, white school and housing officials planned a housing project and school village "in a swampy section of the Ninth Ward that was cut off from the rest of New Orleans."[13] While housing officials and white residents sought Black containment in certain areas, school officials aimed to build and "equalize" schools to ease demands for desegregation. Charles Colbert, head of the school district's planning division, was intent on reducing land costs and suggested a "school village" on "an isolated ninety-acre tract in the city's Ninth Ward, roughly six miles from Central City."[14] The tract was bought for three hundred thousand dollars in 1952—six to eight million less than the same amount of land in Central City—and was surrounded on four sides by railroad tracks in addition to nearby drainage canals. Colbert's plan was presented in 1952 as *Brown* awaited trial before the Supreme Court.[15]

This same year, the Housing Authority of New Orleans learned that it would receive twenty-four million dollars under the 1949 federal Housing Act to build a Black housing project near the proposed school village.[16] The Desire Housing Project and Carver school complex would be built as part of a coordinated scheme. Colbert emphasized that "the price of real estate in this outlying section . . . would enable the Board to give the Negroes a school with facilities such as they had never had before—a football field, gymnasium, track space."[17] He emphasized as well that the board "would be able to assist in city planning by helping to direct populations," a clear statement on maintaining racial and geographic segregation.[18] Notably, the building contract was approved one month after the *Brown* decision and went to Curtis and Davis Architects.[19]

The curriculum anticipated by architects, embedded in their plan book with classroom designations, included English, foreign language, speech, journalism and business English, social studies, math, business education (typing, bookkeeping), science, home economics, industrial arts (electrical shop, woodworking, masonry, mechanical drawing, automotive shop), music, art, and physical education.[20] The high school, named by the school board for George Washington Carver, a Black botanist who taught industrial education at Tuskegee Institute, offered an education that spanned the trades, career preparation, and ultimately, college preparation.[21]

Although built for racial containment, teachers and students made the school their own. In the very first year, *The Carver Times*, a school newspaper highlighting clubs, accomplishments, and relevant issues, was published. One issue described the ceremony commemorating the school's opening: "On Sunday evening, December 7, 1958, at two-thirty, the Carver Site Dedication Program stimulated and impressed the people of this City."[22] A biographic portrait of Carver was presented, and a list of first-year faculty—Hatfield, Smith, Hicks, Busch, and others—who ultimately invested decades nurturing students was included in the program.[23] Notably, the school adopted the "RAM"—its letters standing for righteousness, achievement, and mastery—as its mascot.[24] Teachers' pedagogy reflected these principles, which surfaced in oral histories and documents.[25] A chart features the pedagogic elements highlighted in the following profiles (Figure 1).

School Culture and Pedagogy at Carver Senior High School
Intergenerational Network
• Developing and sustaining meaningful relationships across time • Appreciating connections between past, present, and future generations
Ethic of Self-Determination and Achievement
• Fostering a sense of intrinsic capacity, inner authority, and self-determination • Embracing high expectations and supporting achievement
Dual Commitment to Academic Content and Civic Character/Context
• Valuing traditional measures of education (content mastery), while also demonstrating concern for development of the whole person (civic character and consciousness) • Accounting for students' life circumstances (race, income, social context) as part of the pedagogic process

CHARLES HATFIELD: LANGUAGE TEACHER
AND TEACHER UNION LEADER

Charles Hatfield was a scholarly man, political scientist, civil rights advocate, and labor organizer. He held multiple graduate degrees, taught Spanish and English for nearly three decades at Carver, acted as longtime yearbook advisor, and was a pivotal figure in the history of the city's teacher union. At great risk, he was also the first Black person to apply to the all-white law school at Louisiana State University (LSU), which resulted in litigation that opposed racial segregation.[26]

Hatfield was born in 1915, but his family roots in Louisiana go back much further. His grandfather fought in a Union regiment with free people of color during the Civil War. Hatfield came from a line of educators, including his mother.[27] During his youth, Hatfield lived in a house on Iberville Street in New Orleans. After his father died in 1931, the family lost the house and moved to the Lafitte Housing Project. The Great Depression was in full force, and Hatfield terminated schooling to assist his mother and siblings. Despite the circumstances, he read philosophy, history, and political science intently—and later graduated from Gilbert Academy, a private Black high school, in 1938.[28]

During this same period, Hatfield worked a range of jobs—building the Lake Pontchartrain seawall through the Depression-era Works Progress Administration (WPA) and laboring with iron workers and longshoremen. "That was the time," he explains, "when I became interested in organized labor," as the Depression "made me even more conscious . . . of the necessity [of organizing]."[29] Only

21 years old, Hatfield was one of the few African Americans in Louisiana with a voter registration card.[30]

In 1940, Hatfield enrolled at Xavier University, a historically Black institution in New Orleans, while he labored as a postal worker and WPA employee.[31] A newspaper article penned during this period conveys his disgust with racial discrimination:

> Several days ago, I visited a certain park in this city. . . . There is a fine golf course, excellent tennis courts, [and] swimming pools. . . . About ten years ago, this same park was poorly developed. . . . [Then] plans were made to develop [it]. . . . As usual the labor had to come from the ranks of the Negroes. . . . As I walked through this place I saw . . . all other nationalities taking part in the amusements. . . . The Negro was the only person who was forbidden to use this public park. . . . This is one among the many instances where the colored man has been denied the right to enjoy the products of his toil. While his sons drown in bayous . . . others spend exciting moments in the fine public pools.[32]

In 1946, Hatfield graduated with a bachelor's degree, majoring in history, Spanish, and English, and minoring in economics and political science. Just before graduation, he requested an application for admission to the all-white LSU Law School, indicating that he was nearly complete at Xavier. Instead, he got a letter indicating that Louisiana maintains racially separate schools.[33]

He approached A. P. Tureaud, one of only two Black attorneys in New Orleans, about a lawsuit. Tureaud invited Thurgood Marshall with the National Association for the Advancement of Colored People (NAACP) Legal Defense and Education Fund, and Louis Berry, a Howard Law professor from Louisiana, to act as co-counsel.[34] Hatfield soon learned that a special committee involving LSU had decided to advocate the establishment of a law school at the all-Black Southern University. Tureaud filed a lawsuit.[35]

Hatfield faced a wave of threats. In one instance, he received a letter asking him to meet at the Pythian Temple to discuss funds to withdraw his suit and study elsewhere. Hatfield was infuriated and proceeded to the meeting to tell the solicitor he planned to attend LSU. He recollected:

> I went there and walked up to the 6th or 7th floor. When I got up there, the elevator door was open, and the elevator was down at the bottom. It was dark and there was nobody around, and you can believe I got out of there right quick. I ran down the stairs as fast as I could . . . I don't know if they wanted to push me down the shaft or not, but I didn't wait to see.[36]

While Hatfield's case was moving through the courts, Tureaud advised him to leave New Orleans for his safety.[37]

Hatfield was offered a fellowship at Atlanta University in 1947 and was pursuing his master's degree when Southern's law program opened. Hatfield was invited to join the Alpha Kappa Delta National Honor Sociology Fraternity, completed his Master of Arts (MA) in sociology in 1948, and was invited to join the faculty.[38] However, he opted to leave Atlanta because of threats from a racist hate group on Spelman's campus, where he supervised student teachers. On returning to New Orleans, he had trouble finding employment because of fears surrounding his lawsuit. Thus, he returned to the post office while he taught religion, history, Spanish, and English at Gilbert Academy.[39]

Hatfield also continued taking graduate courses, receiving his MA degree in education from Xavier in 1950. He completed student teaching at Joseph Clark Senior High School and received an "exceptional" rating. Hatfield's lawyers appealed his case, but the program at Southern was opened with forty thousand dollars in appropriations.[40] Meanwhile, Hatfield was among only 13 percent of public school teachers in Louisiana with an MA degree. Despite this, he faced challenges getting his teaching certificate because of retaliation, ultimately requiring Tureaud to submit a formal request to the state. Hatfield's certificate was issued for social science, Spanish, and English in 1952. He joined the faculty at Clark in 1953. When Carver opened five years later, he transferred there.[41]

Hatfield headed Carver's language department.[42] Ten years into his tenure, Russian, Latin, French, and Spanish were taught to the eight hundred students enrolled in courses.[43] Ella Shaw, a student of Hatfield's who graduated in 1974, said that he would tell "class clowns . . . you can do better" and "was a very good teacher" who "tried his best to work with us." After forty-seven years, she remarks, "I still remember the Spanish."[44] However, Hatfield intended more for the students than language mastery. He was concerned about "the poor unfortunate Negro who is infected with the idea of white superiority" and thankful for those "who have never nor will [ever] permit our children to become infected by this dreadful ideology."[45]

Not long after Hatfield began teaching, he found himself "amazed" at the challenges teachers faced; not only did these challenges shape their work lives, "but it affected the child in the classroom."[46] He thus became active with the teacher union, Local 527 of the American Federation of Teachers (later United Teachers of New Orleans). He was the building representative at Clark and Carver, and as an organizer, he brought in two thousand new members. He also served as secretary-treasurer, was elected vice president, and worked as a legislative lobbyist. In 1966, Hatfield and Local 527 began a campaign for the school board to grant collective bargaining, which was rejected. This led to a three-day strike, the first teachers' strike in the South; efforts persisted, and in 1974, the board agreed.[47] For Hatfield, collective bargaining was a critical component of respecting teachers' labor, which did not, in any way, compromise their commitment to students or the understanding of teaching as a distinctly human profession. Hatfield believed:

> Teaching is not just an ordinary thing. . . . You're dealing with human beings and human lives, and especially little young lives. . . . I've given hours of my time and I've seen other teachers give hours of their time, even weekends. . . . But they did it voluntarily, they weren't doing it under a demand. And that's the difference.[48]

Union organizing enabled Hatfield to shift power imbalances that affected Black teachers and address the intergenerational needs of "children and teachers," not just teachers as antiunion forces liked to suggest.[49] Marilyn Pierre, a business education teacher at Carver during the 1960s, described Hatfield as a "union guy," noting, "If we had a strike, Hatfield organized it." Hatfield, she said, was "large and in charge."[50] Finally, under Hatfield's initiative in 1972, the teacher union established a federal credit union, with twenty million dollars in assets by 1999.[51]

Hatfield seamlessly wove his organizing with his teaching, including extracurricular activities. For years, he acted as advisor for Carver's yearbook.[52] The 1973 yearbook staff included the tribute: "Hatfield has worked untiringly with us. He has given unaccountable [countless] hours [of] advice, criticism, and legwork in helping us to realize the completion of the project. We salute you, 'Mr. Hat.'" Above the tribute is a photo of Hatfield, wearing what appears to be a union pin on his jacket.[53]

Hatfield retired in 1979, saying he "spent thirty years trying to help young minds improve."[54] He was honored in 1983 by the union with the Pioneer Award "for untiring efforts . . . in helping to build a viable teacher union movement."[55] In 2002, Southern University Law Center bestowed its first honorary doctorate on Hatfield in a hooding ceremony—one month before he passed.[56] Regarding his activism and teaching, Hatfield concluded, "I just followed the course of right as it came along. Of course, I tried to make things happen that wouldn't happen otherwise."[57]

LAMAR SMITH: SCIENCE TEACHER AND CARVER COMMUNITY SCHOOL PRINCIPAL

Lamar Smith was a Lower 9th Ward resident in New Orleans for over sixty years. A Navy veteran of World War II and the Korean War, Smith later became a beloved science educator, with a bachelor of science degree in chemistry and biology from Xavier and a master's degree in educational leadership from the University of New Orleans. Smith first worked at Samuel Green Junior High, and then Clark High School from 1952 to 1958. He transferred to Carver its opening year, where he headed the science department and taught chemistry and physics until his retirement in 1986.[58]

Theron Lewis, a Carver student-athlete who graduated in 1962, said that Smith inspired an interest in science. "I wanted to be a biologist," said Lewis. Thinking back to science class with Smith, Lewis said "he taught chemistry, but he always had this life lesson." Students would explore "what would happen if you mixed this with that," but whatever the scientific content of the day, "Smith almost always ended his class with a life lesson" that addressed broader issues. "He was very majestic in his speech and in his classes," concluded Lewis.[59] Important to note, Smith's teaching emphasized both content mastery and social consciousness.

In addition to daytime teaching, in 1972, Smith became the founding principal of the G. W. Carver Community School, an evening program open to neighborhood residents. In its inaugural year, Smith described the Community School as a "human development center," explaining:

It provides opportunities for education, the development of vocational skills, cultural enrichment, special interest, and recreation for all citizens. It makes available . . . services such as educational guidance, testing, vocational counseling, job information [and] welfare and social security information. The community school cuts across all ages, racial lines, religious, and economic interest[s], needs, and abilities.[60]

As the Community School's "backbone," Smith employed at least 50 workers through the Comprehensive Employment and Training Act, passed in the 1970s to prepare low-income communities for public service positions. In doing so, he enabled students with economic challenges to remain in school while assisting their families.[61] He served in this capacity until his retirement, providing critical social and educational supports across multiple generations.

Like Hatfield, Smith was an active member of the city's teacher union. He acted as chair of the union's human relations committee and sat on its executive board. After a 1969 strike, he wrote:

The [New Orleans] School board was forced to give some token recognition to the Teacher Union. The strike witnessed a group of predominantly Black teachers starting at 1,200 and dwindling to [269], who for ten hectic days with sore feet, wet eyes, and fallen hopes courageously endured threats and fear tactics of every conceivable denomination. The question is: why did they persevere? Was this the beginning of something new—the prime step in demonstrating to the white power structure that Black teachers are determined to solve their own problems and, moreover, plan, shape, and direct their own destiny?[62]

Smith declared that "the double-standard educational system in [New Orleans] has been far more productive than its white designers had originally planned, for it has been more than successful in keeping the races separated and relegating to a position of near serfdom the Black protagonist of the classroom."[63] He hoped that the "gears of the system" could be reversed, urging that "Who would be free themselves must strike the blow."[64] Self-determination for teachers and students was central to his work.

Smith was a respected community activist, affiliated not only with the teacher union but also with the NAACP, the political organization SOUL (Southern Organization for Unified Leadership), and the neighborhood-based Black Club, which monitored the "economic and political changes that affect the community" and sought "solutions for these ills."[65] Along these same lines, Smith was a member of St. David's Holy Name Society, a Catholic organization that "spreads the teaching of the church through examples in the community."[66]

His son, Lamar Smith Jr., and former student Douglass Haywood described Smith as an "astute theologian" who knew the bible "in and out" and was constantly reading books. After high school, Haywood operated a barbershop, where Smith came for haircuts and often discussed politics. Haywood recollects: "He'd come to the shop. He would sit three or four hours. He always had a book in his hand."[67] Married to Shirley Guidry Smith, Smith had nine children—all of whom obtained college degrees, with several in the education field. At church, the Smith family took up "the whole bench."[68]

Smith received various awards during his life, including the NAACP Jessie Vickman Special Teacher Award and the Outstanding Science Teacher of the Year Award from New Orleans Public Schools. He was recognized by Ernest Morial and Sydney Barthelemy, Black mayors in New Orleans, for his teaching and was named "Honorary State Senator" as well.[69]

After Smith passed in 2003, the Louisiana State Senate passed Senate Resolution No. 41 to honor his legacy of encouraging "students to further their education," with "many becoming influential members of the community."[70] Smith Jr. said that his father's students were successful, among them congressmen and mayors. He shared, "I meet so many people and they tell me, 'Man, your daddy was just an inspiration to me.'"[71] Ultimately, Smith "encouraged his students to be self-disciplined and to help light the torch for another individual."[72]

Haywood remembers when this "little guy, Ray," came to the barbershop. He checked Ray's homework and noticed spelling problems, showing them to Smith. Smith told Ray to come back the next evening to the shop. In the meantime, Smith brought Haywood some flashcards to assist Ray. Years later, when Haywood and Ray crossed paths, Ray expressed gratitude: "Tell Mr. Smith, 'Thank You,' and I want to thank you, too. Because if it wasn't for you and him, I wouldn't have graduated" from college.[73]

"My dad would always iron his shirt in the morning," said Smith Jr., "I mean, white shirt with the tie. That was his thing."[74] Smith picked up Coach Enos Hicks each morning, and they rode together to Carver.[75]

ENOS HICKS: PHYSICAL EDUCATION
TEACHER AND HEAD COACH

Coach Enos Hicks was five feet, six inches tall and weighed one hundred sixty pounds, but he was "mighty in presence to most." He was a world-class athlete: the fastest sprinter in the South during his years at Xavier; winner of the sixty-yard dash in Madison Square Garden; runner in the Penn and Drake Relays; and participant in the Olympic trials.[76] He began teaching and coaching at Clark and became head coach of track and football and athletic director when Carver opened. His mentorship of student-athletes spanned nearly four decades from 1939 to 1976. Hicks held a bachelor of arts (BA) degree and an MA degree from Xavier University.[77]

Hicks had ten children of his own—seven boys and three girls—with nearly all earning college degrees.[78] Enos Hicks Jr., also a coach of forty-plus years in New Orleans, attests that his father was a guidepost for most students he encountered. Hicks was soon regarded as one of the best track coaches in the state.

Theron Lewis, who ran track in the 1964 Olympics, reminisced about Coach Hicks. He had "heard about the legendary Enos 'Hoopy' Hicks," so it was phenomenal "to finally be in the man's presence" at Carver. Hicks was not only an excellent mentor but also "a near-world's record runner." Lewis noted that Hicks "was coached by Ralph Metcalfe at Xavier, who ran with Jesse Owens in the '36 Olympics, so Coach Hicks came through that lineage."[79] Lewis remembered Hicks receiving Carver's "Teacher of the Year Award" in 1961 and seeing "the bag of medals that he won in track and field," which were visible during the ceremony. "We thought . . . we could win a bag full of medals," too, said Lewis.[80] In describing Hicks's legacy, Lewis referenced the movie *Camelot*, in which King Arthur asked a young man why he wanted to be a knight of the Round Table. "Because of the stories people tell," the young man replied. "It was the stories people told about Coach Hicks," Lewis passionately conveyed, "He was larger than life to us."[81]

Lewis recalled being nervous about a race in the city championships. "I went to talk to Hicks . . . I can't remember what he said to me, but it calmed me because . . . he said he had confidence that I would pull it off. . . . He just helped me work through it."[82] Lewis recalls that Hicks was "high on trying to secure scholarships for his top athletes" and "was always talking to athletic directors."[83] Lewis got a scholarship to Southern University and held multiple world records.[84]

A Curriculum Council at Carver High School, pictured in the 1962 yearbook, worked "to improve the learning situation for children in the New Orleans public schools." Hicks, Hatfield, and Smith are first, second, and fifth from the left, respectively (UNO, OPSB–147, Carver Junior-Senior High School, Box 5).

Hicks Jr. recalled that Carver coaches were always together at his house. "When we would be home and all the other coaches would come over there socializing," he says, "it was always about sports and who was gonna get a scholarship." Along with his father, he explains, the coaches were "preparing students" years in advance. He contends, "These cats always wanted the betterment of the students. I'm not just saying athletes—other students [too]. [My dad] was always trying to make them better and prepare them for the future."[85]

Hicks was also a disciplinarian, as "that was a part of coaching." "His whole thing was respect. . . . If you had any sense, you immediately knew who was in charge," conveyed Hicks Jr.[86] Former student Lloyd Wills, who ranked nationally in the four-hundred-meter dash and became a coach himself, reflected on Hicks's "can-do" philosophy, which pushed students to new heights. Wills remembers a challenging time as a Carver athlete:

I had just finished a hard-won race and felt sick to my stomach and drained of all energy. I told Coach [Hicks] that I couldn't go anymore—I was exhausted. He put his hand around the back of my neck and calmly walked me off to a semi-secluded spot. He imparted to me in very colorful language that I was the best runner in the next event and I could defeat anyone, even if I was sick. Coach was right. I ran the next race and was victorious. Coach Hicks never gave up on his athletes—even when we wanted to give up on ourselves.[87]

Herman Gray, a Clark student, remembered when, in 1955, Hicks disciplined him because he "was too smart to be a damned hoodlum." Hicks had heard that Gray was doing things that would lead to trouble. After speaking for an hour and coming to an agreement that "I was about to throw my life away," Hicks brought Gray to his next class. Gray credits Hicks: "I am firmly convinced that if he had not gotten my attention, I would be either in jail, or dead." Gray went on to receive a BA degree in physical education from Dillard University.[88]

Hicks was committed to supporting and developing students fully, not only as disciplined athletes. His son recollects that "When a kid have a problem, they would come to the gym. You're a coach, you're a counselor. He was mama, he was daddy, he was parent." Perhaps most important, Hicks:

set . . . in a kid's mind that there is a lot of ways to be successful. . . . You gotta have what he would call the safety net. What you gonna be when you grow up? Can't play football forever. Can't run track. . . . They're [Carver coaches] not trying to make you the athlete they was, they trying to make you the person they want you to be and they just using sports as a vehicle to get you there. That was his philosophy.[89]

Hicks Jr. was recruited as an athlete by McNeese State University, where he desegregated the track team.[90] However, track was not at the forefront of his father's mind as he prepared him for his future. When the McNeese coach came to recruit Hicks Jr., he told Coach Hicks, "I'm gonna do all I can for your kid to graduate." He remembered his father's response with clarity:

My dad told [the coach], "A lot of coaches have come here to talk to me and my wife about recruiting my kid." He said, "But you one of the first ones to talk about education." He said, "I like that, Coach. I'm gonna see if you a man of your word." [The McNeese] Coach said, "What that mean?" [My dad] say, "He'll sign with you."[91]

For all his children—those at home and at Carver—Hicks emphasized the importance of educational achievement and personhood before anything.

Ernest Charles, a 1965 graduate, similarly reflected on Hicks and several other Carver coaches, emphasizing, "As a young Black man who didn't have a father, these guys talked to you about being a man." Reflecting on Hicks's influence five decades later, Charles attests:

Coach Hicks was just there. . . . Different things, dealing with ladies and stuff like that, different little things that I still hold to right now. He used to tell us, look fellows, if ya'll gonna court [date] . . . get you a mint and put it in your mouth. . . . If anybody know me, they say, "Damn, why you got those two mints in there?" I'll be seventy years old and I still do the same thing now [that Hicks taught me then].[92]

It is important to note that Hicks attended to the full range of matters relevant to students coming of age. Hicks died one year after his retirement in 1976.[93]

YVONNE BUSCH: MUSIC TEACHER AND BAND DIRECTOR

Yvonne Busch was a legendary music teacher and band director who spent most of her career at Carver. Although short in stature, her talents, commitment, and command were unrivaled. She trained countless musicians in New Orleans, many of whom built not only local and national but international reputations.

Born in 1929, Busch grew up in New Orleans' Tremé neighborhood, where brass bands and second lines often passed her way. From a young age, Busch exhibited a passion for music, even though her parents could not afford an instrument for joining the band at Joseph Craig Elementary School. Her cousin, James Clifton Polite, however, was a student at Piney Woods Country Life School in Mississippi, known for its instrumental music program, and persuaded the school's founder to admit fifth-grader Busch in 1940. There, Busch learned multiple instruments (e.g., alto horn, trumpet) and traveled nationally with student singers of the "Swinging Rays of Rhythm" to raise school funds. This included performing in states throughout the South and beyond.[94]

Busch returned to New Orleans in 1943 and played trumpet in the band at Albert Wicker School during eighth grade. She next attended Gilbert Academy, also attended by Hatfield. Under band leader T. LeRoy Davis, she mastered additional instruments (e.g., baritone horn, trombone). In 1947, she won first place in the Tristate Music Festival in Arkansas. By the twelfth grade, Busch aspired to be a music teacher.[95]

Busch followed Davis to Southern University in Baton Rouge, where he became band director. She majored in trombone and joined the teacher training program in instrumental music.[96] In her freshman year, Busch was appointed student conductor of the Southern University Concert Band in which it became "routine for [her] to organize, teach, and discipline students who were several years older."[97] In addition to the instruments that she already played, she played bass clarinet, bassoon, and oboe and took additional classes in woodwinds, percussion, and arranging. She also assumed first seat in trombone in what had been, up to that point, the all-male Southern Jazz Band. Notably, when the Jazz

Band traveled, Busch "was making contacts that would help her students obtain music scholarships in the future."[98] She graduated in 1951.

After graduating, Busch was hired for a short-term position at Booker T. Washington High School. She discovered a band program in which "many of the instruments were too old or damaged to be used."[99] Relying on personal funds, she had instruments repaired and obtained sheet music for students. Impressed with her capacity to play an astonishing number of instruments, students "instantly understood that Yvonne Busch meant business."[100] Although somewhat ragged, Washington's band uniforms became a symbol of pride, and Busch's halftime shows set a new performance standard. Student Tony Bazley later participated in recitals with Langston Hughes.[101]

When Washington's band director returned, Busch was assigned to teach at three schools—Clark High School, McDonogh No. 41 Junior High School, and Craig Elementary School.[102] Busch spent a half day at Clark and divided afternoons at Craig and McDonogh No. 41. Moving from one underresourced school to another required bringing music stands and books to the afternoon school and returning them to Clark. For a time, Busch's parents paid someone to assist her in getting from one place to the next. Busch invested additional time on weekends to prepare students for football games, parades, and competitions. During all of this, she initiated work on a master's degree in instrumental music at VanderCook College of Music in Chicago over summers.[103]

When Carver opened in 1958, Busch was assigned with Hatfield, Smith, and Hicks.[104] There, she kept students practicing for halftime shows until nine o'clock at night. In 1961, Louisiana Weekly named Carver the "Band of the Year," and other awards followed, with the marching band repeatedly winning first place recognition. Busch also received Carver's "Teacher of the Year" award in 1962.[105] Student teachers sought her mentorship, including Cynthia Sheeler Perkins, who ultimately taught music for twenty-one years in the city's public schools.[106] Jazz pianist Ellis Marsalis likewise was a student teacher under Busch.[107] Herlin Riley, one of the top three drummers worldwide, also studied under Busch at Carver.[108]

Riley spoke to the precision of Busch's teaching and her demanding standards. Recalling Ms. Busch and his junior high band teacher, Mr. Lloyd Harris, Riley stressed, "Those two teachers, they really, really instilled a sense of discipline in me as far as music is concerned." Ms. Busch, in particular, "taught me about paying attention to details because the small details will make something that's good great." He says they "taught me the method of how to count and how to figure out . . . the rhythm," which "served me so well playing with the Lincoln Center Jazz Orchestra" as well as with the New York Philharmonic. Under Busch's direction, the band did not march until the music was perfected. On a Monday, she would tell students to "go out on your porch and know [a

Yvonne Busch with Band Students in 1973 Yearbook
(Personal Collection of Avis and Vermon James)

song] by heart by Friday," and on Friday, she would "go down the line to each
and every person, 'Let me hear you.'" Riley emphasized that it was not about just
"putting on a show"; rather, "you had to have some substance," first learning the
music, then the steps. In this way, Riley secured the "solid foundation" for future
achievements.[109]

Providing students with a foundation for future achievements was central to
Busch. Student Leonard Smith recollected Busch telling students that they "better stop tryin' to chase them little nickel gigs" and instead refine their musical
knowledge and skills. Students were steered away from easy-to-get, low-paying
work toward higher pursuits that required double the effort in a racist system.
Such admonitions "were very low key," says Smith, but they came from the
teachers' experience of racism.[110] Highly accomplished and disciplined herself,
Busch offered students "detailed instructions about every instrument in the
band room," said Paul Batiste, once a student teacher under Busch.[111] Beyond
the band room, Busch offered music lessons free of charge to students during
summers.[112] Former students and student teachers became veteran music teachers and musicians of the next generation.

In 1983, Busch retired with thirty-two years of teaching in her musical reper-
toire. To honor her, Smith, also a former band member, produced the documentary, "A Legend in the Classroom: The Life Story of Miss Yvonne Busch."[113] In
the film, Clyde Kerr portrays Busch as part of a pantheon of Black women leaders, asserting that "A woman like that in our midst to me is like being around a
Mary Bethune or a Harriet Tubman or a Phyllis Wheatley."[114]

When Busch died in 2014, 1963 Carver graduate Rhea Dokes saw many
former students and musicians at her funeral. "They played some music before
the service, and then after," she explained, everyone did "what we do in New

Orleans, we have the second line [procession that follows the brass band]—it was just beautiful."[115]

Lenora Condoll Gray taught social studies at Carver from 1958 to 1996, nearly four decades. She says that she was a "little cutie pie" when she began—and she still is. This descriptor, however, does not capture Condoll's untiring efforts as an incubator of young citizens. After majoring in social studies and minoring in library science at Southern University, Condoll accepted a post at Carver teaching civics, US history, world history, free enterprise, and applied economics during her career. She also traveled annually with students to Washington, DC, and other sites of political importance.[116]

Condoll grew up in New Orleans' 7th Ward and graduated from McDonogh No. 35. Her father worked on plantations outside New Orleans and on the city's railroads; her mother was a seamstress. Although her family was poor, her mother bought her books about places around the world, fueling an interest in human geography, world cultures, and travel. Growing up, Condoll "was discriminated against," experiencing racism from whites and colorism in parts of the Black community.[117] These life experiences shaped how she taught: She wanted students to see the world and recognize that they could exercise influence as politically engaged citizens.

Condoll was aware of the ways in which racism affected Black students at Carver and other New Orleans schools, reflecting:

> One of the things you may notice is the location of all the Black schools. . . . Do you see any schools on a main thoroughfare? They're all stuck back in a corner someplace where nobody could actually see them or know where they are. . . . In spite of that, so many of our kids succeeded.[118]

Her commentary on Carver's geography speaks directly to white supremacy and the steadfast commitment of Black teachers to the achievement of students, despite racially oppressive conditions.

For Condoll, teaching social studies meant more than engaging students in traditional study; she sought to ignite political consciousness and foster agency. To accomplish this, Condoll focused mostly on local government. She "always loved" teaching civics and said she "used to take kids out to work in campaigns." They would stand on corners, hand out fliers, and learn the work of organizing. Then came a letter from the white school board, stating "teachers are not allowed to involve their students in political activities." Condoll was "getting emotional" recollecting her efforts, because "in the Black community, this is . . . the only exposure [students] had." Condoll sought to develop civic consciousness through active participation, but the board "found a way . . . to take away from our kids the ability to work in politics and learn." This pained Condoll, who believed in engaging young people on the ground.[119]

Dwan Julien, a student of Condoll's in the 1980s, credits her as "the one who kinda convinced me to become a registered voter when I turned 18." By Julien's account:

> Condoll always talked about having your voice heard and it's not always something you have to say [verbally], but it can be something as simple as a . . . check on the paper in the voting booth. She said, there are so many ways our youth don't get their voices heard and it would be a good way to exercise your right after so many have fought for you to have it. It was one of the reasons that I registered to vote.[120]

Hasan Sparks, who grew up in Desire and attended Carver in the 1990s, likewise had Condoll as a teacher. He said that students "read a lot, and we did a lot of essays, but it wasn't dull though. We learned in that class."[121] Condoll helped turn on a light.

Condoll also "exposed [students] to the world of economics." She took them to neighborhood businesses to "find out what they did, how did they want us to advertise." Students would then create ads. Some businesses found it so helpful that they "wanted us to work during the summer," with one class generating substantial income. Condoll reflected, "Those are the kinds of things I did that did not look [traditional]—was not down on a lesson plan." In short, Condoll says she focused on "entrepreneurship," to "find out whatever your passion is and try to make it work for you."[122] It was a strategy of self-determination.

Beyond local politics, Condoll used Close Up to introduce students to national politics. Close Up is a Washington, DC-based program initiated in 1971 to advance students' knowledge of government and social issues. Under Condoll's direction, students took annual trips to political sites.[123] Condoll reports:

> Each year for about 23 years, I would take a group of students to Washington, DC, so that they would get firsthand knowledge of the government as it worked from the ground up . . . I mean, literally sitting on the floor of the House of Representatives, interacting with our Congress people. . . . It opened their world.[124]

While in DC, Condoll planned visits to nearby universities, including Howard University, an HBCU, where students later applied.[125]

Getting students to Washington, DC, required funds, and Condoll never balked. In 1982—one of many instances in which Condoll secured student resources—she organized a French Quarter flea market to raise funds.[126] Not surprisingly, in 1983, she was recognized by the *Times Picayune/States Item* for her "dedication to students."[127] In 1985, Condoll was designated by students as the "Best All Around Teacher" and described as a "beacon light" for Carver youths.[128] The very next year, Condoll was, again, among their "favorite" teachers, noted for her service as "senior class advisor, student council and Close Up advisor, coordinator of Teacher Appreciation Week, and one thousand other student related activities."[129] Commendations such as this came when Condoll was thirty years deep in teaching, demonstrating the kind of persistence typically associated with activism.

Condoll taught more than subject matter. Condoll recalled an "expensive Black cashmere skirt," which she wore "to school four days a week." One day she would wear it long, and the next day, she rolled it up. She overheard students talking about clothing costs and mentioned that she wore her skirt frequently. In disbelief, the students observed the next week. "You told the truth," they said, conceding, "Now we know we don't have to always spend all that money." Condoll summed up the lesson, "It's not about how much or how many. It's what you do with what you have."[130] She taught students to maneuver in the face of barriers.

Condoll "taught the person," not only academic content, and supported students holistically in all life's aspects. In cases where girls' mothers could not assist, Condoll stepped in. She recollected students who asked her to "help us pick our dresses" for prom. Condoll's response:

> Not only did I do it, I said, "Okay, we're gonna run to the bridal shops. You're gonna try on some dresses and see which ones look good on you." Then they said, "Well, we can't afford it." A former student of mine who was in homemaking, now a teacher at Clark, made those dresses, but we wanted to bead 'em up. . . . Laid out some paper in the library . . . [and] I taught them how to bead. . . . When they walked in that prom . . . they were fabulous.[131]

Condoll wanted Black youths to know that "They are important people." When students wrote names on papers with initials, such as "Jon B.," she demanded their full names. "Who are you?" she asked, because "This is not your name." It may have been "something simple," Condoll reflected, but it taught students to "Be proud of who you are." When marijuana came on the scene, she instructed students that drugs were "a form of slavery."[132]

Condoll's radiant smile in yearbooks betrays the rigorous work required to teach as she did, especially over a forty-year time span as post-*Brown* disinvestment took its toll on Black public schools. Speaking of such neglect, Condoll shared, "I can recall one year, I had 66 students in every class. No place to sit. No books. Those are the kinds of things we put up with" from the 1970s onward. She likewise recalled problems with the auditorium, which propelled her "for a solid year" to request repairs from the school board. They wanted Condoll to

Lenora Condoll in 1982 Yearbook
(Personal Collection of Avis and Vermon James)

take students to another high school for senior events. Condoll put down her foot, conveying that "It would not happen." She personally met with someone at headquarters, making clear, "This is totally unacceptable. These things will have to be repaired."[133] Repairs were made, and seniors convened in Carver's auditorium. This kind of advocacy defined Condoll's day-to-day work.

Despite the challenges, Condoll conveyed with deep sincerity, "I loved that school. That's the only place I ever wanted to [teach]."[134]

"MAKING THINGS HAPPEN THAT WOULDN'T HAPPEN OTHERWISE"

Reflecting on teachers during the civil rights movement, Riley emphasized that their pedagogy went beyond academic content to address the life circumstances and prospects of Black youths: Teachers "saw some glimpse of light" in the '70s and wanted students to "get outta that dark hole we were in socially and economically." He believes that students were not fully aware of how much this sensibility drove the small things that teachers did. "Looking back on it, we can see why they were like that," teaching not just school subjects but also how students might successfully prevail, given the racial-political climate.[135]

Whether organizing teachers like Hatfield, teaching life lessons in science class like Smith, inspiring student-athletes and seeking scholarships like Hicks, providing disciplined music instruction on school nights like Busch, or taking students to DC to develop political consciousness like Condoll, this was deeply challenging work. However, Carver teachers did it with determination and vision for the next generation. Carver's culture, shaped by teachers' practices along a continuum of organized interventions to everyday interactions, is best characterized by Hatfield's invocation of trying to "make things happen that wouldn't otherwise happen." This is the classic definition of activism; despite the challenges of racism, teachers taught students to inhabit a world that did not yet exist—one in which they could thrive as fully human beings.

As Condoll alluded, this took immense effort in underresourced and over-crowded schools. A 1978 school board report indicates that, from 1963–1964 to 1977–1978, the total number of white students in public, private, and Catholic schools in Orleans Parish was cut in half from eighty-four thousand to forty-four thousand. Meanwhile, the number of Black students in public schools increased.[136] In 1977–1978, Carver had the second highest enrollment of all Black public high schools in New Orleans, with a student body of more than two thousand.[137] With white went green, and investment in Black public schools further stagnated.

A 1978 School Plant Survey provides insight into resource deprivation in a majority Black district.[138] The cost of rehabilitating the entire system was estimated at one hundred thirty million dollars but was closer to two hundred eight million dollars, considering inflation and the ten-year construction timeline.[139] Total building repairs proposed for 1978–1979 were only six million dollars, with a meager nine thousand dollars given to Carver to replace the gym's folding partition and fourteen thousand dollars for auditorium electrical work.[140] Half of the fire alarm systems were wholly or partially inoperative in the district. Eleven buildings were under continual structural observation. Of the one hundred thirty cafeterias inspected, floors were found unsatisfactory in fifty-nine, walls and ceilings were found unsatisfactory in seventy-six, lavatories were unsatisfactory in fifty-two, and nine needed rat-proofing.[141] Black educators such as those at Carver labored daily to support student achievement despite these conditions.

A 1987 report on Carver by the Southern Association of Colleges and Schools, which accredits educational institutions, underscores the herculean efforts of veteran teachers lacking infrastructural resources. Reviewers made it clear that they were "deeply impressed by the high morale of the faculty," with the school demonstrating "a significant influence on the lives of students."[142] However, the report is replete with statements about the lack of school resources, such as "plumbing for water in the science labs needs to be installed or repaired" and "bleachers and furniture in the gym should be replaced."[143] Despite such shortcomings, faculty are lauded as "well qualified, dedicated, with a positive professional approach to education" and do "an excellent job with limited resources," including "very low" teacher turnover.[144]

Grasping the depth of racism in New Orleans may have been what prompted Busch and choral teacher Zenobia Stewart to pen the words of Carver's school song, which pronounced:

> Hail to Carver, Alma Mater Forever aye.
> Though life be perilous
> Carver will guide the way. . . .[145]

Things were happening that otherwise would not *because* experienced teachers wisely and proactively showed students the way.

"Dedication to the Highest of Callings"

Florence Coleman Bryant, School Desegregation, and the Black Freedom Struggle in Postwar Virginia, 1946–2004

ALEXANDER HYRES

For Florence—1984
"She moved among us, quiet and contained,
Always bearing herself with natural grace
As one who has accepted a duty
And acknowledged its fitness and her own
Dedication to the highest of callings-
To teach, to lead, and to inspire. . . ."

— *The English Department, Charlottesville High School,*
Charlottesville, Virginia

The faculty of Charlottesville High School's English Department penned the poem above, "For Florence—1984," in tribute to Florence Coleman Bryant.[1] Bryant tendered her retirement papers with the school division during the spring of 1984, after working in the Charlottesville City Schools Division for nearly four decades. "As it turned out, the time of my retirement was most appropriate," asserted Bryant, "Education in the United States was at somewhat of a crossroad." She noted the publication of *A Nation at Risk* in 1983 and how, on the basis of her long tenure in education, she suspected that the report would lead to a shift in American educational reform efforts. "It was obvious to me that education would be in a state of flux for some time," recalled Bryant. Although Bryant retired from teaching and leading in schools, she stayed busy reflecting and writing about her experiences as a Black woman living, teaching, parenting, and leading in Charlottesville, Virginia.[2]

Bryant was born and educated in rural Caroline County, Virginia, in the midst of Jim Crow. After graduating from Union High School and Virginia State University, she started her teaching career at Charlottesville's segregated Black schools: Jefferson Elementary, Jefferson High School, and Jackson P. Burley

High School. After the *Brown v. Board of Education* decisions and in the midst of massive resistance, Bryant helped desegregate the University of Virginia as a graduate student and, soon after, the Charlottesville City School Division as a teacher. Bryant was not the first Black student to attend the nearby University of Virginia. However, she became part of the first wave of Black graduate students who entered a formerly white, male space in a university founded by enslaver and third president of the United States, Thomas Jefferson. In addition to navigating school desegregation as a student and later as a teacher, Bryant experienced the process and its consequences as a parent and administrator. This chapter traces the full arch of Florence Coleman Bryant's career and reveals how, in her various roles as an educator across various school settings, she sought justice for Black students, including her own children, amid the political, social, and economic milieu of post–World War II Virginia.[3]

This chapter broadens our understanding of the Black freedom struggle in Virginia during the twentieth century. Because Robert Pratt observed a lack of civil rights scholarship in the state, broadly, and in education, specifically, scholars such as Jill Ogline Titus, Christopher Bonastia, Brian Daugherity, Matthew D. Lassiter, and Andrew B. Lewis, Jeffrey L. Littlejohn, and Charles Howard Ford have revealed the particularities of the Black freedom struggle in the Commonwealth of Virginia. This recent work, however, has only just begun the process of filling the gap identified a few decades ago by Pratt. By focusing on a Black teacher in Charlottesville, Virginia, this chapter further illuminates the convergences and divergences between Virginia and other states during the Black freedom struggle of the twentieth century. In particular, we see how Bryant faced both the opportunities and the limitations of the "Virginia Way." The "Virginia Way" represents the specific form of racism and white supremacy in the Commonwealth of Virginia that, on one hand, projects genteel and paternalistic race relations and, on the other hand, produces the same inequality and injustices for Black people found in other regions of the South and throughout the United States.[4]

By illuminating the life and work of Bryant, this chapter also engages with the growing scholarship on Black teacher activism, organizing, and protest. It spotlights one theme that scholars still have much to uncover and recover: Black teacher desegregation. Adam Fairclough, Michael Fultz, Sonya Ramsey, Vanessa Siddle Walker, and others have chronicled the displacement, demotion, and firing of Black teachers in the aftermath of the *Brown* decisions. These accounts have revealed what happened across the South to Black teachers as a group. However, not all Black teachers faced displacement, demotion, and firing; some teachers joined Black students in desegregating all-white schools throughout the South. Indeed, Barbara Shircliffe has provided the most substantive account of teacher desegregation. She builds on the work of Fairclough, Fultz, Ramsey, and Walker by centering southern public school teachers in the desegregation process. Shircliffe focuses primarily on the legal changes and consequences for Black and white teachers, but we know less about the individual experiences of Black teachers in desegregated settings during the 1960s and beyond. Furthermore, we know even less about how Black teachers balanced and navigated their multiple roles and identities. Building on this work, this chapter spotlights the experience of school desegregation from Florence Bryant's perspective as a student, educator, parent, and administrator in a southern locale, which was and remains entangled in the politics and economics of a local predominantly white institution of higher education. Focusing on Bryant reveals how her various roles and identities intersected with the process of school desegregation both at the K–12 level and higher education.[5]

EDUCATION

Florence Coleman Bryant came of age in Caroline County, Virginia. Caroline County sits between Richmond, Virginia, to the south and Washington, DC, to the north. In addition to living and working in Caroline County, Bryant and her family attended worship and participated in the life of their local church, St. John Baptist. In 1866, Reverend J. F. Wright helped organize the congregation and served as St. John Baptist's first pastor. By the 1920s, the church had the most members of any church in the county and possessed property worth approximately five thousand dollars. Located just a few miles from the Coleman home, St. John Baptist Church served as an important institution for Florence Bryant, both when she lived in Caroline County but also throughout her life. "We were taught [at St. John Baptist] to be faithful stewards of our time, talent, and financial resources," Bryant remembers, "I attribute my ability to cope with crises in my life to the strong religious beliefs fostered by our parents, our school, our community, and our church." Her early and ongoing involvement in the church shaped her consciousness about her faith but also what her faith meant in the context of her future life and career.[6]

Indeed, Bryant's life in the church shaped her relationship to education and civil rights. Reverend Chester A. Lindsay served as the pastor at St. John Baptist during her formative years at the church in the community. Reverend Lindsay preached on a range of topics, including, most notably, power and politics. On political power, he highlighted the demographics of Caroline County, where Black people constituted nearly half of the population by 1924, to try and persuade his congregants of the collective power they could possess and wield. "Blacks owned almost as much property as whites and held an almost equal social and economic status; generally, we were all struggling farmers," remembers Bryant. Reverend Lindsay had a difficult time organizing his congregants to seek more political power in the context of Jim Crow Virginia. Several factors kept

Black people from engaging in the political process and seeking office, including systemic electoral disenfranchisement and the rise of the second Klu Klux Klan in Virginia. To be clear, those factors did not keep *all* Black people from fighting for political, social, and economic justice. Some Black people, particularly in the Commonwealth's urban areas, organized and protested segregation and racism throughout the Jim Crow era.[7]

In addition to the push for greater civil rights, Reverend Lindsay worked to expand access to secondary and higher education. Bryant remembers, "Rev. Lindsay unceasingly encouraged young people with whom he had contact to acquire as much education as possible." Reverend Lindsay's work went beyond words, too. He served as a moderator for the Mattaponi Association. The Mattaponi Association, a collaborative endeavor of seventy-three Baptist churches, sought to create greater and better educational opportunities for youths in Virginia. It supported students attending historically Black colleges and universities (HBCUs), including Virginia Union University, Virginia Seminary and College, and the Hampton Institute. St. John Baptist Church offered spiritual sustenance and fellowship for Bryant and many others in Caroline County, but it also spotlighted the power of education and the need to expand educational opportunities. These values and beliefs were ingrained in Bryant's consciousness as she approached her own education and, eventually, her career as an educator.[8]

Bryant attended public schools in Caroline County. Formalized schooling in Caroline County for Black people emerged during the Civil War. A mixture of public and private schools for Black residents opened in the county during and after the war, with elementary schools appearing first and secondary schools appearing later, during the early twentieth century. Alongside the other neighborhood children, Bryant attended St. John Elementary School. St. John sat approximately two miles from her childhood home. The school consisted of two rooms with a porch running across the entirety of the building. Within the classrooms, which were similarly sized, there were large windows and a wall-length blackboard on the opposite side. Bolted wooden desks were arranged in two rows, all turned toward the blackboard. One room held students in Grades One to Three, and the other held students in Grades Four to Seven. "It epitomized the neighborhood school concept, in that the parents and teachers worked together, not only in school activities, but in church and community activities as well," recalls Bryant, "Working as a unit, the school, home, and church fostered the development of the whole child." The experience at St. John Elementary, and in other community institutions including the church, built a strong foundation for Bryant as she moved onto the next steps in her formal education.[9]

Bryant's time at St. John Elementary ended earlier than her peers. Halfway through seventh grade, she transferred to Union High School. "I missed my chance to be one of the honored participants at seventh grade commencement, which was an important event, but having the opportunity to become acclimated to the high school environment to ease my transition there was worth it," remembers Bryant. She observed stark differences between the two schools. Whereas St. John Elementary consisted of students from the nearby community, Union High School drew from students throughout the county. As a result, the student population at Union exceeded that of St. John Elementary. Union High School proved to be more challenging than St. John Elementary, too. "The classwork was much more concentrated and competitive," Bryant recalls, "I had to study harder on my homework in order to teach up with the class and to become better adjusted to its pace. My best friend had already transferred to Union High, so I didn't feel entirely alone. The class of forty-plus students remained largely intact throughout high school." Bryant's entry into secondary schooling coincided with more and more Black students in Virginia and across the South gaining greater access to education beyond elementary school. Access to secondary schooling for Black students still lagged behind access for white students in Virginia as a whole, however.[10]

Similar to some other areas in Virginia, including Charlottesville, Lynchburg, and Richmond, the Caroline County School Division expanded to include a Black high school during the first half of the twentieth century. In 1903, Bowling Green Industrial Academy opened; it was replaced by Caroline County Training School in 1914, which, in turn, was replaced by Union High School in 1929. When Bryant attended Union High School, the school's teachers lived primarily in Richmond. Some of the teachers lived in the Union's dormitory from Monday to Thursday and returned to the capital city on the weekends. The school's teachers possessed "degrees in their areas of specialties." Few teachers left the school. Union High School served all the Black students seeking a secondary education in Caroline County. There was a single curriculum track at the school: college preparation. The course offerings included English, mathematics, social studies, science, foreign language, health and physical education, and agriculture or industrial arts for the boys and home economics for the girls. Union High School's extracurricular activities were limited to baseball, softball, basketball, and choir. Bryant sang in the choir throughout high school, but she did not take part in any sports or other activities beyond the classroom at school. "Our tight schedules allowed no flexible or free time," recalls Bryant.[11]

Bryant has fond memories of her teachers at Union High School. Mrs. Virginia Scott Jackson and Mrs. Louise B. Carter left an indelible mark on Bryant's education and future career as an educator herself. Mrs. Jackson taught both math and science. Although Bryant struggled a bit more in math and science than in other courses, she still enjoyed the coursework, especially in science, where she was "enthralled by the use of Bunsen burners and test tubes, studying microbes, and writing up analyses of the experiments." Bryant's favorite subjects were English and French. Mrs. Carter taught both classes, and Bryant viewed her as a role model. "I regarded Mrs. Carter as the epitome of what a school teacher should be: intelligent, articulate, interesting, and friendly," remembers Bryant, "I especially loved the literary selections we studied. Vicariously, I shared the romance, intrigue, and adventure in which the characters were involved." Witnessing the work of her teachers, in the segregated Black schools of Caroline County, provided Bryant with models of how to engage students and make the most of the available curriculum and pedagogy materials.[12]

After graduating from Union High School, Bryant did not immediately attend college. "Following my graduation from Union High School in 1940, I was like a leaf caught in the breeze," recalls Bryant, "Because of my family's limited financial resources, I did not consider going to college as an option." For two years, Bryant traveled north to Philadelphia, Pennsylvania to work as a domestic for a few different families. After two years in what Bryant deemed the "school of life," she enrolled at Virginia State College. She majored in English and minored in French. "My freshman year at Virginia State College was primarily a year of adjustment," recalls Bryant. Despite the adjustment period during her freshman year, Bryant excelled throughout the remaining years at Virginia State. Bryant made the dean's list throughout her time in college and, during her senior year, earned the Top English Student and Student Teacher of the Year awards. These awards were in addition to working throughout college both during the school year and during the summer months.[13]

During college, Bryant took an active role in campus life. She attended performances by the drama and music department. She worked for the college newspaper, the *Virginia Statesman*, where she served as both a feature editor and a columnist. The column was called "The People's Pulpit," and Bryant earned a certificate of recognition for her contributions. Another critical aspect of Bryant's college experience was joining Delta Sigma Theta. She was not initiated until her senior year. "Even though that left me little time to become involved in the activities of the sorority, I appreciated the support the sisterhood provided me. It became another anchor for my life and another avenue for productive, fulfilling involvement after graduation," recalls Bryant. After graduating from Virginia State College, Bryant applied to and received a job offer to teach at the Jefferson School in Charlottesville, Virginia.[14]

In 1946, Bryant started her teaching career at Charlottesville's Jefferson Elementary School. Similar to Caroline County's public schools, Charlottesville's public schools originated during the Civil War and Reconstruction. Eventually, the Jefferson School emerged as the segregated elementary school for Black students in the city. In 1926, after several decades of organizing by the city's Black community, the Jefferson School expanded to include a high school. At the time, Jefferson High School was one of the few Black high schools in Virginia. During the early twentieth century, leading up to Florence Coleman Bryant's arrival in Charlottesville, the student population at both the Jefferson School and Jefferson High School grew exponentially. Jefferson High School transformed from a school educating a relatively small population of Black students to a mass institution educating greater numbers of students each year particularly after World War II.[15]

Bryant faced several challenges during her first year. "In the beginning, I felt like almost a complete failure," recalls Bryant, "The more I taught, tested, and graded, the more discouraged I became. The students continued to perform poorly. I blamed their poor performance on my inexperience and ineffective teaching methods." Bryant was not satisfied with how she or her students were performing in the classroom. As a result, she sought out help from a more veteran colleague of the school, Miss Maude Gamble. Gamble had taught for several years and even held administrative positions at the school. Bryant recalls, "We reviewed my curriculum and evaluated my teaching methods, my student assignments, and my general expectations, I revamped my whole program. Almost immediately the students' performances began to improve." Although Bryant had witnessed exemplary teaching during her time growing up in Caroline County, Virginia, and trained as a teacher at Virginia State University, she realized that her approach was not meeting the curricular and pedagogical needs of her students. This realization and willingness to continue developing as an educator shows why Bryant had such a profound influence as a teacher in the Charlottesville City Schools.[16]

After just a year at the segregated Jefferson School, Bryant moved to Jefferson High School. On curriculum and pedagogy at the high school, Bryant observed, "We had the same books as the other schools. We didn't see any black faces in those books. There were state textbooks. In the high school we had *Uncle Tom's Cabin*, that was about it." The curricular and pedagogical materials provided by the Charlottesville City Schools Division at Jefferson High School often failed to represent the Black experience—or worse, misrepresented it—so Bryant and her fellow teachers organized and participated in Negro History Week at the Jefferson School and Jefferson High School. Bryant remembers, "Negro History Week . . . during that week, we all dealt with African-American history in the fields we were teaching in." Woodson's Negro History Week started in 1926, the same year that Jefferson High School opened, and the materials centered Black people and critiqued the master narratives of white supremacy propagated in the pages of the state-sanctioned textbooks. During her time in the classroom at Jefferson High School, Bryant developed as a professional and, through her curriculum and pedagogy, provided her students with counternarratives to the representations of Black inferiority and white supremacy provided by the city of Charlottesville and its school division. This work occurred behind closed doors and in the spaces of Black segregated schools. Although this work did not draw the headlines in the way that overt protest during the civil rights movement would, it was no less impactful to the multitude of students who crossed paths with Bryant and her fellow teachers at Jefferson High School. William Gilmore, a graduate of Jefferson High School in 1948, asserted that ". . . the people who are basically pillars of this town would not have been had it not been for a school like Jefferson."[17]

In 1951, the Charlottesville City School Division replaced Jefferson High School with Jackson P. Burley High School. The new high school memorialized Jackson P. Burley, a Black educator in the area during the early twentieth century and a leader in the fight for the establishment of Jefferson High School. Whereas only Black students from Charlottesville attended Jefferson High School, Black students from Charlottesville and the surrounding Albemarle County attended Burley High School. Florence Bryant, along with several colleagues and students, transitioned from Jefferson over to Burley. Bryant's time at Burley was brief; she left in the same year as the first *Brown* decision. "I was transferred to Burley High School, along with many of the faculties of the consolidated schools. Operating under a new administration, the school staff underwent an extensive readjustment period. Inspired by the beautiful new facilities, the faculty put forth a special effort to design an exciting new, vital, and dynamic educational program. The expanded facilities made possible additional course offerings such as art, speech and drama, practical nursing, and the building trades." Virginia, along with other southern states, aimed to equalize facilities for Black students to create the appearance that they were attempting to uphold the standard of "separate but equal" conditions in public facilities set out by the Supreme Court's ruling in *Plessy v. Ferguson* (1896). The building of Burley to replace Jefferson High School was just one of many examples to equalize facilities.[18]

Much of what the teachers and students built and practiced at Jefferson High School remained part of the curriculum and pedagogy at Jackson P. Burley High School. "Burley continued the tradition of academic excellence already established at Jefferson High School," Bryant recalls, "It had an active National Honor Society, and each year had its share of Merit Semi-Finalists. The students continued to perform well at institutions of higher education. Both schools won repeated state championships in both basketball and football." Jackson P. Burley High School remained open throughout the school desegregation era, as only a small group of Black students enrolled at the city's previously segregated white high school, Lane High School. Burley High School closed in 1967, however, as full-scale desegregation took hold in the Charlottesville City Schools and in school divisions across Virginia. Bryant did not stay long at Burley. Her departure from Burley coincided with a critical juncture in her own education. Soon after the Supreme Court's ruling in the *Brown* case, she would become one of the first Black women students at the nearby University of Virginia.[19]

DESEGREGATION

The University of Virginia, founded by enslaver and former US president Thomas Jefferson, served only white males of a high socioeconomic class for the entirety of the nineteenth century and well into the twentieth century. However, the university became slightly more open to women and Black people. In 1950, Gregory Swanson was admitted to the university's law school; ultimately, Swanson did not complete his degree. Swanson was followed by Walter Ridley in 1951. Just two years later, Ridley graduated with his doctorate in education. Alongside Louise Stokes Hunter, who, in 1953, also earned her doctorate in education, Florence Coleman Bryant became one of the first Black women to desegregate the University of Virginia. Bryant took a leave of absence from Burley during the 1955–1956 school year for the birth of her second child. Around the same time, she enrolled in a master's degree program at the University of Virginia. Rather than having to travel and stay in the dorms at Howard University in Washington, DC—as Bryant had done for previous graduate courses—she could attend graduate courses within walking distance of her home in Charlottesville.[20]

Beginning in January 1956, Bryant enrolled in the Graduate School of Arts and Sciences at the University of Virginia. She had taught speech and drama at Burley High School during the previous year. She pursued a graduate degree in combining those two subjects. In Virginia, at the time, Bryant remembers, "Black students were admitted into only those graduate programs that were not offered at the black state institution of higher learning, Virginia State College in Petersburg, Virginia." Bryant decided to start anew with credits for her degree in speech and drama at the University of Virginia, although it is doubtful that they would have accepted credits from Howard University. Throughout her life, Bryant had only attended schools with other Black students and only Black teachers. Of her experience in a desegregated setting, Bryant recalls, "Often I was not only the only black student in class but the only woman and the oldest student. My classmates were not particularly serious about their work. They were respectful to the 'old, black lady,' but for the most part, they paid me no mind. The professors did not appear fazed by my presence either, which suited me fine. I was glad to be 'invisible,' at least until I had become adjusted to my new environment." Bryant's mere presence at the University of Virginia represented a subversive act. For the previous nearly one hundred thirty years at the time, only white men were welcomed to "the Grounds" at the university as students.[21]

To complete her degree, Bryant wrote a thesis on General Douglas MacArthur's speeches. "The purpose of the study was to make an objective analysis of selected speeches delivered by General MacArthur at climatic points in his life while fulfilling his role of civic and military leader," remembers Bryant, "It focused on all of the elements of the speaking situations: the speaker, the speech, the audience, and the occasion." Bryant spent significant time at the University of Virginia's Alderman Library poring over newspapers and periodicals for nearly two and a half months. Her advisor was nearing retirement, which forced her to complete the degree on an ambitious timeline. All of her hard work resulted in a degree; however, according to Bryant, "The librarian told me she feared for my health and sanity." Bryant graduated with a master's degree from the University of Virginia in 1956—becoming one of the first Black students to do so not only at the university but also throughout the South. Bryant has not received the same publicity as her University of Virginia contemporaries such as Gregory Swanson, Walter Ridley, and Mary Louise Hunter. Along with her contemporaries, however, Bryant contested the white, male, and aristocratic exclusivity of the University of Virginia. Generations of women and Black students have followed in their footsteps.[22]

When Bryant returned to the classroom, she spent a brief time back at the Jefferson School before school desegregation took hold in the Charlottesville City Schools. The Charlottesville City Schools joined other cities and counties across Virginia, during the late 1950s, in both massive and passive resistance schemes to avoid the implementation of the *Brown v. Board of Education* decision. Rather than desegregate their schools in the fall of 1958, local politicians and school officials closed Venable Elementary School and Lane High School. Venable and Lane reopened, to white students, in the spring of 1959; Black students did not gain entry until the fall of 1959. Full-scale school desegregation did not occur until well into the late-1960s in Charlottesville and across the Commonwealth. As school desegregation took hold, Black teachers and administrators across the South lost their jobs at a staggering rate.[23]

In 1965, Bryant became one of the few Black teachers to desegregate the Charlottesville City Schools. The school division assigned her to teach ninth-grade English at Walker Junior High School. Because the school division had not adequately prepared for school desegregation, the city's two junior high schools met at the former Jefferson Elementary School. The two schools met in shifts, too; the Walker students attended school during the morning shift, and the Buford Junior High School students attended during the afternoon shift. School officials determined the shift assignments by flipping a coin. As a result of the truncated schedules for both schools, they only offered core courses in English, mathematics, social studies, and science. Not only was the curriculum limited, but neither school could offer the normal load of elective courses, extracurricular activities, or even lunch on site. The school's library had limited resources available in the Jefferson School, too.[24]

Beyond the building limitations, Bryant faced a number of additional challenges in the classroom, during her initial year at Walker. First, she had not taught ninth-grade English before this teaching assignment. "I spent most of the summer prior to the opening of school preparing for my new teaching assignment," remembers Bryant, "Since it was my first experience teaching ninth-grade English, I had to review all of the instructional materials I was expected to use or planned to use." She also prepared to teach students with various ability levels within the classroom. Second, Bryant had limited curriculum resources. To help support her students, she combed through the collections available at the local public libraries and created reading lists for her students. Third, Bryant had little experience teaching white students. She recalls, "For a few days there wasn't much participation. They sat very politely, but they didn't participate. Then, I encouraged participation and it began to happen." Bryant's experience in the classroom mirrors those of other Black teachers in Virginia who recall facing various forms of resistance from white students. Not only was Bryant entering a new classroom setting, but she also faced it without the support of many other Black educators or Black administrators in the building.[25]

In addition to the challenges in the classroom, Bryant was also faced with a toxic work environment beyond the classroom. She dealt with two individuals on a regular basis: one white woman and one white man. The woman was "an intelligent, well read, career educator from an old Virginia family." She often asked Bryant about her opinions on "racial topics." For example, when her colleague asked about why Black people sought integration in the public sphere, including schools, Bryant "pointed out to her that the United States Constitution guarantees equal rights to all Americans, and that those rights would never be fully enjoyed by black people under the separate but equal policy." She also explained that, although some Black people did succeed despite discrimination and racism, their success should not be used as justification for the continuation of the status quo. Furthermore, Bryant asserted "that there may have been scores of other blacks to excel had they been afforded equal opportunities, and those who had excelled might have contributed far more than they did to the world." Bryant's interactions and conversations, according to her, did seem to have an impact on her colleague's worldview. It is difficult to determine its extent, however, drawing upon the available source materials from the time. On the basis of Bryant's characterizations of those conversations, it seems as though she viewed them as dialogues. The same cannot be said of her interactions with the other colleague mentioned in her memoir.[26]

Bryant's conversations with her white male colleague were more contentious. In her overall accounting of this man's ideological perspective, Bryant asserts, "He was thoroughly indoctrinated with the myths and stereotypes usually associated with racism." She worried not only about how those beliefs affected his relationship with her but also about how he related to the Black students in his classes. "If he reacted that way toward me, I wondered how the black students assigned to his classes would fare," recalls Bryant. She never cites anything directly occurring with this white male teacher and Black students in his class. However, the lack of any cited incident still leaves open the possibility that Black students faced a discriminatory and racist environment in that teacher's classroom. The experiences of Black students in the Charlottesville City Schools during desegregation suggest that the perspective and behavior of her white male colleague were more common than not. The experience of Bryant's children gives credence to this claim.[27]

Not only did Bryant face and navigate school desegregation as a student and as a teacher, but she also dealt with it as a parent. Bryant's three children, Audrey, Ronnie, and Clint Bryant, all participated in the school desegregation process. They each faced hostile environments. "When Audrey was first assigned to Venable Elementary School, she was immediately placed in a remedial reading class," recalls Bryant, "Being placed in that remedial reading class destroyed her confidence to such an extent that she stopped reading almost entirely." Audrey Bryant had been a "voracious reader" before school desegregation and having a white teacher for the first time. Bryant confronted the teacher about the remedial designation; the teacher did not relent on her decision to place Audrey in the remedial reading class. Audrey Bryant was not alone in dealing with racism in Charlottesville's desegregated classrooms. When Ronnie Bryant received a perfect score on a geometry test, the white teacher believed that he cheated. She required him to retake the test. He repeated the perfect score. In both cases, Florence Bryant advocated on behalf of her children in ways she did not have to before the onset of school desegregation.[28]

Clint and Audrey Bryant attended Lane High School at the height of the school's racial tensions in the late 1960s. During a Negro History Week assembly, Black students requested that all students stand for "Lift Every Voice and Sing." Not only did white students and teachers refuse to stand for the "Negro National Anthem," but one of the white teachers also led a procession of white students and teachers out of the assembly. "In protest, the black students staged a sit-out of classes for several days," remembers Bryant, "I was extremely proud that my children had the courage to stand up for what they believed was right." She did not participate in any protests as a teacher during her time in the Charlottesville City Schools; however, she started teaching at the Jefferson School in a slightly different social, political, and economic context. Her activism manifested in her curricular and pedagogical approach. Bryant's children, who were some of the first Black students to experience desegregation, sought justice and equity using their own means of protest alongside many other Black students at Lane High School. Despite her children using a different approach from her own, Bryant still supported their means and ways of protesting injustice.[29]

All three of Bryant's children graduated from the Charlottesville City Schools. Of their ability to survive and thrive during the era of school desegregation in Charlottesville, Bryant cited several factors. She noted that their behavior, intelligence, and confidence helped them avoid problems with their predominantly white teachers. She also observed how their friends helped provide a strong support system within and beyond the classroom and school. Finally, she noted their positive experiences as students in segregated schools who participated in the full range of activities. Bryant's support of her students, including their protest of racism and injustice at Lane High School, also surely helped them survive the various and overlapping challenges they faced as the first wave of students to desegregate the Charlottesville City Schools. All of Bryant's children attended HBCUs. Their choices reflected a desire to focus on their education and not deal with a desegregated, predominantly white environment beyond their high school experience.[30]

After spending several years in the classroom and seeing her children graduate, Florence Bryant became an administrator. The Charlottesville City Schools closed Lane High School and opened Charlottesville High School in 1974. Because of a lack of planning by the school division, Lane High School had quickly become overcrowded and outdated during the school desegregation era. The new high school, with a new building and new name, offered the chance at a fresh start for the school division. However, the same issues that plagued Lane High School followed students, teachers, and administrators to Charlottesville High School. The Charlottesville City Schools hired Bryant as vice principal at Charlottesville High School in 1979. Even after graduating from the University of Virginia with a master's degree, Bryant continued taking postgraduate courses. The accumulation of these courses yielded an additional certification, which allowed Bryant to serve as administrator. In the 1980s, Bryant, as an administrator, would become entangled with the racist actions of white students and teachers at the school.[31]

Initially, Bryant spent most of her time as an administrator working to reform the new school's curriculum. She was proud of all the work completed during those initial years at Charlottesville High School. "I had established a credible reputation as an effective administrator," asserts Bryant, "I had developed a good working relationship with the other members of the administrative staff and faculty; and I had gained the respect and trust of my students." Like her experience as a teacher during the desegregation era, Bryant was one of the few Black administrators in the Charlottesville City Schools. Unfortunately, Bryant's final year proved to be the "most tumultuous." One event contributed most to the tumult.[32]

On Monday, March 5, 1984, Charlottesville High School closed for the day. An article in the *Knighttimes*, the school's student newspaper, caused the closure. The article, "Grading Black-White Relations: 17 Years After Integration," included several racist quotes from anonymous white students. A white sophomore student claimed that the school's Black students "hang around the hall. They just come to get heat. They just mess around . . . come to school 'cause they have nothing else to do . . . they just come to smoke herb and all that stuff." Another white student quoted in the article claimed that Black students "like to start fights." Regardless of whether the school newspaper's advisor actually read the article, a white teacher approved the article for publication. A day after the article was published, students, teachers, and administrators arrived at the school and found racist epithets spray-painted on the parking lot surface. Fights broke out between Black and white students throughout the morning. After bookcases were overturned in the library and several students refused to vacate the school buses in front of the school, administrators called the police. Although the police did not arrest anyone, the administrators decided by eleven o'clock that morning to close school for the day. Teachers and administrators stayed at school in the afternoon to discuss the situation and decide how to handle it.[33]

Bryant stood in the middle of the controversy. In reflecting on the situation years later, Bryant wrote, "More than once I, who had a reputation of remaining cool, calm, and collected under all circumstances, became emotional and strident in my attempt to make some sense of the sudden explosive situation." Although Bryant had dealt with similar situations as a parent, she had never been placed in a position of authority where she had to make a decision about how to handle a racist incident in the school. Bryant witnessed firsthand the changes and continuities in high school education in Charlottesville as a teacher, parent, and administrator. However, her position as an administrator placed her in a difficult position from which to navigate and respond to the situation at Charlottesville High School. "I felt mostly angry with myself because I failed to detect the degree of pent-up frustrations the students harbored by not having their needs adequately met," remembers Bryant.[34]

Overall, Bryant's response to the situation reflected her multiple identities as a Black woman within the school and the community. "I felt caught between my position as an administrator, who needed to defend the integrity of the school's program, and my position as a black person, who needed to defend the legitimacy of the black students' perceptions of racism and inequality at Charlottesville High," reflected Bryant, "I felt totally ineffectual on both counts." Although Bryant took personal responsibility for the situation, the Charlottesville City

Schools placed her in a situation where she would be caught between those two worlds. Bryant did not seek out the vice principal position. The Charlottesville City Schools sought her out. During school desegregation across the county, the number of Black administrators plummeted. In the 1970s and 1980s, however, school districts, including the Charlottesville City Schools, sought out a select number of Black people to serve as administrators.[35]

Bryant aimed to do everything in her power to reach all students at Charlottesville High School. She had always aimed to do so since her early days at Jefferson School and Jefferson High School. "Many special programs had been implemented, especially to raise the achievement levels of underachievers, but obviously the success in that regard had not been fully attained," asserts Bryant, "On the other hand, I was equally sure that, because racism was so deeply ingrained in the fabric of the American society, Charlottesville High School could not possibly have been immune." In retrospect, Bryant realized both the limits of her capacity to shape change and the enduring nature of racism in the United States. Becoming the vice principal and developing programs for Charlottesville High School could help students who underachieved. At the same time, the institutional racism prevalent and constant within the Charlottesville City Schools throughout her tenure as an educator in the school division made reform efforts difficult, even for someone with immense skill and institutional knowledge as Bryant did. Bryant was placed in a difficult position as one of the few Black administrators in the school division; her place in the crisis at Charlottesville High School said more about how the school division failed to systemically support Black students than anything about Bryant's personal capacity to create change in the school.[36]

WITNESS

Bryant stayed busy in retirement. She spent a significant portion of her time making sense of and witnessing to all she had seen as a Black person, educator, parent, and community member. In 1987, she appeared in a documentary titled *The Road to* Brown: *The Untold Story of the Man Who Killed Jim Crow*, about Charles Hamilton Houston, one of the legal architects of the strategy to end "separate, but equal schooling." Standing in front of the Jefferson School, Bryant discussed the activism of Black teachers in the fight for equal pay in Virginia, her experience with school desegregation in Charlottesville, and the need for teaching Black history in public schools. Her appearance in the documentary was just the beginning of her move from educator to public intellectual in the retirement phase of her life.[37]

Bryant published her first book, *Memoirs of a Country Girl*, just four years after her retirement from Charlottesville High School. The book—one of the sources drawn upon for this chapter—offered a comprehensive account of

Bryant's life from her upbringing and education in Caroline County to her experience as an administrator at Charlottesville High School. The book's intended readership includes Bryant's children, grandchildren, and other members of her extended family. When Bryant detailed the book's aims, she wrote, "My purpose for writing the book was mainly to illustrate how our family was able to survive and triumph over the adversities of our conditions and attain our goals through tenacity, perseverance, and determination."[38] Beyond her family, Bryant also seems intent on meditating on the experience of rural America. She wrote, "Even though the experiences and events related in the book were drawn from my life, they represent similar experiences in the lives of numerous other rural black and white families throughout America, many members of which, unlike me, never get an opportunity to develop their talents and participate fully in the American Dream." From Bryant's vantage point at the time, it is not surprising that she would describe America as a desegregated society, because the forces of resegregation, especially in education, were only starting to take root during the decade when she was writing. Specific to the Charlottesville context, all the schools projected the outward appearance of being desegregated spaces— even as they resegregated within the schools including at Charlottesville High School.[39]

After writing about her own life, Bryant turned her attention to another legendary Black educator. In 2001, Bryant published a book on Rebecca Fuller McGinness. In *Rebecca Fuller McGinness, A Lifetime: 1892–2000*, Bryant chronicled McGinness's life as a student, educator, and community member in Charlottesville. "The life she related to me was a testament to her indomitable spirit, to her grace, and to her fortitude, as she overcame great odds to achieve a long, productive life," wrote Bryant, "For more than a century she was not only an eyewitness to history but a completely active participant." McGinness lived in Charlottesville nearly her entire life and contributed in significant ways to the life and education of the city's Black residents throughout the twentieth century. McGinness represented the generation of Black students and teachers in Charlottesville who attended and taught at Charlottesville's Black segregated schools.[40]

The collaboration between Bryant and McGinness yielded a wide-ranging account of both the changes and continuities in Charlottesville for Black residents during the twentieth century. Obviously, McGinness's perspective was limited by centering her own experience living in the city, and her socioeconomic standing exceeded that of many other Black residents; at the same time, the account that emerged has also kept McGinness's contributions and memories in a physical place for generations of people in and around Charlottesville. "Rebecca Fuller McGinness seems to have been one of those people who had 'greatness thrust upon them,'" wrote Bryant, "The accumulation of small heroic deeds, one day at a time, the touching, influencing, and changing lives in positive ways—all merge to create a portrait of a great lady, a profoundly inspiring human being: Rebecca Fuller McGinness." Bryant not only captured the life of another Black woman who was heavily involved in education and community in Charlottesville, but she also tried to make sense of her own life and work.[41]

In 2003, Bryant sat for an interview with Alexandria Searls. At the time, Searls and Liz Sargent were interviewing individuals who had been associated with the Jefferson School. The fate of the Jefferson School building was in the balance; Searls and Sargent hoped to collect stories about the Jefferson School to ensure that the building would continue to stand. When asked about how she feels about the school, Bryant asserted, "I have warm feelings." Although Bryant's interview is shorter than those of other participants in the archive of interviews, her willingness to be involved in the project reveals a strong association with the Jefferson School and its meaning to the community—several decades after the school stopped educating Black youths, ultimately closing its doors. On the basis of the testimony of Bryant and others, the Jefferson School building became a hub for the city's nonprofit sector and, more important, a heritage center for Black life and history in the city. The Jefferson School Heritage Center continues that work today.[42]

Three years after publishing the book on McGinness, Bryant self-published *One Story About School Desegregation*. Only a few physical copies of the text exist; however, Bryant not only wrote about the specific case of school desegregation in Charlottesville, but she also situated the city's experience within broader political, social, and economic contexts. The text blends together well-known secondary sources on the *Brown* decision, such as Richard Kluger's *Simple Justice*, with evidence from oral history interviews with a range of stakeholders during the school desegregation era. It has a timeline, beginning in 1955 and ending in 1965, of major events in the "Desegregation of Schools in Charlottesville, Virginia" and transcripts with those aforementioned oral history interviews. This work provided yet another account into school desegregation in the South yet centered the voices of local participants in the process, including students. It also another entry into the personal archive that Bryant has cultivated over the course of several decades since her retirement.[43]

These efforts as a public intellectual by Bryant manifest an effort to witness, surface, and remember the Black educational heritage present in Charlottesville, Virginia. Whereas individuals such as Mary McCleod Bethune, Ida B. Wells, W. E. B. Du Bois, Carter G. Woodson, and, more recently, Cornel West have been thought of as public intellectuals, Bryant evinces a more local example of public intellectualism. Bryant sought not a national audience but a local one with her writing. In Charlottesville, Virginia, a city deeply immersed and invested in the hagiography of Thomas Jefferson and the heritage of the Lost Cause, Bryant's writing contributed to the making and remaking of the city in a

Black image. Certainly, she was not the only one before, during, or after her time to revise the city's history. However, she collected and cultivated a personal archive, which offers insight into her own experience not only as an educator but also as an individual with multiple identities experiencing school desegregation both at the K–12 and higher education levels.[44]

CONCLUSION

Beyond Charlottesville, Virginia, Florence C. Bryant may not be well known. However, Bryant's contributions to the local Black freedom struggle and schooling in Charlottesville were constant and are ongoing and significant. As an educator, Bryant sought improvement in her practice to better meet the needs of Black youths in her classes, which led to both onsite professional development in segregated and desegregated schools but also seeking additional education in graduate schools including the nearby historically white institution of higher education. Previous work on school desegregation has focused significant attention on how Black teachers were fired, displaced, and demoted. This is an important part of the story, but it's only part of the story. Tracing the contours of Bryant's life reveals the experience of Black graduate students desegregating predominantly white institutions of higher education during the postwar era, the experience of Black teachers navigating school desegregation, and how Black teachers made sense of their experiences while cultivating an archive through the written word.

This is one story of a Black woman educator in the South. However, Bryant's life reveals the many challenges facing, and opportunities available to, Black women educators, parents, and public intellectuals in the postwar era. Bryant's story embodies some of the prevailing themes within the recent literature on Black teacher activism, organizing, and protest. Although she did not participate in overt activism beyond the classroom, Bryant's pedagogical activism, including the participation and coordination of Negro History Week in segregated school settings and the continued promotion of learning Black history, manifests a commitment to counternarratives in the curriculum. Although she did not participate in overt activism beyond the classroom, Bryant's support of her children—and their peers—protesting at Lane High School shows a commitment to justice for Black students in the Charlottesville City Schools during the era of desegregation. Furthermore, although she did not participate in overt activism beyond the classroom, Bryant spent her retirement witnessing to all she had seen and done as an educator during the post–World War II era. All in all, Bryant was dedicated to "the highest of callings"—education and justice for Black Americans.

Hidden in Plain Sight

Black Educators in the "Militant Middle" of
Alabama's Municipal Civil Rights Battlegrounds

TONDRA L. LODER-JACKSON

In the Invited Distinguished Address to the meeting of the Society for the Psychological Study of Social Issues of the American Psychological Association (APA) in Washington, DC, in September 1967, Dr. Martin Luther King Jr. exhorted social scientists to use their professional acumen and privilege to tackle social ills, the most pressing of which were urban riots in the North.[1] He declared that the "most urgent task at hand" was a moderately aggressive strategy to ignite civic action that would compel the federal government to act more swiftly.[2] After acknowledging that mass nonviolent resistance was "effective in Montgomery, Birmingham, and Selma" in yielding landmark congressional legislation for Black Americans, King resigned himself to the reality that this strategy was ineffective in dismantling intransigent urban Northern problems. Consequently, he proposed: "I believe we will have to find the militant middle between riots on the one hand and weak and timid supplication for justice on the other hand. That middle ground, I believe, is civil disobedience. It can be aggressive but nonviolent; it can dislocate but not destroy. The specific planning will take some study and analysis to avoid mistakes of the past when it was employed on too small a scale and sustained too briefly."[3]

Beyond addressing urban riots, King set forth three key foci where social scientists could help advance civil rights:

1. Addressing the problem of Negro leadership—namely, social class divisions, studied by Black sociologist E. Franklin Frazier and others, that undermined coalition building.[4]
2. Initiating a scientific examination of political action, with voter enfranchisement as its focal point.
3. Understanding psychological and ideological changes in Negroes, which he described as "an inner transformation that is liberating them" from internalized racism.[5]

During this era, King's APA audience was undoubtedly overwhelmingly white and male.[6] He referenced psychologist Kenneth Clark in his address, who, in collaboration with his wife, psychologist Mamie Phipps Clark, tilted the landmark *Brown v. Board of Education* school desegregation Supreme Court case toward victory with their dolls test of Black children's racial identification and preference.[7] As APA's preeminent Black member—elected its first Black president in 1969—Clark likely extended King the invitation to speak. Notably, Clark had interviewed King on television in 1963 on the topic, "The Negro and the American Promise," secerning King's perspectives on the best course of action for Black liberation with those of Malcolm X and James Baldwin.[8] King clearly respected Clark as a socially conscious social scientist and co-champion in forging a new integrationist world order.

Given the juxtaposition of the APA audience's probable demographics and the racial repression of Black America during that time, King, perhaps understandably, positioned Black Americans passively in an address intended to spur psychologists to redirect their academic focus to the movement. However, there were, indeed, Black social scientists during that time beyond the Clarks and Frazier, who were deeply engaged in King's threefold foci both empirically and in practice. Many of them would have also identified as "teachers" whether they worked in schools or colleges and universities. In fact, it was common in many southern Black communities during this time for schoolteachers and administrators to be reverently referred to as professor or "'fessor," as well as to associate with college professors and administrators in Black teachers associations, suggesting their status as intellectuals regardless of their role as a teacher or administrator in a grade school or college.[9]

RECASTING BLACK EDUCATORS IN CIVIL RIGHTS HISTORIOGRAPHY

As do all the chapters in this volume, this chapter contributes to a fervent aim to revise the extant, primarily US Southern, civil rights historiography by unearthing data on an elaborate local, state, and national network of Black educators across schools, colleges, and communities that advanced the movement through their professionalism.[10] The chapter augments my previous historical case study of Black educators' relatively overlooked civil rights activism and resistance in Birmingham, Alabama, while also extending this investigation into the municipal civil rights bastions of Tuskegee, Montgomery, and Selma between the 1930s and 1960s.[11] Their unassuming contributions entailed: researching and documenting racial inequities in educational, social, economic, and political life; acknowledging and addressing intraracial hindrances to coalition building; teaching students and community members about Black history when it was discouraged; tacitly endorsing student protests; negotiating civil rights reforms with the white power structure behind the scenes; and marshaling a "collective cultural capital" by strategizing activism in Black teachers associations as well as in solidarity with civic, social, religious, and civil rights organizations.[12]

This scholarly endeavor is akin to collecting "grains of sand," to borrow, in homage, from a Black educator who self-effacingly applied this metaphor to her contributions to the civil rights movement.[13] During the height of Birmingham's movement, as a student, Evelyn Dilworth (now Dilworth-Williams) penned the poem, "The '63s," and later used it to help students in her own classroom make connections between the 1863 signing of the Emancipation Proclamation and the 1963 Children's March in Birmingham's Kelly Ingram Park, where Public Safety Commissioner Theophilus Eugene "Bull" Connor ordered his firemen and policemen to unleash water hoses and dogs on youth activists.[14] From her perspective, her pedagogical contributions seemed as infinitesimal as a grain of sand compared with the sacrifices that other civil rights leaders and foot soldiers were making on the front lines. Her metaphor hearkens the image of a jar filled with grains of soil from the ground where Black teacher Elizabeth Lawrence was lynched near Birmingham in 1933 for scolding white children who were rude to her on her way home. This jar, displayed among several others memorializing Alabama's lynching victims in the Equal Justice Initiative's Legacy Museum in Montgomery, is a harrowing yet sacred reminder of Black teachers' sacrifices—even martyrdom—in their long struggle for freedom and human dignity.[15]

Elizabeth Lawrence's jar-of-soil memorial is revelatory of Black educators as missing-persons cases in civil rights historiography.[16] These educators are seldom mentioned in seminal southern civil rights histories, and when they are, they are typically dismissed with "fear narratives" postulating their tepidness about getting involved in the movement for fear of losing their livelihoods.[17] For example, Glen Eskew portrayed Black educators in Birmingham who stood in the doorway to prevent students from skipping classes to participate in the Children's March.[18] However, in afterthought, he acknowledged that "[s]ome teachers joined their pupils in protest."[19] In his critically acclaimed examination of Mississippi civil rights struggles, John Dittmer concluded that "as a group, black teachers in the 1950s refused to take a stand and the movement of the early 1960s passed them by."[20] Similarly, Idus Newby proposed that the civil rights movement in South Carolina happened despite the appreciable involvement of Black schools and colleges.[21] Adam Fairclough heralded teachers' behind-the-scenes contributions to the movement yet surmised that they were averse to protesting publicly because "the disruption of school routine and discipline violated the professional instincts of many black educators."[22] These portrayals tell only a part of the story of Black educators' civil rights legacy.

Truth be told, being a Black teacher during the Jim Crow era was a symbol of middle-class status, self-respect, and learnedness that inherently threatened

Soil Collection Jar of Elizabeth Lawrence, The Legacy Museum,
Montgomery Alabama. Courtesy of Equal Justice Initiative.

white supremacy and could engender hostility and violence.[23] At the extreme,
Black teacher activists such as Harry T. and Harriette Moore in Brevard County,
Florida, were killed when their home was bombed by the Ku Klux Klan on
Christmas night in 1951—the day of their twenty-fifth wedding anniversary.[24]
At the lesser but, nonetheless, demoralizing extreme, Black teacher activists
were fired, were demoted, were denied promotions, and had their tenure re-
voked.[25] Therefore, conventional definitions of activism—marches, sit-ins, and
boycotts—must be interrogated and expanded to make room for activism and
resistance enacted through educators' professionalism.[26] Using their professionalism in this manner risked their livelihoods—and even their very lives.[27]
In fact, King was known to assure Black professionals, particularly those with
celebrity, of their value to the movement whenever they expressed their chagrin
for not being actively involved on the front lines like him and other activists. He
affirmed that their professionalism and celebrity alone were a worthy platform
for advancing the aims of the movement.[28]

FOUR MUNICIPAL CIVIL RIGHTS BATTLEGROUNDS

These four municipal cases of Tuskegee, Montgomery, Birmingham, and Selma
portray how Black educators advanced the movement, perhaps more so than
King realized, in spite of crossing paths with them in all four cities and addressed his threefold foci concerning Black leadership, political action, and psychological and ideological changes among Black Americans. They sometimes
did so through deliberate "study and analysis" to avoid the mistakes of their
predecessors.[29] These municipalities were selected because they are deemed

pivotal Alabama civil rights battlegrounds, although not all share the same notoriety. Their municipal demographics are distinctive. Two are somewhat rural
and intertwined governmentally with their respective county seats: Selma in
Dallas County and Tuskegee in Macon County. The other two are larger cities,
Birmingham and Montgomery, the latter of which is the state's capital and a former capital of the Confederacy during the Civil War. Today, all four cities have
a majority-Black population. To the extent that Black mayoralty is deemed a
marker of racial progress, notably, two of these municipalities first elected Black
mayors in 1972 (Tuskegee) and 1979 (Birmingham), whereas the other two did
so only recently, in 2000 (Selma) and 2019 (Montgomery).

All four municipalities are homes to historically Black colleges and universities (HBCUs) that were significant to the movement, although Selma University,
historically a seminary training ground for Black male ministers and layper-
sons, was arguably the least activist compared with Alabama State College (now
Alabama State University in Montgomery), Tuskegee Institute (now University),
and Miles College (city of Fairfield near Birmingham). Traditionally overshadowed and intermittently honorably mentioned in US Southern civil rights
historiography, faculty activism at HBCUs (sometimes supported by Black
college presidents) is crucial to understanding these cities' civil rights histori-
ographies.[30] Furthermore, the presence of thriving state Black teachers associations—in this case, the Alabama State Teachers Association (ASTA)—served as
an instrumental intermediary for mobilizing Black schoolteachers, principals,
college faculty, administrators, and personnel from across the state.[31]

These narratives are presented in chronological order demarcating the
timeframes of Black educators' most visible and sustained participation in the
Alabama movement.[32] Each one underscores a distinctive brand of activism that
typified their involvement; namely, democratizing Black communities, boycotting buses and insisting on dignity for its Black riders, transgressing professional boundaries expected of public schoolteachers, and marching alongside
fellow teachers and civil rights leaders for voting rights. Black educators who
made especially noteworthy contributions—Charles G. Gomillion (Tuskegee);
Mary Fair Burks, Jo Ann Robinson, and Lawrence Reddick (Montgomery);
Lucinda Robey and Lucius Pitts (Birmingham); and Reverend Frederick D.
Reese (Selma)—are highlighted, with their fellow educators' supporting roles
and collective cultural capital duly recognized.[33]

TUSKEGEE EDUCATORS DEMOCRATIZING

Tuskegee's role in Alabama's civil rights movement is overshadowed by those of
its sister cities, Selma and Montgomery.[34] The city is located forty miles east of
Montgomery and approximately seventy-seven miles east of Selma in central
Alabama. One of its most famous civil rights heroines, Rosa Parks, was born

there yet is fatefully linked to the Montgomery bus boycott. Tuskegee's renown tends to be intertwined with the legacies of Booker T. Washington, the founding principal of Tuskegee Institute, and the belatedly decorated heroes of World War II, the Tuskegee Airmen. It has also drawn infamy for the US government–sponsored Tuskegee Syphilis Study of indigent Black men without their knowledge or consent between 1932 and 1972.[35]

Charles G. Gomillion

The life of one Tuskegee professor, Dr. Charles G. Gomillion, spanned all these historical markers, yet his contributions and those of his pedagogical contemporaries remain woefully unsung. His contributions to the civil rights movement, as well as those of his fellow Tuskegee educators, encompassed all three of King's foci with a primary emphasis on voting rights. To be effective, they quickly determined that their enfranchisement mission had to be deeply intertwined with addressing intraracial class tensions and inspiring psychological and ideological changes in Black Americans. Tuskegee's Black community was unlike many other communities in Alabama during that time, in that it did not depend heavily on local whites for employment or income, given its residents' employment at Tuskegee Institute and the Veterans Administration (VA) Hospital. In fact, the formal education of Black people in Macon County exceeded that of whites because of the influence of Tuskegee Institute. The *Chicago Daily Tribune* once stated: "Any educational test for voting, no matter how rigorous, if fairly applied, would probably result in the enfranchising of more Negroes than whites in Macon County."[36] This cadre of professionals unceremoniously laid the groundwork in the 1930s and 1940s for subsequent high-profile civil rights events that came to fruition in the 1960s—namely, *Gomillion v. Lightfoot*, a landmark unanimous 1960 Supreme Court decision that helped pave the way for the 1965 Voting Rights Act.[37] To understand the significance of this case, one must trace Gomillion's biography in tandem with the painstaking efforts of Tuskegee Institute faculty, local schoolteachers, Black professionals at the VA Hospital, and community residents to establish a premiere civic organization dedicated to defeating Jim Crow segregation in Tuskegee–Macon County.[38]

Formative Years

Gomillion enrolled in Paine College, an HBCU in Augusta, Georgia, at age sixteen to complete his secondary education and obtain a postsecondary degree shortly thereafter. A white Methodist teacher and missionary—one whom he recalled as the first white person who treated him as a person—encouraged him to become a teacher. However, Gomillion dropped out of school after two years to support his parents, then married, and did a stint at the US Post Office in Philadelphia. After teaching school briefly in Georgia, he returned to Paine in the fall of 1926 to complete his college degree, switching his major to sociology.

Reserved and professorial in demeanor, after his first wife left the family, which he blamed partly on his intense disposition, Gomillion raised their two young daughters on his own for several years after obtaining a teaching position at Tuskegee. Always mindful of being a role model to his daughters and students, Gomillion avoided smoking, drinking, and gambling. Before his departure for Tuskegee, he confided with someone that "Booker Washington had taught blacks how to make a living," but that he "was going to teach them how to live."[39] He eventually remarried, and his second wife worked alongside him in his civic endeavors.

A group of schoolteachers whom Gomillion taught during summer school in 1929 influenced his thinking about civic involvement.[40] These teachers detailed the abysmal racial inequities in Alabama's public education system. Their revelations inspired Gomillion to pursue a yearlong leave from Tuskegee Institute in 1933 to extend his sociology studies at Fisk University. There, he was mentored by Charles S. Johnson, a leading figure in the Harlem Renaissance and a race man trained in the tradition of the University of Chicago sociology school of thought.[41] Gomillion admired Johnson's ease in associating with whites. He acknowledged, "I got from him some idea about how a group would need to work to get the kinds of help necessary to improve educational opportunities for Negroes."[42] Johnson stirred Gomillion's change of heart about Booker T. Washington's accommodationism. Gomillion had been swayed by W. E. B. Du Bois's diatribes about Washington in the National Association for the Advancement of Colored People's (NAACP) magazine, *The Crisis*. On the contrary, Johnson was an ardent supporter of Washington, publicly defending him in Black media. As Gomillion learned more about the racial oppression of Tuskegee–Macon County, he concluded sympathetically that Washington was constrained in being "assertive about black rights."[43]

On returning to Tuskegee in fall 1934, Gomillion moved to the Institute's college department to teach sociology. He worked as an assistant to Monroe Work, who directed the Institute's Department of Records and Research. Work was responsible for assembling data for the Institute's annual report on lynching and for the *Negro Yearbook*.[44] In this position, Gomillion learned important lessons about the power of documenting educational inequities in wielding a battle to dismantle Jim Crow.

Tuskegee Men's Club

Gomillion's most consequential early civic affiliation was the Tuskegee Men's Club, an organization formed in 1910 and made up of male faculty and administrators. These men were approximately the same age as Gomillion or younger and, like him, came of age and attained their education outside Tuskegee.[45] The Club included Tuskegee Institute economics professor Hollis Price; dean of the business school, James Johnson; psychology professor Alonzo David Sr.; and other Tuskegee staff and local professionals. The Club's purpose was to improve public services in the surrounding areas of the campus. These men took pride in keeping the grounds of the school immaculate with truly little help from the white-led government, despite their appeals for assistance. One of their accomplishments included founding the Tuskegee Institute Federal Credit Union, which helped Black Tuskegeeans avoid indebtedness to white business owners. However, a far more vexing issue than lobbying for better public services was the disenfranchisement of Black Tuskegeeans, particularly its middle-class professionals.

Gomillion encouraged others, especially Black educators, to register to vote and pursued this goal personally as early as his 1934 return to campus. However, he was not successful registering himself until 1939, when he met the requirement of finding a second white person to vouch for him.[46] To register, he had to pay the back poll taxes owed for the years 1928–1939. He was not alone in facing such barriers. Gomillion and his fellow educators understood that the major hindrances to enfranchisement occurred at the local level at the behest of the notorious county Board of Registrars. This Board "exercised great discretion in deciding whether an applicant met the requirement of either property or literacy."[47] Gomillion documented some of these barriers in the *Journal of Negro Education*, meticulously tabulating the disproportionality in the number of Black registered voters compared with their majority population in the city and county.[48] His major premise was "voting is the most vital of the civil rights because upon it rests all of the other basic rights."[49] Furthermore, he advocated for an educated voting populace, noting in an interview: "We were interested in increasing numbers of persons registered to vote, but I was of the opinion that we needed not only voters, but knowledgeable voters, and that was the reason for this so-called responsible citizenship course in political science."[50]

Tuskegee Civic Association

After a name change and an expansion of the club in 1941 to include the wives of the male members as well as other women, the Tuskegee Civic Association (TCA) was born. The new name reflected Gomillion's commitment to the idea of civic democracy that he taught in both his secondary and postsecondary school classrooms. For Gomillion, "civic democracy was color-blind democracy, a concept that Gomillion took largely from his high school civics textbook."[51] However, he understood clearly that democracy was not viewed as such by

Tuskegee's white segregationists. Therefore, the TCA launched the "Crusade for Citizenship" in Alabama, which included a multipronged strategy to promote democracy in the Black community. The TCA addressed the "political apathy of many Negroes" who had grown weary with making multiple futile attempts to register to vote.[52] These strategies included appeals to professionals, especially schoolteachers and ministers. The TCA's 1949 slogan was "every eligible teacher and preacher a voter" where members asked schoolteachers pointedly: "Can you continue to teach good citizenship to Negro boys and girls without making an effort to obtain first-class citizenship for yourself, your colleagues, and/or the parents of the children whom you teach?"[53]

Gomillion, who served as the TCA's president between 1941–1945 and 1951–1970, was supported by other Tuskegee educators such as Frank Toland Sr., who chaired Tuskegee Institute's Department of History between 1968 and 1984 and emerged as a TCA leader during that time.[54] Also, TCA member Jessie Parkhurst Guzman, a former historian and director of the Department of Records and Research at Tuskegee Institute, meticulously documented the history and activities of the Association in her book *Crusade for Civic Democracy: The Story of the Tuskegee Civic Association, 1941–1970*.[55] The TCA's major activities included civic education, Negro History Week observance, weekly mass meetings, voter registration, legal cases, and several other activities involving political education, economic education, community welfare programs, and collaboration with other civic educational organizations and agencies. Civic education was the cornerstone of the TCA, with monthly Sunday meetings featuring "the churches as classrooms."[56] Guests who spoke on civic, political, and racial reconciliation matters were invited to speak.

After making several impassioned tactical appeals to the Board of Registrars and elected officials that went unheeded, the TCA organized Black citizens to boycott businesses owned and operated by segregationists in response to a recent gerrymander bill intended to dilute the strength of the Black vote.[57] The boycott was labeled a "selective buying campaign" to circumvent the state's antiboycott law.[58] Tuesday evening weekly mass meetings served as "an instrument through which aggrieved citizens could discuss their plight and harness their efforts in their attempt to cause the legislative act which gerrymandered Negroes out of the city of Tuskegee to be rescinded or repealed."[59] These mass meetings were convened primarily to address State Senator Samuel Engelhardt's Senate Bill Number 291, which "proposed to gerrymander Tuskegee in such a manner that 3,000 of the 5,397 Negro citizens would lose urban residence, while all of the 1,310 White citizens would retain theirs."[60] Furthermore, the bill would not only reduce the size of the city but would also change its shape from a simple four-sided rectangle to a complex, twenty-eight-sided plane. Legislators and other public officials said this exclusion was necessary to 'prevent [Negroes] from gaining prominence at the polls.'"[61]

Churches and community members helped fund the TCA's legal efforts through their donations at weekly mass meetings and special programs "plus donations made by friends of the movement."[62] Gomillion received support for his case from across the country, including a check for one hundred dollars from Dr. King after his guest-speaking engagement at a TCA mass meeting in July 1957.[63] Beyond high-profile civil rights leaders such as King; Reverend Ralph Abernathy, a confidant of King and leading figure in the Southern Christian Leadership Conference (SCLC); and Reverend Fred Shuttlesworth, the pastor of Bethel Baptist Church in Birmingham and foremost leader of his city's movement, other mass meeting speakers included a notable number of Black schoolteachers and college administrators and personnel, including Selma University president Dr. James H. Owens; faculty and administrators from Alabama State College; and faculty and college presidents from HBCUs such as Morehouse College and Howard University.[64]

In addition to the activities of the TCA, other Tuskegee Institute educators such as Lewis Wade Jones documented the volatile tenor of race relations through research.[65] Jones, a sociology professor, had pioneered studies of Black people in the rural South. To seek a better understanding of white perspectives about Tuskegee's race relations for a booklet that he was writing for the Anti-Defamation League of B'nai B'rith, Jones commissioned a questionnaire and hired white graduate students from the University of Alabama to interview ninety-five white Tuskegeeans. The respondents brazenly expressed their hatred, fears, and disdain for Black progress. Many whites were convinced by Engelhardt of Gomillion's Communist ties. As a remedy for Tuskegee's ills, one respondent declared, "Get rid of Gomillion."[66] A college-educated Methodist housewife retorted cavalierly, "We could start [with] hanging Gomillion," as a remedy to problems. Another respondent surmised: "remove all Negro agitators from jobs at [the] V. A. Hospital and Tuskegee Institute and the rest will take care of itself."[67]

Intergenerational Tensions

Through the lens of presentism, and even the historicism of comparing pre- and post-*Brown* activism, a crusade for civic education seems insipid compared with the dramatic direct action of boycotts, sit-ins, marches, and tactically instigated arrests that characterized the 1950s and 1960s—but this was far from being the case. Gomillion was investigated by the Federal Bureau of Investigation (FBI) in 1942, under the suspicion that his civil rights activism was influenced by Communism.[68] The FBI informant who took notes at a TCA meeting noted that the "old school type of Negro leader such as Booker T. Washington and George Washington Carver who believed in conservative progress . . . by achievement and meritorious service, was passing out of control at the Institute and a 'modern' school of thought has been gradually replacing the old.'"[69] The FBI informant named Gomillion and Tuskegee Institute president Frederick Patterson, as a part of this "modern group" that was pushing for full and equal rights. The TCA's office and a Tuskegee printing shop were also raided by the Alabama Attorney General and his assistants, who seized records, membership lists, and other materials related to the TCA and NAACP operations.[70]

Although Gomillion filled a critical civic leadership void in Tuskegee Institute's post-Washingtonian era, Tuskegee president Luther H. Foster, who led the Institute during the tumultuous 1950s and 1960s, supported his students, faculty, and staff activism more so than not. He shepherded the campus through the death of one of his student activists, Samuel Younge Jr., who was killed by a white man while allegedly trying to use a whites-only restroom in 1966.[71] Student activist Gwendolyn Patton characterized Tuskegee as more of a bourgeois than an activist institution, recollecting how she and other student activists nudged Patterson to do more for the movement; for example, feeding marchers on campus during the Selma-to-Montgomery March.[72] However, she acknowledged that Tuskegee's curriculum reflected a diverse range of Black intellectual and political thought that inspired her activism as well as that of other students. She recalled: "Negro history was compulsory. So when you read Du Bois, whatever his limitations, or Booker T. Washington, whatever his limitations, how are you supposed to come out of that? I mean, I thought education was to inform you and change your behavior, And so, it changed our behavior to be more revolutionary."[73] Patton went on to acknowledge unequivocally: "This institution ha[d] prepared us to be Freedom Fighters."[74]

However, there were mounting tensions between students and administrators at Tuskegee during the 1960s. Over time, TCA's strategies began to vex student activists in the Tuskegee Institute Advancement League, who advocated more direct action to break Jim Crow's hold on their futures.[75] Impatience was expressed even by veteran activists such as Detroit Lee, who—after returning from World War II, and although civil in his interactions with Gomillion—had once advocated the establishment of a NAACP branch to upstage the TCA when he felt TCA was moving too slowly on civil rights.[76] In the 1960s, Lee pressed the TCA to support his school desegregation lawsuit on behalf of his children and other students, but Gomillion was reluctant to redirect the organization's efforts away from voting rights. Gomillion eventually joined ranks with Lee after *Gomillion* was decided favorably, and *Lee v. Macon County Board of Education* (1964) became a landmark federal district court ruling resulting in mandatory school desegregation statewide.[77]

Tuskegee Institute was not the only HBCU in Alabama where tensions between administrators, faculty activists, and student activists flared around optimal strategies for advancing social change. Alabama State College (ASC) was at the forefront of Montgomery's civil rights battles. ASC, the state's oldest public HBCU, has institutional roots as a teacher preparation school, drawing aspiring Black teachers from across the state.[78] Even after ASC broadened its focus to include other majors, Jim Crow still circumscribed Black professional opportunities to teaching. Many of Alabama's renowned civil rights leaders were educated at ASC, including Montgomery attorney Fred Gray and Selma teacher activist Reverend Frederick D. Reese (discussed later in this chapter). Reese said his professors inspired his involvement in the movement through their classroom dialogues.[79] Many ASC faculty and students were actively involved in the Montgomery bus boycott challenging the view that middle-class professionals would not risk their livelihoods for the movement. Notably, several women faculty members, led by ASC faculty Mary Fair Burks and Jo Ann Robinson, were instrumental in strategizing the bus boycott through their political and civic organizing efforts outside of the college.

Mary Fair Burks, Jo Ann Robinson, and the Women's Political Council

The Montgomery bus boycott cannot be fully understood without chronicling the history of the Women's Political Council (WPC). Its founder, Mary Fair Burks, once distinguished between a trailblazer who pioneered the civil rights movement and a torchbearer who "follows the trailblazer imparting tested knowledge or truth provided originally by the pioneer in its rudimentary form."[80] According to Burks, "Rosa Parks, Jo Ann Robinson, and members of the WPC were trailblazers. Martin Luther King, Jr. was a torchbearer."[81] She praised Parks for challenging classist perspectives that undermined intraracial coalition building, noting that her arrest on a Montgomery bus "penetrated the indifference of the middle class and shook the passivity of the masses."[82]

Inspired by a fiery sermon delivered by her activist pastor, Vernon Johns, Burks organized and served as founding president of the WPC between 1946 and 1950. Burks recalled, "The Women's Political Council was the outgrowth of scars I suffered as a result of racism as well as my desire to arouse black middle-class women to do something about the things they could change in segregated Montgomery."[83] Underscoring precisely how prescient the WPC was in pioneering civil rights advancements, she noted: "*Brown v. the Board of Education* was just an idea being discussed by lawyers of the NAACP. *Plessy v. Ferguson* remained unchallenged in the deep South. Yet these forty women were willing [sic] try to improve conditions for blacks."[84] The women at the initial meeting of the WPC bonded around their collective experiences of being demeaned on Montgomery's buses. They agreed on three strategies: political action, protest, and education and decided that teaching younger generations of Black Montgomery students would be central to their strategy. Although tension arose around what to name the organization—the WPC versus the more "neutral-sounding Women's Human Relations Council"—the WPC barely edged out the latter much to Burks's satisfaction.[85]

One of the WPC's early initiatives was Negro Youth City, a civic education program patterned after Youth City sponsored for white high school students. Students modeled municipal and state governance structures and simulated leadership as the governor, state legislators, the mayor, and commissioners. However, Negro Youth City's import far exceeded teaching Black students about governance. The program was what Burks referred to as "a subversive tactic" to teach Black youths "what democracy could and should mean."[86] The WPC felt vindicated in their efforts when they witnessed the students they mentored registering to vote when they reached age twenty-one, actively engaging in politics, and becoming attorneys, judges, and elected officials in Montgomery.[87]

Jo Ann Robinson, an ASC professor of English, who assumed the helm of the organization as its second president in 1950, was instrumental in taking the WPC's long-deliberated strategies to boycott buses to the next level. In fact, the WPC had entertained a bus boycott of its own prior to both Parks's defiance and the bus arrest of teenager Claudette Colvin.[88] Robinson, like Burks, "had experienced her own humiliation on a Montgomery bus in 1949."[89] She was also a co-leader of the Montgomery Improvement Association (MIA), over which King was elected to preside at twenty-six years old.[90] Immediately after Parks's arrest, Robinson and civil rights attorney Fred Gray strategized a plan for the boycott.[91] In concert with the WPC's previous boycott deliberations, Robinson corralled WPC members and ASC students to assist her with mimeographing at her office and distributing approximately fifty-two thousand leaflets calling for a bus boycott.[92]

ASC President Harper Councill Trenholm's Dubious Legacy

Robinson's use of ASC resources to mimeograph leaflets for the boycott was a point of contention in her otherwise cordial relationship with the college's president, Harper Councill Trenholm.[93] Robinson regarded Trenholm's wife, Portia, as a close friend, and she made many overtures to keep Trenholm abreast of her involvement in the boycott through Portia. She recalled that, although "Dr. Trenholm did not participate personally in the boycott . . . he was mentally and spiritually involved—and deeply so!"[94] Robinson also acknowledged that Trenholm supported the movement financially, particularly for people who lost their jobs because of their participation in the movement. She explained: "He never went onto the housetop and screamed of what his contributions had been, but his actions, his constant advice, his donations, and his guidance amounted to much more than dollars and cents."[95] Even after his terse meeting with Robinson about mimeographing leaflets on campus, she maintained that she "worked on the boycott with Dr. Trenholm's approval."[96]

Robinson had the benefit of reflecting on her relationship with the Trenholms in her memoir after much time had passed. In contrast, King's last words on Trenholm's legacy, penned in the heat of the Montgomery movement, were far less sympathetic.[97] Perhaps because he felt kindred to him as a fellow Morehouse alumnus and because of Trenholm's role as a deacon at King's Dexter Avenue Baptist Church. By all accounts, Trenholm's relationship with King was initially amicable. He invited King to give the baccalaureate sermon at ASC's commencement in 1955. King also agreed to speak and accepted a dinner invitation at Trenholm's home before the ceremony.

After sit-ins began in Montgomery during 1960, Alabama Governor John Patterson threatened to withhold state funds and fire Trenholm if he would not quell ASC students and faculty activism. By some accounts, Trenholm, with support from ASTA, attempted to subvert Governor Patterson's demands that he deter student activism.[98] However, he eventually yielded to Patterson's demands and threatened to expel or probate any students and fire any faculty who demonstrated.[99]

King voiced dismay about the governor's threat, particularly because of his friendships with Burks and Robinson, both congregants of his church, and ASC faculty activist Lawrence Reddick. Reddick was a confidant of King's who wrote speeches for him, and both participated in and documented the unfolding of the Montgomery movement.[100] Reddick and Robinson served together on the MIA, where they, along with junior ASC history faculty member Norman Walton, collaborated on MIA's history committee. The committee's charge was to ensure "a reliable and orderly record of the bus protest plus an accurate record of the origin, growth and future development of the Montgomery improvement Association."[101] In support of their collective scholarly and activist contributions to the Montgomery movement, King called Trenholm's actions "cowardly" and expressed his concerns in a letter to Burks:

> I had hoped that Dr. Trenholm would emerge from this total situation as a national hero. If he would only stand up to the Governor and the Board of Education and say that he cannot in all good conscience fire the eleven faculty members who have committed no crime or act of sedition, he would gain support over the nation that he never dreamed of.[102]

However, King's exhortations were ignored. Patterson openly chastised Trenholm for permitting "'agitators' to run the school."[103] In 1960, Patterson and the State Board of Education launched an investigation of ASC, which led to Reddick's firing, Robinson's and Burks's resignations, and Trenholm's forced retirement.[104] Sadly, Trenholm died three years later at age sixty-three.[105]

This surely was not the epitaph that Trenholm desired after such a long legacy of admirable leadership. Born on June 16, 1900, in Tuscumbia, Alabama, Trenholm succeeded his father as president of ASC in 1926. More sympathetic accounts of his life emphasize his legacy as a Negro Renaissance man who innovated a "second curriculum that emphasized idealism and encouraged race consciousness undergirded by history."[106] Trenholm has been portrayed as a college president who "transformed ASU into an oasis of race consciousness even as it was simultaneously enveloped by hostility and racial violence."[107] He and Carter G. Woodson forged a long-lasting friendship and alliance that helped to infuse an incomparably comprehensive Black history curriculum throughout schools and colleges during the first half of the twentieth century.[108] According to historian Jelani Favors, "When Woodson published his *Negro History Bulletin* in May 1937, Trenholm wrote, 'I think that it will be very serviceable and will be started at a very opportune time because there is a mounting enthusiasm now for this approach to Negro history.'"[109] However, the tenor of the times had changed toward the end of his leadership tenure, with successively younger generations of Black Montgomery residents calling for bolder direct action. Trenholm found himself caught between a previous era characterized by subtler strategies for change and a new one that demanded more personal and professional sacrifices for the cause. The fallout at ASC—by Robinson's account "it lost many of its best professors, student enrollment plummeted, and the school lost its accreditation and faced censure from the AAUP for two decades for its violation of academic freedom and due process"—surely took its toll on Trenholm personally and professionally.[110]

BIRMINGHAM EDUCATORS TRANSGRESSING

Compared with Black educators in Tuskegee and Montgomery, those in Birmingham especially tend to be cast as too fearful to participate visibly in the movement. In worst-case scenarios, they have been portrayed as obstacles to the movement, typified by Parker High School principal R. C. Johnson's efforts to prevent his students from skipping school to participate in the Children's March.[111] One exception to this fear narrative is Lucinda Robey, who challenged the view that middle-class professionals in Birmingham were categorically averse to participating in the movement. In a vein similar to Montgomery's WPC, she strove to change the psychological and ideological perspectives of Black youths about their treatment as second-class citizens.

Lucinda Robey and the Alabama Christian Movement for Human Rights

Lucinda Robey was a highly regarded school principal and ASTA member.[112] Fellow teacher activist Carlton Reese, renown for founding the Alabama Christian Movement for Human Rights (ACMHR) choir that inspired the songs of the Birmingham movement, recalled that Robey was one of the few teachers whom he remembered playing a visible role in the movement, noting that she "didn't give a rip" about white retaliation.[113] According to Reese, Robey "knew her rights" and "she was there at the movement, day in and day out."[114] Voted Teacher of the Year by her community and Principal of the Year by the Birmingham Progressive Education Association, Robey served as local and state NAACP youth director and spoke at the Alabama State Sixth Annual Conference of the NAACP, headlined by the organization's executive director, Walter White.[115] In this capacity, she established youth councils throughout the state of Alabama, preparing fertile ground for mentoring emerging student activists. She was also a guest speaker for the TCA's special anniversary program on June 28, 1960.[116]

Notably, Robey was the sole woman listed on the charter of the ACMHR. She was highly regarded by Reverend Fred Shuttlesworth, founder of the organization and considered by many observers as the foremost leader of the Birmingham civil rights movement.[117] He described her as a friend who was "very aggressive and progressive."[118] Shuttlesworth recalled that, during a meeting that he and Robey had with civil rights attorney Arthur Shores, a former teacher and an ASTA member, to discuss Alabama's recent injunction against the NAACP operating in the state, Robey was adamant about determining a workaround to continue resistance efforts, even if it meant going to jail.[119] Shuttlesworth once cautioned her about her public activism: "Lucinda, you can't teach school from jail." She replied, "I'll do what I can do."[120] Robey invited Shuttlesworth to speak at her elementary school where he marveled at her command of the classroom. He was blushful when recalling her public devotion that there were only two men in her life whom she was willing to follow: her husband, Bruce Brown Robey, and Shuttlesworth, whom she christened, "The Black Prince of Peace."[121] Shuttlesworth lauded her as "one of the greatest women I ever met."[122]

Robey defied Jim Crow laws by supporting her students' decisions to protest in the streets without reporting them to school authorities for suspension and expulsion. While serving as a principal in the Birmingham Public Schools, Robey led an SCLC youth group. Former Birmingham student protestor Annetta Streeter Gary recalled that Robey would drive her and other students to mass meetings if they did not have transportation.[123] Undoubtedly in retaliation to her activism, the Birmingham Board of Education denied her resources to run her school.

Other teachers and civil rights activists admired Robey as well. Former Birmingham Public Schools teacher Lillie Fincher remembered Robey as a role model whose car "always had her toothbrush and a change of underwear in it just in case she had to go to jail."[124] It was Robey who strengthened Fincher's resolve when she fretted about losing her job because of her NAACP membership. According to Fincher, Robey attended "every one of those [mass] meetings at night."[125] When the school district refused to grant Robey a secretary to support her in her role as principal, Fincher recalled that she paid for her own secretary and purchased school supplies from both her and her husband's (who was also an educator) salaries. Robey's civil rights comrade, Lola Hendricks, remembered that "Robey was under constant threat of the loss of her job but was bold."[126] Hendricks also recalled that Robey threatened to sue the school superintendent if he fired her from her job.[127]

Miles College President Lucius Pitts and Faculty Activists

Miles College president Dr. Lucius Pitts and his faculty and students also led the charge for a pivotal precursor to the 1963 Birmingham civil rights strategies.[128] Pitts served as president between 1961 and 1971. He grew up in a sharecropping family and was ordained as a Colored Methodist Episcopal preacher. He once declined King's and Mississippi civil rights activist Ella Baker's requests to lead the Atlanta chapter of the SCLC. Like other teacher activists, Pitts had ties to Black teachers associations, serving as the executive secretary of the Georgia Teachers and Educators Association and president of the national American Teachers Association.

Similar to what was done in Tuskegee, Pitts inspired and endorsed both his students' and faculty members' involvement in an Easter season selective buying campaign. In 1962, Miles faculty and student activists strategized a campaign to stop doing business with white merchants who refused to hire Black sales clerks or get rid of segregated bathrooms and water fountains. Local Black residents were urged to spend their money selectively only in those business establishments where they would not be discriminated against. As one flier proclaimed: "Join the fight for freedom. Let's celebrate a true Easter by not buying at stores which uphold segregation, discrimination, and inequality."[129]

The selective buying campaign had mixed results. Student activists had demanded the hiring of Black retail workers, equal job opportunities in civil service careers, and desegregation of lunch counters, restrooms, and all drinking fountains. On the positive side, the selective buying campaign was credited with engaging 90 percent of the Black community at the pinnacle of the campaign, putting a major dent in pre-Easter shopping with sales reportedly 12 percent lower than the previous years. In response, Shuttlesworth used the selective buying campaign to persuade Martin Luther King and other SCLC members to select Birmingham as the site for "Project C," which stood for the "confrontation" that would ensue between activists and Bull Connor in Kelly Ingram Park.[130] Although a significant number of Black citizens supported the campaign, Frank Dukes recalled that they had a little trouble convincing some teachers "who dressed sharp" to stop buying attire at their favorite shops.[131] In retaliation to the campaign, some of the few Black retail workers at white-owned stores were fired, and segregated water fountain signs were reinstalled.[132]

Similar to other larger-than-life figures, Pitts was "different things to different people."[133] By some accounts, he was viewed as an activist; by other accounts, he was viewed as an accommodationist who was cautious about some of the direct-action strategies planned by Birmingham's civil rights leaders and some radical factions among his own student body. Although he capitalized on Miles College's selective buying campaign, even Shuttlesworth equivocated on Pitts's legacy, noting that Pitts never said anything against him or the movement but also never stood out too publicly because he had real fears of losing donors who kept Miles College afloat.[134] In his own words, ultimately, Pitts espoused that "a Black college president has to encourage activism and create a climate where it can come out."[135]

SELMA TEACHERS MARCHING

Perhaps the most dramatic display of Black educators' collective heroism during the movement occurred on January 22, 1965, in Selma, Alabama, when an unassuming group of teachers marched to fight for their voting rights.[136] Led by Reverend Frederick D. Reese, a science and mathematics teacher who headed the Selma City Teachers Association and the Dallas County Voters League, by varying accounts, an estimated one hundred to three hundred Black teachers marched from Clark Elementary School to the Dallas County Courthouse, resolute on registering to vote.[137]

Reese and his fellow Selma activists and teachers fought the same battles as Tuskegee's and Montgomery's educators to break Jim Crow's stronghold in the arenas of voting, education, and other facets of public life. Selma educators, like their counterparts in Tuskegee, Montgomery, and Birmingham, had made several attempts to register to vote before their courageous act of solidarity. Selma's teachers also faced a skeptical Black community that could not fathom that they would put their livelihoods on the line in this manner. Even Reese once acknowledged that Black teachers in Selma "had somewhat divorced themselves from participating in the movement at that point, and the common laborers and . . . people who were workers were carrying the main load for demonstrations and marches at that time."[138] Using a strategy similar to that of the TCA, Reese posed this penetrating question to Selma's Black teachers: "How can you teach citizenship and you're not a first-class citizen yourself?"[139] Reese was also inspired by the Montgomery bus boycott.[140] He recalled, "It was very motivating to see what was happening in Montgomery and to see the courage that took place on the part of Dr. King and those people in Montgomery."[141] Reese understood the economic impact of teachers in Selma–Dallas County, notably that "the absence of 'teacher dollars' would have caused an economic collapse in the community."[142]

The Selma teachers marched while under the threat of being fired by their school board. In fact, the white superintendent of the Selma City Schools was reportedly inside the courthouse but never made a public appearance during the protest. Dallas County sheriff Jim Clark shouted his characteristically combative command: "Get off my steps!" The teachers made three attempts to enter the courthouse. Reese endured violent assaults from Clark as he tried to walk into the courthouse to register. Sheriff Clark poked Reese's fellow teacher, Lawrence Huggins, in the stomach with his nightstick. Although Reese and the teachers were pressed to divert their march toward Brown Chapel African Methodist Episcopal (AME) Church, their brave protest spurred other groups of Black professionals to organize to support voting rights in Alabama. Reese recalled: "There were all kinds of groups after the teachers march. Then the undertakers got a group and they marched. The beauticians got a group; they marched. Everybody marched after the teachers marched because the teachers had more influence than they ever dreamed in the community."[143] Reese, who had his salary cut and was eventually fired from his teaching position (although later reinstated with honor), proclaimed this teacher-led demonstration the first of its kind during the movement.[144] His fellow teachers at R. B. Hudson High School refused to sign their employment contracts in protest of his firing. In turn, ASTA influenced the National Education Association to pledge money in support of these teachers, but Reese dissuaded the teachers from sacrificing their jobs and livelihoods, opting to stand alone in his termination.[145] Notably, the Selma Teachers March preceded the original attempted Selma-to-Montgomery March (also called Bloody Sunday) by six weeks. Some of the teachers who participated in the Selma Teachers March also marched in Bloody Sunday.[146]

Much like Shuttlesworth, Reese tends to be overshadowed as a key leader of the movement. In fact, he and Shuttlesworth crossed paths during Reese's early teaching career in Wilcox County and Shuttlesworth's early ministerial vocation before his popularity skyrocketed in Birmingham.[147] Reese acknowledged that Shuttlesworth inspired him in the early 1950s through his sermon at a small Presbyterian church on the Wilcox County school's campus. Before the Selma Teachers March, Reese had already made waves in Wilcox County, leading the way for the integration of the County's segregated teachers associations.[148] Eventually, Reese became a member of a core group of voting rights activists dubbed the "Courageous Eight," which, in addition to Reese and five others, included a teacher and a principal.[149] In fact, it was Reese who initially invited King and the SCLC to Selma for the events leading up to the Selma-to-Montgomery March. Reese marched on the front lines hand-in-hand with Coretta Scott King, and alongside Dr. King, during what became the third and only fully completed iteration of the Selma-to-Montgomery March at that time on March 21, 1965.[150] Reese was also arrested and charged with "contributing to the delinquency of minors" when he participated in a youth march in 1964.[151]

CONCLUSION

The Selma Teachers March, and many other acts of civil disobedience enacted both inside and outside of the schoolhouse, reveal the critical but overlooked role of Black educators in advancing the civil rights movement in Alabama. Black educators in Alabama exemplified King's "militant middle" strategy, although they were sometimes tepid about leading the way. The same way in which King, Abernathy, and Shuttlesworth mobilized Black pastors, congregants, and the masses, educator activists such as Gomillion, Burks, Robinson, Robey, and Reese did similarly for Black educators while mentoring and encouraging nascent student activists along the way. King crossed paths with virtually all the educators featured in this chapter—most notably, Gomillion, Burks, Robinson, Reddick, Trenholm, Pitts, and Reese. By all accounts, he respected and was very close to some of them. As King recommended to his 1967 APA audience, these educators were already using "militant middle" tactics to address the problem of Black leadership, initiate scientific examinations of political action, and seek to understand psychological and ideological changes in Black Americans. However, even King may not have been cognizant of the true breadth and depth of their collective import as Black teachers and social science faculty advancing social change through their professionalism.

Historical case studies inevitably raise questions about generalizability. How typical was the activism and resistance of Black educators in these four municipalities compared with others in Alabama (e.g., Huntsville, Mobile, and rural Black Belt counties and towns)? There is evidence of notable teacher activism in the rural Wilcox County, Alabama, where teachers were fired or lost tenure in retaliation for their civil rights activities.[152] Huntsville's land-grant HBCU, Alabama A&M (Agricultural and Mechanical) University, does not publicize its civil rights history in the same way that Alabama State University does, although at least one alumnus from Alabama A&M recounted his deep involvement in Huntsville protests while he was a student in the 1960s.[153] Would more intentional efforts to unearth archival data on Black educators in Alabama municipalities who were not a part of King's ambitious circuit that cut across Alabama, Georgia, Tennessee, and even up to Chicago reveal similar stories?

Undoubtedly, there are countless stories like these that should be anthologized in states beyond Alabama. Is there compelling evidence of Black educators' involvement in the movement in US Southern cities with similar high-profile activism and HBCU presence like Atlanta, Georgia, or Nashville, Tennessee?[154] The parallel and intersecting struggles to collect grains of sand in Alabama and beyond, where lost souls were lynched and where valiant Black educators were overlooked, must continue.

Hopefully, an irrefutable case has been made to revisit Black educators' legacy in civil rights historiography. To do justice to this case, the boundaries of activism must be expanded to account for the unique contributions that Black educators made through their professionalism (e.g., teaching, leading, researching, and mentoring). Furthermore, the time span for examining their involvement must include pre- and post-*Brown* eras that encompass their roles in establishing Black schools and teachers associations, joining ranks with the NAACP in teacher salary equalization cases, and integrating schools and national teachers organizations.[155] Finally, Black educators rich cultural capital arising from their deep ties to Black civic, political, educational, religious, and social organizations must be focal, because their unassuming contributions to the movement are often hidden in plain sight.

From Jim Crow to the
Civil Rights Movement

The University of Missouri's Black Faculty, Staff,
and Student Organizations Fight Back!

VANESSA GARRY &
E. PAULETTE ISAAC-SAVAGE

This chapter, part of a much larger body of research, is a case study of the Black Faculty and Staff Organization (BFSO) established in 1970 at the University of Missouri (MU). Its purpose was to explore the self-reliant networks that constituted the organization and their efforts to gain equity and inclusion in all aspects of MU campus life. Similar to other BFSOs established at predominantly white institutions (PWIs) nationwide, the MU BFSO served as a safe space for Blacks to insulate themselves from a hostile campus environment and develop survival mechanisms to exist and prosper. Members of the organization emulated the Black neighborhood activists who monitored city and school officials and pushed for educational parity for their children during the Jim Crow era. MU Black students initiated the Black power movement on campus, but Dr. Arvarh Strickland, the first Black faculty hire on campus, fueled it with his pedagogical activism. From the 1960s through the 1970s, the faculty, staff, and students morphed into a Black community. Senior faculty honed students' activist skills and watched over new, vulnerable, and enterprising colleagues and students as they pressed the university for equity. The BFSO also extended their advocacy to Black Columbia, the community that developed as a result of the use of covenants to restrict Black Americans to certain sections of the city and prevent them from integrating white neighborhoods.

In this chapter, before examining the early years of MU's BFSO, we contextualize how Missouri's laws and policies influenced MU's treatment of Black students, faculty, and staff, which facilitated the eventual birth of the BFSO on its campus. To illustrate the point, Missouri, a border state, adhered to the rule of law of the South. Like its southern neighbors, Missouri denied free and enslaved Black children a public school education during the antebellum period. After the Civil War, the state permitted Black children to attend segregated schools that were inferior to those of their white peers. The law made it easy for Missouri colleges and universities to admit only white students and hire only white faculty. For example, MU served as the university for white students, whereas Lincoln University in Jefferson City, Missouri—thirty-one miles from MU and originated by the Sixty-Second US Colored Infantry after the Civil War—served as the university for Black students.[1]

Although MU opened in 1839, it did not admit Black students until 1950. Before 1950, MU denied Black students admittance, even when Lincoln University did not offer their desired degree programs. Rather than admit them, state legislators passed a law in 1921 authorizing the payment of tuition fees for Black students to attend institutions outside of Missouri.[2] The Supreme Court's landmark case, *Missouri ex rel. Gaines v. Canada* illustrates the point. In 1931, Lloyd Gaines graduated from Vashon High School, one of two segregated Black high schools in St. Louis, Missouri. A history major, Gaines graduated from Lincoln University in 1935 and applied to MU's law school the summer of the same year. MU's refusal to admit Gaines prompted a long-protracted litigation process. In 1938, Gaines, with support from the NAACP, eventually won the case when the US Supreme Court ruled in his favor. Gaines's disappearance in 1939 prevented him from attending MU's law school. During the same year, Missouri lawmakers established a law school at Lincoln University to prohibit other Black students from applying to MU.[3]

Laws and policies regarding real estate property equally supported MU's discriminatory stance. In the early 1900s, Missouri's cities used covenants to keep Black citizens from living among white homeowners; Columbia, founded in 1821 and home to MU, followed suit. For example, the St. Louis 1916 Ordinance relegated Blacks to several neighborhoods.[4] Like St. Louis, such agreements prevented Black Americans from moving into Columbia's white enclaves. From the early to mid-1900s, the Black and white neighborhoods were starkly different, with white neighborhoods having paved roads and indoor plumbing, whereas Black homes went without either. The germination of Black Columbia, a thriving independent community was a product of covenants. MU's Black students, faculty, and staff new to Columbia found it to be a home away from home, and existing residents working at or attending MU lived in the community; all relied on its cultural resources, Black churches, and its historical Black activism for support.

The civil rights movement also shaped MU's posture on Black students, faculty, and staff. The movement in the 1960s and early 1970s and the sweeping federal policies that followed it inspired MU's growing Black student population to voice their discontent. They demanded that the administration hire Black faculty and develop a Black studies program. Once fervently opposed to admitting Black students, the administration agreed to the students' first demand. In 1969, they hired Dr. Arvarh Strickland, a full professor and MU's first Black faculty member. With the inaugural win, students began to formally organize, a hallmark of the MU's BFSO. Although students initially obtained only one Black faculty hire, Strickland was instrumental in helping realize the demands of the students—hire Black faculty and create a Black studies program. In 1979, students, faculty, and staff networks officially organized into a collective, forming the MU BFSO in support of initiatives supported by MU's Black students, faculty, and staff. Their campaigns during the years that bound this study and the fruits of their labor are studied in the narrative. Last, we considered the implications of the autonomous BFSO membership's abilities to net gains on campuses at PWIs.

A historian, Strickland kept comprehensive records of correspondence regarding his recruitment efforts, BFSO's initiatives, and memoranda to his colleagues. All were useful data, especially his informal notes that captured his ideas for formal correspondence as well as newspaper clippings of salient events and milestones of successes and setbacks for Blacks. Archival data— from both Strickland's and the MU Archive's BFSO collection comprising student newspapers such as *The Black Letter, The LBC Newspaper, UMOJO,* and others—revealed MU's Black students' activism during the 1960s and 1970s. These sources were replete with examples of how Black faculty, staff, and students were instrumental in advocating on behalf of each other. Additionally, the documents corroborated how Black students amplified their voices and would not take "no" from MU's administration as they forced the advancement of employment of Black faculty. They also reveal counternarratives to MU's treatment of Black Americans, even though it attempts to whitewash its dishonorable deeds with actions such as placing a portrait of Lloyd Gaines in its law school or awarding a journalism degree to Lucile Bluford, both Black Americans denied admittance during the Jim Crow era.

THE RISE OF BFSOS AT PWIS

During the 1940s through the early 1960s, Black Americans' quest for the same liberties as those enjoyed by the majority were peaceful demonstrations. By the mid-1960s, a series of hate crimes against Blacks proved so heinous that protests that were mostly isolated in the South expanded to every region in America. Disruptions became the norm in response to racial strife, as media exposure of acts of violence against Blacks made local issues into national ones. The news media's coverage also catapulted the civil rights movement campaigns from the streets to college campuses, especially where most of the violence occurred—in the South.

Student demonstrations on college campuses proliferated across the country at historically Black colleges and universities (HBCUs) and PWIs. Although Black activism at coastal PWIs such as Columbia University and the University of California, Berkeley, increased along with its Black enrollment, so did Black activism at PWIs in the Midwest. Equally active were the Black student collectives at MU and other midwestern PWIs such as the University of Illinois and Indiana University.[5] Students at their respective colleges and universities led their own demonstrations.[6] Student-run national organizations such as the Congress of Racial Equality (CORE) or the Student Nonviolent Coordinating Committee (SNCC) influenced the campaigns of Black students, while the Students for a Democratic Society (SDS) shaped white agendas. For example, white and Black Columbia University's student-run organizations such as CORE and SDS advocated for the Black community in opposition to Columbia's asset acquisition and construction projects during the late 1960s.[7] Similarly, the MU Black student-led organization the Legion of Black Collegians (LBC) organized demonstrations that represented interests of the Black community. In the fall of 1974, its members organized a demonstration against racism at MU. Activist attendees included Black MU and Lincoln University students; Black citizens of Columbia; politicians; and Reverend John Barber, keynote speaker.[8]

Additionally, college and university students of both races advocated for participatory governance, with Blacks' top demands being increasing Black student enrollment, hiring Black faculty, and inclusion in matters relating to them. Conversely, white students, sympathizing with their Black peers, also campaigned to end the Vietnam War, remove the Reserve Officers' Training Corps from university campuses, and demanded things that affected their daily lives. For example, Harvard's students demanded lower rents in university-owned buildings.[9]

Black students' activism was similar to that of their HBCU counterparts during the 1940s, who demanded the replacement of white presidents with Blacks.[10] They adhered to the same practice of relying on themselves to achieve change. Not willing to wait for change to occur naturally, they were the catalyst to make it happen sooner rather than later as they ramped up their campaigns with risks equal to or, in some cases, unparalleled to that of their ancestors. Unlike their predecessors who often surreptitiously outmaneuvered their foe, this generation did so by confronting them eye-to-eye, no matter the risks.[11] For example, Black students from NC Agricultural and Technical College in Greensboro, North Carolina, disrupted Jim Crow cafeterias when they took the war on racism to a downtown discount store's lunch counter reserved for whites only. Students elsewhere replicated their protest. Additionally, college students affiliated with the integrated CORE organization commenced the dangerous Freedom Rides that tested the US Supreme Court's 1960 ruling in the *Boynton v. Virginia* case, which desegregated bus terminals. Although Black students found support from their white peers who joined CORE or SNCC, it was *their* mission to end Jim Crow.[12] Their fixation on the mission remained with them, as more PWIs surrendered to desegregation and admitted Black students for the first time.

The arrival of Black students on campuses at PWIs outpaced that of Black faculty and staff. For instance, MU admitted a few Black students in 1950, but it hired its first Black full professor in 1969, almost two decades later. Accelerated appointments of Black faculty occurred because it topped the students' list of demands, which prompted PWIs to hire them. As PWIs recruited faculty from HBCUs, they unwittingly hired the faculty responsible for training Black student activists. Many who were hired away from HBCUs were experienced activists themselves.[13] The newly hired faculty could easily see that these institutions were microcosms of America, where inequalities for Blacks prevailed; therefore, both Black faculty and students needed to organize in order to survive.[14]

BFSOs emerged in the 1960s and 1970s, as Black faculty, staff, and students found themselves without support from the administration when confronted with racism and isolationism. The organizations created support systems for Blacks in higher education. One of the earliest BFSOs established was at the University of Pittsburgh. Case in point, University of Pittsburgh admitted its first Black student in 1829. However, lack of support for its students in the 1960s resulted in their obtaining a meeting with the chancellor after hijacking the computer center. Although the chancellor denounced their method, he conceded to their demands.[15]

At California State University, Fullerton, the Black Faculty and Staff Association (BFSA)—formerly known as the African American Faculty and Staff Association—was founded in the late 1960s by John Anderson. Anderson, a custodian at the university, was able to foresee the need to create a community to support one another. At the time, the purpose of the organization included bridging the gap between staff and faculty and developing a "system of advocacy for employees of African descent, and to bring African/African American cultural activities."[16]

The 1970s ushered in other BFSOs at universities across the United States, including Iowa State University and the University of Alabama. At the University of Maryland, the BFSA was one of many Black organizations on the campus that emerged between 1968 and 1972 because of the proliferation of Black students attending the university.[17] Conversely, in 1972, the University of South Florida's Black faculty and staff, along with community members, developed its BFSA in response to the decreasing retention rates of Black students, the racist hiring and firing practices of Black faculty, and the tenure and promotion practices and processes.[18] MU's BFSO would also be among those established in the 1970s.

According to the MU timeline, the BFSO, founded in 1970, evolved as the university began to slowly hire Black faculty. As outlined in its 1978 constitution, the purposes of the organization included communicating the concerns and interests of Blacks; serving as recruitment and retention advocates and increasing the number of Black faculty, staff, and students; promoting upward mobility among Blacks; fostering the educational mission of the institution; and establishing a line of communication with the chancellor's office as well as with the Office of Equal Opportunity.[19] Nested in the BFSO was the advisory council. The council presented concerns and points of view to administrators, committees, and others. It consisted of a president, two faculty, two exempt staff, and two nonexempt staff.[20] The council members served for two years. For example, at the Black faculty meeting held on April 29, 1979, their first agenda item was determining topics for the meeting with the chancellor the next day. At the top of the list was recruitment and retention of Black faculty.[21] Several Black faculty members had recently departed MU, and some members of the Black community felt that the administration did little to try to retain them. In a letter to Strickland dated March 1, 1979, Prentice Gautt thanked him for his support and shared his reasons for leaving. He stated, "It will, I believe, provide a good perspective on professional administration, something I believe I need for professional development. The other issue is I got a tremendous salary increase!"[22] Gautt's letter was another piece of evidence that Blacks could use to press the administration to hire and retain Black faculty.

HISTORIED COLUMBIA, HOME TO MU

"What is there for a Black person to do in Columbia?" Wynna Faye Elbert asked Mark Noblin, staff writer for the *Columbia Daily Tribune*.[23] The article, published Monday, February 25, 1974, was the second in a five-part series on minority hiring in Columbia's public institutions. Attracting Black professionals to Columbia was likely a daunting task in the 1970s, as the Black population languished in the single digits. At its greatest point, 51%, it exceeded the white population prior to the Civil War before it experienced its highest decline, 30%, in the 1930s during the Black migration.[24] The first article published Sunday, February 24, 1974, explained that the university, the city, and the public schools were all grappling with how to hire more minorities for professional positions. Blacks featured in the article along with Elbert, youth director for the city parks, were Walter Anderson, attendance counselor for Columbia Public Schools; T. Charles McKinney, MU associate professor; Harold Warren, city councilman; and Arvarh Strickland, MU professor of history. In response to Noblin's inquiry on the appeal of the city to persuade Black job seekers to look for opportunities in Columbia, the interviewees shared deterrents that caused Blacks to exclude

Columbia from their job search. Disincentives included their lack of presence in public relations literature, the absence of a Black middle class, the dearth of Black teachers in Columbia Public Schools, nonexistent social engagements for Blacks, and racism. Elbert affirmed racism by sharing her experiences, which included firecrackers activated nightly in her yard and a little neighborhood girl who quoted her parents to her, "We don't want no niggers here."[25]

Probably, none of the interviewees' remarks shocked Strickland, because he was tapped at the beginning of his tenure at MU by the chancellor to help recruit Black faculty. However, from Strickland's letters to the college deans, it appears that the deans were not as enthusiastic as the chancellor was to interview Black candidates, especially the dean of the law school. He questioned Strickland's recruits and ultimately stopped the search. In his letter to Strickland on April 1, 1972, Eckhardt wrote:

> On Friday morning after you gave me the name of . . . Hattiesburg, Missis-sippi, I telephoned the University of Mississippi Law School, and talked to two former teachers who remembered him well as a student, but neither of whom gave any indication of having followed his career since graduation six years or so ago.
>
> Both remembered him as bright but lazy, ending up in the lower half of his class, about low middle (the records were not checked to ascertain his exact standing). Neither believes him to be qualified to teach law. These evaluations were given to me on a confidential basis.[26]

Although Strickland did not state whether the dean's actions were racially mo-tivated, his reply to the dean clearly revealed his dissatisfaction with the dean's unprincipled behavior. On April 21, 1972, Strickland wrote the following re-sponse to him regarding one of his recommendations.

> I received your two letters dated April 17 concerning recruiting black candi-dates for the School of Law faculty. It was a great surprise to learn that you had decided that Mr. . . . was not worthy of further investigation as a candi-date. It was even more surprising to read the method you used in making this decision.
>
> For a number of reasons, I turned Mr. . . . name and information about how to contact him over to you without further comment. In the first place, since you had already filled the position, it seemed pointless to pursue the matter with you. But, even had the request for assistance been made in good faith, it seemed more appropriate that evaluation of candidates and any nec-essary investigation be made in the Law School. I have been available to help with any special problems in evaluating black candidates.[27]

The dean's behavior troubled Strickland because, as he stated, the dean did not act in good faith by asking for the candidate's information although he had filled the position. In addition to his questionable motives, the dean was unprofessional in relying on the hearsay of a couple of law school professors instead of evidence. The dean's lack of professionalism warranted Strickland's criticism and his follow-up with the chancellor about the incident.

Strickland's recruitment work and comments by Columbia's Black leaders revealed that the city had to improve its image if it was interested in attracting Blacks to the community. Strickland's experience working with the MU deans to recruit Black faculty likely did not surprise his colleagues. Likewise, the comments the Black professionals shared with Noblin probably did not phase the *Columbia Daily Tribune* readership. Nothing seemed out of the ordinary, because both MU and Columbia, similar to other institutions and cities in the border state, have a history of discriminatory practices against Black Americans. However, the interviewees' remarks about the Columbia School District's lack of progress since desegregation likely got the attention of Black professionals with children. Both Councilman Warren and Professor Strickland commented on the lack of Black teachers in the school system and the need for Black children to see role models.

The 1974 five-part article series on the hiring of Black Americans put the city on notice that its past was responsible for its plight. Key factors for its dilemma included the community's culture, institutional attitudes, and the total level of Black education in Columbia.[28] Instead of confronting past discriminatory actions, leaders of the institutions laid the blame elsewhere or, worse yet, presented a solution that did not address the problem. For example, instead of assuming responsibility for MU's contributions to the problem, the MU president blamed Black Americans. "MU President C. Brice Ratchford responded, . . . not many Blacks have [gold-plated credentials] required by the university, but they still have the potential to do the job."[29] Conversely, Assistant Superintendent Hank Steere stated that he applied for a federal grant for funds to provide professional development to help Columbia Public Schools' white teachers relate better to Black children. Hiring Black teachers did not appear to be an option.

The institutional decision makers did not acknowledge the past transgressions of their organizations that contributed to the issues Columbia experienced in the 1970s. Meanwhile, the Black interviewees jeopardized their careers by speaking up. They took calculated risks, but history reveals that Black Americans coalesce around issues that matters most to them and attempt to remove barriers that stymies the race from moving forward. After twenty-six years, Strickland retired from MU, so he was apparently not going to let fear of losing a job mute him.

HISTORIED SHARP END, HOME TO
COLUMBIA'S BLACK AMERICANS

MU and Columbia Black communities were tethered together by their cultural norms and the long-standing racist Missouri laws that, for decades, shuttered MU's doors to both. In addition to MU being off limits to Blacks, so were most of Columbia's neighborhoods. Like most Black neighborhoods in Missouri's cities during the Jim Crow era, Black Columbia was born out of racial animus, as the white majority used covenants to confine Blacks to a specific geographical region in Columbia. Similar to the Black middle-class residents who lived in St. Louis's The Ville neighborhood, Black Columbia residents built an independent enclave where they lived, worked, and worshipped with self-respect and dignity. By the mid-1900s, they had a thriving business district with eateries, a barber shop, and other amenities normally found in a downtown proper.[30] Black MU students likely visited some of these businesses in the district as they searched for their favorite cultural foods or a barber who could cut their hair.

The vicissitudes of Columbia Blacks' prosperity mirrored the times from post-Civil War to the mid-1900s. Like most segregated Black communities, it experienced short-lived boom periods immediately after the Civil War and during the early to mid-1900s. Conversely, it also suffered busts in the late 1800s, when there were few jobs for Blacks, and during the 1960s, as federal laws such as the Fair Housing Act of 1968 stemming from the civil rights movement shuttered Black enclaves because many Black people moved to neighborhoods formerly closed to them.[31]

As early as 1865, educating their children and worshipping in their own churches were important to Black Columbians. Regardless of the economic strength of the neighborhood, two strongholds—schools and churches—bolstered their community. Douglas High School eventually fulfilled their wish. It was the pride of the neighborhood, like Sumner High School was to St. Louis' Black community and Lincoln High School was to Kansas City's Black population. Equally as important were the different denominational churches and the services they provided in uniting both the Black Columbia and MU communities.

Built in the late 1800s, two of the oldest Black churches in Columbia that exist today include Second Baptist Church and St. Paul's African Methodist Episcopal Church. *UMOJO*, the MU Black student newsletter singled out Second Street Baptist Church in its paper, signaling the connectedness between students and its congregation.[32] It was common for MU students and the church congregation to worship together and protest against injustices alongside one another. Historically, the Black church in the United States was a vehicle for activism; it served as a cultural and social center, so it is not surprising that Second Baptist Church served in that capacity. It provided the escape Black Americans needed from the onslaught of social and economic deprivation.[33] Farris, one of the deacons at Second Baptist, indicated that the church helped strengthen "people to overcome the obstacles of discrimination."[34] According to one parishioner, the young people were enthused about the church's ministries.[35]

MU BFSO AS COMMUNITY ADVOCATE
AND THE FRUITS OF ITS LABOR

Two articles reported in the *Columbia Missourian* newspaper two years apart revealed that, in 1977, Black student enrollment at MU from 1970 to 1977 increased from 2.0% to 2.9%; and, in 1979, new MU Black faculty hires from 1972 to 1979 increased from twelve to twenty-nine. Although, at a glance, both data points were encouraging, the following paragraphs reveal why Strickland, seemingly excited about the possibilities for Blacks at MU when he accepted the position at MU, was troubled by the data. After all, the young Black scholar likely took the job because he could teach Black history and assist with the development of a Black studies program. Reported in the 1979 *Columbia Missourian* article, is a quote of Strickland's reminiscence of the promise of MU during his early years.[36]

> Strickland began his teaching career at the University in 1969, when "there was an atmosphere of hope and optimism pervading the campus." Both Black and White students in 1969 asked the chancellor to create a committee for the evaluation of minorities on campus. The resulting Committee on Ethnic Minorities and another group, the LBC, which also formed at this time, brought considerable change to the University, he said. And in April 1971 the Board of Curators passed a statement committing the University to affirmative action.[37]

In 1977, the *Columbia Missourian* newspaper reported that the enrollment of minority students decreased at the MU campus between 1970 and 1976 but that it increased at the other three universities. The university system included MU; the University of Missouri–St. Louis (UMSL); University of Missouri–Kansas City (UMKC); and the University of Missouri–Rolla (UMR), now named the Missouri University of Science and Technology. The period observed was from 1970 to 1977. The following data illustrate the increase in Black student enrollment by each institution: Black enrollment at MU increased from 2% to 2.9%; at UMSL, it increased from 7.6% to 12.2%; at UMKC, it increased from 5.8% to 7.9%; and at UMR, it increased from 1.3% to 3.1%.[38] Joe Saupe, director of institutional research, University of Missouri, stated that the numbers were not 100% correct but reasonably correct.[39] The former full professor in institutional research at Michigan State in the late 1960s returned home to Columbia, Missouri, in the late 1960s or early 1970s. He, along with his coauthor, James R. Montgomery, of the article, "The Nature and Role of Institutional Research: Memo to a College or University,"[40] garnered attention for their research on defining the role of institutional research in higher education. In the article, they discussed analytics, modeling, reporting, and decision making. Given his research and position at MU, it is no wonder that he contributed to the data discussion regarding the enrollment of Black students at the four Missouri system institutions.

Although the MU numbers showed an increase in Black students over a seven-year period, Strickland noted that the numbers reflected mostly undergraduate and graduate students; there were minimal Black students enrolled in professional classifications. He asked the question, "If the strength of the campus is the professional schools, why don't these schools reflect greater minorities?"[41] Strickland went on to answer his own question. He stated that there was a need for Black doctors, lawyers, and veterinarians, but it would not happen with only about 1 percent enrolled in the professional schools.

Two years later, in 1979, another writer from the *Columbian Missourian* newspaper reported on the hiring progress of Black faculty at MU. Strickland, the guest speaker at the Black Culture Center's dedication services for archival photographs of Black faculty, chose the newspaper's topic for his talk. He summed up MU's progress by stating, "We seem to run in order to stand still."[42] Strickland reported an increase in Black faculty members from twelve to twenty-nine between 1972 and 1979 but, compared with the total faculty increase from one thousand six hundred sixteen to twenty-two hundred, the number was minuscule.[43] Strickland did not share the Black faculty disaggregated data that he recorded on a yellow legal pad—likely because the data were even more discouraging. The twenty-nine educators equated to nine tenured-track professors, thirteen nontenured faculty, and seven nonregular instructors. The recruitment and retention of Black faculty, staff, and students remained the BFSO's top priority and its most elusive one.

It is understandable why Strickland likely felt the way he did. He was in his eighth year at MU, and in addition to performing his professorial job, he spent many hours on and off the road recruiting Black faculty. He additionally supported new faculty, the Black studies program, and students. Seeing the minimal growth of new faculty hires and students in the professional schools surely was disheartening. However, Strickland did not let it deter his efforts in advancing Black causes.

Examining the LBC, Black faculty, and staff provides a better understanding of the MU BFSO's contribution to the advancement of Blacks at MU during the 1960s and 1970s. Although each group had unique needs, the demand for equity for all Blacks on MU's campus served a larger purpose, which was to lift up all three. As mentioned earlier, the organization's purpose is to (a) serve as recruitment and retention advocates and increase the number of Black faculty, staff, and students; (b) communicate the concerns and interests of Blacks; (c) promote upward mobility among Blacks; (d) foster the educational mission of the institution; and (e) establish a line of communication with the chancellor's office as well as with the Office of Equal Opportunity.

The LBC

As Strickland was integral to the recruitment of Black faculty during his early years, the LBC was the backbone of student activism on MU's campus. Not to diminish the contributions of the many Black Americans who contributed to the improvement of Black lives on MU's campus during the 1960s and 1970s, but the LBC and Strickland were essential as MU admitted Black students and hired its first Black faculty members. The LBC's work resides in all areas of the BFSO's constitution. However, we situate it mostly in three areas: increasing the number of Black faculty, staff, and students; communications (e.g., communicating with MU's leadership); and promoting Black upward mobility.

Similar to demonstrations at other PWIs during the 1960s, student unrest on MU's campus had no particular pattern. Students demonstrated to gain the attention of administrators, because their needs were continually unmet. Ultimately, they wanted to be involved in the decision-making process. Although Black students shared similar concerns, their protests were contingent on the situations. In the Midwest, there were both nonviolent protests and violent unrest on campuses. One example was the destruction of university property by Black Southern Illinois University (SIU) students who protested SIU's president for withdrawing its invitation for Stokely Carmichael to speak at a campus seminar. Carmichael, a former SNCC member, challenged [he arguably never embraced it fully] the organization's nonviolent movement and embraced Black Power. His message likely caused grave concerns for the SIU administrators, which then prompted them to rescind the invitation.[44] At the University of Wisconsin, Black students demonstrated for ten days and demanded an autonomous Black studies department, twenty Black faculty for the department, and Black counselors.[45] On April 29, 1969, at St. Louis University in St. Louis, Missouri, Black students occupied the administration building. The act prompted a meeting with the administration. They shared their concerns, which included increased Black student enrollment, hiring more Black faculty, adding courses in Black studies to the curriculum, and stopping police harassment.[46]

The approach of MU's Black students was comparable; they pressed for a meeting with the administration. Before their meeting, Black students convened to discuss student life on campus and developed a list of concerns. Then, students secured a meeting with the chancellor.[47] Afterward, they officially formed the LBC in March 1969 and returned to the chancellor's office with several demands. Similar to Black students at other universities, they wanted the ad-ministration to increase the Black faculty and develop a Black studies program. Additionally, they wanted more Black cheerleaders and pom-pom girls propor-tionate to Black athletes on the football and basketball teams. Other student-related concerns included the active recruitment of and scholarships for Black students and implementation of tutoring sessions for incoming Black freshmen. Furthermore, they wanted a Black culture center where students could congre-gate and hold meetings, a building dedicated to a slain Black leader, and their own office space. They also requested that MU sponsor an annual Black week and periodically promote Black service employees and staff.[48]

Black students at MU wanted to feel welcomed and included in campus life. Unfortunately, they had to ask for things that made them feel that way. Compa-rable with their fellow Black activists, if the administration ignored, stalled, or refused their requests, they were relentless in getting the university leadership to meet their demands. The top three requests on the MU students' list were hiring Black faculty, implementation of a Black studies program, and providing students with a Black cultural center.

By the fall of 1969, MU addressed two demands by hiring Arvarh Strickland as its first full professor of history to teach Black history courses. Because his scholarship interest was Black history, he was also instrumental in helping cre-ate a Black studies program. Strickland, an alumnus of Tougaloo and former faculty member of Chicago State College, could also assist MU deans with their recruitment of Black scholars. After Strickland accepted the position, the chan-cellor quickly solicited his help with the recruitment of Black faculty candidates. Although an excellent hire, he was the only tenured faculty appointed that year, which meant that the LBC needed to continue to push for Black faculty.

The LBC undoubtedly had little trouble agitating for Black faculty. The fact that they communicated like a small business would not surprise Black Ameri-cans familiar with organizing and advocating for themselves. The students had access to a small cadre of Black faculty—experienced activists who, on occasion, likely augmented the students' knowledge on the nuts and bolts of advocating for their rights. Oral and written communication skills were essential. After all, MU decision makers during the 1960s and 1970s had their own ideas about Blacks' abilities, because there were so few Black faculty appointments and grad-uate students enrolled in professional programs. Cognizant of others judging them or presuming they produced inferior work, the LBC removed any doubt by communicating as a professional organization.

They promoted the Black community on and off campus with the publica-tions of several newspapers and newsletters enabling them to reinforce their messaging. Newspaper articles informed readers about guest speakers at MU that included Black politicians and activists such as Angela Davis, Julian Bond, and Stokely Carmichael. During her 1974 rap session at the Black Culture Center, Angela Davis warned students, "If you don't get involved in the struggle against racism, you are going to be a victim."[49] Students wrote articles about the LBC's demonstrations and the rationale for them. One article detailed how the LBC disrupted the Missouri Students Association (MSA) senate hearing to protest the cuts made to the LBC budget. Twenty-four LBC members marched in a single file with signs protesting racism and oppression. The motivation for the demonstration was to inform them of how the cuts affected their yearly programming. For instance, the speakers, concerts, and costs associated with the publication of the organization's newspapers were in jeopardy.

Another responsibility of the LBC was promoting upward mobility. There are many ways the organization accomplished this through messaging in the newspapers and newsletters or providing training. For example, in 1979, forty-seven LBC members attended the Big Eight Conference in Norman, Oklahoma, on organizing. They attended numerous workshops that helped them develop people to run effective student governments. LBC also promoted upward mobility in the Black community by participating in Project Growth. It involved the collaboration of students from several colleges in the Columbia region. Their mission was to work with Black Columbia teenagers by tutoring them or teaching a specialty class, such as a Black pride class.

Black Faculty and Staff

The MU BFSO got its start when there were only a handful of MU faculty on the tenure track. Blacks were probably excited about their potential at MU because of its unchartered territory. MU was one of the last holdouts in Missouri to admit Black students and hire Black faculty. By the time MU hired Strickland, many PWIs were hiring Black scholars to develop Black studies programs. For instance, "Dr. Byrum E. Carter, Chancellor of the University of Indiana Bloomington Campus commented, [It is not snap courses. It's a fascinating area. Unfortunately, we had to be hit over the head to call our attention to it]."[50] He conceded, "We're open to the tokenism charge but because of an awareness of this charge we are making a much more deliberate effort to find black scholars." In fact, there were likely some HBCUs experiencing faculty shortages because PWIs recruited heavily from those institutions.[51]

When MU hired the talented scholar Strickland, he had a difficult time finding candidates acceptable to the deans. Unquestionably, he possibly avoided putting his reputation on the line by not suggesting that a potential candidate consider a job when a dean showed no interest in the candidate. The last thing he probably wanted to happen was for a colleague to consider an interview only for the candidate to walk into a lukewarm reception at MU or not receive an interview.

As stated earlier, MU appointed Strickland in 1969, but it was not until two years later when it hired Sandra Gautt, assistant professor in social work, in 1971. MU appointed William Robertson, associate professor in regional and community affairs, in 1972; and in 1973, MU added both Araminta Smith in social work and Walter Daniel in English. It took five years for the university to hire five Black professors, but the following year, 1974, five additional Black faculty members joined the teaching faculty.

Noblin's findings from his five-part series on the employability of Blacks in Columbia appear to ring true when reflecting on MU's slow-paced hiring of Blacks. MU's practice was likely attributed to its institutional attitudes toward Black scholars. It was also likely that the university's inability to hire Blacks was because of its own doings. Additionally, hiring Black faculty was the number-one student demand, and by failing to hire Black faculty, it chose not to listen to their students. MU's actions were similar in some ways to those of the Columbia Public Schools' superintendent, who decided to provide training for white teachers instead of hiring Black teachers. Although MU was hiring few Black faculty, the BFSO continued to recruit them.

The MU faculty and staff had competing concerns. The faculty wanted more Black tenure-track hires, while the staff wanted to focus on promotions. Yet, on the faculty side, the number was rather deceiving, as the term *faculty* encompassed individuals in nonacademic departments. In a document dated October 11, 1979, listing Black faculty, there were thirty-eight Black faculty in all titles. Undoubtedly, MU sought to give the impression that they had significantly increased their numbers. However, a closer examination revealed that the list comprised full-time and part-time faculty as well as research associates, medical residents, instructors and assistant instructors, assistant coaches, and a postdoctoral fellow to generate the total number.[52]

Undoubtedly, Blacks were employed at MU but primarily in low-level positions such as custodial staff, for decades. One such employee, John T. Scott, a janitor in the early 1920s and a member of Second Baptist Church, was lynched by a mob who falsely accused him of raping a white woman.[53] As the century progressed, professional staff increased in number simultaneously with faculty. As early as 1961, Barbra A. Horrell was hired as a training/development coordinator for the Medical Center Personnel.[54] George Brooks joined the staff as assistant director of financial aid in 1964. Having been reared in Columbia during the Jim Crow era, he undoubtedly knew about MU's history. Although he may have experienced some trepidation about joining the staff, he eventually accepted the position. He later served as director of financial aid for seventeen years.[55] Another hire in the 1960s was Prentice Gautt. He worked in the athletics department as an assistant coach for the football team. As the first Black football player for the University of Oklahoma, he probably experienced his share of racism and thus would be ready to tackle any injustices he or others encountered.[56] By 1972, Joe Davis, Donald Johnson, and Clarence Wine worked for Minority Student Programs. Keener Tippin and Muriel Paul were assistant directors of admissions.[57] The following year, Harold Sims Jr. and Jennifer Hill became program advisors for Minority Student Programs, filling a gap left by Joe Davis, who left for Lincoln University.[58]

LEGACY OF NET GAINS
Student Voice

"The Black activist students left the meeting singing [Power to the People] and happy to have finally asserted themselves as the vanguard they were meant to be."[59] These words in the article, "Militants Take Over Meeting" by an anonymous writer for the *Black Letter* richly captured the essence of how one Black LBC member felt as he departed the MSA meeting. Just minutes before the disruption, white students convened to conduct the business of the majority and had no idea that their Black peers would interrupt their meeting, much less accuse them of what they had blamed the establishment for in the 1960s—not allowing them to be part of the decision-making process. When the LBC students marched in a single file into the meeting wearing signs that read "oppression" and "racism," it likely stunned the students who wanted to reduce LBC's allocation.

LBC members protested this meeting because the MSA members, representative of the white majority, were voting to reduce funding that LBC would receive in the next year for its programs. It had already planned its calendar for the year, and every dollar in the budget was spent. If they did not receive the money requested, they would need to cut something out of the budget, which meant that Black students would end up with one less guest speaker, fewer newspapers, or something else that benefited them.

One contributor of an article published in LBC's spring of 1974 *Black Letter* wrote, "the time has come when Black students on this campus have come to realize there are some principles that transcend practicality and logic."[60] The incident and even the words written in the newsletter aptly described the work of the LBC on MU's campus. The attempt to reduce the organization's budget by the MSA was the tipping point for Black MU students, like the assaults on Blacks in Birmingham in the early 1960s was the tipping point for the civil rights movement. In turn, the movement fueled the Black students' uprisings on the campuses of PWI campuses across the nation. Black people, like the LBC members, stepped out of the shadows, made eye-to-eye contact with their oppressors, and told them they would not allow them to continue to oppress them.

This brief episode exemplifies the work of the MU BFSO's student partner who, in their small numbers, fueled the movement that caused the administration to start hiring its first Black faculty. Their work was also the catalyst for the Black studies program and the Black Culture Center, a gathering place for Black students. LBC's membership is also credited for the implementation of the tutoring program and the gradual increase of Black students on MU's campus. They also had a hand in crafting communications with the chancellor as the BFSO continued to push for what students demanded in 1969, an increase in Black faculty.

In addition to campaigning for more Black faculty and staff, the BFSO sought to promote unity and diversity and to pool their knowledge of what worked and did not work to make conditions better at MU. Undoubtedly, many members were familiar with how Strickland's recruitment efforts of Black faculty were initially derailed by the deans, particularly the law dean. Nonetheless, with his storied career at MU, Strickland served as a role model for Black faculty and staff of how one could advance.[61] Strickland and the BFSO would continue their recruitment efforts, and eventually, gains were made in the number of Black faculty and staff. BFSO members would not be deterred from past experiences. New strategies would have to be used. This included meeting with the chancellor at the beginning of the school year to express concerns and goals for the year and to discuss how to rectify the problems at hand. Even as they fought their own battles, BFSO members never lost sight of helping students.

When LBC first received funding from the MSA, it was a meager sixteen hundred dollars. With the help of Joe Davis, coordinator of Minority Student Programs, it increased to approximately ten thousand dollars by 1973. Joe Davis believed that MU was resistant to change; therefore, he used his knowledge to advocate for students.[62] One piece of the puzzle instrumental to students' success was financial aid. Muriel Paul, assistant director of financial aid, not only assisted students with money but also provided them with advice and love.[63]

The Collective of Black Faculty, Staff, and Students

The MU BFSO that assembled in 1970 from two small groups representative of its name were successful in seeding an organization at MU not always fertile ground for it to take root. MU, as well as the city where it is located, has a history that reveals that it is not always welcoming to Black Americans. Therefore, like other BFSOs established in the 1970s at PWIs, its collective comprising the three groups—Black faculty, staff, and students—insulated itself from harsh realities and provided space to nurture the development of its members.

A few BFSO faculty responsible for the development of the organization include Drs. Arvarh Strickland, William Gene Robertson, and Ellis Ingram. Strickland and Robertson joined the faculty within three years of each other, and Ingram joined in 1978. Dr. Charles Nilon, of the MU School of Natural Resources and a former BFSO president, worked with Strickland toward the end of his career and attributed the success of the organization to its leadership. Nilon stated, "Dr. Strickland was a role model on how to advance . . . Robertson was an activist." The strengths of these men and others who joined them were critical to the development of young activists on the MU campus as the disparate groups fighting for equity evolved into a cohesive network to accomplish the BFSO gains.

MU Black activists advocated for Black faculty, Black students, and Black studies similarly to other Black activists in PWIs during the 1960s and 1970s. MU's narrative contributes to the literature on activism pedagogy, because Black faculty put what Jelani Favors calls the second curriculum (Black history) into practice. Strickland, a Tougaloo alumnus, learned the second curriculum as an undergraduate and honed those skills as a faculty member at the HBCU Chicago State University. Serendipitously, when MU hired him, he was the right man at the right time, at the right place. For example, as soon as he came on board, the chancellor charged him with assisting deans in the hiring of Black faculty. With an existing active Black student body, Strickland wasted no time looking for additional Black faculty who could bolster student activism. Although there was a gap in years before MU hired more Black faculty, it did not stall their drive for equity. Perhaps the South's race perspective and Missouri's racist policies drove the intensity of MU's Black faculty and students. Whatever the rationale, they were unstoppable.

The strength of the MU BFSO was the collective leadership of all three groups who implemented its constitution—recruited Black faculty and students; created a Black studies program; and established the Black Culture Center, now named Gaines/Oldham Black Culture Center. The BFSO was successful because they communicated among themselves, developed relationships, cared for one another, and was committed to support the group's upward mobility. All of these things and more continue to be necessary, because the campus grounds at PWI nationwide continually need to be fertile for all minoritized groups to take root and feel welcomed so there is no longer a need for BFSOs. According to Robert E. Weems, Strickland's colleague and former MU BFSO president, there is a continuing need for BFSOs.[64] As long as PWIs continue to have closed-door policies toward Blacks, they will continue to find their own pathways for advancement.

W. E. B. Du Bois and the
University of Berlin

The Transnational Path to Educational Activism

BRYAN GANAWAY

At the beginning of the first chapter in *The Souls of Black Folk*, Du Bois wrote that people asked him all the time about racial injustice in the South. He reflected that behind these queries lay the real issue; "How does it feel to be a problem? I answer seldom a word."[1] There are now hundreds of scholarly books and articles dealing with the life and work of W. E. B. Du Bois, but we are still wrestling with the racial problems that occupied his scholarship and activism. Today, we recognize him as one of the most important figures from the civil rights movement in the twentieth century, as a pan-African nationalist who converted to Marxism later in his life, and as a professor who was one of the founding fathers of the modern discipline of sociology in the United States.[2] However, is it possible to shed new light on Du Bois and the "problem" by looking at his life through a transnational perspective?

Many of the scholars working on Du Bois are specialists in American history. They are well equipped to deal with his English-language writing and the cultural context of race in the United States, but they do not speak German or French, and so they cannot engage as effectively with the time he spent in Europe and Africa. This article argues that Du Bois's time at the University of Berlin in the 1890s illuminates several important things. It shows why he decided to embrace sociology as a public intellectual and why he helped form the National Association for the Advancement of Colored People (NAACP) at its founding; it helps us understand his evolving position on education; and it makes the case that, along with Max Weber, he is the most important sociologist of the first half of the twentieth century. Du Bois's time at Humboldt University of Berlin, the world's premier graduate institution, provided him with both social science methodology and an analytical category that helped him identify solutions to the "race" question in the United States. Du Bois embraced the federal model articulated by his professors suggesting that government could use its power over education to strengthen its citizenry by providing economic and political opportunities. This would increase the power of a country by integrating social minorities into the same rights as those of other citizens and build the best society possible. Therefore, Du Bois the educator fits smoothly into this volume's thesis that Black academics embraced pedagogical activism out of conviction and necessity in ways that would not have occurred to their white peers. Although it is not the case that Du Bois regularly participated in marches (he was too much of an elitist for that), his activist impact was as an educator of Black college students and as a writer of editorials for the NAACP. It is remarkable enough that Du Bois came to this type of activism in imperial Berlin, but even more stunning when we recall that he spent lots of time listening to lectures from Heinrich von Treitschke, a notorious race baiter and crank.[3]

This specific re-evaluation of Du Bois is significant because it fits into a broader re-estimation of his importance as an intellectual. Du Bois has long been recognized as a pre-eminent Black intellectual. Today, however, there is a growing consensus that he is one of the most important academics and public intellectuals of the past century. This is because the comparative, or transnational, methods that he used are now mainstream in the academy. We can get a feel for this reappraisal by looking at recent developments in American studies. Starting in the 1990s, but picking up speed in the first decade of this century, a number of historians looked for ways to reintegrate US national history into the context of global history. Although this has clear historiographical implications, part of the motivation also involved the political situation after September 11, 2001. For example, in an influential article in the *Journal of American History*, David Thelen argued that, in the nineteenth century, history was codified around the nation-state. He suggested that the term *transnationalism* offered a way to interrogate this category. Drawing inspiration from the work of Aihwa Ong and W. E. B. Du Bois, of all people, he argued that American historians could recover things that had been submerged by national history. Thelen suggested that transnationalism offered a number of advantages. It encouraged comparative approaches to how nations developed. It enabled authors to focus on individuals and events that shaped the construction of nations and nationalist policies to show the "contingency of the moment." Transnationalism also provided a way for scholars to integrate the individuals, goods, and ideas that crossed national borders into the broader stream of history by engaging with borderlands, mobility, and diaspora communities.[4] Similarly, Thomas Bender wrote, "About a decade ago [in the mid-1990s] I began to think more seriously and quite differently about the way American history has been written . . . What were the true boundaries of the American experience." After much soul searching, Bender came to the conclusion that the United States made no sense unless it was placed in a transnational framework, and the first sentence of his 2006 book begins, "this [text] proposes to mark the end of American history as we have known it."[5] Bender, one of the deans of American studies, argued that traditional US national history, based on notions of exceptionalism, had exhausted itself. Standard markers of the uniqueness of the American experience such as revolution, democracy, slavery, individualism, and civil war all could be viewed within a global context. Bender reasoned that, because truly global history (defined as the interconnection of the entire globe within networks of trade, exchange, and power such as those created by the Portuguese) and the arrival of Europeans in the Western Hemisphere began at roughly the same time, we can only understand later US history in a transnational framework. He inscribes this argument within a nineteenth-century tradition of scholarship that always accepted the United States as part of the Atlantic World and included Frederick Jackson Turner, his frontier thesis notwithstanding. Like Thelen, the historian that Bender most admires from this period for his transnational grip on the world is Du Bois.[6]

There are other reasons that transnationalism gained such wide appeal in American studies this century. It is, at least in part, a reaction against the way George W. Bush tried to define US national identity and market the war in Iraq by taking advantage of people's fear and shock after September 11, 2001. In her keynote address to the American Studies Association on November 12, 2004 (barely a week after the president's reelection), Shelley Fisher Fishkin made a plea for a transnational history that explored the borders of American experience to expose "racism, sexism and brutality." She recounted a story about withdrawing a manuscript from Oxford University Press because they refused to include a poem that suggested that violence did not always lead to progress. She then stated, "[I]magine this: if those young soldiers imbued in our memories forever in those horrible photos of prisoner abuse in Abu Ghraib had had the chance back in high school to read and discuss and really confront [Gloria] Anzualdua's shocking poem about wanton brutalization, might not one of them have though twice before perpetrating analogous violence?"[7] In a passionate speech, Fishkin mobilized Mark Twain to argue that there is little that we can define as "exclusively American." The United States needed to be put back into a global system, and transnationalism offered one way to accomplish this goal. Fishkin suggested that, in the future, scholars of American studies would learn foreign languages; engage with borderlands; and focus on the African, Native American, and Asian influences on the US story. They would also explore the global construction of race and read international literature. The end result will be to demolish the notion that the United States is the logical outcome of world history and, hopefully, thwart any more presidents with pretentions of martial and religious glory from using the military to remake human geography in other parts of the globe. It also means acknowledging that Du Bois is a figure of significance not only in the United States but also globally in terms of the method and categories he learned in Germany and brought back to the United States.[8]

This more flexible way of looking at global capitalism as a series of networks that can produce positive and negative outcomes is useful when we return to Du Bois and his views on education. Du Bois's background is well known; he grew up in a middle-class Black family with a mixed-race background in Great Barrington, Massachusetts. His mother's family had been in New England for generations, and his father Alfred came from Haiti. Because of financial constraints, he could not attend Harvard University, but his neighbors collected enough money for him to attend Fisk University in Nashville, Tennessee (one of the Jim Crow states).[9] He completed three years there and apparently already had an interest in Germany of all places. He gave a commencement speech on German Chancellor Otto von Bismarck. In 1940, he recalled:

> This choice in itself showed the abyss between my education and the truth in the world. Bismarck was my hero. He made a nation out of a mass of bickering peoples. He dominated the whole development with his strength until he crowned an emperor at Versailles. . . . This foreshadowed in my mind the kind of thing that American Negroes must do . . . I did not understand at all . . . anything of current European intrigue . . . of the industrial revolution built on slave trade . . . I was blithely European and imperialist in outlook.[10]

Nonetheless, Du Bois gained an opportunity to transfer to Harvard. He had to redo his undergraduate degree before beginning graduate studies in sociology, a brand-new discipline. Harvard did not have a sociology department, so Du Bois took classes from philosophers, historians, and political economists. One of these was William James, a founder of modern psychology and also a proponent of pragmatism (which assumed that you could tell if something was good or bad through its practical uses and consequences). Even more important to him was Albert Bushnell Hart, a historian who pioneered the use of statistical data collection in the social sciences. In the late nineteenth century, many academics believed that subdisciplines of philosophy such as history and sociology could be made to operate on the same principles as the natural sciences. Today, we see sociology as a social science, meaning that practitioners are comfortable using quantitative and qualitative methods of analysis. Harvard taught Du Bois the importance of rigorous method, and there is good evidence that it was a refuge from some of the all-pervasive scientific racism of the late nineteenth century.[11]

It was not protection against everything, however. Although his Harvard professors certainly thought in conceptual terms, their chief category was race. Charles Darwin's *On the Origin of Species* appeared in an American edition in

1860 and immediately shaped thinking regarding race. Unfortunately, most of his American readers seemed to have misunderstood the concept of natural selection. Darwin emphasized that most of evolution was random and that one of the most successful strategies was cooperation (commensalism). Almost immediately, other scientists assumed that natural selection proceeded solely by means of competition and thus provided a scientific basis for racism. We refer to this today as social Darwinism, although the term was not common in the late nineteenth century. Herbert Spencer and Francis Galton coined the term *survival of the fittest* (Darwin used *struggle for survival*) to articulate the notion that all species fought for life. It was a normal process for some to win and others to go extinct. For men like Spencer and Galton, race and species functioned as synonyms. If the white race dominated people of color, then that was simply a sign of progress and could not be stopped, moral sentiments notwithstanding. Dalton's misunderstanding of Darwin eventually led to the development of eugenics, or the notion that the gene pool can be selectively controlled and directed by humans. Collectively, scholars refer to these ideas as scientific racism. Race was an immutable category because it was grounded in evolution. Indeed, superior races had a duty to humanity to dominate the inferior ones. In theory, the superior white races could slowly improve Colored races, but the subtext was clear. Black people were inferior because they were Black; this was a failure that could not be redeemed.[12]

If we return specifically to the case of Harvard, those professors who hoped to ground their theories in science latched on to social Darwinism because it provided a simple solution to the race question that validated the existing political structure in the United States. People of African heritage were irredeemably inferior as proven by history, and nothing could be done about this.[13] There was no hope of ever really enfranchising Blacks because they represented an inferior gene pool. This conceptualization drove Du Bois to despair. Looking back on this period, he recalled, "This was the race concept which has dominated my life . . . it had . . . all sorts of illogical trends and irreconcilable tendencies. . . . All this led to an attempt to renationalize the racial concept and its place in the modern world."[14] His primary mentor at Harvard, Albert Bushnell Hart, supported Du Bois academically, but his sociological method had no room for a study of Blacks. Du Bois experimented with a number of solutions. He engaged with Booker T. Washington and the Tuskegee Institute's focus on self-reliance through regular academic subjects supplemented with trades skills and moral instruction. There is evidence that Du Bois envisioned creating a college curriculum for Blacks that would focus on cultural awareness (teaching the humanities, middle-class social behavior) as a way of contributing to this project. In other words, Black people would slowly move up the social hierarchy in step-like fashion. They might never reach the heights of their white counterparts, but they would move as far as their racial heritage allowed.[15] This solution did not really satisfy Du Bois, however, and he went looking for new ideas. He found these in Imperial Germany, of all places.

Among many other things, nineteenth-century capitalism brought us the railroad, the telegraph, the steamship, and bank-wire transactions. Du Bois was able to take advantage of all of those things to leave Cambridge and go to Berlin. His ability to go to a new place was a product of transnationalism (it was temporally specific). However, today we might not think that Germany was a good place to go to unlearn race as a category. Imperial Germany had only unified in 1871 on the back of the Prussian military and the Hohenzollern dynasty. It had an emperor, avowedly anti-Semitic parties, and it was aggressively nationalistic. It also had the fastest growing economy in the world, the best modern research universities, the largest Social Democratic Party in Europe, and a vigorous civil society that had room for a gay rights movement.[16] Du Bois was able to climb aboard one of the transnational networks linking the United States and Imperial Germany, that of higher education.

How did he do this? He won a grant from the Slater Fund. This was important for the young scholar because Harvard refused to fund him. Charles Eliot wrote "Du Bois would be considered a very promising candidate if he were white." The Slater Fund, chaired by former President Rutherford B. Hayes, was tasked with finding Negro men with a talent for "art or literature" and providing scholarship money for study at university. Apparently, Hayes did not believe that such a specimen of homo sapiens existed, but Du Bois wrote him an angry reply, and the shocked board of the Slater Fund gave him about seven hundred dollars to take a steamship to Berlin.[17] They arranged for him to stay with a family in the summer before classes started and then saw to it that he had a bank account where they could wire him money. When he went to Germany, Du Bois joined a parade of Americans who journeyed to Europe to study at the Reich's peerless research institutions. Of these schools, the Humboldt University in Berlin was acknowledged as the best of the best.[18] Indeed, to be a top-flight intellectual in the nineteenth century, one had to spend time in Germany. His two years in Germany (1893–1895) transformed him.

Du Bois attended lectures and seminars with major intellectuals. The two most important were Gustav Schmoller and Heinrich von Treitschke. Schmoller was one of Imperial Germany's famous liberals. He was a historian focused on economic policy. In particular, he believed that the state could influence economic policies in ways that could improve people's lives and strengthen the nation in the process. Schmoller founded the *Verein für Sozialpolitik*, which included Max Weber, Lujo Brentano, and Werner Sombart. Its affiliates believed that the nation could only achieve its full potential if all members had access to economic opportunity.[19] Schmoller called its members the "pre-eminent representatives of the idea of the state [who] must seize the initiative for a great legislative program of social reform."[20] These men used the new field of social science research and surveys to accumulate data that could then be used to convince legislators to pass reform bills that tamed the rougher edges of the market and improved the condition of working citizens. At the time when Du Bois arrived, they were heavily invested in *Hausarbeiter*, or piece workers, who operated out of the home for low wages with no benefits.[21] Du Bois joined their organization and went to rural Eastern Germany to conduct research on Polish peasants. Du Bois learned a new social science method that assumed that research only truly had value if it positively intervened in the social life of the nation. This was radically different from what he learned at Harvard, where race was an immutable category. There was nothing the government or anyone else could do to improve the condition of Blacks, according to Albert Bushnell Hart and his colleagues. In Berlin, Du Bois learned that history, which was the study of people's irrational and contingent decision making, could be turned into a social science through the use of statistics. The economic data gained from the statistics could then be used to frame laws and policies that could improve the lives of the Polish minority in Germany, or the Black minority in the United States. In his lecture notes, Du Bois wrote that "science allows [the researcher] to bring order to world . . . the scientific method is the proper way of representing reality."[22] Within ten years, and still a young man, Du Bois mobilized this new theory in *The Philadelphia Negro* (1899) and then more famously in *The Souls of Black Folk* (1903).

Du Bois did not merely acquire social science methods from Berlin. He came back with a new primary category of analysis. At Harvard, he learned that race was the prime factor for understanding social conditions. Indeed, as we have seen, the category of race at Harvard was immutable. This flawed understanding of Darwin assumed that Black people were genetically (historically) coded for inferiority in ways that could not be redeemed. If race was indeed immutable, this represented a terrible dilemma for a Black man. Du Bois's professors in Berlin also recognized race, but they saw it as subservient to another category: the nation. Nations could use the power of the state to remake race to at least some degree. Nobody made this argument more loudly than the notorious, race-baiting historian Heinrich von Treitschke (1834–1896). Given the chair in Modern German History at Humboldt University by Otto von Bismarck, he shaped generations of the Empire's best students with his spectacular, populist lectures filled with screaming and flying spittle. I will pass over his style, but we need to examine the substance.[23] For Treitschke, the only legitimate subject of historical inquiry was the nation. Other categories such as class or race only had value insofar as they informed us about the creation of the nation. Nations developed organically and depended on ethnicity. The strongest nations gained power by means of war and suffering. Once a nation had developed, people of an outside ethnicity could join but only on the condition that they assimilated into the dominant culture (*Leitkultur*). Indeed, war became the prime calling of the nation in this conceptualization, whether it was fighting foreign enemies or struggling to educate minorities and turn them from Poles into Germans.[24] Because Treitschke believed that nations should be homogenous, you can imagine what he thought about Jews. In his history of Germany, Treitschke wrote, "The Jews play a quite abnormal part in this singular whirlpool of national antagonisms. Because they want to continue being Jews even though they lived in Germany they represented an element of national decomposition. . . . In an age of unified and homogenous nations, however, Jews must admit that after a nation has become conscious of its own personality there is no place left for the cosmopolitanism of the Semite."[25] Treitschke believed that the dominant culture in any nation had to subsume minorities by assimilating then. Minorities who refused to do this might need to be eliminated. Du Bois recorded that, after getting suitably lathered up one afternoon, Treitschke declared "during a lecture on America: 'Die Mullattin sind niedrig! Sie fühlen sich niedrig! [Mulattoes are inferior! They feel themselves to be substandard!]'"[26] This was undoubtedly a very painful moment, but Du Bois kept attending the lectures because he was getting something from them that Treitschke had not intended.

It appears that Du Bois slowly realized he had a conceptual answer to the race problem in the United States. The key was to take Treitschke's notion that the state could assimilate willing minorities and strengthen the nation and change it to "the state could strengthen the nation by giving minorities the same rights and educational access" as members of the dominant culture. For Du Bois, the most important moment seems to be the change in categories from race to nation. Rather than assuming that race was immutable, as his American colleagues did, he assumed that the state could circumvent race in a way that would empower the whole nation. Clearly, he imagined this process differently from what Treitschke had intended. This fits in very nicely with the ways in which transnational theory accounts for the flow of ideas across boundaries; they are constantly being modified to fit new conditions. Treitschke assumed the state would erase difference by eradicating inferior cultures; Du Bois eventually came to the conclusion that the state would guarantee access to education and equal treatment before the law as a way to make race irrelevant by proving that notions of race immutability rested on totally unscientific grounds. This makes for some strange permutations. Imperial Germany was a land riven by hatred and controversy, but it was also a nation where people believed in progress and improvement. Treitschke, who was one of Bismarck's strongest acolytes on the right, also supported the Chancellor's policies for giving national health insurance, unemployment insurance, pensions, and workers' compensation to the industrial classes, because these things were all seen as strengthening the nation. We see these things today as social, or socialist, but Treitschke (and, at this point, Du Bois as well), saw it as nation building, or nationalist. Du Bois's biographers and scholars have long recognized that he saw himself as a member of a patriotic Black elite in the United States, leading his people to a better future.[27] He recalled that Treitschke taught him to think as a patriot, and that, "Negroes simply did not speak or think of patriotism for the nation which held their fathers in slavery for 250 years."[28] The patriotic "category" he learned from Treitschke helped Du Bois think about how to use the methods he digested from Schmoller and the *Verein für Sozialpolitik*.

Today, of course, we naturally see Du Bois as a fully formed intellect who left the United States for Ghana and embraced Communism as the best means of ensuring equality for people of color. We tend to forget that he took a long-winding path to reach that point, and early in his intellectual history it was Germany that provided his model for understanding politics. It is possible to glean empirical evidence of this transition by returning to an article that Du Bois wrote in Germany in 1893 called *The Present Condition of German Politics*. This article covered the first big election in Germany after the ouster of Bismarck by the new German Emperor, Wilhelm II. Historians of Germany (as well as some Du Bois experts) have known about this article for several decades, but they have not been sure what to do with it.[29] On the one hand, it is a sensitive, social science analysis of voting behavior in Germany, complete with statistics. Du Bois explained the German multiparty system and showed which groups were anti-Semitic and which one was demagogic. What perplexes scholars is his defense of the kaiser and his interpretation of the Social Democrats. On the one hand, he explained that Germany needs a "military monarchy" because that is what built the nation. Germany sat in the middle of Europe between "the whims of the Paris mob" and the "half wild Russian bear." Du Bois then wrote that, "The German government has taken the one middle course and embraced socialism to escape democracy."[30] This is one of the most remarkable descriptions of Germany's monarchy and constitutional systems I have ever read. When we combine it with Du Bois's apparent disdain for democracy (the Paris mob) and racial others (the Russian bear), it seems very difficult to interpret. If we take into consideration that he spent the last four semesters listening to Treitschke speak about the state being the only entity that can protect the nation from enemies, then this statement seems more plausible. If he believed, as Treitschke did, that Central Europe was a scary place, then the need for a strong state made sense. We know that Du Bois believed that the United States was a racist state enforced by legalized violence for Blacks, so we can see that he might have been willing to leave his laissez-faire Harvard professors behind and ask for a stronger state that would intervene to protect and cultivate its most vulnerable citizens. That state had the power to exclude threats and include marginalized citizens.

Later in the article, which was written for an American audience, Du Bois presents a truly perplexing interpretation of the Social Democratic Party. The Social Democratic Party was the largest and most progressive Socialist party in the world at this time and would form the first democratic government in Germany in 1919. In other words, it was the biggest party on the left. That's not how Du Bois saw it. He placed the party on the far right. Du Bois wrote that against the governmental or nationalist parties stood "a right wing of ultra-socialist tendencies."[31] He recalled going to a Social Democratic rally with ten thousand people and called them "a typical Coney Island throng"; in other words, lower middle-class and working-class types who are not educated and who cannot compete in the contemporary world.[32] No nation could look to people like that for leadership. Du Bois portrayed Social Democrats as backward, premodern types who did not understand the modern world. This seems strange, given that Du Bois eventually ended up as a convinced Marxist. On the one hand, we could perhaps attribute these views to the influence of his professors at Harvard. That is not particularly convincing, however, because although socialists scared people in Cambridge, they were not seen as backward. Rather, they represented dangerous radicals and revolutionaries. Du Bois recalled in his autobiography that Hart and other professors simply ignored Marx or ridiculed his social science methods. Kenneth Barkin, the only contemporary German historian who tried to engage deeply with Du Bois, wrote "this analysis gives the historian pause, and one can only speculate about such a political taxonomy." If we return to his lectures at Berlin, we can do more than speculate. This placement of the Social Democratic Party on the political right makes perfect sense if your frame of reference is Heinrich von Treitschke. His category was the nation, not class. Any party that accepted the nation as the locus of human progress became modern and possibly democratic, whereas any party that did not became premodern and backward. Treitschke saw class as a remnant of the medieval era. People did not get their rights from their class but from the nation. Class did not protect people; the national government with its army did. Indeed, Du Bois argued that the true parties of the left (i.e., liberal parties) actually supported the Kaiser. Needless to say, no contemporary German historian would define the two Conservative Parties and the National Liberals (much less, the Catholic Center) as parties on the left. It makes sense in Du Bois's taxonomy, however, because as supporters of the nation, they were progressive in his view. They moved history forward. Even if they supported the Kaiser now, they were simply laying the framework for long-term democracy and inclusion, because that was the logical outcome of a nation-state. By holding on to an antiquated social category (class) the social democrats became obstacles to progress in a fascinating inversion of Marx's concept of false consciousness. This is, perhaps, the earliest moment when we can see Du Bois grappling with his new categories and methods.

There is no doubt that Germany was the pivotal intellectual experience for Du Bois, aside from his acquisition of method and category. In 1960, reporter William Ingersoll visited Du Bois in Africa and castigated him for his continued support of the Kaiserreich. How could he continue to support a place that was monarchical, militaristic, and anti-Semitic after the Holocaust? Du Bois replied, "I had a very interesting time [there]. I learned to realize that White people were human."[33] Like him, the Germans seemed to be trying to build a better life in a dangerous world surrounded by enemies who despised them. I don't think that this is what Treitschke (or even Schmoller, for that matter) had in mind, but Du Bois interpreted them in ways they did not imagine. For him, Germany was the first place he felt human. This is where he learned that a racial minority could be part of a nation. If we return to the socialist meeting he attended, he recalled dancing (twice) with a white woman who did not bat an eye at him. This is not surprising; he was young, handsome, and educated. She apparently assumed that, because he spoke excellent German, he could be part of the nation. Cultural experiences such as these also changed him. In his autobiography, he wrote, "I met men and women as I had never met them before. Slowly they became, not white folks, but folks. The unity beneath all life clutched me. I was less fanatically a Negro, but 'Negro' meant a greater, broader sense of humanity and world fellowship."[34] In a note from 1894, he wrote, "I have finally proved to my entire satisfaction that my race forms slight impediment between me and kindred souls . . . I am here free from most of those iron bands that bound me at home. Therefore, I have gained for my life's work a new hope and zeal."[35] In other words, race is the wrong category. Nation is the right category. The key to the long-term solution to the Negro question in the United States was to get the federal government to guarantee that everyone had equal civil rights.

Du Bois's experience in Germany helps us understand his position on Booker T. Washington and the Atlanta Compromise, his well-known elitism regarding education, and even his decision to support the creation of the NAACP. It appears that, before he went to Germany, Du Bois was sympathetic to Booker T. Washington and the political philosophy that lay behind the so-called Atlanta Compromise formalized in 1895. This is not surprising; Du Bois was still quite young, and before 1893, all of his professors taught him that race was an immutable category. Once back from Berlin and armed with new categories and a refined method, his position changed. By 1896, he ended up at the University of Pennsylvania and took a commission to do a modern, sociological study of the Black community in Philadelphia. The white men who commissioned the study assumed that it would confirm that Blacks were not suitable for full citizenship, but Du Bois showed that the crime, unemployment, and lack of education among members of this community did not derive from moral failings but from disinvestment and discrimination; so he called for the city, the state, and the federal government to intervene. Because these people were citizens, the nation could never achieve its full potential until they had been integrated into the mainstream culture of rights and opportunities.[36]

The Philadelphia Negro was not a widely read text, but today, academics see it as one of the most important early works of modern sociological method in the United States. For us, its lack of impact at the time is less important than the trajectory it laid out. Du Bois identified education—particularly, higher education—as a key component of empowering Blacks. His next project involved contacting state superintendents of education across the United States to learn what educational opportunities currently existed for Black residents of the United States. He wanted to know which states provided "normal" education, by which he meant full preparation to attend university, and which limited Blacks to "industrial" education, thus closing the doors permanently to any postsecondary credentialing, and then compare the results. This project eventually fell apart, because the state agencies refused to provide information.[37] Therefore, the first really strong rejection of Washington's "accommodationist" model accepting Black inferiority in return for an end to violence appeared in *The Souls of Black Folk*, in the chapter titled "Of Mr. Booker T. Washington and Others." Du Bois scholars such as Derrick P. Alridge and Eugene F. Provenzo Jr. consider this to be his most important text.[38] In a stunning statement, the 35-year-old Du Bois mobilized his training in Germany and wrote the following:

> It has been claimed that the Negro can survive only through submission. Mr. Washington distinctly ask that Black people give up, at least for the present, three things—
> First, political power,
> Second, insistence on civil rights
> Third, higher education of the negro youth, and concentrate all their energies on industrial education.[39]

If we recall that Washington's position was in line with race thinking as practiced by almost all Americans, including men such as Hart and James at Harvard, we have to ask where this critique is coming from. It comes from Germany. Treitschke taught Du Bois that race was a category secondary to the nation. Nations and peoples succeeded by fighting; but, indeed, the nineteenth century had shown that nations that invested in diverse people could unify them. Individuals who were fully part of a nation had a future; those who were not did not. If Germany had taken Bavarians, Prussians, Saxons, Franconians, Swabians, etc., and turned them into one people, then the United States could do that with white, Black, and Brown citizens. To fully develop the nation, all citizens needed two

things: access to full civil rights and normal education. The top levels of education would only be available to an elite, Du Bois's "talented tenth," but secondary
education had to be made available to everyone. Here, we can see him applying
the methods from his article on German politics to the United States. Parties in
Germany that rejected the category nation or concepts such as race or class were
backward. Du Bois applied the same logic to Booker Washington. However, Du
Bois clearly ignored Treitschke's belief that people of color and Jews were not
redeemable in the same ways as "white" citizens such as Poles and Sorbs (a small
Slavic minority). Finally, the method through which he would interrogate the
category of the nation comes from Schmoller's *Verein für Sozialpolitik*. For Du
Bois, sociology is not merely an analytical tool; it is a means of achieving lasting
political change through the nation.

To conclude this brief overview, we can see how *The Souls of Black Folk* logi-
cally flowed into Du Bois's participation in the Niagara Movement of 1905 and
then to his decision to become a founding member of the NAACP in 1909. The
very first word is the new social science category that he learned fifteen years
earlier in Imperial Germany. We also tend to forget that Du Bois and his colleagues carefully chose the term "Colored" rather than "Negro" or "Black." To
achieve its potential, the nation would need to enfranchise all citizens. This
would have to be done by lobbying the federal government to ensure civil rights,
and state and local governments to provide access to education. Not surprisingly, Du Bois edited the NAACP's magazine *The Crisis*. The choice of title was
also deliberate. Nations and their states existed to fight for the rights of all citizens. Because Black people did not enjoy rights, there was a crisis in the United
States. Du Bois began, "The object of this publication is to set forth those facts
and arguments which show the danger of race prejudice, particularly as manifested today toward colored people. It takes its name from the fact that the editors believe that this is a critical time in the history of the advancement of men.
. . . Finally, its editorial page will stand for the rights of men, irrespective of color
or race, for the highest ideals of American democracy, and for reasonable but
earnest and persistent attempts to gain these rights and realize these ideals."[40]
There we have it laid out. Racism is a danger to the nation because it deprives
the United States of the services of Black citizens. The magazine stands for the
rights of every man in the nation as the best way to guarantee the triumph of
democracy. It is a truly remarkable moment, and the intellectual inspiration did
not come from Cambridge or Tuskegee; it developed between Brandenburger
Tor and Alexanderplatz in Berlin.

I would like to close by returning to the transnational approach to US history that Thomas Bender has advocated this century. Du Bois saw himself as
a member of the Western world's transnational elite. Interpreting Du Bois in
the same way he saw himself gives us a richer understanding of his intellectual

genealogy. Drawing on work by sociologists, we can define transnationalism as the ways in which capitalist economic systems both strengthen nation-states and their often-authoritarian leaders while simultaneously providing ordinary citizens with the means to escape from control and redefine their identity through a series of networks that cross borders. Global capitalism made authoritarian Germany the most powerful country in Europe by 1900, but it also produced the best universities in the world, institutions that accepted a Black American and gave him a world-class education. Admittedly, he used it in ways they did not expect. He took their social science method and their category (the nation), but he divorced its racial components. He used the networks of knowledge and capitalism linking Boston and Berlin to move these ideas across continents. I believe that it took him ten to fifteen years to digest everything that he had learned and experienced, but "The Present Condition of German Politics" (1893) informed *The Philadelphia Negro* (1899), which informed *Souls of Black Folk* (1903). From there, it seemed logical to Du Bois to become a public intellectual (more Schmoller and Treitschke, and less Hart and James), even if that meant giving up his faculty status. Therefore, his decision to be a part of the Niagara Movement in 1905 and then the NAACP some years later makes perfect sense. The NAACP can be seen as a more rigorous and engaged version of the *Verein für Sozialpolitik*, if only because the condition of Black Americans was far worse than those of home workers and ethnic Poles in Imperial Germany. This comparative, transnational approach links Du Bois to the major intellectual currents of the late nineteenth century and makes him (in my opinion, at least) not so much a Black intellectual of astonishing creativity and depth but an intellectual of world-historical significance (as the Germans would say) who showed the power of sociology as a method to identify problems and anticipated the system of education that the vast majority of us assume to be inseparable from a healthy democracy.

Afterword

DERRICK P. ALRIDGE, JON N. HALE,
& TONDRA L. LODER-JACKSON

The time could not be more opportune to revisit the historical legacy of Black educators' involvement in the civil rights movement. Nearly seven decades after *Brown v. Board of Education*, the issue of race is no less divisive than it was when the Supreme Court ruled in 1954 that race should not be a constraining factor in how we provide an education. Not surprisingly, today's most glaring battle is being played out in the long-contested site of American public education. A Black principal of a school in Colleyville, Texas, near Dallas-Fort Worth was suspended by his school board in fall 2021, and later resigned, after white parents voiced complaints about his perspectives on race. One parent charged that he promotes "conspiracy theories about systemic racism." In addition, when pictures of him embracing his wife, who is white, during their wedding anniversary surfaced publicly, some parents charged that they were "inappropriate." The principal acknowledged: "I am the first African American to assume the role of Principal at my current school in its 25-year history, and I am keenly aware of how much fear this strikes in the hearts of a small minority who would much rather things go back to the way they used to be." This controversy began brewing in July 2021, underscoring how the past remains enduringly present.[1]

It is as if many Americans have had an epiphany about the power of teaching and curriculum in our nation's classrooms. Arguably, the governmental response to the COVID-19 pandemic to close schools and teach remotely has made matters of curriculum and instruction more transparent to parents, guardians, and families than they have ever been. Moreover, there appears to be a throughline across the racial reckoning that followed the murder of George Floyd by police officers in Minneapolis, Minnesota, in 2020; the interracial makeup of the national and global protests that followed; and the appetite of younger generations of Americans for a deeper knowledge and understanding of diversity and social justice. The notion of "wokeness," and the awareness of racism and systemic injustice it implies—a term now appropriated and referred to derisively by many on the political right—captures the zeitgeist of the present moment.[2]

Many observers believe that we are in the midst of a new iteration of the civil rights movement as long-standing conflict over the curriculum rage, this time with critical race theory (CRT) and the legitimate origins of US history (1619 vs. 1776) being vociferously contested at the time of this writing. Parents have organized to protest a perceived threat to CRT in the schools.[3] Parents who oppose discussions of race (and sexuality) stormed school board meetings in 2020. They organized to remove school board members and remove administrators and teachers who supported or taught CRT in the schools. The ferocity, scope, and anger of board meetings transformed often sleepy board rooms into sites of unusually hostile political discord.[4] They also inspired a legislative movement. Since the outset of 2021, thirty-five states have introduced bills or taken steps to restrict teachers from teaching CRT.[5] Republican gubernatorial candidates have been hedging their bets on winning campaigns partly on anti-CRT platforms, with the most recent election upset in 2021 leveled by Virginia's Republican Governor Glenn Youngkin, who has vowed to abolish CRT in public education and government.[6] Even in the historic Supreme Court nomination hearings convened in March 2022, where the first Black woman, Judge Ketanji Brown Jackson, was vying to be appointed to the highest court of the nation, her record was scrutinized for any smattering of CRT.[7] In response, many educators of grades K–12 and higher and school administrators across the country are confused, worried, and cautious about whether and how they should be teaching about race and racism in US history and current events. There are reports of libraries removing content deemed controversial or divisive from their holdings.[8] Yet many educators are joining ranks with legal, civic, and academic organizations to fight back. Faculty, teacher, student, and even some parent organizations across the country are testifying at statehouses, pleading their cases at school board meetings, and protesting in their communities.[9]

Today's pedagogical and intellectual activism is not occurring in the reified Black–white segregated context of the US South's Jim Crow era. The Colleyville, Texas, principal is a part of an interracial marriage and family where he encountered an overwhelming majority of white-parent resistance but also garnered support from an interracial coalition of students, parents, and community members. Even the statehouses and boards of education where anti-CRT laws and regulations are originating include contingents of Black lawmakers and their legislative allies who are fighting internally, and joining ranks with their diverse constituents, to stem the tide of restraints on academic and intellectual freedom.[10] Higher education groups fighting lawmakers in their respective states reflect, at least to a degree, some of the racial and ethnic diversity of their surrounding communities.[11] The two most prominent national teacher organizations, the National Education Association (NEA) and the American Federation of Teachers (AFT), which were desegregated post-*Brown* primarily through the dissolution of Black teacher associations, are joining ranks to fight legislation banning the teaching of accurate history and diverse perspectives.[12]

The legislative and political racist posturing at the publication of this volume is an iteration of the historic assault on Black teachers, even those who challenged a violent state behind classroom walls. After *Brown*, Black teachers experienced wholesale dismissal, demotion, and displacement. Once all-white districts were forced to desegregate, Black teachers found themselves in a precarious professional position. Within the first decade of the position, approximately forty thousand Black teachers—nearly one-half of the southern Black teaching force—lost their positions, and thousands of others were displaced or demoted.[13] Well over one-half of a century after *Brown*, Black teachers constitute only 7 percent of a public school system in which 53 percent of all students are Black, Latinx, Asian American, Indigenous, or other students of color.[14] Not only did the nation lose a committed teaching force and a sizable portion of the Black middle class, but the nation also lost a highly skilled teaching force that acquired the knowledge of an antiracist curriculum and pedagogy that challenged the racist curriculum deeply embedded in public schools.

Many of the issues that define the contemporary educational climate have deep roots and will continue to shape our schools in how and what we teach. The history examined in this volume also looks forward and provides a historic path of sorts for teachers currently in the classroom. Black teachers and administrators have continued to engage in modes of pedagogical activism since the social and political movements of the 1960s and 1970s. Black educators and allies carried forth the insurgent tradition of writing antiracist curriculum and shaping antiracist teaching in the "multicultural education" movement of the 1990s. Like their predecessors, educators integrated the histories and cultures of Black communities and other communities of color sidelined by a mainstream white history. Multicultural education, as James Banks and others conceived it, moved beyond the traditional figureheads like Dr. Martin Luther King Jr. and Rosa Parks to incorporate a more robust understanding of our past. It made these truths central to a refashioned multicultural curriculum. Banks also helped popularize the idea of promoting civic action and commitment to broader social change. Through serious study and close introspection, students developed the knowledge and skill set to actualize the ideals on which our country was founded.[15] The principles of multicultural education became more popular and even inspired newer versions of it—such as culturally relevant teaching or, its latest manifestation, culturally sustaining pedagogy.[16] However, the idea never became the core or essence of how we teach, and ideas presented in the controversial *1619 Project* remain vilified well into the twenty-first century.[17]

We, as coeditors of and contributing authors to this volume, have spent considerable time advancing the revision of the civil rights historiography to include the undeniably relevant role of Black educators in the US South, but not all lessons learned from these narratives can be applied to the present moment. Yes, some of the threats are still the same, especially as we observe an alarming spate of bomb threats against historically Black colleges and universities.[18] Black history curriculum and programming are under threat.[19] White and other allies to Black social movements are also being targeted, which is not new.[20] However, the powerful media images of interracial groups of primarily younger people but also multigenerations of protestors marching in the streets in 2020, both in the United States and across the globe, to protest George Floyd's murder-as-tipping-point for all the murders of unarmed Black people that preceded him left a lasting impression both on people who are fighting for social justice and people who are threatened by this fight.[21] Teaching Black students in Black schools about Black pride and history in the 1960s and 1970s was one thing. Teaching all students, especially young white students, about race and other social identity matters is something altogether different for many in America. It is what many white segregationists during Jim Crow feared all along. Therefore, the stakes for "schooling the movement" are perhaps higher than they have ever been. The lessons learned from these exemplary Black educators are timely and timeless, but they cannot teach us everything we need to know moving forward. We are trailblazing a new movement for a new time within a new context. Let's hope we get the unfolding historiography right this time.

NOTES

ALRIDGE, HALE, AND LODER-JACKSON: INTRODUCTION

1. Nikole Hannah-Jones and the *New York Times Magazine* (eds.), *The 1619 Project* (New York: One World, 2021); "1619 Project," *New York Times,* August 18, 2019; Clint Smith, *How the Word Is Passed: A Reckoning with the History of Slavery Across America* (New York: Little, Brown and Company, 2020).

2. Cathryn Stout and Thomas Wilburn, "CRT Map: Efforts to Restrict Teaching Racism and Bias Have Multiplied Across the US," *Chalkbeat* (February 1, 2022), https://www.chalkbeat.org/; Tondra L. Loder-Jackson et al., "Critical Race Theory and Educational Research Utilizing Qualitative Methods," in *International Encyclopedia of Education*, 4th ed., edited by Robert J. Tierney, Fazal Rizvi, and Kadriye Erkican (New York: Elsevier, 2023), 67–77; Caitlin O'Kane, "Nearly a dozen states want to ban critical race theory in schools," *CBS News,* May 20, 2021, accessed at; Bobby Caina Calvan, "Florida Bans 'Critical Race Theory' from its classrooms," *AP News,* June 10, 2021, https://apnews.com/; Alexandra Kelley, "Texas passes law banning critical race theory in schools," *The Hill,* June 17, 2021, https://thehill.com/; https://www.cbsnews.com/news/critical-race-theory-state-bans/; Bobby Caina Calvan, "Florida Bans 'Critical Race Theory' from its classrooms," *AP News,* June 10, 2021, https://apnews.com/; Alexandra Kelley, "Texas passes law banning critical race theory in schools," *The Hill,* June 17, 2021, https://thehill.com/.

3. American Association of University Professors, American Historical Association, Association of American Colleges & Universities, PEN America "Joint Statement on Legislative Efforts to Restrict Education about Racism and American History," June 2021.

4. Jan Vansina, *Oral Tradition as History* (Madison: University of Wisconsin Press, 1985). For further discussion on the use of oral history in exploring teachers' pedagogy, see Derrick P. Alridge, "Teachers in the Movement," https://teachersinthemovement.com/. See also Michele Foster's *Black Teachers on Teaching* published by New Press in 1997.

5. James D. Anderson, *The Education of Blacks in the South, 1860–1935* (Chapel Hill: University of North Carolina Press, 1988); R. Scott Baker, *Paradoxes of Desegregation: African American Struggles for Educational Equity in Charleston, South Carolina, 1926–1972* (Columbia: University of South Carolina Press, 2006); David S. Cecelski, *Along Freedom Road: Hyde County, North Carolina and the Fate of Black Schools in the South* (Chapel Hill: University of North Carolina Press, 1994); Vanessa Siddle Walker, *Hello Professor: A Black Principal and Professional Leadership in the Segregated South* (Chapel Hill: University of North Carolina Press, 2009); Vanessa Siddle Walker, *Their Highest Potential: An African American School Community in the Segregated South* (Chapel Hill: University of North Carolina Press, 1996); Sonya Ramsey, *Reading, Writing, and Segregation: A Century of Black Women Teachers in Nashville* (Champaign: University of Illinois Press, 2008); Tondra L. Loder-Jackson, *Schoolhouse Activists: African American Educators and the Long Birmingham Civil Rights Movement* (New York: State University of New York Press, 2015); Adah Ward Randolph, "The Memories of an All-Black Northern Urban School: Good Memories of Leadership, Teachers and Curriculum," *Urban Education* 39, no. 6 (Nov. 2004), 596–620; Hilton Kelly, *Race, Remembering, and Jim Crow's Teachers* (New York: Routledge, 2010); Karen A. Johnson, Abul Pitre, and Kenneth Johnson, *A Critical Examination of Their Pedagogies, Educational Ideas, and Activism from the Nineteenth to the Mid-Twentieth Century* (Lanham, MD: Rowman & Littlefield Education, 2014); Patrice Preston-Grimes, "Fulfilling the Promise: African American Educators

Teach for Democracy in Jim Crow's South," *Teacher Education Quarterly* 37, no. 1 (Winter 2010): 35–52; Derrick P. Alridge, "Teachers in the Movement: Pedagogy, Activism, and Freedom," *History of Education Quarterly* 60, no. 1 (February 2020), 1–23; Jon N. Hale, *The Freedom Schools: Student Activists in the Mississippi Civil Rights Movement* (New York: Columbia University Press, 2016); Hilary Green, *Educational Reconstruction: African American Schools in the Urban South, 1865–1890* (New York: Fordham University Press, 2016); Wayne Urban, *Why Teachers Organized* (Detroit: Wayne State University Press, 1982); Wayne Urban, *Gender, Race and the National Education Association: Professionalism and its Limitations* (New York: Routledge, 2000); Carol Karpinski, *A Visible Company of Professionals: African Americans and the National Education Association During the Civil Rights Movement* (New York: Peter Lang, 2008). On the Black intellectual tradition, see Derrick P. Alridge, Cornelius L. Bynum, and James B. Stewart (eds.), *The Black Intellectual Tradition: African American Thought in the Twentieth Century* (Champaign: University of Illinois Press, 2021); Dionne Danns, Michelle A. Purdy, and Christopher M. Span (eds.), *Using Past as Prologue: Contemporary Perspectives on African American Educational History* (Charlotte, NC: Information Age Publishing, 2015).

6. Walker, *Their Highest Potential*, 201–5; Vanessa Siddle Walker, "Can Institutions Care? Evidence from the Segregated Schooling of African American Children," in M. Shujaa (ed.), *Beyond Desegregation: The Quality of African American Schooling* (Thousand Oaks, CA: Corwin Press, 1996): 209–26. On the argumentation based on inferiority, see Jonna Perillo, *Uncivil Rights: Teachers, Unions, and Race in the Battle of School Equity* (Chicago: University of Chicago Press, 2012), 100–102; Michael Fultz, "Teacher Training and African American Education in the South, 1900–1940," *Journal of Negro Education*, vol. 64, no. 2 (Spring 1995): 196–210; Daryl Scott, *Contempt and Pity: Social Policy and the Image of the Damaged Black Psyche, 1880–1996* (Chapel Hill: University of North Carolina Press, 1996).

7. Benjamin E. Mays with Orville Vernon Burton, *Born to Rebel: An Autobiography* (Athens: University of Georgia Press, 2003); Randal Jelks, *Benjamin Elijah Mays, Schoolmaster of the Movement: A Biography* (Chapel Hill: University of North Carolina Press, 2012); Katherine Charron, *Freedom's Teacher: The Life of Septima Clark* (Chapel Hill: University of North Carolina Press, 2009); Karen A. Johnson, "Septima Poinsette Clark's Literacy Teaching Approaches for Linguistic Acquisition and Literacy Development for Gullah-Speaking Children," in *African American Women Educators: A Critical Examination of their Pedagogies, Educational Ideas, and Activism from the Nineteenth to the Mid-Twentieth Century*, edited by Karen A. Johnson, Abdul Pitre, and Kenneth L. Johnson (Lanham, MD: Rowman and Littlefield, 2014), 73–105; Derrick P. Alridge, *The Educational Thought of W. E. B. Du Bois: An Intellectual History* (New York: Teachers College Press, 2008); Valinda Littlefield, *South Carolina Women: Their Lives and Times* (Athens: University of Georgia Press, 2009); R. Scott Baker, "Pedagogies of Protest: African American Educators and the History of the Civil Rights Movement, 1940–1963," *Teachers College Record*, 113, no. 12 (2011): 2777–2803.

8. Charron, *Freedom's Teacher*; Afro American and Richmond Planet, "NAACP Carries Teacher Salary Fight into VA," (November 5, 1938), quoted in *Encyclopedia Virginia*, accessed March 27, 2022, https://encyclopediavirginia .org/; Mississippi Encyclopedia, "Gladys Noel Bates, 1920–2010 Educator and Activist," accessed March 27, 2022, https://mississippi encyclopedia.org/.

9. Adam Fairclough, *A Class of Their Own: Black Teachers in the Segregated South* (Cambridge, MA: Belknap Press, 2007), 345–49; Charron, *Freedom's Teacher*, 242–47; John F. Potts, *A History of the Palmetto Education Association* (Washington, DC: National Education Association, 1978), 66–67; Jerome A. Gray, Joe L. Reed, and Norman W. Walton, *History of the Alabama State Teachers Association* (Washington, DC: National Education Association, 1987); 151–154. On activism at the university level, see Jeffrey A. Turner, *Sitting In and Speaking Out: Student Movement in the American South, 1960–1970* (Athens: University of Georgia Press, 2010), 167–169; Joy Ann Williamson, "This Has Been Quite a Year for Heads Falling": Institutional Autonomy in the Civil Rights Era, *History of Education Quarterly* 44, no. 4 (Winter 2004): 554–76; Karen A. Johnson, "Septima Poinsette Clark's Literacy Teaching Approaches," 73–106.

10. Valinda Littlefield, "Teaching Survival and Combat Strategies During the Jim Crow Era: Ruby Middleton Forsythe and Fannie Phelps Adams" in *South Carolina Women: Their Lives and Times*, Marjorie Julian Spruill, Valinda W. Littlefield, and Joan Marie Johnson, eds. (Athens: University of Georgia Press, 2012), 17–34; Charron, *Freedom's Teacher*, 3–5; Tiyi M. Morris, *Womanpower Unlimited and the Black Freedom Struggle in Mississippi* (Athens: University of Georgia Press, 2015).

11. Maurice J. Hobson, *The Legend of the Black Mecca: Politics and Class in the Making of Modern America* (Chapel Hill: University of North Carolina Press, 2019); Jerome E. Morris and Carla R. Monroe, "Why Study the U.S. South? The Nexus of Race and Place in Investigating Black Student Achievement," *Educational Researcher* 38, no. 1 (2009): 21–36; Tomiko Brown-Nagin, *Courage to Dissent: Atlanta and the Long History of the Civil Rights Movement* (Oxford, England: Oxford University Press, 2012).

12. On the professional networks of Black educators, see Walker, *Hello Professor*; Carol Karpinski, *"A Visible Company of Professionals": African Americans and the National Education Association During the Civil Rights Movement* (New York: Peter Lang, 2008); Wayne Urban, *Gender, Race and the National Education Association: Professionalism and its Limitations* (New York: Routledge, 2000). On the organization of White teacher associations, see Marjorie Murphy, *Blackboard Union: The AFT and the NEA 1900–1980* (Ithaca, NY: Cornell University Press, 1990); Jonna Perillo, *Uncivil Rights: Teachers, Unions, and Race in the Battle of School Equity* (Chicago: University of Chicago Press, 2012); Wayne Urban, *Why Teachers Organized* (Detroit: Wayne State University Press, 1982). On the historiography to situate the professional association of teachers as labor, see Robin Kelley, *Hammer and Hoe: Alabama Communists During the Great Depression* (Chapel Hill: University of North Carolina Press, 1990); Theodore Rosengarten, *All God's Dangers: The Life of Nate Shaw* (New York: Random House, Vintage Books, 1974); Michael Honey, *Southern Labor and Black Civil Rights: Organizing Memphis Workers* (Champaign: University of Illinois Press, 1993). On the work of Black dockworkers and interracial labor struggles in New Orleans, see Eric Arnesen, *Waterfront Workers of New Orleans: Race, Class, and Politics, 1863–1923* (New York: Oxford University Press, 1991); Daniel Rosenberg, *New Orleans Dockworkers: Race, Labor, and Unionism, 1892–1923* (Albany: State University of New York Press, 1988); Herbert Gutman, "The Negro and the United Mine Workers of America: The Career and Letters of Richard L. Davis and Something of Their Meaning, 1890–1900," 121–208; Henry M. McKiven Jr., *Iron and Steel: Class, Race, and Community in Birmingham, Alabama, 1875–1920* (Chapel Hill: University of North Carolina Press, 1995); Bruce Nelson, *Divided We Stand: American Workers and the Struggle for Black Equality* (Princeton, NJ: Princeton University Press, 2001); Nell Irvin Painter, *The Narrative of Hosea Hudson: His Life as a Negro Communist in the South* (Cambridge, MA: Harvard University Press, 1979); Leon F. Litwack, "Working," in *Trouble in Mind: Black Southerners in the Age of Jim Crow* (New York: Random House, 1998), 114–178.

13. Jarvis R. Givens, "'There Would be No Lynching if It Did Not Start in the Schoolroom': Carter G. Woodson and the Occasion of Negro History Week, 1926–1950," *American Educational Research Journal* 56 no. 4 (August 2019): 1457–1494; Imani Perry, *May We Forever Stand: A History of the Black National Anthem* (Chapel Hill: University of North Carolina Press, 2018).

14. Tondra L. Loder-Jackson, Lois M. Christensen, and Hilton Kelly, "Unearthing and Bequeathing Black Feminist Legacies of *Brown* to a New Generation of Women and Girls," *Journal of Negro Education* 85, no. 3 (Summer 2016): 199–211; Ronald Roach, "The Scholar-Activists of *Brown*," *Black Issues in Higher Education* 21, no. 7 (May 2004): 26–31.

15. Loder-Jackson, *Schoolhouse Activists*, 6–13.

16. John Dittmer, *Local People: The Struggle for Civil Rights in Mississippi* (Champaign: University of Illinois Press, 1994), 143–55; Aldon D. Morris, *The Origins of the Civil Rights Movement: Black Communities Organizing for Change* (New York: Free Press, 1984), 195–228; Charles Payne, *I've Got the Light of Freedom: The Organizing Tradition and the Mississippi Freedom Struggle* (Berkeley: University of California Press, 1996); François N. Hamlin, *Crossroads at Clarksdale: The Black Freedom Struggle in the Mississippi Delta after World War II* (Chapel

Hill: University of North Carolina Press, 2012); Emilye Crosby, *A Little Taste of Freedom: The Black Freedom Struggle in Claiborne County, Mississippi* (Chapel Hill: University of North Carolina Press, 2005); Doug McAdam, *Freedom Summer* (New York: Oxford University Press, 1988); Bruce Watson, *Freedom Summer: The Savage Season That Made Mississippi Burn and Made America a Democracy* (New York: Viking Press, 2010).

17. On the origins of the earliest documentation of teacher activism and the organization to overturn "White-only" teaching laws in the South, see Michael Fultz, "Charleston, 1919–1920: The Final Battle in the Emergence of the South's Urban African American Teaching Corps," *Journal of Urban History* 27, no. 5 (July 2001): 633–49; Howard N. Rabinowitz, "Half a Loaf: The Shift from White to Black Teachers in the Negro Schools of the Urban South, 1865–1890," *Journal of Southern History* 40, no. 4 (November 1974): 565–94. On the organization of Black teacher associations, see Walker, *Hello Professor*; Karpinski, *A Visible Company of Professionals*; J. Rupert Picott, *History of the Virginia Teachers Association* (Washington, DC: National Education Association, 1975); Cleopatra D. Thompson, *The History of the Mississippi Teachers Association* (Washington, DC: NEA Teachers Rights, 1973); John F. Potts Sr., *A History of the Palmetto Education Association* (Washington, DC: National Education Association, 1978); Percy Murray, *History of the North Carolina Teachers Association* (Washington, DC: National Education Association, 1984); Thelma D. Perry, *History of the American Teachers Association* (Washington, DC: National Education Association, 1975). See also Tondra L. Loder-Jackson, *Schoolhouse Activists: African American Educators and the Long Birmingham Civil Rights Movement* (Albany: State University of New York Press, 2015); R. Scott Baker, "Pedagogies of Protest: African American Teachers and the History of the Civil Rights Movement, 1940–1963," *Teachers College Record* 113, no. 12 (December 2011), 2777–2803.

18. As Nelson Lichtenstein noted, "teachers... had been largely unorganized in the 1950s and expected to remain so"; see Nelson Lichtenstein, *State of the Union: A Century of American Labor* (Princeton, NJ: Princeton University Press, 2002), 189; Nelson Lichetenstein and Elizabeth Tandy Shermer, *The Right and Labor in America: Politics, Ideology, and Imagination* (Philadelphia: University of Philadelphia Press, 2012); Elizabeth Tandy Shermer, "Counter-Organizing the Sunbelt: Right-to-Work Campaigns and Anti-Union Conservatism, 1943–1958," *Pacific Historical Review* 98, no. 1 (February 2009): 81–118.

19. Fairclough, *A Class of Their Own*, 357.

20. John Dittmer, *Local People: The Struggle for Civil Rights in Mississippi* (Champaign: University of Illinois Press, 1994), 75. Scholars have tempered such accounts by thoroughly documenting the integral role of Black public schools in local communities across South, see Baker, *Paradoxes of Desegregation*; David S. Cecelski, *Along Freedom Road: Hyde County, North Carolina and the Fate of Black Schools in the South* (Chapel Hill: University of North Carolina Press, 1994); Walker, *Their Highest Potential*; for a larger context on the role of pedagogy, including John Dewey and progressive education theory and practice in fostering activism in Burke High School, see R. Scott Baker, "Pedagogies of Protest."

21. For more information, see https://teachersinthemovement.com, accessed September 28, 2021.

22. Jacquelyn Dowd Hall, "The Long Civil Rights Movement and the Political Uses of the Past," *Journal of American History* 91, no. 4 (2005): 1233–1263.

GIVENS: TEACHING TO "UNDO THEIR NARRATIVELY CONDEMNED STATUS"

1. Jarvis Ray Givens, "'A Grammar for Black Education beyond Borders': Exploring Technologies of Schooling in the African Diaspora," *Race, Ethnicity and Education* 19, no. 6 (2016): 1288–1302; Achille Mbembe, *Critique of Black Reason*, trans. Laurent Dubois (Durham, NC: Duke University Press Books, 2017), 28.

2. Vanessa Siddle Walker, *Their Highest Potential: An African American School Community in the Segregated South* (Chapel Hill: The University of North Carolina Press, 1996); Vanessa Siddle Walker, "African American Teaching in the South: 1940–1960," *American Educational Research Journal* 38, no. 4 (December 21, 2001): 751–779; V. P. Franklin, "'They Rose and Fell Together': African American Educators and Community Leadership, 1795–1954," *Journal of Education* 172, no. 3 (1990): 39–64; Tondra L.

Loder-Jackson, *Schoolhouse Activists: African American Educators and the Long Birmingham Civil Rights Movement* (Albany: SUNY Press, 2015); Michael Fultz, "African American Teachers in the South, 1890–1940: Powerlessness and the Ironies of Expectations and Protest," *History of Education Quarterly* 35, no. 4 (1995): 401–22; Michael Fultz, "An African American Educator in the Context of His Time: George Washington Trenholm, 1871–1925," *The Alabama Review* 73, no. 3 (2020): 246–67.

3. Benjamin Quarles, "Black History's Antebellum Origins," *Proceedings of the American Antiquarian Society* 89, no. 1 (1979): 89–122; Charles H. Wesley, "Creating and Maintaining an Historical Tradition," *Journal of Negro History* 49, no. 1 (1964): 13–33; Pero Dagbovie, *The Early Black History Movement, Carter G. Woodson, and Lorenzo Johnston Greene* (Champaign: University of Illinois Press, 2007); Jeffrey Aaron Snyder, *Making Black History: The Color Line, Culture, and Race in the Age of Jim Crow* (Athens: University of Georgia Press, 2018); Jarvis R. Givens, "'There Would Be No Lynching If It Did Not Start in the Schoolroom': Carter G. Woodson and the Occasion of Negro History Week, 1926–1950," *American Educational Research Journal* 56, no. 4 (2019): 1457–94; Jarvis R. Givens, "'He Was, Undoubtedly, a Wonderful Character': Black Teachers' Representations of Nat Turner during Jim Crow," *Souls* 18, no. 2–4 (October 2016): 215–34.

4. Sylvia Wynter, "No Humans Involved: An Open Letter to My Colleagues (May 1992)," *Forum N.H.I. Knowledge for the 21st Century* 1, no. 1 (Fall 1994): 70, 58.

5. Woodson, *The Mis-Education of the Negro*, 3.

6. Sylvia Wynter, "Textbooks and What They Do: The Conceptual Breakthrough of Carter G. Woodson," in *Do Not Call Us Negro: How "Multicultural" Textbooks Perpetuate Racism* (San Francisco: Aspire, 1990).

7. "[G]ender is the modality in which race is lived." Paul Gilroy, *The Black Atlantic: Modernity and Double-Consciousness*, Reissue edition (Cambridge, MA: Harvard University Press, 1993), 85. Gilroy references and directly builds on Stuart Hall's former (1978) claim that "race is the modality in which class is lived." See Stuart Hall, *Policing the Crisis: Mugging, the State, and Law and Order* (London: Macmillan, 1978), 394.

8. Wynter, "No Humans Involved: An Open Letter to My Colleagues," 58, 62.

9. Khalil Gibran Muhammad, *The Condemnation of Blackness: Race, Crime, and the Making of Modern Urban America* (Cambridge, MA: Harvard University Press, 2011).

10. Quarles, "Black History's Antebellum Origins"; Wesley, "Creating and Maintaining an Historical Tradition."

11. James W. C. Pennington, *The Fugitive Blacksmith; or, Events in the History of James W. C. Pennington, Pastor of a Presbyterian Church, New York, Formerly a Slave in the State of Maryland, United States* (London: Charles Gilpin, 1849), iv. "The being of slavery, its soul and body, lives and moves in the chattel principle, the property principle, the bill of sale principle; the cart-whip, starvation, and nakedness, are its inevitable consequences. . . ."; Pennington's concept of "the chattel principle" is further theorized by Walter Johnson. See Walter Johnson, *Soul by Soul: Life inside the Antebellum Slave Market* (Cambridge, MA: Harvard University Press, 1999), 20.

12. James W. C. Pennington, *Text Book of the Origin and History of the Colored People* (Hartford: L. Skinner, 1841); Webster, quoted in Stephen G. Hall, *A Faithful Account of the Race: African American Historical Writing in Nineteenth-Century America* (Chapel Hill: University of North Carolina Press, 2009), 49.

13. The fugitive slave William Wells Brown also wrote a textbook. William Wells Brown, *The Black Man: His Antecedents, His Genius, and His Achievements* (New York: Thomas Hamilton; Boston, MA: R. F. Wallcut, 1863).

14. The intellectual task embodied by Pennington was at the foundation of black literary practices; cf. Nathaniel Mackey, "Other: From Noun to Verb," *Representations*, no. 39 (1992): 55.

15. Benjamin Quarles, *Allies for Freedom: Blacks and John Brown* (New York: Oxford University Press, 1974), 119.

16. Charlotte L. Forten, *The Journal of Charlotte L. Forten*, Ray Allen Billington, ed. (New York: W. W. Norton & Company, 1981), 194–95; see also 72, 112.

17. Quoted in Benjamin Quarles, *Black Mosaic: Essays in Afro-American History and Historiography*, First edition (Amherst: University of Massachusetts Press, 1988), 112.

18. Forten, *The Journal of Charlotte L. Forten*, 55.

19. Forten, 55.

20. Charlotte Forten Grimké, "Life on the Sea Islands (1864)," in *The Portable Nineteenth-Century African American Women Writers*, *Edited by Hollis Robbins and Henry Louis Gates* (New York: Penguin Classics, 2017), 138.

21. Heather Williams, *Self-Taught: African American Education in Slavery and Freedom* (Chapel Hill: University of North Carolina Press, 2007), 126, 136.

22. Grimké, "Life on the Sea Islands" (1864), 138–39.

23. Frederick Douglass quoted in Quarles, *Black Mosaic*, 65.

24. Richard Robert Wright, "The Possibilities of the Negro Teacher," *The AME Church Review* 10, no. 4 (April 1894): 460.

25. Wright, 461.

26. Wright, 464–65.

27. Wright, 464–65.

28. Rayford W. Logan, *The Betrayal Of The Negro: From Rutherford B. Hayes To Woodrow Wilson* (New York: Hachette Books, 1965).

29. August Meier and Elliott Rudwick, *Black History and the Historical Profession, 1915–1980* (Champaign: University of Illinois Press, 1986), 3–4; John David Smith et al., *The Dunning School: Historians, Race, and the Meaning of Reconstruction* (Lexington: The University Press of Kentucky, 2013); see also "Looking Backward" in W. E. B. Du Bois and David Levering Lewis, *Black Reconstruction in America 1860–1880* (New York: Simon and Schuster, 1935).

30. Oliver R. Pope, *Chalk Dust* (New York: Pageant Press, 1967), 4.

31. Benjamin Mays, *Born to Rebel: An Autobiography* (Athens: University of Georgia Press, 2003), 2–4.

32. For more on Benjamin May's early education, see Randal Maurice Jelks, *Benjamin Elijah Mays, Schoolmaster of the Movement: A Biography* (Durham: University of North Carolina Press, 2014), 33.

33. Jelks, *Benjamin Elijah Mays, Schoolmaster of the Movement*, 33.

34. Roscoe C. Bruce, "Report of the Assistant Superintendent in Charge of Colored Schools," *Report of the Commissioners of the District of Columbia*, July 1, 1915, 249–50; E. Renee Ingram, "Bruce, Roscoe Conkling, Sr.," in *Harlem Renaissance Lives: from the African American National Biography*, Henry Louis Gates Jr. and Evelyn Brooks Higginbotham, eds. (New York: Oxford University Press, 2009), 84–86.

35. Jessie Fauset, "What to Read," *The Crisis*, August 1912, 183.

36. Pendleton, *A Narrative of the Negro*, 6.

37. Arthur Alfonso Schomburg, *Racial Integrity: A Plea for the Establishment of a Chair of Negro History in Our Schools and Colleges, Etc.* (New York: A.V. Bernier, 1913).

38. Schomburg, *Racial Integrity*.

39. Schomburg, *Racial Integrity*.

40. William H. Watkins, "Black Curriculum Orientations: A Preliminary Inquiry," *Harvard Educational Review* 63, no. 3 (1993): 321–38.

41. Schomburg, *Racial Integrity*.

42. Randall K. Burkett, Pellom McDaniels, and Tiffany Gleason, *The Mind of Carter G. Woodson as Reflected in the Books He Owned, Read, & Published* (Atlanta: Emory University, 2006).

43. Bruce, "Report of the Assistant Superintendent in Charge of Colored Schools," July 1, 1915, 249–50.

44. Bruce, "Report of the Assistant Superintendent in Charge of Colored Schools," July 1, 1915, 249–50.

45. W. E. B. Du Bois, "Slanderous Film," *The Crisis*, December 1915, 76–77; Ed Guerrero, *Framing Blackness: The African American Image in Film* (Philadelphia: Temple University Press, 1993), 11–13.

46. Dagbovie, *The Early Black History Movement*.

47. Roscoe Bruce, "Report of the Assistant Superintendent in Charge of Colored Schools," *Report of the Commissioners of the District of Columbia*, June 30, 1916, 249–250.

48. Carter G. Woodson, "Notes," Journal of Negro History 1, no. 1 (1916): 98; J. R. Fauset, review of The Haitian Revolution, 1791 to 1804, by T. G. Steward, 93; W. B. Hartgrove, "The Story of Maria Louise Moore and Fannie M. Richards," Journal of Negro History 1, no. 1 (1916): 23–33.

49. Roscoe Bruce, "Report of the Assistant Superintendent in Charge of Colored Schools," *Report of the Commissioners of the District of Columbia*, June 30, 1916, 249–50.

50. "The Challenge to the Negro," 1926–1927, Box 1 Folder 33, CGW Papers, Emory University.

51. Ernest J. Middleton, *History of Louisiana Education Association* (Washington, DC: National Education Association, 1984), 65.

52. Ernest Becker, "Correspondence from Ernest O. Becker (Assistant Superintendent) to Miss Sue Hafley (Supervisor of School Libraries) and CC: Mr. George Longe," December 19, 1947, George Longe Papers Box 1, Folder 1, Amistad Research Center, New Orleans, LA.

53. Ira B. Bryant, "Study Guide Negro History, Public School, Houston, Texas," 1936, Thelma S. Bryant and Ira B. Bryant Collection, MSS 0452, Box 4, Folder 3, Houston Metropolitan Research Center, The African American Library at the Gregory School; George Longe, "A Tentative Approach to Negro History for Use in Grades 1–4, New Orleans Colored Public Schools, Literature and Music," 1936, George Longe Papers Box 2, Folder 7, Amistad Research Center, New Orleans, LA; Bessie King and Madeline Stratton, "Supplementary Units for the Course of Study in Social Studies, Grades 7–8" (Chicago: Bureau of Curriculum, Board of Education, City of Chicago, 1942), Madeline Stratton Morris Papers Box 2, Folder 2, Vivian G. Harsh Research Collection of Afro-American History and Literature, Chicago Public Library.

54. Jonathan Zimmerman, "Brown-ing the American Textbook: History, Psychology, and the Origins of Modern Multiculturalism," *History of Education Quarterly* 44, no. 1 (Spring 2004): 52.

55. E. Belfield Spriggins, "Dr. Du Bois Holds Audience Spellbound on 'Negro and Reconstruction,'" *Louisiana Weekly*, February 24, 1934, Louisiana Weekly Microfilm Collection, Amistad Research Center, New Orleans, LA.

56. W. E. B. Du Bois, "Does the Negro Need Separate Schools?" *Journal of Negro Education* 4, no. 3 (1935): 328–35.

57. Albert White, "Historians Hold Session," *Louisiana Weekly*, November 17, 1934, Amistad Research Center, New Orleans, LA.

58. Vivian Robinson, "Black Reconstruction, W. E. B. Du Bois," *The Moving Finger*, 1937, Box 2 Folder 10, Fannie C. Williams papers, Amistad Research Center, New Orleans, Louisiana.

59. Tamah Richardson and Annie Rivers, "Progress of the Negro: A Unit of Work for the Third Grade," *Virginia Teachers Bulletin* (May 1936): 3–8.

60. Richardson and Rivers, "Progress of the Negro: A Unit of Work for the Third Grade," 3–8.

61. "Proceedings of the Annual Meeting of the ASNLH, Held at Virginia State College, Petersburg, Virginia, October 25–28, 1936." *Journal of Negro History* 22, no. 1 (January 1937): 11.

62. Dagbovie, "Black Women, Carter G. Woodson, and the Association for the Study of Negro Life and History, 1915–1950."

63. Mary McLeod Bethune, "The Association for the Study of Negro Life and History: Its Contributions to Our Modern Life," *Journal of Negro History* 20, no. 4 (October 1935): 408.

64. "Proceedings of the Annual Meeting of the ASNLH, Held at Virginia State College, Petersburg, Virginia, October 25–28, 1936," 11.

65. John Hope Franklin, "The Place of Carter G. Woodson in American Historiography," *Negro History Bulletin* 13, no. 8 (May 1950): 176.

66. Carter G. Woodson to Lorenzo Greene, June 8, 1937, Box 74, Lorenzo Johnston Green Papers, Manuscript Division, Library of Congress, Washington, DC.

67. Carter G. Woodson to Pearl Schwartz, November 10, 1937, Box 75 in Lorenzo Johnston Green Papers, Manuscript Division, Library of Congress, Washington, DC; Lorenzo J. Greene to Carter G. Woodson, November 13, 1937, Box 74 in Greene Papers.

68. Greene to Woodson, June 22, 1938, Box 74, Greene Papers; Woodson to Greene, July 2, 1938, Box 74, Greene Papers.

69. Vanessa Siddle Walker, *The Lost Education of Horace Tate: Uncovering the Hidden Heroes Who Fought for Justice in Schools* (New York: The New Press, 2018); Jon Hale, "'The Development of Power Is the Main Business of the School': The Agency of Southern Black Teacher Associations from Jim Crow through Desegregation," *Journal of Negro Education* 87, no. 4 (Fall 2018): 444–59.

70. E. Horace Fitchett to Carter G. Woodson, May 30, 1941, Papers of Carter G. Woodson and the Association for the Study of Negro Life and History, 1915–1950 [Microfilm Collection, University Publication of America).

71. Carter G. Woodson, "Notes," *Journal of Negro History* 5, no. 7 (April 1942), 242–43.

72. Dr. D. O. W. Holmes, "Spent Life Bringing About Respect for Race, Heritage," *The Afro-American*, May 12, 1950.

73. Thelma D. Perry, *History of the American Teachers Association* (Washington, DC: National Education Association, 1975), 195.

74. "Teachers Urged By Dr. Woodson to Adopt More Realistic Approach: Delegates Pack Sisters Chapel," *Atlanta Daily World*, April 17, 1942, 1 and 6.

75. Woodson, *The Mis-Education of the Negro*, chapter 3.

76. "Teachers Urged by Dr. Woodson to Adopt More Realistic Approach: Delegates Pack Sisters Chapel," *Atlanta Daily World*, April 17, 1942, 1 and 6.

77. Carter G. Woodson, *Early Negro Education in West Virginia*, Vol. 3, no. 6, Studies in Social Science (Charleston: The West Virginia Collegiate Institute, 1921); see chapter 6.

78. Albert Brooks, "Organizing Negro Leadership," *NHB* (May 1945): 180.

79. Muhammad, *The Condemnation of Blackness*.

80. Jarvis R. Givens, *Fugitive Pedagogy: Carter G. Woodson and the Art of Black Teaching* (Cambridge, MA: Harvard University Press, 2021), 2–4.

JOHNSON, WINGFIELD, AND ALRIDGE: CYNTHIA PLAIR RODDEY

1. Pat Robertson, "Rock Hill Teacher is First Negro at Winthrop," *Evening Herald*, July 20, 1964; "Winthrop College Admits First Negro" (Greenwood, SC), *Index Journal*, July 20, 1964, 1.

2. Cynthia Roddey, interview by Derrick Alridge, September 12, 2015. James Wright, an educator in South Carolina, noted the perception of Rock Hill as a more progressive town compared with others in South Carolina. See James Wright, interview by Derrick Alridge, January 20, 2020. Teachers in the Movement Project Collection, University of Virginia (all interviews with Cynthia Plair Roddey hereafter are in the TIM Collection unless otherwise noted).

3. "Winthrop Alumna Cynthia Roddey to be Honored as Local Hero," November 18, 2019, https://www.winthrop.edu/.

4. Cynthia Roddey, interview by Derrick Alridge, September 12, 2015, TIM Collection, University of Virginia; A. J. Angulo and Leland Graham, Winthrop College in the Sixties: Campus Protests, Southern Style, *Historical Studies in Education/Revue d'histoire de l'éducation* 23,

no. 2 (Fall 2011), https://doi.org/10.32316/hse/rhe.v23i2.3222.

5. Tondra Loder-Jackson, *Schoolhouse Activists: Educators and the Long Birmingham Civil Rights Movement* (New York: SUNY Press, 2016), 24.

6. V. P. Franklin, *The Young Crusaders: The Untold Story of the Children and Teenagers Who Galvanized the Civil Rights Movement* (New York: Basic Books, 2021); Martha Jones, *Vanguard: How Black Women Broke Barriers, Won the Vote, and Insisted on Equality for All* (New York: Basic Books, 2020); Tondra Loder-Jackson, *Schoolhouse Activists: Educators and the Long Birmingham Civil Rights Movement* (New York: SUNY Press, 2016).

7. Adam Fairclough, "The Costs of *Brown*: Black Teachers and School Integration," *Journal of American History* 91, no. 1 (June 2004): 43–55; and Adam Fairclough, *Teaching Equality: Black Schools in the Age of Jim Crow* (Athens: University of Georgia Press, 2001); Sonya Ramsey, *Reading, Writing, and Segregation: A Century of Black Women Teachers in Nashville* (Champaign: University of Illinois Press, 2008).

8. James D. Anderson, *The Education of Blacks in the South, 1860–1935* (Chapel Hill: University of North Carolina Press, 1988); Vanessa Siddle Walker, *Their Highest Potential: An African American School Community in the Segregated South* (Chapel Hill: University of North Carolina Press, 1996); Vanessa Siddle Walker with Ulysses Byas, *Hello Professor: A Black Principal and Professional Leadership in the Segregated South* (Chapel Hill: University of North Carolina Press, 2009); Vanessa Siddle Walker, *The Lost Education of Horace Tate: Uncovering the Hidden Heroes Who Fought for Justice in Schools* (New York: The New Press, 2018); Jarvis Givens, *Fugitive Pedagogy: Carter G. Woodson and the Art of Black Teaching* (Cambridge, MA: Harvard University Press, 2021).

9. R. Scott Baker, *Paradoxes of Desegregation: African American Struggles for Educational Equity in Charleston, South Carolina, 1926–1972* (Columbia; University of South Carolina Press, 2006); Candace Cunningham, "'Hell Is Popping Here in South Carolina': Orangeburg County Black Teachers and Their Community in the Immediate Post-*Brown* Era," *History of Education Quarterly* 6, no. 1 (February 2021), 35–62; Jon Hale, "'The Development of Power Is the

Main Business of the School': The Agency of Southern Black Teacher Associations from Jim Crow through Desegregation," *Journal of Negro Education*, 87, no. 4 (Fall 2018): 444–59; Scott Baker, "Pedagogies of Protest: African American Teachers and the History of the Civil Rights Movement, 1940–1963," *Teachers College Record*, 13, no. 12 (December 2011): 2077–83.

10. Sonya Ramsey, *Reading, Writing, and Segregation: A Century of Black Women Teachers in Nashville* (Champaign: University of Illinois Press, 2008).

11. See https://teachersinthemovement.dev8 .uvaits.virginia.edu, accessed September 28, 2021.

12. The 2005 interview was conducted before the establishment of the TIM project in 2014. The first two interviews were conducted by Derrick Alridge, director of the TIM project. The 2021 interview was conducted by Alridge and the project's associate director, Alexis Johnson. TIM Collection.

13. Sandi Ludwa, *Ashes to Incense: Emancipation from Jim Crow* (Bloomington, IN: Xlibris, 2017), 31.

14. Ibid., 33–34.

15. David Perlmutt, "From one man's wheelchair: A dignified historical stand," *Evening Herald*, February 14, 2010, 1B and 5B.

16. William "Dub" Massey, interview by Derrick P. Alridge, Rock Hill, SC, September 17, 2017, TIM Collection; Fred Sheheen, "Lunch Counters: Police Arrest 10 at Rock Hill Sit-In," *Charlotte Observer*, February 1, 1961, A series of sit-ins took place before the 1961 sit-in. The first sit-in at McCrory occurred on February 12, 1960.

17. John Hope Franklin and Evelyn Brooks Higginbotham, *From Slavery to Freedom: A History of African Americans* (New York: McGraw Hill, 2021), 600.

18. Cynthia Plair Roddey, interview by Derrick Alridge, September 12, 2015.

19. Cynthia Plair Roddey, interview by Derrick Alridge, September 12, 2015.

20. Cynthia Plair Roddey, interview by Derrick Alridge, September 12, 2015. For an examination of Emmett Scott High School, see Terrance J. Alridge, "A Case Study of Emmett Scott High School from 1965–1970," (PhD diss., University of South Carolina, 2009).

21. Cynthia Plair Roddey, interview by Derrick Alridge, September 12, 2015.

22. Cynthia Plair Roddey, interview by Derrick Alridge, September 12, 2015. See W. E. B. Du Bois, *The Negroes of Farmville, Virginia: A Social Study* (Washington, DC, 1898) and W. E. B. Du Bois, "The Upbuilding of Black Durham: The Success of the Negroes and Their Value to a Tolerant and Helpful Southern City," *The Worlds Work* 23 (January 1912): 334–38.

23. Cynthia Roddey, interview by Derrick Alridge and Alexis Johnson, June 5, 2021.

24. Cynthia Roddey, interview by Derrick Alridge and Alexis Johnson, June 5, 2021.

25. Cynthia Roddey, interview by Derrick Alridge and Alexis Johnson, June 5, 2021.

26. Cynthia Roddey, interview by Derrick Alridge and Alexis Johnson, June 5, 2021.

27. Cynthia Roddey, interview by Derrick Alridge, September 12, 2015.

28. Cynthia Roddey, interview by Derrick Alridge, September 12, 2015.

29. Cynthia Roddey, interview by Derrick Alridge, September 12, 2015.

30. Cynthia Roddey, interview by Derrick Alridge, September 12, 2015.

31. Cynthia Roddey, interview by Derrick Alridge and Alexis Johnson, June 5, 2021.

32. Cynthia Roddey, interview by Derrick Alridge, September 12, 2015.

33. Jelani M. Favors, *Shelter in a Time of Storm: How Black Colleges Fostered Generations of Leadership and Activism* (Chapel Hill, NC: University of North Carolina Press, 2019), 17.

34. Before 1975, North Carolina had twelve HBCUs. After the closing of Kittrell College in 1975, it now has eleven HBCUs. "North Carolina's Historically Black Colleges and Universities (HBCUs)," accessed June 14, 2021, https://www.ncpedia.org/.

35. Tom Hanchett, interview by Alexis Johnson, July 29, 2020.

36. Favors, *Shelter in a Time of Storm*, 15.

37. Clayborne Carson, *In Struggle: SNCC and the Black Awakening of the 1960s* (Cambridge, MA: Harvard University Press, 1981).

38. Cynthia Roddey, interview by Derrick Alridge, September 12, 2015.

39. Cynthia Roddey, interview by Derrick Alridge, September 12, 2015; Cynthia Roddey, interview by Hope Murphy, May 17, 2004, transcript and recording Special Collections, J. Murrey Atkins Library, University of North Carolina at Charlotte.

40. Cynthia Roddey, interview by Derrick Alridge, September 12, 2015.

41. "Partnership History," accessed June 14, 2021, https://tougaloo.brown.edu/.

42. Jill Ogline Titus, *Brown's Battleground: Students, Segregationists, and the Struggle for Justice in Prince Edward County, Virginia* (Chapel Hill, NC: University of North Carolina Press, 2011), 56–94.

43. Cynthia Roddey, interview by Derrick Alridge, September 12, 2015.

44. Cynthia Roddey, interview by Derrick Alridge, September 12, 2015. Cynthia Roddey, interview by Hope Murphy, May 17, 2004, transcript and recording Special Collections, J. Murrey Atkins Library, University of North Carolina at Charlotte.

45. Cynthia Roddey, interview by Derrick Alridge, September 12, 2015; Cynthia Roddey, interview by Hope Murphy, May 17, 2004, transcript and recording Special Collections, J. Murrey Atkins Library, University of North Carolina at Charlotte; Cynthia Roddey, interview by Derrick Alridge and Alexis Johnson, June 5, 2021.

46. Cynthia Roddey, interview by Derrick Alridge, 2005; Cynthia Roddey, interview by Derrick Alridge, September 12, 2015; Cynthia Roddey, interview by Hope Murphy, May 17, 2004, transcript and recording, Special Collections, J. Murrey Atkins Library, University of North Carolina at Charlotte.

47. Cynthia Roddey, interview by Derrick Alridge and Alexis Johnson, June 5, 2021.

48. Cynthia Roddey, interview by Derrick Alridge and Alexis Johnson, June 5, 2021.

49. Cynthia Roddey, interview by Derrick Alridge and Alexis Johnson, June 5, 2021.

50. Cynthia Roddey, interview by Derrick Alridge, 2005.

51. "Chronology: Early Achievements," accessed June 17, 2021, https://www.winthrop.edu/.

52. Cynthia Roddey, interview by Derrick Alridge, 2005; Cynthia Roddey, interview by Derrick Alridge and Alexis Johnson, June 5, 2021.

53. Cynthia Roddey, interview by Derrick Alridge, 2005.

54. Cynthia Roddey, interview by Derrick Alridge and Alexis Johnson, June 5, 2021.

55. Cynthia Roddey, interview by Derrick Alridge, September 12, 2015.

56. Alumni Association, Alumni Awards, Alumni Distinguished Service Award, Cynthia Plair Roddey '67, https://www.winthrop.edu/.

57. Cynthia Roddey, interview by Derrick Alridge and Alexis Johnson, June 5, 2021.

58. Cynthia Roddey, interview by Hope Murphy, May 17, 2004, transcript and recording, Special Collections, J. Murrey Atkins Library, University of North Carolina at Charlotte.

59. Cynthia Roddey, interview by Derrick Alridge and Alexis Johnson, June 5, 2021; Cynthia Roddey, interview by Hope Murphy, May 17, 2004, transcript and recording, Special Collections, J. Murrey Atkins Library, University of North Carolina at Charlotte.

60. Edward A. Hatfield, "Desegregation of Higher Education," last modified February 25, 2021, https://www.georgiaencyclopedia.org/.

61. Thomas James Carey, "Desegregation of Public Colleges and Universities," last modified April 13, 2018, https://mississippiencyclopedia.org/.

62. Claude Sitton, "Enrolling of Meredith Ends Segregation in State Schools," *New York Times*, October 1, 1962.

63. South Carolina State University is the state's historically Black land-grant institution.

64. Cathy Sams, "Introduction: 'Quiet Courage,'" in *Integration with Dignity: A Celebration of Harvey Gantt's Admission to Clemson*, Skip Eisminger, ed. (Clemson, SC: Clemson University, 2003), 2.

65. Cathy Sams and Harry Durham, "40 years ago: Gantt breaks Clemson color barrier," *Times and Democrat* (Orangeburg, SC), January 26, 2003), 8A.

66. Cathy Sams and Harry Durham, "40 years ago: Gantt breaks Clemson color barrier," *Times and Democrat* (Orangeburg, SC), January 26, 2003), 8A.

67. Ibid., 3.

68. Glen Luke Flanagan, "Jan. 28, 1963: The Day Clemson University Integrated," *The State* (Columbia, SC), January 28, 2016.

69. Jeffrey Collins, "USC marks 50 years since desegregation," *Associated Press* (Columbia, SC), September 10, 2013.

70. Cynthia Roddey, interview by Derrick Alridge, 2005.

71. Cynthia Roddey, interview by Hope Murphy, May 17, 2004, transcript and recording,

Special Collections, J. Murrey Atkins Library, University of North Carolina at Charlotte.

72. Ibid.

73. Ibid.; Cynthia Roddey, interview by Derrick Alridge, 2005.

74. Cynthia Roddey, interview by Derrick Alridge, 2005.

75. Ibid.

76. Ibid.

77. Ibid.

78. Ibid.

79. Angulo and Graham, Winthrop College in the Sixties, 116.

80. Cynthia Roddey, interview by Derrick Alridge and Alexis Johnson, June 5, 2021.

81. "History of CMS: Desegregation," Charlotte-Mecklenburg Schools, accessed June 28, 2021, https://www.cms.k12.nc.us/.

82. Ibid.

83. "The Green Decision of 1968," Virginia Museum of History and Culture, accessed July 1, 2021, https://virginiahistory.org/.

84. "History of CMS: Desegregation," Charlotte-Mecklenburg Schools, accessed June 28, 2021, https://www.cms.k12.nc.us/.

85. Cynthia Roddey, interview by Derrick Alridge and Alexis Johnson, June 5, 2021.

86. For examples of the pedagogy of Black teachers, see Scott Baker, "Pedagogies of Protest: African American Teachers and the History of the Civil Rights Movement, 1940–1963," *Teachers College Record* 113, no. 12 (December 2011): 2777–2803.

87. Cynthia Roddey, interview by Derrick Alridge, September 12, 2015.

88. Cynthia Roddey, interview by Derrick Alridge and Alexis Johnson, June 5, 2021.

89. Cynthia Roddey, interview by Derrick Alridge, September 12, 2015.

90. Cynthia Roddey, interview by Derrick Alridge, September 12, 2015.

91. See Joy Ann Williamson, *Black Power on Campus: University of Illinois, 1965–1975* (Champaign: University of Illinois Press, 2003); Ibram X. Kendi (formerly Rogers), *The Black Campus Movement: Black Students and the Racial Reconstitution of Higher Education, 1965–1972* (New York: Palgrave Macmillan, 2012); Martha Biondi, *The Black Revolution on Campus* (Berkeley: University of California Press, 2012).

92. For example, see Dwayne C. Wright,

"Black Pride Day, 1968: High School Student Activism in York, Pennsylvania," *Journal of African American History* 88, no. 2 (2003).

93. Cynthia Roddey, interview by Derrick Alridge and Alexis Johnson, June 5, 2021.

94. Cynthia Roddey, interview by Derrick Alridge and Alexis Johnson, June 5, 2021.

95. See Gloria Ladson-Billings, *Culturally Responsive Pedagogy: Asking a Different Question* (New York: Teachers College Press, 2021).

96. Cynthia Roddey, interview by Derrick Alridge and Alexis Johnson, June 5, 2021.

97. Cynthia Roddey, interview by Derrick Alridge and Alexis Johnson, June 5, 2021.

98. Cynthia Roddey, interview by Derrick Alridge and Alexis Johnson, June 5, 2021.

99. Alumni Association, Alumni Awards, Alumni Distinguished Service Award, Cynthia Plair Roddey '67, https://www.winthrop.edu/.

HALE: "IT ONLY TAKES A
SPARK TO GET A FIRE GOING"

1. Peter H. Wood, *Black Majority: Negroes in Colonial South Carolina from 1670 through the Stono Rebellion* (New York: Knopf: Distributed by Random House, 1974); Bernard E. Powers Jr., *Black Charlestonians: A Social History, 1822–1885* (Fayetteville: University of Arkansas Press, 1994); "Burke High School," *Public School Review*, https://www.publicschoolreview.com/.

2. Lois Averetta Simms, *A Chalk and Chalkboard Career in Carolina* (New York: Vantage Press, 1995), 9–10; As a result of the *Duvall* decision, the South Carolina General Assembly put in place a procedure for teachers like Duvall to file a salary complaint. Their plan restricted complaints to an individual basis and required a teacher to first file a complaint with her local school board. If her complaint was denied locally, she could then appeal to the State Board of Education. This process could take up to two months. Additionally, if a teachers' complaint reached the state level, the salaries of all teachers in her school district would be reviewed, thereby affecting not only the plaintiff but all of her peers and colleagues. Charron, *Freedom's Teacher*, 164–65; "Court Orders Negro Teacher Pay Equality," *The News and Courier* (Charleston, SC), February 15, 1944.

3. Lois Simms papers, Box 8, "Professional Records, Charleston High School, 1937–2003" Folder 46, "Burke High School Attendance

Record, 1959–1960"; Lois Simms, interview with the author, December 5, 2011; Carmen Gaston, interview with the author, October 4, 2019; *A New Kind of Youth: Historically Black High Schools and Southern Student Activism, 1920–1975* (Chapel Hill: University of North Carolina Press, 2022).

4. Betty Collier-Thomas and V. P. Franklin (ed.), *Sisters in the Struggle: African-American Women In the Civil Rights and Black Power Movements* (New York: New York University Press, 2001); Belinda Robnett, *How Long? How Long? African American Women in the Struggle for Civil Rights* (New York: Oxford University Press, 1997); Belinda Robnett, "African-American Women in the Civil Rights Movement, 1954–1965: Gender, Leadership, and Micromobilization" *American Journal of Sociology* 101, no. 6 (May 1996): 1661–1693; Katherine Mellon Charron, *Freedom's Teacher: The Life of Septima Clark* (Chapel Hill: University of North Carolina Press, 2009), 4–8; Valinda W. Littlefield, "Ruby Forsythe and Fannie Phelps Adams: Teaching for Confrontation during Jim Crow," in Marjorie Julian Spurill, Valinda W. Littlefield, and Joan Marie Johnson, eds., *South Carolina Women: Their Lives and Times, Volume 3* (Athens: University of Georgia Press, 2012), 17–34.

5. Clark, quoted in Charron, *Freedom's Teacher*; Septima Poinsette Clark and Cynthia Stokes Brown (eds.) *Ready from Within: Septima Clark and the Civil Rights Movement* (Navarro, CA: Wild Trees Press, 1986), 83.

6. Carmen Gaston, interview with the author, October 4, 2019.

7. On the origins of the earliest documentation of teacher activism and the organization to overturn "whites-only" teaching laws in the South, see Michael Fultz, "Charleston, 1919–1920: The Final Battle in the Emergence of the South's Urban African American Teaching Corps," *Journal of Urban History* 27 no. 5 (2001): 633–49; Howard N. Rabinowitz, "Half a Loaf: The Shift from White to Black Teachers in the Negro Schools of the Urban South, 1865–1890," *Journal of Southern History* 40 no. 4 (1974): 565–94. On the organization of Black teacher associations, see Walker, *Hello Professor*; Karpinski, *A Visible Company of Professionals*; J. Rupert Picott, *History of the Virginia Teachers Association* (Washington, DC: National Education Association, 1975); Cleopatra D. Thompson,

The History of the Mississippi Teachers Association (Washington, DC: NEA Teachers Rights, 1973); John F. Potts Sr., *A History of the Palmetto Education Association* (Washington, DC: National Education Association, 1978); Percy Murray, *History of the North Carolina Teachers Association* (Washington, DC: National Education Association, 1984); Thelma D. Perry, *History of the American Teachers Association* (Washington, DC: National Education Association, 1975). See also Tondra L. Loder-Jackson, *Schoolhouse Activists: African American Educators and the Long Birmingham Civil Rights Movement* (Albany: State University of New York Press, 2015); R. Scott Baker, "Pedagogies of Protest: African American Teachers and the History of the Civil Rights Movement, 1940–1963," *Teachers College Record* 113 no. 12 (2011): 2777–2803.

8. Walker, *Their Highest Potential*, 201–5; Vanessa Siddle Walker, "Can Institutions Care? Evidence from the Segregated Schooling of African American Children," in M. Shujaa (ed.), *Beyond Desegregation: The Quality of African American Schooling* (Thousand Oaks, CA: Corwin Press, 1996). On the argumentation based on inferiority, see Jonna Perillo, *Uncivil Rights: Teachers, Unions, and Race in the Battle of School Equity* (Chicago: University of Chicago Press, 2012), 100–102; Michael Fultz, "Teacher Training and African American Education in the South, 1900–1940," *Journal of Negro Education* 64, no. 2 (Spring 1995): 196–210; Daryl Scott, *Contempt and Pity: Social Policy and the Image of the Damaged Black Psyche, 1880–1996* (Chapel Hill: University of North Carolina Press, 1996).

9. Lois Simms, notes in *Exploration in Personal Adjustment*, 9 (Box 1, Folder 8 "Biographical Records: Academic Work: Howard University 1948–1986," Avery Research Center; Lois Simms, interview with the author, December 5, 2011; "Lois Simms, Biographical Notes, Inventory of the Lois A. Simms Papers, 1920–2003, and undated," Avery Research Center, accessed at https://avery.cofc.edu/.

10. Simms, notes in *Exploration*, 12–13, Avery Research Center.

11. Simms, interview with the author, December 5, 2011.

12. Lois Simms, interview with the author, December 5, 2011.

13. Simms, notes in *Exploration*, 20–21, Avery Research Center.

14. Simms, notes in *Exploration*, 19, Avery Research Center.

15. Simms, notes in *Exploration*, 39, Avery Research Center.

16. Simms, notes in *Exploration*, 41, Avery Research Center.

17. Lois Simms, interview with the author, December 5, 2011; "Lois Simms, Biographical Notes, Inventory of the Lois A. Simms Papers, 1920–2003, and undated," Avery Research Center, accessed at https://avery.cofc.edu/; *Initiative, Paternalism, and Race Relations: Charleston's Avery Normal Institute* (Athens: University of Georgia Press, 1990), 48–53; Katherine Mellon Charron, *Freedom's Teacher: The Life of Septima Clark* (Chapel Hill: University of North Carolina Press, 2009), 38–39; Scott R. Baker, *Paradoxes of Desegregation: African American Struggles for Educational Equity in Charleston, South Carolina, 1926–1972* (Columbia: University of South Carolina Press, 2006), 25–29.

18. Simms, notes in *Exploration*, 43, Avery Research Center; W. E. B. Du Bois, "The Talented Tenth," from *The Negro Problem: A Series of Articles by Representative Negroes of Today* (Miami: Mnemosyne Printing, 1903/1969).

19. Counts, *New Social Order?* 40, 43; Lawrence A. Cremin, *The Transformation of the School: Progressivism in American Education, 1876–1957* (New York: Vintage Books, 1964), 224–34. For a broader history of Counts and the radical progressives, see Gerald L. Gutek, *The Educational Theory of George S. Counts* (Columbus: Ohio State University Press, 1971); Gutek, *George S. Counts and American Civilization: The Educator as Social Theorist* (Macon: Mercer University Press, 1984).

20. Baker, "Pedagogies of Protest: African American Teachers and the History of the Civil Rights Movement, 1940–1963," *Teachers College Record* 113, no. 12 (December 2011): 2777–2803; on education of Black teachers during the 1930s, see Fairclough, *A Class of Their Own*, 339–40; Walker, *Their Highest Potential*, 26–27; Dr. Clinton Irving Young, who served as principal during the time of the Kress sit-in, is emblematic of the well-educated Black administrator that led institutions during the last decade of segregation. He held degrees in education from the Teachers College and Columbia University and Wilberforce University in Ohio. The 1959 *Bulldog* (Burke High School Yearbook) in Lois A. Simms Papers, Box 2, Folder 23, "Burke High School Yearbook, 1959," Avery Research Center. Dr. Eugene Hunt completed graduate school courses at University of Chicago and Northwestern University," Vita Sheet, Eugene C. Hunt," Eugene Hunt Collection, Box 1, Folder 1, "Vita," Avery Research Center. For a thorough and impressive examination of the legal context and social experiences of out-of-state study programs in which Southern states subsidized the education of Black students who studied outside the South, see Donna Jordan-Taylor, "'I'm Not Autherine Lucy': The Circular Migration of Southern Black Professionals Who Completed Graduate School in the North during Jim Crow, 1945–1970," (PhD diss., University of Washington, 2011).

21. Adam Fairclough, A Class of Their Own, 319–20; Christine A. Ogren, "Out-of-Class Project: American Teachers' Summertime Activities, 1880s–1930s," *History of Education Quarterly* 56, no. 1 (2016): 22–23; Michael Fultz, "Determination and Persistence: Building the African American Teacher Corps through Summer and Intermittent Teaching, 1860s–1890s," *History of Education Quarterly* 61, no. 1 (2021): 4–34. On teacher education during the progressive era, see *A New Kind of Youth: Historically Black High Schools and Southern Student Activism, 1920–1975* (Chapel Hill: University of North Carolina Press, 2022).

22. For a provocative illustration of the divergence of opinion among educational and civil rights leaders, see W. E. B. Du Bois, "Does the Negro Need Separate Schools?" *Journal of Negro Education* 4, no. 3 (July 1935): 328–35; Randal Jelks, *Benjamin Elijah Hays: Schoolmaster of the Movement* (Chapel Hill: University of North Carolina Press, 2012); Katherine Mellon Charron, *Freedom's Teacher: The Life of Septima Clark* (Chapel Hill: University of North Carolina Press, 2009); Derrick P. Alridge, *The Educational Thought of W. E. B. Du Bois: An Intellectual History* (New York: Teachers College Press, 2008); Jarvis R. Givens, *Fugitive Pedagogy: Carter G. Woodson and the Art of Black Teaching* (Cambridge: Harvard University Press, 2021).

23. Jarvis R. Givens, *Fugitive Pedagogy:*

Carter G. Woodson and the Art of Black Teaching (Cambridge, MA: Harvard University Press, 2021).

24. John Dewey, "My Pedagogic Creed." *The School Journal*, LIV, no. 3 (January 1897), 77.

25. John Dewey, *Experience & Education* (New York: Touchstone, 1938, 1997), 20.

26. R. Scott Baker, "Pedagogies of Protest: African American Teachers and the History of the Civil Rights Movement, 1940–1963," *Teachers College Record* 113 no. 12 (2011): 2777–2803.

27. Simms, Chalk and Chalkboard, 24.

28. Simms, "An Analysis of the Biological Factors in Race Relations," 1, in Box 1, Folder 8 "Biographical Records: Academic Work: Howard University 1948–1986," Avery Research Center.

29. Simms, "An Analysis of the Biological Factors in Race Relations," 6–7.

30. Simms, *A Chalk and Chalkboard Career*, 26–27.

31. Mark V. Tushnet, "Securing the Precedents: *Gaines* and *Alston*," in *The NAACP's Legal Strategy Against Segregated Education, 1925–1950* (Chapel Hill: University of North Carolina Press, 1987), 70–81; this strategy was adopted across the South, see Charles Bolton, "A Last Gasp to Maintain a Segregated System: Mississppi's Failed Effort to Make Separate Education Truly Equal," in *The Hardest Deal of All: The Battle Over School Integration in Mississippi, 1870–1980* (Jackson: University Press of Mississippi, 2005), 33–60.

32. Simms, "A Comparative Study of Provisions," 3, Box 1, folder 13.

33. Simms, "A Comparative Study of Provisions," 5, Box 1, folder 13.

34. School districts could receive the money they needed to equalize schools up front, allowing them to begin "establishing and maintaining adequate physical facilities, see Rebekah Dobrasko, "Architectural Survey of Charleston County's School Equalization Program, 1951–1955," University of South Carolina, Public History Program, April 2005, 11–13.

35. Simms, "A Comparative Study of Provisions," 77–79, Box 1, folder 13.

36. Frank A. DeCosta, "The Education of Negroes in South Carolina," *Journal of Negro Education* 16, no. 3; *The Availability of Education in the Negro Separate School* (Summer 1947): 405–16.

37. Mrs. Lois Simms, interview with the author, December 5, 2011; L. A. Simms, "A Comparative Study of Provisions for the Education of Negro and White Pupils in the Public Schools of South Carolina," in Lois A. Simms Papers, Box 1, Folder 13, "Biographical Records: Academic Work, Howard University," Avery Research Center; Lois Averetta Simms, *A Chalk and Chalkboard Career in Carolina* (New York: Vantage Press, 1995), 26–27, 33. The Avery Normal Institute benefited from the mission of the American Missionary Association; see Richardson and Jones, *Education for Liberation*, 29–45; for a full history on the Avery Normal Institute, see Edmund L. Drago, *Initiative, Paternalism, and Race Relations: Charleston's Avery Normal Institute* (Athens: University of Georgia Press, 1990); "Avery: the Spirit That Would Not Die," Lowcountry Digital Humanities Initiative (Charleston: College of Charleston, 2015), accessed at https://ldhi.library.cofc.edu/; on teacher equalization, see Vanessa Siddle-Walker, *The Lost Education of Horace Tate: Uncovering the Hidden Heroes Who Fought for Justice in Schools* (New York: The New Press, 2018); Charles H. Thompson, "Editorial Comment: Discrimination in Negro Teachers' Salaries in Maryland," *Journal of Negro Education* 5, no. 4 (1936): 539–42; Adam Fairclough, "Teachers Organize," in *A Class of Their Own: Black Teachers in the Segregated South* (Cambridge, MA: Harvard University Press, 2007), 309–53; Mark V. Tushnet, "The Campaign in the 1940s: Contingencies, Adaptations, and the Problem of Staff," in *The NAACP's Legal Strategy Against Segregated Education, 1925–1950* (Chapel Hill: University of North Carolina Press, 1987), 82–104.

38. Tondra Loder-Jackson, Lois M. Christensen, and Hilton Kelly, "Unearthing and Bequeathing Black Feminist Legacies of *Brown* to a New Generation of Women and Girls. *Journal of Negro Education* 85, no. 3 (Summer 2016): 199–211.

39. Simms, Chalk and Chalkboard Career, 10; Peter F. Lau, *Democracy Rising: South Carolina and the Fight for Black Equality Since 1865* (Lexington: University of Kentucky Press, 2006), 129–31; Charron, *Freedom's Teacher*, 162–67.

40. Tinsley E. Yarbrough, *A Passion for Justice* (New York: Oxford University Press, 1987), 196 (emphasis is original); see also Orville Vernon Burton, Beatrice Burton, and Simon Appleford,

"Seeds in Unlikely Soil: The *Briggs v. Elliot* School Segregation Case: 191; Baker, *Paradoxes of Desegregation*, 87–107.

41. Fairclough, *A Class of Their Own*, 312.

42. Givens, *Fugitive Pedagogy*; C.G. Woodson, "Negro History Week," *Mississippi Educational Journal: A Monthly Magazine for Teachers in Colored Schools* 18, 57, MDAH; Fairclough, *A Class of Their Own*, 320–22.

43. Perry, *History of the American Teachers Association*, 199–201.

44. Mississippi Educational Advance, *Mississippi Educational Journal: A Monthly Magazine for Teachers in Colored Schools* 18, 74–76, MDAH.

45. W. A. Walters, "Why Limit the Study of the Negro," *Mississippi Educational Journal: A Monthly Magazine for Teachers in Colored Schools* 18, 88–89, MDAH; Fairclough, *Teaching Equality*, 43–44.

46. Letter to "Mother Simms," November 14, 1969: Box 2, Folder 17, "Biographical Records; Personal Papers, 1931–1944, and undated"; Letter from Ervin Lessington to Lois Simms, Box 2, Folder 18, "Biographical Records; Personal Papers, 1931–1944, and undated"; Simms, *Chalk and Chalkboard*, 72.

47. Littlefield, "Ruby Forsythe and Fannie Phelps Adams," 17.

48. Reverend John Dart, Dart Family Papers, Box 1, Folder 6, "Colored and Industrial School Stationary," Avery Research Center.

49. "Prospectus of the Charleston Industrial School," in Dart Family Papers, Box 1, Folder 6, "Colored Industrial School Prospectus," Avery Research Center.

50. For further history of Burke High School, see Sherman E. Pyatt, *Burke High School, 1894–2006* (Charleston, SC: Arcadia Publishing, 2007); *Who Is Burke High?: The History of the Burke High School Family* (Charleston: South Carolina Humanities Society, 2010); Jon Hale, "History of Burke High School in Charleston, South Carolina since 1894," Lowcountry Digital Humanities Initiative (Charleston, SC: College of Charleston, 2015), accessed at https://ldhi.library.cofc.edu/.

51. For the ideology and pervasiveness of vocational and industrial educational discourse, see James Anderson, "The Hampton Model of Normal School Industrial Education, 1868–1915," in *Education of Blacks in the South,*

1860–1935 (Chapel Hill: University of North Carolina Press, 1988), 33–78.

52. Mrs. Lois Simms, interview with the author, December 5, 2011; see also Lois Averetta Simms, *A Chalk and Chalkboard Career in Carolina* (New York: Vantage Press, 1995). L. A. Simms, "Assignments for English II and III," in Lois A. Simms Papers, Box 2, Folder 20, "Plan Books for English and History, 1956–1957 and 1959–1960," Avery Research Center; for a contextual description of John Dewey, progressive education, and the impact on Black educators, including teachers at Avery and Burke, see Baker, "Pedagogies of Protest," 2785–88.

53. "Mrs. Lois Simms, Assignment for English II and III, 1959–1960," Lois A Simms Papers, Box 2, Folder 20 "Professional Records: Burke High School, 1937, 1956–2003, undated," Avery Research Center.

54. "Negroes and the War" (US Office of War Information, 1943) in Lois Simms Papers, Box 9, "Publications, 1920–1975, and undated," Folder 49, "Negroes and the War, 1943."

55. "Mrs. Lois Simms, Lesson plans, 1956–1957," and "Mrs. Lois Simms, Assignment for English II and III, 1959–1960," Lois A Simms Papers, Box 2, Folder 20 "Professional Records: Burke High School, 1937, 1956–2003, undated," Avery Research Center.

56. "Mrs. Lois Simms, Assignment for English II and III, 1959–1960," Lois A Simms Papers, Box 2, Folder 20 "Professional Records: Burke High School, 1937, 1956–2003, undated," Avery Research Center.

57. Lois Simms, interview with the author, December 5, 2011.

58. "Programme of the Forty-Ninth Commencement of Burke High School" and "Programme of the Fiftieth Commencement of Burke High School" in Lois A. Simms Collection, Box 2, Folder 21. "Professional Records: Burke High School, 1937, 1956–2003, undated, Commencement and Event Programs."

59. "Choose Your College," in Lois A. Simms Collection, Box 2, Folder 21, "Professional Records: Burke High School, 1937, 1956–2003, undated."

60. "News in Brief," *Parvenue*, March 1952, June 2, 1953, Avery Research Center.

61. "Student Council Agenda Includes Nat'l Society," *Parvenue*, October 27, 1952, Avery Research Center.

62. "1960 Bulldog (Burke Yearbook)," in Lois A. Simms Papers, Box 2, Folder 24, "Professional Records, Burke High School 1937, 1956–2003, Burke High School Yearboo," Pyatt, *Burke High School*, p. 57.

63. "This I Believe" (essay by Larry Tolbert), "Burke High School Student and Related Papers," Eugene Hunt Collection, Box 3, Folder 6, Avery Research Center.

64. "This I Believe" (essay by Uyron Smith), "Burke High School Student and Related Papers," Eugene Hunt Collection, Box 3, Folder 6, Avery Research Center.

65. "Education: The Freedom of Knowledge vs. Mankind," *Parvenue*, March 1952, Avery Research Center.

66. "History Department to Give Program About Negroes," Significance of Negro History," *Parvenue*, February 1956, Avery Research Center; "Negro History Course Proposal, 1958," Charleston County School District, Box 863; Sherman E. Pyatt, *Burke High School, 1894–2006 (The Campus History Series)* (Chicago: Arcadia Publishing, 2007), 113.

67. "Let's Discuss the Race Problem Intelligently," *Parvenue*, June 1953, Avery Research Center; Pyatt, *Burke High School*, 97–118.

68. Eugene Hunt, "Burke High School Teaching Materials," Eugene Hunt Collection, Box 3, Folder 2, Avery Research Center.

69. Simms, *Chalk and Chalkboard Career*, 78.

70. Jon Hale, "'The Fight Was Instilled in Us': High School Student Activism and the Civil Rights Movement in Charleston, South Carolina," *The South Carolina Historical Magazine*, 114, no. 1 (January 2013), 20; Reverend James Blake in the "South Carolina Voices of the Civil Rights Movement," transcript, Avery Research Center, p. 218

71. Simms, *Chalk and Chalkboard Career*, 44.

72. Minerva Brown King, interview with the author, December 12, 2011; Harvey B. Gantt, interview with the author, November 28, 2011; Hale, "The Fight Was Instilled in Us," 22–23.

73. Hale, "'The Fight Was Instilled in Us," 23–25; Baker, Paradoxes of Desegregation, 158–76; Charles McDew, interview with Katherine Shannon, August 24, 1967, Civil Rights Documentation Project, Moorland Spingarn Research Center, Howard University (transcript in possession of author, courtesy of Joellen ElBashir); *Brown v. School District No. 20*, Charleston, South Carolina, 226 F. Supp. 819 (E.D.S.C. 1963); Martin Oppenheimer, *The Sit-In Movement of 1960* (Brooklyn: Carlson Publishing, 1989), 154–57; William C. Hine, "Civil Rights and Campus Wrongs: South Carolina State College Students Protest, 1955–1968," *The South Carolina Historical Magazine* 97, no. 4 (October 1996): 320–25.

74. Lois Simms, interview with the author, December 5, 2011.

75. Lois Simms, interview with the author, December 5, 2011.

76. Lois Simms, interview with the author, December 5, 2011; Kerry Taylor, "The Charleston Hospital Workers Movement, 1968–1969," (Charleston, SC: Lowcountry Digital History Initiative, 2013), http://ldhi.library.cofc.edu/; Stever Estes, "'I Am Somebody': The Charleston Hospital Strike of 1969," *The Avery Review* 3 no. 2 (Spring 2000): 8–32; Leon Fink and Brian Greenberg, *Upheaval in the Quiet Zone: A History of Hospital Workers' Union, Local 1199* (Champaign: University of Illinois Press, 1989).

77. Simms, *Chalk and Chalkboard Career*, 78.

78. Simms, *Chalk and Chalkboard Career*, 78.

79. Simms, *Chalk and Chalkboard Career*, 78.

80. Simms, "Black Is Beautiful," in *Chalk and Chalkboard Career*, 78–87.

81. Simms, *Chalk and Chalkboard Career*, 120.

82. Jon N. Hale, "'We Are Not Merging on an Equal Basis': The Desegregation of Southern Teacher Associations and the Right to Work, 1945–1977," *Labor History* (March 2019), accessed at https://doi.org/10.1080/002 3656X.2018.1561103; for an overview of the numbers of displaced and dismissed teachers in the wake of *Brown*, see James Anderson, "'A Tale of Two *Browns*': Constitutional Equality and Unequal Education," in *Yearbook of the National Society for the Study of Education* 105, no. 2 (2006): 30–32; Fultz, "The Displacement of Black Educators Post-*Brown*," 28; Adam Fairclough, "The Costs of *Brown*: Black Teachers and School Integration," *Journal of American History* 91 (June 2004): 53–56.

83. Hale, "We Are Not Merging on an Equal Basis"; Jon Hale, "'The Development of Power is the Main Business of the School': The Agency of Southern Black Teacher Associations from Jim Crow Through Desegregation," *Journal of*

Negro Education 87, no. 4 (Fall 2018): 444–59; "Your Schools, March 1970" in "Dual Association Merger–South Carolina," folder 5, Box #0519," NEA Papers.

84. Simms, *Chalk and Chalkboard Career*, 10; Baker, "Testing Equality, 1936–1946," *Paradoxes of Desegregation*, 44–62.

85. Simms, *Chalk and Chalkboard Career*, 88–90.

86. "New Faces Among Faculty," *The Bantam* (December 21, 1973), in BHS/CHS scrapbook, Box 4, Lois Simms Collection.

87. Lois Simms, interview with the author, December 5, 2011.

88. "C.H.S. Work History and English, 1973–1974," in Lois A. Simms Papers, Box 7, folder 29, "Professional Records, Charleston High School, 1961–1976, Plan Books, 1972–1976" and folder 30, "Papers from Plan Books, 1972–1976"

89. Lois Simms, interview with the author, December 5, 2011.

90. "C.H.S. Work History and English, 1973–1974," in Lois A. Simms Papers, Box 7, folder 29, "Professional Records, Charleston High School, 1961–1976, Plan Books, 1972–1976" and folder 30, "Papers from Plan Books, 1972–1976"; Simms, *Chalk and Chalkboard Career*, 80–82.

91. Lois Simms, interview with the author, December 5, 2011.

92. Jeanne-Marie A. Miller "Angelina Weld Grimké: Playwright and Poet," *CLA Journal* 21, no. 4 (June 1978): 513.

93. Lois Simms papers, Box 8, "Professional Records, Charleston High School, 1937–2003" Folder 46, "Burke High School Attendance Record, 1959–1960"; Lois Simms, interview with the author, December 5, 2011; Carmen Gaston, interview with the author, October 4, 2019.

MCCULLUM AND HOLT: "WE EXPERIENCED OUR FREEDOM"

1. Clayborne Carson, *In Struggle: SNCC and the Black Awakening of the 1960s* (Cambridge, MA: Harvard University Press, 1981). Note that, before the movement of the 1960s, Pauli Murray organized a sit-in in 1943 in a cafeteria in Washington, D.C. See "Pauli Murray Organizes Howard Student Sit-Ins," *SNCC Digital Gateway*, SNCC Legacy Project and Duke University, https://snccdigital.org/.

2. For more on Ella Baker, see Barbara Ransby, *Ella Baker and the Black Freedom Movement: A Radical Democratic Vision* (Chapel Hill: University of North Carolina Press, 2003); and J. Todd Moye, *Ella Baker: Community Organizer of the Civil Rights Movement* (Lanham, MD: Rowman & Littlefield, 2013).

3. For a selection of works on student and civil rights activism in North Carolina, see Howard Zinn, *SNCC: The New Abolitionists* (Cambridge, MA: South End Press, 1964); William Chafe, *Civilities and Civil Rights: Greensboro, North Carolina, and the Black Struggle for Freedom* (New York: Oxford University Press, 1980); Carson, *In Struggle*; Tom Dent, *Southern Journey: A Return to the Civil Rights Movement* (New York: William Morrow, 1997); Wesley Hogan, *Many Minds, One Heart: SNCC's Dream for a New America* (Chapel Hill: University of North Carolina Press, 2007); Iwan Morgan and Philip Davies, *From Sit-Ins to SNCC: The Student Civil Rights Movement in the 1960s* (Gainesville: University Press of Florida, 2012); Jelani M. Favors, *Shelter in a Time of Storm: How Black Colleges Fostered Generations of Leadership and Activism* (Chapel Hill: University of North Carolina Press, 2019); Brian William Suttell, "Campus to Counter: Civil Rights Activism in Raleigh and Durham, North Carolina, 1960–1963" (PhD diss., University of North Carolina at Greensboro, 2017). Also see *SNCC Digital Gateway*, SNCC Legacy Project and Duke University, https://snccdigital.org/.

4. Vanessa Siddle Walker, *Their Highest Potential: An African American School Community in the Segregated South* (Chapel Hill: University of North Carolina Press, 1996). For other literature about the value and importance of all-Black schools in the segregated South, see David S. Cecelski, *Along Freedom Road: Hyde County, North Carolina and the Fate of Black Schools in the South* (Chapel Hill: University of North Carolina, 1994); Carter J. Savage, "'Because We Did More With Less': The Agency of African-American Teachers in Franklin, Tennessee: 1890–1967," *Peabody Journal of Education* 76, no. 2 (2001): 170–203; Carter J. Savage, "Cultural Capital and African American Agency: The Economic Struggle for Effective Education for African Americans in Franklin, Tennessee, 1890–1967," *Journal of African American History* 87, no. 2 (2002): 206–35; Alison Stewart, *First Class: The Legacy of Dunbar, America's First Black Public High School* (Chicago: Lawrence

Hill Books, 2013); Sharon G. Pierson, *Laboratory of Learning: HBCU Laboratory Schools and the Alabama State College Lab High in the Era of Jim Crow* (New York: Peter Lang, 2014); Karida L. Brown, *Gone Home: Race and Roots through Appalachia* (Chapel Hill: University of North Carolina Press, 2018); and Kristan L. McCullum, "'They will liberate themselves': Education, Citizenship, and Civil Rights in the Appalachian Coalfields," *History of Education Quarterly* 61, no. 4 (2021): 449–77.

5. The historiography of community and educational segregation discusses educative spaces outside the walls of the formal classroom, examining their impact in nurturing youth and community advocacy. In his study of Franklin, Tennessee, Carter J. Savage describes how the Black community was able to create cultural capital and demonstrate agency within, despite and because of their segregated contexts. See Carter J. Savage, "Cultural Capital and African American Agency." See also Kristan L. McCullum, "They will liberate themselves." Additionally, David G. Garcia discusses Mexican American playgrounds as sites of community building and organizing, despite these spaces having been intentionally segregated by white community members. David Garcia, *Strategies of Segregation: Race, Residence, and the Struggle for Educational Equality* (Berkeley: University of California Press, 2018).

6. bell hooks, *Teaching to Transgress: Education as the Practice of Freedom* (New York: Routledge Taylor & Francis Group, 1994), 207.

7. Although we chose to only focus on three individuals for this chapter, the themes and arguments we present here are supported by multiple interviews with Black educators who taught in Raleigh and North Carolina, including: Helen Adams, JoAnne Smart Drane, Esther Dunnegan, Carolyn Fox, Algeania M. W. Freeman, Mattie Goode, Joyce Hilliard-Clark, Mattie Jones, Jackie Selby, Virginia Tally, Gladys Walker, and others. These interviews were conducted through the Teachers in the Movement (TIM) oral history project at University of Virginia's School of Education and Human Development, www.teachersinthemovement.com (hereinafter referred to as TIM Collection).

8. Delores Revis, interview by Kristan McCullum, April 7, 2021, TIM Collection.

9. Delores Revis, interview by McCullum, April 7, 2021, TIM Collection.

10. Delores Revis, interview McCullum, April 7, 2021, TIM Collection.

11. Genevieve M. Farmer, interview by Kristan McCullum, June 18, 2021, TIM Collection.

12. This idea in which Black students "experienced freedom" in their segregated spaces designated by Jim Crow is similar to other studies of segregated education and communities. It is also a common theme across interviews conducted through the Teachers in the Movement oral history project. Drawing from Robin D. G. Kelley's concept of "freedom dreams," Kristan L. McCullum explores the all-Black school and other communal spaces as "freedom spaces" that allowed Black students to dream and plan for their futures within and despite the Jim Crow system. See Kristan McCullum, "(Re)locating Sites of Memory in Appalachia Through Black Spaces and Stories," *Black Perspectives*, December 10, 2021, https://www.aaihs.org/; Robin D. G. Kelley, *Freedom Dreams: The Black Radical Imagination* (Boston: Beacon Press, 2002); and Kristan L. McCullum, "'They will liberate themselves.'"

13. Genevieve M. Farmer, interview by McCullum, June 18, 2021, TIM Collection.

14. Genevieve M. Farmer, interview by McCullum, June 18, 2021, TIM Collection.

15. Delores Revis, interview by McCullum, April 7, 2021, TIM Collection.

16. Dorothy Thompson, interview by Kristan McCullum, April 21, 2021, TIM Collection.

17. Delores Revis, interview by McCullum, April 7, 2021, TIM Collection.

18. Dorothy Thompson, interview by McCullum, April 21, 2021, TIM Collection.

19. Genevieve M. Farmer, interview by McCullum, June 18, 2021, TIM Collection.

20. Delores Revis, interview by McCullum, April 7, 2021, TIM Collection.

21. Genevieve M. Farmer, interview by McCullum, June 18, 2021, TIM Collection.

22. Genevieve M. Farmer, interview by McCullum, June 18, 2021, TIM Collection.

23. Delores Revis, interview by McCullum, April 7, 2021, TIM Collection.

24. Delores Revis, interview by McCullum, April 7, 2021, TIM Collection.

25. Genevieve M. Farmer, interview by McCullum, June 18, 2021, TIM Collection.

26. Dorothy Thompson, interview by McCullum, April 21, 2021, TIM Collection.

27. Dorothy Thompson, interview by McCullum, April 21, 2021, TIM Collection.

28. Dorothy Thompson, interview by McCullum, April 21, 2021, TIM Collection.

29. Dorothy Thompson, interview by McCullum, April 21, 2021, TIM Collection.

30. Dorothy Thompson, interview by McCullum, April 21, 2021, TIM Collection.

31. Delores Revis, interview by McCullum, April 7, 2021, TIM Collection.

32. Genevieve M. Farmer, interview by McCullum, June 18, 2021, TIM Collection.

33. Genevieve M. Farmer, interview by McCullum, June 18, 2021, TIM Collection.

34. Dorothy Thompson, interview by McCullum, April 21, 2021, TIM Collection.

35. For considerations on the role of teachers in relation to activism and the Black freedom struggle, see Jerome E. Morris, "Forgotten Voices of Black Educators: Critical Race Perspectives on the Implementation of a Desegregation Plan," *Educational Policy* 15, no. 4 (September 2001), 575–600; Sonya Ramsey, *Reading, Writing, and Segregation: A Century of Black Women Teachers in Nashville* (Champaign: University of Illinois Press, 2008); Hilton Kelly, *Race, Remembering, and Jim Crow's Teachers* (New York: Routledge, 2010); Scott Baker, "Pedagogies of Protest: African American Teachers and the History of the Civil Rights Movement, 1940–1963," *Teachers College Record* 113, no. 12 (December 2011): 2777–2803; Zoë Burkholder, *Color in the Classroom: How American Schools Taught Race, 1900–1954* (New York: Oxford University Press, 2011); Adah L. Ward Randolph, "'It Is Better to Light a Candle than to Curse the Darkness': Ethel Thompson Overby and Democratic Schooling in Richmond, Virginia, 1910–1958," *Educational Studies* 48, no. 3 (May 2012), 220–43; Jon Hale, "'The Fight Was Instilled in Us': High School Activism and the Civil Rights Movement in Charleston," *South Carolina Historical Magazine* 114, no. 1 (January 2013), 4–28; Karen A. Johnson, Abdul Pitre, and Kenneth L. Johnson, eds., *African American Women Educators: Critical Examination of Their Pedagogies, Educational Ideas, and Activism from the Nineteenth Century to the Mid-Twentieth Century* (Lanham, MD: Rowman & Littlefield Education, 2014); Vanessa Siddle Walker, "School 'Outer-gration' and 'Tokenism': Segregated Black Educators Critique the Promise of Education Reform in the Civil Rights Act of 1964," *Journal of Negro Education* 84, no. 2 (Spring 2015): 111–24; Tondra L. Loder-Jackson, *Schoolhouse Activists: African American Educators and the Long Birmingham Civil Rights Movement* (Albany: State University of New York Press, 2015); Derrick P. Alridge, "Teachers in the Movement: Pedagogy, Activism, and Freedom," *History of Education Quarterly* 60, no. 1 (2020): 1–23; Candace Cunningham, "'Hell Is Popping Here in South Carolina': Orangeburg County Black Teachers and Their Community in the Immediate Post-*Brown* Era," *History of Education Quarterly* 61, no. 1 (February 2021): 35–62; Jarvis R. Givens, *Fugitive Pedagogy: Carter G. Woodson and the Art of Black Teaching* (Cambridge, MA: Harvard University Press, 2021); and Alexander Hyres, "Persistence and Resistance: African American High School Teachers and Students During the Long Civil Rights Movement in Charlottesville, Virginia, 1926–1974" (PhD diss., University of Virginia, 2018).

36. Dorothy Thompson, interview by McCullum, April 21, 2021, TIM Collection.

37. Dorothy Thompson, interview by McCullum, April 21, 2021, TIM Collection.

38. Dorothy Thompson, interview by McCullum, April 21, 2021, TIM Collection.

39. Dorothy Thompson, interview by McCullum, April 21, 2021, TIM Collection.

40. Dorothy Thompson, interview by McCullum, April 21, 2021, TIM Collection.

41. Dorothy Thompson, interview by McCullum, April 21, 2021, TIM Collection.

42. Dorothy Thompson, interview by McCullum, April 21, 2021, TIM Collection.

43. Dorothy Thompson, interview by McCullum, April 21, 2021, TIM Collection.

44. Dorothy Thompson, interview by McCullum, April 21, 2021, TIM Collection.

45. Genevieve M. Farmer, interview by McCullum, June 18, 2021, TIM Collection.

46. For more on the history of civil rights activism at Hampton University and in Norfolk,

Virginia, see Earl Lewis, *In Their Own Interests: Race, Class, and Power in Twentieth-Century Norfolk, Virginia* (Berkeley: University of California Press, 1991); Thomas C. Parramore, Peter C. Stewart, and Tommy L. Bogger, *Norfolk: The First Four Centuries* (Charlottesville: University of Virginia Press, 2000); Mary C. Doyle, "From Desegregation to Resegregation: Public Schools in Norfolk, Virginia 1954–2002," *Journal of African American History* 90, nos. 1–2 (2005): 64–83; Hoda M. Zaki, *Civil Rights and Politics at Hampton Institute: The Legacy of Alonzo G. Moron* (Champaign: University of Illinois Press, 2007); Denise M. Watson, "'I Guess That Was Our Little Protest': Hampton Roads Natives and Residents Remember the 1960 Sit-in Movement," in *The Virginian-Pilot*, March 8, 2020; The Civil Rights History Project: Survey of Collections and Repositories, Norfolk State University, Harrison B. Wilson Archives and Art, https://libguides.nsu.edu/; School Desegregation in Norfolk, Virginia, Old Dominion University Libraries Digital Collections, https://dc.lib.odu.edu/; Oral history interviews with Audrey Perry Williams, Bernice Bundick, Aubrey S. Escoffery, Renee Escoffery-Torres, Harriet Johnson, Hattie Suber, Jennifer Petticolas, and Sylvia Elder, TIM Collection, www.teachersinthemovement.com.

47. Economic reprisals were a common strategy by the white power structure in response to civil rights activism. See Cecelski, *Along Freedom Road*; Michael W. Fuquay, "Civil Rights and the Private School Movement in Mississippi, 1964–1971," *History of Education Quarterly* 42, no. 2 (2002): 159–80; Hasan Kwame Jeffries, "SNCC, Black Power, and Independent Political Party Organizing in Alabama, 1964–1966," *Journal of African American History* 91, no. 2 (2006): 171–93; Jon N. Hale, "'The Student as a Force for Social Change': The Mississippi Freedom Schools and Student Engagement," *Journal of African American History* 96, no. 3 (2011): 325–47; Jill Ogline Titus, *Brown's Battleground: Students, Segregationists, and the Struggle for Justice in Prince Edward County, Virginia* (Chapel Hill: University of North Carolina Press, 2011); Crystal R. Sanders, "More than Cookies and Crayons: Head Start and African American Empowerment in Mississippi, 1965–1968," *Journal of African American History* 100, no. 4

(2015): 586–609; and Hyres, "Persistence and Resistance."

48. Delores Revis, interview by McCullum, April 7, 2021, TIM Collection.

49. Genevieve M. Farmer, interview by McCullum, June 18, 2021, TIM Collection.

50. Delores Revis, interview by McCullum, April 7, 2021, TIM Collection.

51. Delores Revis, interview by McCullum, April 7, 2021, TIM Collection.

52. Delores Revis, interview by McCullum, April 7, 2021, TIM Collection.

53. Loder-Jackson, *Schoolhouse Activists*, 8; Patricia Hill Collins, *Another Kind of Public Education: Race, Schools, the Media, and Democratic Possibilities* (Boston: Beacon Press, 2009), 133; Patrice Preston-Grimes, "Fulfilling the Promise: African American Educators Teach for Democracy in Jim Crow's South," *Teacher Education Quarterly* 37, no. 1 (2010): 41.

54. hooks, *Teaching to Transgress*, 207.

55. hooks, *Teaching to Transgress*, 2.

56. hooks, *Teaching to Transgress*, 2.

57. Dorothy Thompson, interview by McCullum, April 21, 2021, TIM Collection.

58. Delores Revis, interview by McCullum, April 7, 2021, TIM Collection.

59. Delores Revis, interview by McCullum, April 7, 2021, TIM Collection.

60. Delores Revis, interview by McCullum, April 7, 2021, TIM Collection.

61. Dorothy Thompson, interview by McCullum, April 21, 2021, TIM Collection.

62. hooks, *Teaching to Transgress*, 12.

SANDERS: "IN THE FACE OF HER SPLENDID RECORD"

1. Author, unpublished telephone interview with Dr. Willa M. Cofield, December 8, 2020.

2. Interview with Dr. Cofield; Willa M. Cofield, Cynthia Samuelson, and Mildred Sexton, *The Nine O'clock Whistle: Stories of the Struggle for Freedom in Enfield, NC* (forthcoming book). For more on Black teachers being fired for their connection to the Black freedom struggle, see Katherine Mellen Charron, *Freedom's Teacher: The Life of Septima Clark* (Chapel Hill: University of North Carolina Press, 2009); Catherine M. Jannik, "Gladys Noel Bates: Educator and Activist," Master's thesis, University of Southern Mississippi, 1999.

3. Throughout the chapter, I use the words "Black" and "African American" interchangeably to describe people born in the United States who have African ancestry.

4. Michael Fultz, "The Displacement of Black Educators Post-*Brown*: An Overview and Analysis," *History of Education Quarterly* 44, no. 1 (March 2004): 13–14.

5. Dana Goldstein, *The Teacher Wars* (New York: Doubleday, 2014), 112.

6. Richard D. Kahlenberg, "Teacher Tenure Has a Long History, and, Hopefully, a Future," *The Phi Delta Kappan* 97, no. 6 (March 2016): 16–21.

7. "School Ruling Anticipated," *Charlotte News*, May 31, 1955, 1.

8. "Teacher Contract Changes Approved," *News and Observer*, March 25, 1955, 5.

9. Fultz, "The Displacement of Black Educators Post-*Brown*," 28.

10. Adam Fairclough, *A Class of Their Own: Black Teachers in the Segregated South* (Cambridge, MA: Belknap Press, 2007), 369.

11. For notable exceptions to the exclusion of rural areas of North Carolina from civil rights scholarship, see David S. Cecelski, *Along Freedom Road: Hyde County, North Carolina, and the Fate of Black Schools in the South* (Chapel Hill: University of North Carolina Press, 1994); Charles W. McKinney, *Greater Freedom: The Evolution of the Civil Rights Struggle in Wilson, North Carolina* (Lanham, MD: University Press of America, 2010); Crystal R. Sanders, "North Carolina Justice on Display: Governor Bob Scott and the 1968 Benson Affair," *Journal of Southern History* LXXIX, no. 3 (August 2013): 659–80; Jerry Gershenhorn and Anna Jones, "The Long Black Freedom Struggle in Northampton County, North Carolina, 1930s to 1970s," *North Carolina Historical Review* 97 (January 2020): 1–31.

12. Jack Bass and Walter De Vries, *The Transformation of Southern Politics: Social Change and Political Consequence Since 1945* (Athens: University of Georgia Press, 1995), 242.

13. See Jarvis R. Givens, *Fugitive Pedagogy: Carter G. Woodson and the Art of Black Teaching* (Cambridge, MA: Harvard University Press, 2021), especially p. 4. Also see Heather Andrea Williams, *Self-Taught: African American Education in Slavery and Freedom* (Chapel Hill:

University of North Carolina Press, 2005) and Vanessa Siddle Walker, *The Lost Education of Horace Tate: Uncovering the Hidden Heroes Who Fought for Justice in Schools* (New York: The New Press, 2018).

14. Cofield, *The Nine O'clock Whistle*.

15. For more on the political significance of North Carolina's Black Belt, see Eric Anderson, *Race and Politics in North Carolina, 1872–1901* (Baton Rouge: Louisiana State Press, 1980).

16. Anderson, *Race and Politics*.

17. Cofield, *The Nine O'clock Whistle*; Cofield, interview with author; Marcellus Barksdale, "The Indigenous Civil Rights Movement and Cultural Change in North Carolina: Weldon, Chape Hill, and Monroe: 1946–1965," PhD diss., Duke University, 1977, 83, 292.

18. Cofield, interview with author. For more on the financial importance of subscriptions to Black newspapers, see Kim Gallon, *Pleasure in the News: African American Readership and Sexuality in the Black Press* (Champaign: University of Illinois Press, 2020).

19. Cofield, interview with author.

20. Vanessa Siddle Walker, *Their Highest Potential: An African American School Community in the Segregated South* (Chapel Hill: University of North Carolina Press, 3; Cofield, "The Nine O'clock Whistle."

21. Cofield, interview with author: Cofield, *The Nine O'clock Whistle*.

22. Cofield, interview with author: Cofield, *The Nine O'clock Whistle*.

23. Cofield, *The Nine O'clock Whistle*.

24. "Hampton Trustees to Probe," *Philadelphia Tribune*, October 18, 1947, 1.

25. "Bridgman Leaving Hampton Institute," *New York Times*, February 2, 1948, 13.

26. Cofield, *The Nine O'clock Whistle*.

27. "County School Board Asks State to Establish Negro High School for Enfield," *Roanoke Rapids Herald*, September 2, 1948, 1; Barksdale, "The Indigenous Civil Rights Movement," 96.

28. Cofield, interview with author; Cofield, *The Nine O'clock Whistle*.

29. Cofield, *The Nine O'clock Whistle*.

30. Cofield, interview with author; Cofield, *The Nine O'clock Whistle*.

31. Cofield, *The Nine O'clock Whistle*.

32. Cofield, *The Nine O'clock Whistle*.

33. Barksdale, "The Indigenous Civil Rights Movement," 110–17; John W. Wertheimer, *Law and Society in the South: A History of North Carolina Court Cases* (Lexington: The University Press of Kentucky, 2009), 127–57.

34. "14 Candidates Seeking Town Office in Enfield," *Rocky Mount Telegram*, April 21, 1963, 5; "Enfield Election on Slate Today," *Rocky Mount Telegram*, May 7, 1963, 14.

35. Cofield, *The Nine O'clock Whistle.*

36. "14 Candidates Seeking Town Office in Enfield," 5.

37. Cofield, *The Nine O'clock Whistle.*

38. Cofield, *The Nine O'clock Whistle.*

39. Cofield, *The Nine O'clock Whistle.*

40. Cofield, *The Nine O'clock Whistle.*

41. J. B. Harren, "Enfield Youths Picket Theatre," *Carolina Times*, May 25, 1963, 1.

42. Cofield, *The Nine O'clock Whistle.*

43. "Negro Petition Aired in Enfield," *Rocky Mount Telegram*, June 8, 1963, 2.

44. "1,000 Negroes Demonstrate," *The High Point Enterprise*, September 1, 1963, 1; "Enfield Scene of Picketing," *The High Point Enterprise*, September 8, 1963, 6; "Enfield Arrests Continue," *News and Observer*, September 8, 1963, 3.

45. Cofield, *The Nine O'clock Whistle.*

46. Cofield, interview with author; Cofield, *The Nine O'clock Whistle.*

47. "1,000 Negroes Demonstrate," *The High Point Enterprise*, September 1, 1963, 1.

48. "Enfield and Wilson Scenes of Trouble," *Rocky Mount Telegram*, September 2, 1963, 1.

49. Cofield, *The Nine O'clock Whistle.*

50. Cofield, interview with author; Cofield, *The Nine O'clock Whistle.*

51. Cofield, interview with author; Cofield, *The Nine O'clock Whistle.*

52. Cofield, *The Nine O'clock Whistle.*

53. Cofield, interview with author; Cofield, *The Nine O'clock Whistle.*

54. Barksdale, "The Indigenous Civil Rights Movement," 299–300.

55. For more on the Southern Conference Educational Fund, see Irwin Klibaner, "The Travail of Southern Radicals: The Southern Conference Educational Fund, 1946–1976," *Journal of Southern History* 49, no. 2 (May 1983): 179–202.

56. John R. Salter Jr., *Jackson, Mississippi: An American Chronicle of Struggle and Schism* (Lincoln, NE: Bison Books, 2011).

57. Cofield, interview with author.

58. Barksdale, "The Indigenous Civil Rights Movement," 299–300.

59. For more on the Voter Education Project, see Evan Faulkenbury, *Poll Power: The Voter Education Project and the Movement for the Ballot in the American South* (Chapel Hill: University of North Carolina, 2019).

60. Cofield, interview with author; Cofield, *The Nine O'clock Whistle.*

61. "Plan Mass Registration: Political Offices Sought by 11 in Halifax County," *Norfolk Journal and Guide*, May 2, 1964, 12.

62. Cofield, interview with author.

63. "Negroes Say Registration Delayed," *The Charlotte Observer*, May 4, 1964, 4; "Heavy Negro Registration Is Pushed," *Carolina Times*, May 9, 1964, 1.

64. "Halifax Registration Speed Up Is Ordered," *News and Observer*, May 9, 1964, 1.

65. Cofield, interview with author; Cofield, *The Nine O'clock Whistle.*

66. "State Seeks to Intervene in Case of Controversial Teacher's Firing," *News and Observer*, July 21, 1964, 1.

67. "Negro Teacher Sues School Officials," *Asheville Citizen Times*, June 28, 1964, 70.

68. "State Seeks to Intervene in Case of Controversial Teacher's Firing," 1.

69. "Ousted Enfield Teacher is Latest Hood Victim," *Carolina Times*, July 11, 1964, 1.

70. Cofield, interview with author; Cofield, *The Nine O'clock Whistle.* For more on the Citizenship Schools, see Katherine Mellen Charron, *Freedom's Teacher: The Life of Septima Clark* (Chapel Hill: University of North Carolina Press, 2009).

71. "Halifax Teacher Case Is Heard," *News and Observer*, March 16, 1965.

72. "Halifax School Teacher Loses in Court Battle," *News and Observer*, June 14, 1965, 1.

73. Cofield, interview with author; Cofield, *The Nine O'clock Whistle.*

74. "Big Victory for Fired Teacher in High Court," *Norfolk Journal and Guide*, January 4, 1967, 1.

75. "Enfield Teacher is Awarded Damages in Dismissal Case," *The Carolina Times*, June 11, 1966, 1.

76. "Big Victory for Fired Teacher in High Court," 1; "Mrs. Johnson Victorious In Enfield Case," *Carolina Times*, January 14, 1967, 1.

77. For more on the North Carolina Fund,

see Robert R. Korstad and James L. Leloudis, *To Right These Wrongs: The North Carolina Fund and the Battle to End Poverty and Inequality in 1960s America* (Chapel Hill: University of North Carolina Press, 2011).

78. Cofield, interview with author.

BOWMAN: PLANNING, PERSISTENCE, AND PEDAGOGY

1. Two monographs on Elizabeth City State University's history have been written: Evelyn A. Johnson, *History of Elizabeth City State University: A Story of Survival* (New York: Vantage Press, 1980); and Glen Bowman, *Elizabeth City State University, 1891–2016: The Continuity of a Historical Legacy of Excellence and Resilience* (Virginia Beach, VA: Donning Press, 2015). Bowman, "From Confrontation to Conviction: Student Activism at Elizabeth City State Teachers/State College, 1948–1968," *North Carolina Historical Review* 98, no. 2 (April 2021): 183–219.

2. Frances Lee Ansley, "Stirring the Ashes: Race, Class and the Future of Civil Rights Scholarship," *Cornell Law Review* 74, no. 6 (September 1989): 1024, note 129.

3. *State-Supported Traditionally Negro Colleges in North Carolina* (Raleigh, NC: Board of Higher Education, 1967), 39–47.

4. *Catalog of the Eleventh Annual Session of the North Carolina State Colored Normal School, Fayetteville, North Carolina, for the year 1887–'88* (Fayetteville, NC: J. E. Garrett, 1888), 11, https://lib.digitalnc.org/. The institution is now called Fayetteville State University.

5. Nathan Newbold, Founder's Day Address, Elizabeth City State Teachers College, April 8, 1945, in Box "Articles and Speeches, N. C. Newbold, September 1933–December 1948," Division of Negro Education, Department of Public Instruction, State Archives of North Carolina, Raleigh, North Carolina.

6. *A Prospectus of the Elizabeth City State Colored Normal School*, Ballou Papers, Elizabeth City [NC] State University Archive, G. R. Little Library. Scarborough to Moore, October 22, 1894. General Correspondence of the Superintendent, Department of Public Instruction, North Carolina Department of Archives and History, Raleigh, NC. All such correspondence relating to the office of the state superintendent that is located at this collection is hereinafter identified as "General Correspondence."

7. *Public Laws, North Carolina* (1891), Chapter 265, in *Public Laws and resolutions of the State of North Carolina passed by the General Assembly* (Raleigh, NC: Uzzell, 1893–1919), 213.

8. Moore to John Scarborough, September 22, 1893; Moore to Scarborough, October 20, December 14, 1894. General Correspondence.

9. *Third Annual Catalog of the State Colored Normal School, Elizabeth City, N.C., for the year 1893–94* (Elizabeth City, NC: Elizabeth City News, 1894), 13, Elizabeth City [N.C.] State University Archive, G. R. Little University. Unless otherwise noted, all catalogs issued by Elizabeth City State are from the Elizabeth City State University Archive and will be abbreviated by calendar year. "The Life Work of Edward A. Johnson," *The Crisis* 40, no. 4 (April 1933): 81. Edward A. Johnson, *A school history of the Negro race in America, from 1619 to 1890, with a short introduction as to the origin of the race* (Raleigh, NC: no publisher, 1891), iii, iv, https://archive.org/.

10. Givens, "Culture, Curriculum, and Consciousness: Resurrecting the Educational Praxis of Dr. Carter G. Woodson, 1875–1950" (PhD diss., University of California, Berkeley, 2016), 68.

11. Johnson, *History of Elizabeth City State University*, 24.

12. "Reports of Elizabeth City Colored State Normal School for 1894–'95 and for 1895–'96," in *Public Documents, State of North Carolina, Session 1897*, Document 3, in *Public Documents of the State of North Carolina* (Raleigh, NC: Josephus Daniels, 1889–1915), 84–88.

13. Moore to Scarborough, April 17, 1896. General Correspondence.

14. Moore to Charles Mebane, August 8, 1898, and June 8, 1897; S. G. Atkins to Mebane, May 9, 1899. General Correspondence.

15. "Our Colored People," *North Carolinian* (Elizabeth City), December 2, 1896, 3.

16. *Public Laws, North Carolina* (1897), Chapters 119, 225, and 443, in *Public Laws and Resolutions of the State of North Carolina passed by the General Assembly* (Raleigh, NC: Uzzell, 1893–1919), 168, 443, 631.

17. *North Carolina House Journal* (1897), 340, from *Journal of the House of Representatives of the General Assembly of the State of North Carolina* (Raleigh: North Carolina General Assembly, 1869–).

18. *House Journal* (1897), 353, 478; *North Carolina Senate Journal* (1897), 440, from *Journal of the Senate of the General Assembly of the State of North Carolina* (Raleigh: North Carolina General Assembly, 1859–). Moore to Mebane, March 12, 1897. General Correspondence.

19. William A. Mabry, "White Supremacy and the North Carolina Suffrage Amendment," *North Carolina Historical Review* 13, no. 1 (1936): 1; Benjamin R. Justesen, "Black Tip, White Iceberg: Black Postmasters and the Rise of White Supremacy in North Carolina, 1897–1901," *North Carolina Historical Review* 82, no. 2 (2005): 214.

20. For example, "The White Institution for the Blind in the Hands of a Negro," *News and Observer* (Raleigh), August 11, 1898, 4.

21. "White Women of North Carolina Basely Slandered," *Fisherman and Farmer* (Elizabeth City), September 9, 1898, 2; "The Old North State Forever," *Fisherman and Farmer*, September 16, 1898, 4; "Read Carefully, Register and Vote," *Fisherman and Farmer*, October 7, 1898, 4. "Crow, Democrats, Crow," *Fisherman and Farmer*, November 11, 1898, 1; "Resolutions Adopted by the White Man's Union," *Fisherman and Farmer*, November 18, 1898, 1.

22. Mebane to Moore, January 28, 1899; Mebane to Moore, March 23, 1899; Atkins to Mebane, March 1, 1899. General Correspondence.

23. *Biennial Report of the State Superintendent of Public Instruction, State of North Carolina, 1898–1900* (Raleigh: State Superintendent of Public Instruction, 1900), 178–179. Hereinafter, unless otherwise noted, all references to any Biennial Report of the State Superintendent of Education in North Carolina will be referred to as "Biennial Report."

24. Mebane to Moore, October 11, 1899. General Correspondence.

25. The first major monograph on this insurrection was written by H. Leon Prather, formerly a member of the Elizabeth City State faculty. *We Have Taken a City: The Wilmington Racial Massacre and the Coup of 1898* (Rutherford, NJ: Fairleigh Dickinson University Press, 1984).

26. "North Carolina's Coming Battle," *Virginian-Pilot* (Norfolk), May 17, 1900, 7. "Grand Rally," *Fisherman and Farmer*, April 20, 1900, 3. "Elizabeth City's Greatest Day," *Fisherman and Farmer*, May 11, 1900, 3.

27. Electoral fraud in 1900 was not limited only to Elizabeth City. In other areas, the threat of violence hurt turnout, as voters fearfully remembered the Wilmington massacre. James M. Beeby, "Red Shirt Violence, Election Fraud, and the Demise of the Populist Party in North Carolina's Third Congressional District, 1900," *North Carolina Historical Review* 85, no. 1 (2008): 1–28.

28. "The Vote of Pasquotank," *North Carolinian*, August 9, 1900, 2.

29. "Eleven Negroes Register in Greensboro . . . ," *News and Observer* (Raleigh), October 28, 1902, 7. "A Majority of 65, 876," *News and Observer*, November 4, 1902, 1.

30. Gregory Downs, "University Men, Social Science, White Supremacy in North Carolina," *Journal of Southern History* 75, no. 2 (2009): 290.

31. "Elizabeth City's Greatest Day," *Fisherman and Farmer*, May 11, 1900, 3.

32. Mary Jo Jackson Bratton, "Cradled in Conflict: Origins of East Carolina University," *North Carolina Historical Review* 63, no. 1 (1986): 80.

33. "How Is It?" *Tar Heel* (Elizabeth City), October 2, 1903, 4; "White Supremacy Ever," *Tar Heel*, September 5, 1902, 4.

34. *Public Laws, North Carolina* (1901), Chapter 565, in *Public Laws and resolutions of the State of North Carolina passed by the General Assembly* (Raleigh, NC: Uzzell, 1893–1919), 804. For examples that some whites saw consolidation as a way to improve Black normal schools, see M. C. S. Noble to T. F. Toon, January 15, February 18, 1901. Joyner to Leigh, March 29, 1902. Joyner to Leigh, April 7, 1902. All General Correspondence.

35. Minutes, Elizabeth City State Board of Managers, December 11, 1900, at Elizabeth City [NC] State University Archive, G. R. Little Library. "House Journal," *News and Observer*, January 15, 1901, 14.

36. S. L. Sheep to Toon, March 11, 1901. General Correspondence. *Minutes of the State Board of Education*, March 15, 1901 in *Minutes, Deeds, etc, 1890–1905*, in State Archives of North Carolina. Minutes, Elizabeth City Board of Managers, June 6, 1901, Elizabeth City [NC] State University Archive, G. R. Little Library. *Minutes of City Aldermen*, April 30, 1901, 5: 217. City clerk's office, 306 East Colonial Avenue, Elizabeth City, NC. Wade H. Boggs, *State-Supported*

Higher Education for Blacks in North Carolina, 1877–1945 (PhD diss., Duke University, 1972), 159, 160. "Local News," *Economist* (Elizabeth City), June 7, 1901, 3.

37. Thomas J. Jones, *A Study of the Private and Higher Institutions for Colored People in the United States* (Washington, DC: Government Printing Office, 1916), 2: 431–32. "The Colored Normal School," *Economist*, June 14, 1901, 2.

38. S.L. Sheep, quoted in "Benign Influence of Colored Normal School," *Morning Post* (Raleigh), June 29, 1901, 5.

39. *Biennial Report, 1900–02*, in *Public Documents of the State of North Carolina, Session 1903* (Raleigh, NC: Uzzell, 1903), I:3: vii–ix. Joyner, "Address to the People of the South," (c. 1902) in James Yadkin Joyner Papers, University Archives, East Carolina University, Greenville, NC. *Biennial Report, 1900–02*, in *Public Documents of the State of North Carolina, 1903*, I:3: x. *Biennial Report, 1902–04 (Raleigh: State Superintendent of Public Instruction, 1904)*, 80; Joyner to J. H. Hinemon, October 15, 1903. General Correspondence. Hinemon was Arkansas state superintendent); Joyner to J. E. Debman, February 3, 1903, General Correspondence.

40. Joyner to Moore, January 23, 1905. Moore invited Joyner to speak at Greensboro, Moore to Joyner, January 16, 1905. Moore to Joyner, thanks for the address at Greensboro, June 23, 1905. Joyner to Moore, November 3, 1903; January 27, March 19, 1904. W. Buttrick to Joyner, August 28, 1902. All General Correspondence.

41. Moore to Joyner, June 1902 (n.d.), as quoted in Nathan C. Newbold, ed. *Five North Carolina Negro Educators* (Chapel Hill: University of North Carolina Press, 1939), 98. P. W. Moore, Report, September 7, 1903, in Box 16, Special Subject File, Division of Negro Education, Department of Public Instruction, State Archives of North Carolina, Raleigh, North Carolina. Minutes, Elizabeth City State Board of Managers, August 9, 1902; *Biennial Report, 1902–04*, 535–37; Sheep to Joyner, August 12, 1902. Boggs, *State-Supported Higher Education*, 173.

42. "Prof Moore Goes to Tuskegee," *Tar Heel*, February 20, 1903, 3. Moore to Joyner, January 10, 1903. General Correspondence.

43. Moore to Scarborough, July 8, 1896. Moore to Mebane, August 4, 1898. General Correspondence. Leonard R. Ballou, *Gentleman from Pasquotank: Hugh Cale*, 375. Unpublished manuscript in Ballou Collection, Elizabeth City [NC] State University Archive. H. H. Wells, "Colored Normal Teachers Oppose Idea of Work," *Independent* (Elizabeth City), May 27, 1909, 3. This is a special copy only available in the Elizabeth City State University Archive, as microfilm editions of the newspaper preserved by the North Carolina Department of Archives and History begin at 1919.

44. Joyner sent a letter to all boards of Black normal schools, dated May 19, 1903. "Hot Contest Ahead: Will the Seven State Colored Normal Schools Be Consolidated?" *News and Observer*, June 16, 1903, 2.

45. Both petitions are in Box 15, Special Subject File, Division of Negro Education, Office of the State Superintendent of North Carolina, State Archives of North Carolina. Joyner liked the resolution from the teachers. Joyner to Moore, August 19, 1903. The White petition praised Moore for his "orderly and effective work" and his "very beneficial" work in the local Black community. Overman to Joyner, June 13, 1903. All General Correspondence.

46. Moore to Joyner, May 19, 1903. Leigh to Joyner, May 11, 1903. General Correspondence.

47. Minutes of *State Board of Education*, June 30, July 4, 1903, in *Minutes, Deeds, etc, 1890–1905*, State Archives of North Carolina.

48. *Biennial Report, 1902–04*, 559–60. Joyner to W. H. Ward, September 16, 1903. General Correspondence. "Professor Moores [sic] School," *Tar Heel*, July 17, 1903, 1.

49. Minutes, State Board of Education, July 13, 1903. Joyner to Moore, July 20, 1903. General Correspondence. *1903–4 Catalog*, 12–13. Joyner to Moore, September 8, 1903. General Correspondence.

50. Moore to Joyner, September 4, 1903. General Correspondence. *Biennial Report, 1902–04*, 2: 535–37.

51. James D. Anderson, *The Education of Blacks in the South, 1860–1935* (Chapel Hill: University of North Carolina Press, 1988), 28–29. Until 1931, Yale University required incoming students to meet a Latin requirement. Jerome Karabel, *The Chosen: The Hidden History of Admission and Exclusion at Harvard, Yale, and Princeton* (Boston: Houghton Mifflin, 2005), 52.

52. Rayford W. Logan, *Howard University: The First Hundred Years* (New York: New York University Press, 1968), 37–38, 104.

53. The funeral program, titled "In Memoriam: Professor Wiley Lane of the Howard University, Washington, D.C.," can be found in the Elisha Overton Papers, Elizabeth City [NC] State University Archive.

54. *Biennial Report, 1902–04*, 1: 82–83.

55. Moore to Joyner, November 2, 1903; Joyner to Moore, December 8, 1903. General Correspondence.

56. Moore to Joyner, October 13, 1903. General Correspondence.

57. No author, *One Hundred Ten Years of Service, 1892–2002, St James African Methodist Episcopal Zion Church*, 22. Self-printed manuscript, North Carolina Heritage Room, Pasquotank County Library, 100 E. Colonial Ave, Elizabeth City, NC.

58. *Deed Record* 17: 390–91, Pasquotank County Office of the Register of Deeds, 203 E. Main Street, Elizabeth City, NC.

59. Benjamin R. Justesen, "The Class of '83": Black Watershed in the North Carolina General Assembly," *North Carolina Historical Review* 86, no. 3 (2009): 282–308; Mebane, "Have We an American Race Question?" *The Arena* 24, no. 5 (1900): 5–6. *Private Laws, North Carolina* (1893), Chapter 282, in *Private Laws and resolutions of the State of North Carolina passed by the General Assembly* (Raleigh, NC: Uzzell, 1893–1915), 428.

60. M. B. Culpepper to Joyner, May 16, 1903. General Correspondence.

61. Joyner to Samuel Green, August 25, November 15, 1904. Joyner to Moore, March 13, 1905. General Correspondence.

62. *Minutes of the State Board of Education (1905–1916)*, April 19, 1905. On microfilm at State Archives of North Carolina.

63. E. F. Lamb to Joyner, May 14, 1905. Joyner to Lamb, April 29, 1905. Lamb to Joyner, May 18, 1905. General Correspondence.

64. Minutes, Elizabeth City State Board of Managers, April 25, May 18, 1905. *Minutes of the State Board of Education*, June 19, 1905.

65. *Minutes of the State Board of Education*, June 19, 1905. Years later, the other trustees would sue Moore, claiming that he had deceived them when they signed over control of the property. Although they won their case in district court, the North Carolina Supreme Court overturned the decision. *Cases Argued and Determined in the Supreme Court of North Carolina, Spring Term 1914 (in part), Fall Term 1914 (in part)* (Raleigh, NC: Edwards and Broughton, 1914), 462–68.

66. Joyner to Chairmen of Boards of the three (Black) normal schools, including Elizabeth City chair E. F. Lamb, June 22, 1905. General Correspondence. Joyner to Lamb, November 22, 1905. General Correspondence.

67. Minutes, Elizabeth City State Board of Managers, May 8, 1906. Sheep to Joyner, May 25, 1906. Leigh to Joyner, November 22, 1905. General Correspondence.

68. Moore to Joyner, March 11, 1905. C. L. Coon to Joyner, July 19, 1905. General Correspondence. Minutes, Elizabeth City State Board of Managers, September 16, 1905. *Deed Record* 25: 442, *Deed Records* 21: 255–56; 22: 2, both Pasquotank County Office of the Register of Deeds.

69. *Deed Record* 29: 303, Pasquotank County Office of the Register of Deeds. Minutes, Elizabeth City State Board of Managers, November 15, 1906; *Second Annual Catalogue of the State Colored Normal Schools for 1905–1906* (Raleigh, NC: Uzzell, 1906), 5. *1906-7 Catalog*, 12–13.

70. Bowman, *Elizabeth City State University, 1891–2016*, 44–47.

71. Jones, *A Study of the Private and Higher Institutions for Colored People in the United States*, 2: 431–32. R. D. W. Connor, *North Carolina Manual, 1919, issued by NC Historical Commission* (Raleigh, NC: State Printers, 1919), 175. Harold F. Brown, "The History of the Education of Negro Teachers in the State Normal Schools of North Carolina from 1877 to 1943" (master's thesis, East Carolina Teachers College, 1943), 113.

72. Moore to E.E. Sams, December 30, 1916, in *Public Documents of North Carolina, Session 1917* (Raleigh, NC: Edwards and Broughton, 1920), 28: 11.

73. *Biennial Report, 1916–18*, 1: 26–27. *Public Laws, NC* (1917), Chapter 154, in *Public Laws and resolutions of the State of North Carolina passed by the General Assembly* (Raleigh, NC: Uzzell, 1893–1919), 305. In 1919, the 1917 bond issue was amended so Elizabeth City received thirty thousand dollars. *Public Laws, NC* (1919), Chapter 328, 545.

74. Katie Brockett, D. W. White, and Mrs. M. L. Mebane, "State Normal Observes Negro History Week," *Norfolk Journal and Guide*, February 18, 1928, 14. The Negro National Anthem was song at Lyceum functions. "Normal Junior

Class Program," *The State Normal Banner*, December 1, 1928, 5. Elizabeth City State University Archive. W. E. B. Du Bois was the speaker for the 1927 commencement, which coincided with the official dedication and renaming of the administrative building as P. W. Moore Hall. Glen Bowman, "1927: W. E. B. Du Bois comes to Elizabeth City State," *Daily Advance*, July 5, 2015, Lifestyles section, 1.

BURAS: "THEY WERE VERY LOW KEY, BUT THEY SPOKE FROM WISDOM AND EXPERIENCE"

1. The epigraph is Leonard Smith interviewed by Kristen Buras, April 12, 2017, New Orleans, LA.

2. Walter Stern, *Race and Education in New Orleans: Creating the Segregated City, 1764–1960* (Baton Rouge: Louisiana State University Press, 2018).

3. Elizabeth Heavrin, Recordation of Certain Buildings at the George Washington Carver School Campus, New Orleans, Louisiana (Washington, DC: FEMA, June 28, 2010), 5–6. University of New Orleans, Earl Long Library, Louisiana and Special Collections, FEMA G. W. Carver School Collection, Box 1, Folder 1.

4. Derrick Bell, "Serving Two Masters: Integration Ideals and Client Interests in School Desegregation Litigation," in *Critical Race Theory: Key Writings that Formed the Movement*, Kimberlé Crenshaw et al., eds. (New York: New Press, 1995), 5–19.

5. Gwendolyn Mildo Hall, *Africans in Colonial Louisiana: The Development of Afro-Creole Culture in the Eighteenth Century* (Baton Rouge: Louisiana State University Press, 1992); Donald DeVore and Joseph Logsdon, *Crescent City Schools: Public Education in New Orleans, 1841–1991* (Lafayette: Center for Louisiana Studies, 1991).

6. Through oral history and archival research, I sought to answer the following questions: First, what was it like to be a student or teacher at Carver, including experiences inside and outside the classroom? Second, what was the culture of Carver, and how did specific traditions contribute to it? Third, according to students and teachers, did Carver successfully educate students? During 2017–2018, I conducted oral history interviews with nineteen Carver alumni spanning the school's fifty-year history, as well as interviews with or on twelve Carver teachers, most with thirty-plus year of teaching experience spanning a range of subject areas. For deceased teachers, I sought interviews with children, former students, and colleagues. Oral histories were contextualized with primary and secondary sources. In this chapter, I highlight the five teachers in my sample who were at Carver from the very beginning in 1958, as their teaching occurred simultaneous with the civil rights movement and post-*Brown* politics.

7. John Blassingame, *Black New Orleans, 1860–1880* (Chicago: University of Chicago Press, 1973); DeVore and Logsdon, *Crescent City Schools*; Keith Medley, *We as Freeman:* Plessy v. Ferguson, *The Fight against Legal Segregation* (Gretna, LA: Pelican Publishing, 2003).

8. DeVore and Logsdon, *Crescent City Schools*.

9. Alonzo Grace and Citizens' Planning Committee for Public Education in New Orleans, "Tomorrow's Citizens: A Study and Program for the Improvement of the New Orleans Public Schools" (New Orleans, LA: Orleans Parish School Board, 1940).

10. Grace, "Tomorrow's Citizens," 114.

11. DeVore and Logsdon, *Crescent City Schools*.

12. Stern, *Race and Education*.

13. Ibid., 199.

14. Ibid., 212–13.

15. Ibid., 213.

16. Ibid., 221.

17. Ibid, 223.

18. Ibid, 223.

19. Ibid, 225; Nathaniel Curtis and Arthur Davis, George Washington Carver Junior-Senior High School Plan Book (New Orleans, LA: Curtis and Davis Architects-Engineers, c. 1955), University of New Orleans [UNO], Earl Long Library, Louisiana and Special Collections, Orleans Parish School Board [OPSB]-147, G. W. Carver Junior-Senior High School, Box 5.

20. Curtis and Davis, Plan Book.

21. Heavrin, Recordation, 7.

22. *The Carver Times* 1, no. 2 (May 1959): 1. UNO, Long Library, Louisiana Collections, OPSB-147, G. W. Carver Junior-Senior High School, Box 1, Folder 2.

23. Dedication Program (1958, December 1). UNO, OPSB-147, Samuel Scarnato Papers, Box 14, G. W. Carver High School.

24. *The Carver Times*, 1.

25. For a more extensive history, see Kristen Buras, *The World Was Ours: Black Teachers and the Culture They Created in New Orleans (Re-Membering Carver Senior High School, 1958–2005)* (forthcoming).

26. Charles Hatfield interviewed by Al Kennedy, March 12, 1993, Charles Hatfield Papers, Amistad Research Center, Tulane University, New Orleans, LA, Box 4, Item 1 (Videocassette obtained from Charles Hatfield, Jr. by Kristen Buras).

27. Evelyn Wilson, *Laws, Customs, and Rights: Charles Hatfield and His Family—a Louisiana History* (Westminster, MD: Heritage Books, 2008).

28. Wilson, *Laws*, 77.

29. Hatfield, interviewed by Kennedy, Minute Mark 17:30–18:00.

30. Wilson, 78, 83.

31. Wilson, 99.

32. Charles Hatfield, "The Passing Age," news clipping, December 16, 1944, Amistad, Hatfield Papers, Box 1, Folder 16.

33. Wilson, chapter 8; Hatfield's Draft Second Letter to the Registrar at Louisiana State University (1945, January 25), Amistad, Hatfield Papers, Box 1, Folder 16.

34. Wilson, chapter 9; Hatfield, interviewed by Kennedy.

35. Wilson, chapter 11; Hatfield, interviewed by Kennedy.

36. Hatfield, interviewed by Kennedy, Minute Mark 31:00–32:15.

37. Wilson, 190.

38. Ibid.; Hatfield's Alpha Kappa Delta Certificate (1947, December 12), Amistad, Hatfield Papers, Box 1, Folder 14.

39. Wilson, 192–93.

40. Wilson, 193.

41. Wilson, 194; Hatfield, interviewed by Kennedy; Hatfield's Teaching Certificate, State Department of Education of Louisiana (March 7, 1952), Amistad, Hatfield Papers, Box 1, Folder 11.

42. Building Curriculum Council Photo, 1962 Carver Yearbook, UNO, OPSB–147, Carver Junior-Senior High School, Box 5.

43. Programs, Practices, and Progress: A Ten Year Progress Report, *Louisiana Weekly* (1968), UNO, OPSB–147, Scarnato Papers, Box 14; Hatfield Photo in Foreign Language Laboratory, 1972 Carver Yearbook, Personal Collection of Avis and Vermon James, New Orleans, LA.

44. Ella Shaw, interviewed by Kristen Buras, June 11, 2017, New Orleans, LA.

45. Charles Hatfield, "The Passing Age," news clipping (undated version), Amistad, Hatfield Papers, Box 1, Folder 16.

46. Hatfield, interviewed by Kennedy, Minute Mark 1:00:45–1:01:17.

47. Wilson, 201–2; for more on the teacher union, see Kristen Buras, *Charter Schools, Race, and Urban Space* (New Orleans: Routledge, 2015), chapter 5.

48. Hatfield, interviewed by Kennedy, Minute Mark 1:26:45–1:27:10.

49. Ibid., Minute Mark 1:08:15–1:08:50

50. Marilyn Pierre Degrasse interviewed by Kristen Buras, February 5, 2018, New Orleans, LA.

51. Wilson, 202; Hatfield Certificate of Appreciation for Board Membership, Orleans Public School Federal Credit Union (September 30, 1993). Amistad, Hatfield Papers, Box 2, Item 2.

52. Hatfield Farewell to Seniors as Yearbook Advisor, 1962 Carver Yearbook, UNO, OPSB–147, Carver Junior-Senior High School, Box 5.

53. Tribute to Hatfield, 1973 Carver Yearbook, Personal Collection of Avis and Vermon James, New Orleans, Louisiana.

54. Wilson, 202.

55. Hatfield Pioneer Award, April 30, 1983, Amistad, Hatfield Papers, Box 2, Item 1.

56. Wilson, 203–4.

57. Hatfield, interviewed by Kennedy, Minute Mark 46:35–46:45.

58. "Lamar Smith: Back Bone of Community School," 1981 Carver Yearbook, 91, Personal Collection of James; Louisiana Senate Resolution No. 41 (Baton Rouge, LA, 2003).

59. Theron Lewis interviewed by Kristen Buras, April 10, 2017, New Orleans, LA.

60. "The Community School," 1972 Carver Yearbook, 12, Personal Collection of James.

61. "Smith: Back Bone," 1981 Carver Yearbook, 91.

62. Lamar Smith, The Plight of the Black Teacher in New Orleans, pre-published version for Afro-American, circa 1970, 2, UNO, Long Library, Louisiana and Special Collections, United Teachers of New Orleans, Local 527 Collection, Container 135–15.

63. Ibid., 1.

64. Ibid., 4.

65. "Smith: Back Bone," 91.

66. Ibid.

67. Lamar Smith Jr., and Reverend Douglas Haywood, interviewed by Kristen Buras, June 8, 2017, New Orleans, LA.

68. Ibid.

69. Louisiana Senate Resolution No. 41.

70. Ibid., 2–3.

71. Smith and Haywood, interviewed by Buras.

72. "Smith: Back Bone," 91.

73. Smith and Haywood, interviewed by Buras.

74. Ibid.

75. Enos Hicks Jr., interviewed by Kristen Buras, June 8, 2017, New Orleans, LA.

76. "Memories of Daddy by Enos S. Hicks IV," Unpublished essay, Personal Papers of Sarahlilly Hicks; "Ralph Metcalfe, Former Marquette Ace, Has Also Fashioned Enos Hicks into One of the Nation's Best Sprinters" in "J. Herbert Breaks World Record in N.Y.C.," *Indianapolis Recorder*, March 5, 1938, at https://newspapers.library.in.gov/.

77. "Memories of Daddy"; Dedication Program; Building Curriculum Council Photo.

78. Hicks Jr., interviewed by Buras.

79. Lewis, interviewed by Buras.

80. Ibid.; Teacher of the Year 1961, 1962 Carver Yearbook, 125.

81. Lewis, interviewed by Buras.

82. Ibid.

83. Ibid.; Photo, Hicks discusses with Coach Lee, Southern University, scholarships for athletes, 1962 Carver Yearbook; Hicks Jr., interviewed by Buras.

84. Lewis interviewed by Buras; Letter from Carver Principal Milton Becnel to Assistant Superintendent John Monie, February 16, 1967, on Lewis's quarter-mile world record and upcoming Olympics in Mexico City, with newspaper clipping, "Theron Lewis VFW Honoree," *Times-Picayune*, February 16, 1967, OPSB–147, Scarnato Papers, Box 14; "Southern U.'s Best to Run Here," *New York Times*, January 13, 1966, Personal Paper of Theron Lewis.

85. Hicks Jr., interviewed by Buras.

86. Ibid.

87. "Coach Hicks by Lloyd Wills," Unpublished essay (July 26, 2011), Personal Papers of Sarahlilly Hicks.

88. "Coach Herman Gray on Hoopy," Unpublished essay, Personal Papers of Sarahlilly Hicks.

89. Hicks Jr., interviewed by Buras.

90. Ibid.

91. Ibid.

92. Ernest Charles, interviewed by Kristen Buras, April 11, 2017, New Orleans, LA.

93. Hicks Jr., interviewed by Buras.

94. Al Kennedy, *Yvonne Busch: One Teacher's Role in Shaping New Orleans Music* (New Orleans: Louisiana Department of Culture, Recreation, and Tourism, 2000), 2–5.

95. Ibid., 5–7.

96. Ibid., 7.

97. Ibid., 8.

98. Ibid., 8.

99. Ibid., 10.

100. Ibid., 11.

101. Ibid., 10.

102. Ibid., 16.

103. Ibid., 24–26.

104. Dedication Program, 1958.

105. Kennedy, *Yvonne Busch*, 28–29.

106. Ibid., 30.

107. Ibid., 33.

108. Kennedy, *Yvonne Busch*; see also Al Kennedy, *Chord Changes on the Chalkboard: How Public School Teachers Shaped the Jazz and the Music of New Orleans* (Lanham, MD: Scarecrow Press, 2005).

109. Herlin Riley, interviewed by Kristen Buras, April 12, 2017, New Orleans, LA.

110. Smith, interviewed by Buras.

111. Kennedy, *Yvonne Busch*, 34.

112. Ibid., 15.

113. LS3 Studios, 2015.

114. Ibid., Minute Mark 33:00.

115. Rhea Dokes, interviewed by Kristen Buras, April 10, 2017, New Orleans, LA; Busch Funeral Program (March 8, 2014), Personal Papers of Herlin Riley.

116. Lenora Condoll, Carol Righteous, and Clarence Righteous, interviewed by Kristen Buras, June 11, 2017, New Orleans, LA; Lenora Condoll, interviewed by Kristen Buras, April 10, 2021, by phone.

117. Condoll, interviewed by Buras.

118. Condoll, Righteous, and Righteous, interviewed by Buras.

119. Ibid.

120. Dwan Julien, interviewed by Kristen Buras, June 4, 2018, by phone.

121. Hasan Sparks, interviewed by Kristen Buras, June 3, 2018, by phone.

122. Condoll, Righteous, and Righteous, interviewed by Buras.

123. Photo, "Close Up Participants in DC, Outside Smithsonian Institute," 1972 Carver Yearbook; Photos, "Students Tour Nation's Capitol and New York City," 1973 Carver Yearbook; Photos, Close-Up at Lincoln Monument, US Supreme Court, and Williamsburg, VA, 1992 Carver Yearbook; Personal Collection of James.

124. Condoll, Righteous, and Righteous, interviewed by Buras.

125. Ibid.

126. "Introduction '81," 1982 Carver Yearbook, Personal Collection of James.

127. "TP/SI Cites Condoll," 1984 Carver Yearbook, Personal Collection of James.

128. "Teacher Superlatives," 1985 Carver Yearbook, Personal Collection of James.

129. "My Favorite Teacher," 1986 Carver Yearbook, 99, Personal Collection of James.

130. Condoll, Righteous, and Righteous, interviewed by Buras.

131. Ibid.

132. Condoll, interviewed by Buras.

133. Condoll, Righteous, and Righteous, interviewed by Buras.

134. Ibid.

135. Riley, interviewed by Buras.

136. Presentation by Dr. Mack Spears, President, Orleans Parish School Board, to the Business Task Force of the Chamber of Commerce of New Orleans (October 20, 1978), "Student Membership Data, 1977–78," UNO, OPSB–147, Scarnato Papers, Box 14.

137. Presentation by Spears, "New Orleans Public Schools: Comparative Membership Data by Schools, October 1977 and September 1978."

138. Presentation by Spears, "Memorandum to Dr. Gene Geisert, Superintendent, from John Finney, Director of Maintenance Services," (August 4, 1978).

139. Ibid.

140. Presentation by Spears, "Maintenance Services Proposed Budget 1978–79: Contracted Building Repairs."

141. Presentation by Spears, "Memorandum."

142. Report of the Reviewing Committee for G. W. Carver High School, SACS (1987, March 25–27), 1–2, UNO, OPSB–147, Carver Junior-Senior High School, Box 1, Folder 1.

143. Ibid., 7–8.

144. Ibid., 9.

145. 1959 Carver graduate Althea Merricks Haywood, interviewed by Kristen Buras, April 11, 2017, New Orleans, LA; Personal Papers of Merricks, "Alma Mater" mimeograph.

HYRES: "DEDICATION TO THE HIGHEST OF CALLINGS"

1. Florence C. Bryant, *Memoirs of a Country Girl* (New York: Vantage Press, 1988), 182.

2. Bryant, *Memoirs of Country Girl*, 182–83; Florence Bryant, transcript of an oral history conducted March 12, 2003, by Alexandria Searls, Charlottesville, VA: 60–62. Florence Coleman Bryant was born Florence S. Coleman. For the sake of consistency, I will refer to her as Bryant throughout the chapter. On the shift in education reform during the A Nation at Risk era, see Jack Schneider, *Excellence for All: How a New Breed of Reformer is Transforming America's Public Schools* (Nashville, TN: Vanderbilt University Press, 2011); Maris Vinovskis, *From a Nation at Risk to No Child Left Behind: National Education Goals and the Creation of Federal Education Policy* (New York: Teachers College Press, 2015).

3. Bryant, *Memoirs of a Country Girl*; Bryant, transcript of an oral history by Searls, 60–62; Florence Bryant, oral history conducted December 19, 2014, by Lindsey Jones, Charlottesville, VA. For more on the relationship between racism, Charlottesville, Thomas Jefferson, and the University of Virginia, see Louis P. Nelson and Claudrena N. Harold, eds., *Charlottesville 2017: The Legacy of Race and Inequity* (Charlottesville: University of Virginia Press, 2018); Alan Taylor, *Thomas Jefferson's Education* (New York: W. W. Norton, 2019); Maurie D. McInnis and Louis P. Nelson, eds., *Educated in Tyranny: Slavery at Thomas Jefferson's University* (Charlottesville: University of Virginia, 2019).

4. Robert A. Pratt, "New Directions in Virginia's Civil Rights History," *The Virginia Magazine of History and Biography* 104, no. 1 (Winter 1996): 149–56; Robert Pratt, *The Color of Their Skin: Education and Race in Richmond, Virginia, 1954–89* (Charlottesville: University Press of Virginia, 1993); Matthew D. Lassiter and Andrew B. Lewis, eds., *The Moderates' Dilemma: Massive Resistance to School Desegregation in Virginia* (Charlottesville: University Press of Virginia,

1998); Jill O. Titus, *Brown's Battleground: Students, Segregationists, and the Struggle for Justice in Prince Edward County, Virginia* (Chapel Hill: University of North Carolina Press, 2011); Christopher Bonastia, *Southern Stalemate: Five Years Without Public Education in Prince Edward County, Virginia* (Chicago: University of Chicago Press, 2012); Jeffrey L. Littlejohn and Charles Howard Ford, *Elusive Equality: Desegregation and Resegregation in Norfolk's Public Schools* (Charlottesville: University of Virginia Press, 2012); Carmen Foster, "Tension, Resistance, and Transition: School Desegregation in Richmond's North Side, 1960–63," (EdD diss., University of Virginia, 2014); Brian J. Daugherity, *Keep On Keeping On: The NAACP and the Implementation of* Brown v. Board of Education *in Virginia* (Charlottesville: University of Virginia Press, 2018); Danielle Wingfield-Smith, "Navigating the 'Virginia Way': Henry L. Marsh, III, Civil Rights, and Movement Leadership," (PhD diss., University of Virginia, 2018); Derrick Alridge, "Teachers in the Movement: Pedagogy, Activism, and Freedom," *History of Education Quarterly* 60, no. 1 (February 2020): 1–23; Alexander Hyres, "'The Whole Mess Is *American* History': Protest, Pedagogy, and Black Studies at a Desegregated High School in the South, 1974–1974," *Journal of African American History* 107, no. 1 (Winter 2022): 55–78.

5. Adam Fairclough, "The Costs of *Brown*: Black Teachers and School Integration," in *Journal of American History* 91, no. 1 (June 2004): 43–55; Michael Fultz, "The Displacement of Black Educators Post-*Brown*: An Overview and Analysis," in *History of Education Quarterly* 44, no. 1 (Spring 2004): 11–45; Adam Fairclough, *A Class of Their Own: Black Teachers in the Segregated South* (Cambridge, MA: Belknap Press of Harvard University, 2007).

Barbara Shircliffe, *Desegregating Teachers: Contesting the Meaning of Equality of Educational Opportunity in the South Post-*Brown (New York: Peter Lang, 2012); Vanessa Siddle Walker, "School 'Outer-Gration' and 'Tokenism': Segregated Black Educators Critique the Promise of Education Reform in the Civil Rights Act of 1964" in *Journal of Negro Education* 84, no. 2 (Spring 2015): 111–24; Vanessa Siddle Walker, *The Lost Education of Horace Tate: Uncovering the Hidden Heroes Who Fought for Justice in Schools* (New York: The New

Press, 2018); Leslie T. Fenwick, *Jim Crow's Pink Slip: The Untold Story of Black Principal and Teacher Leadership* (Cambridge, MA: Harvard Education Press, 2022).

6. Marshall Wingfield, *A History of Caroline County Virginia: From its Formation in 1727 to 1924* (Richmond, VA: Press of Trevvet Christian & Co., 1924), 171; Bryant, *Memoirs of a Country Girl*, xi, 31, 70; Florence Bryant, interview with Lindsey Jones.

7. Bryant, *Memoirs of a Country Girl*, 72; "Interview with Mrs. Florence Coleman Bryant," from *The Road to* Brown: *The Untold Story of 'the Man Who Killed Jim Crow*, conducted on October 25, 1987, accessed March 27, 2022, https://www.youtube.com/; on Black organizing and activism in Virginia during Jim Crow, see Brent Tarter, *The Grandees of Government: The Origins and Persistence of Undemocratic Politics* (Charlottesville: University of Virginia Press, 2013), 267, 270, 275, 283, 288–90; J. Douglas Smith, *Managing White Supremacy: Race, Politics, and Citizenship in Jim Crow Virginia* (Chapel Hill: University of North Carolina Press, 2002), 78–80, 144–45, 189–90; Blair L. M. Kelley, *Right to Ride: Streetcar Boycotts and African American Citizenship in the Era of Plessy v. Ferguson* (Chapel Hill: University of North Carolina Press, 2010); Marvin Chiles, "'Down Where the South Begins': Black Richmond Activism before the Modern Civil Rights Movement," *Journal of African American History* 105, no. 1 (Winter 2020): 56–82.

8. Wingfield, *A History of Caroline County Virginia*, 175; Bryant, *Memoirs of a Country Girl*, 71.

9. Wingfield, *A History of Caroline County Virginia*, 167; Bryant, *Memoirs of a Country Girl*, 97; on the development of Black schooling in the South during and after the Civil War, see James D. Anderson, *The Education of Blacks in the South, 1860–1935* (Chapel Hill: University of North Carolina Press, 1988); William Watkins, *The White Architects of Black Education: Ideology and Power in America, 1865–1954* (New York: Teachers College Press, 2001); Heather Andrea Williams, *Self-Taught: African American Education in Slavery Freedom* (Chapel Hill: University of North Carolina Press, 2005); Christopher M. Span, *From Cotton Field to Schoolhouse: African American Education in Mississippi* (Chapel Hill: University of North Carolina Press, 2009);

Ronald E. Butchart, *Schooling the Freed People: Teaching, Learning, and the Struggle for Black Freedom* (Chapel Hill: University of North Carolina Press, 2010); Hilary Green, *Educational Reconstruction: African American Schools in the Urban South* (New York: Fordham University Press, 2016); Jarvis Givens, *Fugitive Pedagogy: Carter G. Woodson and the Art of Black Teaching* (Cambridge, MA: Harvard University Press, 2021).

10. Bryant, *Memoirs of a Country Girl*, 107–8; Anderson, *The Education of Blacks in the South*, 235–37.

11. On the origins and development of Black high schools in the South, see Anderson, *The Education of Blacks in the South*, 186–238; Jay Winston Driskell Jr., *Schooling Jim Crow: The Fight for Atlanta's Booker T. Washington High School and the Roots of Black Protest Politics* (Charlottesville: University of Virginia Press, 2014); Wingfield, *A History of Caroline County*, 172–74; Marion Woodfork Simmons, *An Oasis in Caroline County, Virginia, 1903–1969* (Burtonsville, MD: Woodfork Geneaology LLC, 2011); Bryant, *Memoir of a Country Girl*, 111–12.

12. Bryant, *Memoirs of a Country Girl*, 112–14; Givens, *Fugitive Pedagogy*, 199.

13. Bryant, *Memoirs of a Country Girl*, 118–19, 123–24.

14. Bryant, *Memoirs of a Country Girl*, 130–31; Bryant, interview with Lindsey Jones; Bryant, interview for "The Road to *Brown*."

15. Anderson, *The Education of Blacks in the South*, 186–237; Simmons, *An Oasis in Caroline County*, 2–10; Scot A. French, "African American Civic Activism and the Making of Jefferson High School," in *Pride Overcomes Prejudice: A History of Charlottesville's African American School*, Andrea N. Douglas, ed. (Charlottesville, VA: Jefferson School African American Heritage, 2013), 31–72. For more on how the American high school became a mass institution, see Kyle M. Steele, *Making a Mass Institution: Indianapolis and the American High School* (New Brunswick, NJ: Rutgers University Press, 2021).

16. Bryant, *Memoirs of a Country Girl*, 138.

17. Bryant, transcript of an oral history by Searls, 61–62. Jarvis Givens, "'There Would Be No Lynching If It Did Not Start in the Schoolroom," in *American Educational Research Journal* 56, no. 4 (August 2019): 1457–1494; Givens, *Fugitive Pedagogy*, 84, 173, 196; On racist

depictions in Virginia history and US history, see Lawrence D. Reddick, "Racial Attitudes in American History Textbooks of the South," *Journal of Negro Education* 19, no. 3 (July 1934): 225–65; Dan B. Fleming, "A Review of Slave Life in Fourteen United States History Textbooks," *Journal of Negro Education* 56, no. 4 (Autumn 1987): 550–56; William Gilmore, interview conducted by Lynn Carter, August 31, 2002, Charlottesville, VA.

18. Bryant, *Rebecca Fuller McGinness*, 141–42; "Jackson P. Burley High School," http://afrovirginia.org/; Virginia Foundation for the Humanities, "Jackson P. Burley School," *African American Historic Sites Database*, accessed December 5, 2016, http://www.aahistoricsitesva.org/; "Burley High Opens With Fall Session," *New Journal and Guide* (Norfolk, VA), September 15, 1951; Lucille Smith, *Unforgettable Jackson P. Burley High School* (self-published, 2021); for more on equalization in the South, see A. F. Coleman, "The Salary Equalization Movement," *Journal of Negro Education* 16, no. 2 (Spring 1947): 235–41; Doxey A. Wilkerson, "The Negro School Movement in Virginia: From 'Equalization' to 'Integration,'" *Journal of Negro Education* 29, no. 1 (Winter 1960): 17–29; R. Scott Baker, "Testing Equality: The National Teacher Examination and the NAACP's Legal Campaign to Equalize Teachers' Salaries in the South, 1936–63," *History of Education Quarterly* 35, no. 1 (Spring 1995): 49–64; Sarah Thuesen, *Greater Than Equal: African American Struggles for Schools and Citizenship in North Carolina, 1919–1965* (Chapel Hill: University of North Carolina Press, 2013), 159–200; Grace Schultz, "The NAACP Equalization Strategy and the Dismantling of Segregation in Virginia's Public Schools," *Social Education* 84, no. 6 (November–December 2020): 348–54.

19. Bryant, *Memoirs of a Country Girl*, 142; Anna Holden, *The Bus Stops Here: A Study of School Desegregation in Three Cities* (New York: Agathon Press, 1974.), 79–82; Smith, *Unforgettable Jackson P. Burley High School*.

20. McGinnis and Nelson, *Educated in Tyranny: Slavery at Thomas Jefferson's University* (Charlottesville: University of Virginia Press, 2019); Ragosta, Onuf, and O'Shaunessy, eds., *The Founding of Thomas Jefferson's University*; Bryant, *Memoirs of a Country Girl*, 132; "The Long Walk," accessed on October 1, 2021,

https://www.law.virginia.edu/; "The Life of Walter Ridley," accessed on October 1, 2021, https://aig.alumni.virginia.edu/.

21. Daugherity, *Keep On Keeping On*, 18, 33; Bryant, *Memoirs of a Country Girl*, 133.

22. Bryant, *Memoir of a Country Girl*, 133; Florence Coleman Bryant, "Representative Speaking of Douglas MacArthur, General of the Army, During Various Phases of His Life" (MA diss., University of Virginia, 1958).

23. Daugherity, *Keep On Keeping On*, 49–50, 51, 69–70, 75; Paul M. Gaston and Thomas T. Hammond, "Public School Desegregation: Charlottesville, Virginia, 1955–62," (Presentation, The South: The Ethical Demands of Integration, Nashville, TN, December 28, 1962), 1–25; Fultz, "The Displacement of Black Educators Post-*Brown*"; Fairclough, "The Costs of *Brown*"; Wilbert T. Lewis, interview conducted by Derrick Alridge and Alexander Hyres, April 22, 2015, Charlottesville, VA.

24. Bryant, transcript of an oral history by Searls, 61–62; Bryant, interview for "The Road to *Brown*"; Holden, *The Bus Stops Here*, 55–60.

25. Bryant, *Memoirs of a Country Girl*, 133, 161; Johnnie M. Fullwinder, interview conducted by Derrick Alridge and Shontell White, March 11, 2015, Danville, VA; Alridge, "Teachers in the Movement," 9–13; Holden, *The Bus Stops Here*, 53–60.

26. Bryant, *Memoirs of a Country Girl*, 151.

27. Bryant, *Memoirs of a Country Girl*, 153.

28. Bryant, *Memoirs of a Country Girl*, 90; Holden, *The Bus Stops Here*, 39.

29. Bryant, *Memoirs of a Country Girl*, 91; Holden, *The Bus Stops Here*, 87–99.

30. Bryant, *Memoirs of a Country Girl*, 89–90.

31. Bryant, *Memoirs of a Country Girl*, 135.

32. Bryant, *Memoirs of a Country Girl*, 173.

33. "Charlottesville High Reopens as Racial Tension Eases," *Washington Post*, March 7, 1984, accessed June 4, 2018, https://www.washingtonpost.com/.

34. Bryant, *Memoirs of a Country Girl*, 166, 178–79.

35. Bryant, *Memoirs of a Country Girl*, 179; Fultz, "The Displacement of Black Educators Post-*Brown*; Fairclough, "The Costs of *Brown*"; Walker, *The Lost Education of Horace Tate*.

36. Bryant, *Memoirs of a Country Girl*, 179.

37. Bryant, interview for "The Road to *Brown*."

38. Bryant, *Memoirs of a Country Girl*, ix.

39. Bryant, *Memoirs of a Country Girl*, ix.

40. Bryant, *Rebecca Fuller McGinness*, 3.

41. Bryant, *Rebecca Fuller McGinness*, 106.

42. Florence Bryant, transcript of an oral history conducted March 12, 2003, by Alexandria Searls, Charlottesville, VA, Jefferson School Project, Vol. 1: 60–62; Florence Bryant, oral history conducted December 19, 2014, by Lindsey Jones, Charlottesville, VA, Teachers in the Movement.

43. Florence C. Bryant, "One Story About School Desegregation," (Charlottesville, VA: self-published, 2004).

44. For more on the Black educational heritage and teachers, see Givens, *Fugitive Pedagogy*, 123, 231, 241; for more on the work of Black public intellectuals during the progressive era, see Karen A. Johnson, *Uplifting the Women and the Race: The Lives, Educational Philosophies, and Social Activism of Anna Julia Cooper and Nannie Helen Burroughs* (New York: Routledge, 2000); Derrick Alridge, *The Educational Thought of W. E. B. Du Bois: An Intellectual History* (New York: Teachers College Press, 2008); Audrey McCluskey, *A Forgotten Sisterhood: Pioneering Black Women Educators and Activists in the Jim Crow South* (New York: Rowman & Littlefield, 2014).

LODER-JACKSON: HIDDEN IN PLAIN SIGHT

1. Martin Luther King Jr., "The Role of the Behavioral Scientist in the Civil Rights Movement," *American Psychologist* 23, no. 3 (March 1968): 180–86.

2. King, "Role of Behavioral Scientist," 182.

3. King, 182.

4. E. Franklin Frazier, *Black Bourgeoisie: The Rise of a New Middle Class in the United States*, first edition (Glencoe, IL: The Free Press and The Falcon's Wing Press, 1957).

5. King, "Role of Behavioral Scientist," 183.

6. American Psychological Association, "APA President Connects Black History Month to Psychology," accessed August 11, 2021, https://www.apa.org/.

7. King, "Role of Behavioral Scientist," 183; Kenneth B. Clark and Mamie P. Clark, "Emotional Factors in Racial Identification and Preference in Negro Children," *Journal of Negro Education* 19, no. 3 (Summer 1950): 341–50, https://doi.org/10.2307/2966491.

8. American Psychological Association, "APA President Connects Black History Month to Psychology"; Kenneth B. Clark, "Perspectives; The Negro and The American Promise," interview with Dr. Martin Luther King Jr., June 24, 1963, GBH Archives, accessed August 11, 2021, http://openvault.wgbh.org/.

9. Vanessa Siddle Walker, *Hello Professor: A Black Principal and Professional Leadership in the Segregated South* (Chapel Hill: University of North Carolina Press, 2009); Jarvis R. Givens, *Fugitive Pedagogy: Carter G. Woodson and the Art of Black Teaching* (Cambridge, MA: Harvard University Press, 2021), 159–98; Derrick P. Alridge, "HES Presidential Address Teachers in the Movement: Pedagogy, Activism, and Freedom," *History of Education Quarterly* 60, no. 1 (February 2020): 1–23; Tondra L. Loder-Jackson, *Schoolhouse Activists: African American Educators and the Long Birmingham Civil Rights Movement* (Albany: State University of New York Press, 2015), 126–27.

10. This chapter is influenced by the tenets of social history in viewing "the history of ordinary people as contributing greatly to an understanding of the past" and demonstrating more agency than "commonly assumed by conventional historians" (Peter N. Stearns, "Social History," *Oxford Bibliographies*, para. 1, https://www.oxfordbibliographies.com/). See also Jeanne Theoharis, *A More Beautiful and Terrible History: The Uses and Misuses of Civil Rights History* (Boston: Beacon, 2018). As an academic grounded in the "interdisciplinary discipline" of educational foundations with emphases on historical and social foundations, I join ranks with a cadre of educational foundations and history of education scholars, who are dedicated to revising this historiography. A parallel approach in the history discipline is "interdisciplinary history," whereby historians over the past four decades have looked to the social sciences and humanities for innovative ideas and inspiration. See T. C. R. Horn and Harry Ritter, "Interdisciplinary History: A Historiographical Review," *The History Teacher*, 19, no. 3 (May 1986): 427–48 and MIT Press's *Journal of Interdisciplinary History*, https://direct.mit.edu/jinh.

11. Loder-Jackson, *Schoolhouse Activists*; Joy Williamson-Lott and Nancy Beadie, "Forum on Teaching: Constructing Historical Cases," *History of Education Quarterly* 56, no. 1 (February

2016): 115–116; John L. Rury, "The Power and Limitations of Historical Case Study: A Consideration of Postwar African American Educational Experience," *HSE–Social and Education History* 3, no. 3 (October 2014): 241–70, https://doi.org/10.4471/hse.2014.15; Bent Flyvbjerg, "Five Misunderstandings about Case-Study Research," *Qualitative Inquiry* 12, no. 2 (2006): 219–45.

12. V. P. Franklin, "Cultural Capital and African American Education," *Journal of African American History*, 87 (Spring 2002): 175–81.

13. This chapter endeavors to gather as many archival "grains of sand" as possible. These data are collected from: interviews I convened between 2012 and 2015 with over forty educators in Birmingham born before, during, and after the classical phase of the civil rights movement; oral histories from archives at the Birmingham Civil Rights Institute Oral History Project, https://bcriohp.org/; Duke University's John Hope Franklin Center's Behind the Veil Project, https://bcriohp.org/; University of North Carolina's Southern Oral History Program's Long Civil Rights Initiative, https://sohp.org/; and other digital and physical archives, notably HBCUs (e.g., Alabama State University, Tuskegee University, Miles College in Birmingham, and Paine College in Augusta, GA) and the Alabama Department of Archives and History. Artifacts include letters, newspapers, civil rights protest communiques, FBI reports, photographs, oral histories, and a few autobiographies and self-published reports authored by teacher activists, Black teachers associations, and civic and civil rights organizations.

14. Evelyn Dilworth-Williams, "Teachers Symposium," Birmingham Civil Rights Institute, July 25, 2007; *Mighty Times: The Children's March*, directed by Robert Hudson and Bobby Houston (Montgomery, AL: Southern Poverty Law Center and Home Box Office, 2004), DVD.

15. Jefferson County Memorial Project and Equal Justice Initiative, "Elizabeth Lawrence," *Lynching in America: Community Remembrance Project*, p. 14, https://eji.org/; "Negro Woman Lynched in B'ham: Son Narrowly Escapes Same Fate." *Daily ___* (name unreadable on microfilm), July 5, 1933, Tuskegee University Newspaper Archives, Reel #228; "Ala. Boy Tells of Mother's Lynching," *Baltimore Afro-American Newspaper*, July 22, 1933; see also Tammy Blue,

"Elizabeth Lawrence, July 5, 1933, Birmingham," *BirminghamWatch*, accessed September 26, 2021, https://birminghamwatch.org/.

16. Adam Fairclough, *Teaching Equality: Black Schools in the Age of Jim Crow* (Athens: University of Georgia Press, 2001), 46–48.

17. Vanessa Siddle Walker, "Ninth Annual *Brown* Lecture in Education Research: Black Educators as Educational Advocates in the Decades Before *Brown v. Board of Education*." *Educational Researcher* 42, no. 4 (May 2013): 207–22, https://doi.org/10.3102/0013189X13490140.

18. Glen Eskew, *But for Birmingham: The Local and National Movements in the Civil Rights Struggle* (Athens: University of Georgia Press, 1997), 259–97; and *Mighty Times: The Children's March*.

19. Eskew, 264.

20. John Dittmer, *Local People: The Struggle for Civil Rights in Mississippi* (Champaign: University of Illinois Press, 1994), 75.

21. Idus A. Newby, *Black Carolinians: A History of Blacks in South Carolina from 1865 to 1968* (Columbia: University of South Carolina Press, 1973), 82–94, 102–11, 258–73.

22. Adam Fairclough, *A Class of their Own: Black Teachers in the Segregated South* (Cambridge, MA: Harvard University Press, 2007), 382.

23. Ronald E. Butchart, "Courage in the Classroom: When Teachers Faced Violence and Worse for their Activism and Advocacy on Behalf of Black Freedom," *The Georgia Social Studies Journal* 3, no. 1 (Winter 2013), 7–15; Jelani M. Favors, *Shelter in a Time of Storm: How Black Colleges Fostered Generations of Leadership and Activism* (Chapel Hill: University of North Carolina, 2019), 18–21; Givens, *Fugitive Pedagogy*, 167–68; Tondra L. Loder-Jackson, "AATC Keynote Address Schoolhouse Activists: Disrupting Narratives about African American Educators' Involvement in the Alabama Civil Rights Movement," *Curriculum and Teaching Dialogue* 22, nos. 1 and 2 (2020): 17–35; Campbell F. Scribner, "Surveying the Destruction of African American Schoolhouses in the South, 1864–1876," *Journal of the Civil War Era* 10, no. 4, (December 2020): 469–94.

24. Schoolteachers Harry T. and Harriette Moore were martyred civil rights leaders in Florida who founded the Brevard County Branch of the National Association for the Advancement of Colored People (NAACP). Their house was bombed by the Ku Klux Klan on Christmas night, the night of their twenty-fifth wedding anniversary. Moore died on the way to the hospital, and his wife died nine days later. See NAACP, "Harry T. and Harriette Moore," https://naacp.org/; see also a collaboration between the PBS station affiliate, WUCF in Orlando, FL, and students at the University of Central Florida, titled *The Moore Project*, accessed September 26, 2021, https://www.wucf.org/.

25. Jerome Gray, Joe L. Reed, and Norman W. Walton, *History of the Alabama State Teachers Association (ASTA)* (Washington, DC: National Education Association, 1987), 155–56.

26. Loder-Jackson, "AATC Keynote," 20–24; Patricia Hill Collins, *Black Feminist Thought: Knowledge, Consciousness, and the Politics of Empowerment* (New York: Routledge, 2000), 201–25. Previously, I have drawn upon Patricia Hill Collins's seminal work on Black feminist thought to define activism for Black women educators, in particular. Collins has argued that prevailing conceptions of social and political activism and resistance misunderstand the meaning of activism in Black women's lives, as they focus on formalized and visible political activity and miss "unofficial, private, and seemingly invisible spheres of social life and organization," 202. Black women in the US South have been traditionally excluded from or relegated to subordinate roles within formally organized civil rights, women's rights, and labor rights groups. In light of this context, Collins proposed assessing Black women's activism not so much by their ideology (i.e., whether they possess conservative progressive, or radical views) or their association with formal political organizations but by their strategic responses to their daily encounters with domination in their communities, schools, and workplaces. Collins delineated two distinct yet interrelated dimensions of activism: *daily individual struggles for group or professional survival* and *collective struggles for institutional transformation*, 204.

27. Givens, *Fugitive Pedagogy*, 4, 7, 32, 167–69, 213–20.

28. See accounts of King's reassurances to actress Nichelle Nichols, who played the ground-breaking role of Lieutenant Nyota Uhura in *Star Trek*, and American baseball Hall of Famer

Hank Aaron: https://www.npr.org/ and https://www.ajc.com.

29. King, "Role of Behavioral Scientist," 183.

30. Martha Biondi, *The Black Revolution on Campus* (Berkeley: University of California Press, 2012); Favors, *Shelter in a Time of Storm*; *Tell Them We are Rising: The Story of Black Colleges and Universities*, directed by Stanley Nelson and Marco Williams (Arlington, VA: PBS Independent Lens and Firelight Productions, 2018), documentary film; Joy Ann Williamson, *Radicalizing the Ebony Tower: Black Colleges and the Black Freedom Struggle in Mississippi* (New York: Teachers College Press, 2008).

31. Jerome A. Gray et al., *History of ASTA*; Jon Hale, "'The Development of Power is the Main Business of the School': The Agency of Southern Black Teacher Associations from Jim Crow through Desegregation," *Journal of Negro Education* 87, no. 4 (Fall 2018): 444–59; Vanessa Siddle Walker, "Organized Resistance and Black Educators' Quest for School Equality, 1878–1938," *Teachers College Record* 107, no. 3 (2005): 355–88.

32. Jacquelyn D. Hall, "The Long Civil Rights Movement and the Political Uses of the Past," *Journal of American History* 91, no. 4 (March 2005): 1233–1263; Sundiata Keita Cha-Jua and Clarence Lang, "The 'Long Movement' as Vampire: Temporal and Spatial Fallacies in Recent Black Freedom Studies," *Journal of African American History* 92, no. 2 (Spring 2007): 265–88.

33. Franklin, "Cultural Capital."

34. Even Tuskegee's description in the *Encyclopedia of Alabama* is bereft of a section on "civil rights" compared with this theme's insertion in the histories of Selma, Montgomery, and Birmingham. See *Encyclopedia of Alabama*, "Tuskegee," last updated November 21, 2016, http://encyclopediaofalabama.org/.

35. R. A. Vonderlehr, Clark Taliaferro, O. C. Wenger, et al., "Untreated Syphilis in the Male Negro: A Comparative Study of Treated and Untreated Cases," *Journal of the American Medical Association* 107, no. 11 (September 12, 1936): 856–60; Centers for Disease Control and Prevention, "The Tuskegee Timeline," last reviewed April 22, 2021, https://www.cdc.gov/.

36. Global Nonviolent Action Database, "Black Citizens Boycott White Merchants for U. S. Voting Rights, Tuskegee, Alabama,

1957–1961," accessed September 1, 2021, https://nvdatabase.swarthmore.edu/.

37. Gomillion v. Lightfoot, 364 US 339 (1960).

38. William A. Elwood, "An Interview with Charles G. Gomillion," *Callaloo* (published by Johns Hopkins University Press), no. 40 (Summer 1989): 576–99, https://www.jstor.org/; Jessie Parkhurst Guzman, *Crusade for Civic Democracy: The Story of the Tuskegee Civic Association, 1941–1970* (New York: Vantage, 1984); Robert J. Norrell, *Reaping the Whirlwind: The Civil Rights Movement in Tuskegee* (Chapel Hill: University of North Carolina Press, 1998); Gabriel Smith, "A Hollow Inheritance: The Legacies of the Tuskegee Civic Association and the Crusade for Civic Democracy in Alabama" (master's thesis, Auburn University, 2016); the VA Hospital in Tuskegee was established by Black medical professionals, which sparked the ire of the white community.

39. Norrell, *Reaping the Whirlwind*, 34.

40. Norrell, 34.

41. Patrick J. Gilpin and Marybeth Gasman, *Charles S. Johnson: Leadership Beyond the Veil in the Age of Jim Crow* (Albany: State University of New York Press, 2003).

42. Norrell, *Reaping the Whirlwind*, 34–35.

43. Norrell, 35.

44. Robert Cassanello, interview with Tuskegee University archivist Dana Chandler during guest lecture at University of Central Florida, March 2018, produced by Holly Baker as a podcast titled "Episode 7: Tuskegee Archives and Digitization," STARS accessed September 3, 2021, https://stars.library.ucf.edu/.

45. Norrell, Reaping the Whirlwind, 38.

46. Elwood, "Interview with Gomillion," 584.

47. Norrell, *Reaping the Whirlwind*, 36.

48. C. G. Gomillion, "Chapter IX The Negro Voter in Alabama," *Journal of Negro Education* 26, no. 3 (Summer 1957): 281–86.

49. Gomillion, 281.

50. Elwood, "Interview with Gomillion," 597.

51. Norrell, *Reaping the Whirlwind*, 42.

52. Guzman, *Crusade*, 56.

53. Guzman, 57.

54. Guzman, 12; The Historymakers, "Interview with Tuskegee Civic Association Member Frank Toland, Sr.," March 20, 2007, accessed September 24, 2020, https://www.thehistorymakers.org.

55. Guzman, *Crusade*.

56. Guzman, 19.

57. Jack Bass and Walter DeVries, interview with Charles G. Gomillion, July 11, 1974, interview number A-0008 in the Southern Oral History Program Collection (#4007) at the Southern Historical Collection, The Louis Round Wilson Special Collections Library, University of North Carolina–Chapel Hill, 1–5, http://www.sohp.org/; Guzman, *Crusade*, 129–30.

58. Bass and DeVries, "Interview with Gomillion," 4; Norrell, *Reaping the Whirlwind*, 95; Guzman, *Crusade*, 118–23.

59. Guzman, *Crusade*, 22.

60. Charles Johnson and Jared McWilliams, audio recording of Mass Meeting of the Tuskegee Civic Association Meeting #2, July 2, 1957, featuring K. J. Buford, Fred Shuttlesworth, Ralph David Abernathy, and Martin Luther King Jr., Tuskegee University Archives, accessed August 5, 2021, http://hdl.handle.net/; Guzman, *Crusade*, 23.

61. Guzman, *Crusade*, 23; Bass and DeVries, "Interview with Gomillion," 1–10.

62. Guzman, 26.

63. Charles G. Gomillion to Martin Luther King Jr., 18 July 1957, The Martin Luther King, Jr. Research and Education Institute, Stanford University, accessed September 10, 2021, https://kinginstitute.stanford.edu/; The Martin Luther King, Jr. Research and Education Institute, Stanford University, "Gomillion, Charles Goode," Voter Registration Collection, https://kinginstitute.stanford.edu/; King acknowledged in the foreword of his book *Stride Toward Freedom: The Montgomery Story* (New York: Beacon, 2010) "thanks to Professor Gomillion and the Tuskegee Civic Association, an energetic campaign for Negro registration and voting has been conducted."

64. See Tuskegee University Archives, "004 Tuskegee Civic Association Meetings, Speeches, and Records," https://web.archive.org/.

65. Norrell, *Reaping the Whirlwind*, 104–9; David A. Varel, *The Scholar and the Struggle: Lawrence Reddick's Crusade for Black History and Black Power* (Chapel Hill: University of North Carolina Press, 2020), 21, 179.

66. Norrell, *Reaping the Whirlwind*, 105; Norrell ascertained quotes from FBI File Reports on December 21, 1942, and February 3, 1943.

67. Norrell, 105.

68. FBI Vault: Highlander Folk School, Part 19 of 19, "Highlander Friends Rap Critics of Racial Plans," unattributed newspaper clipping, 6; FBI Vault: Highlander Folk School, Part 19 of 19, "3 Atlantians on the Board of Race Integration Hub," *Atlanta Journal and Constitution*, December 15, 1957, 7.

69. Norrell, *Reaping the Whirlwind*, 43.

70. Guzman, *Crusade*, 130–31.

71. Joseph Mosnier and US Civil Rights History Project, published audio-recorded interview with Gwendolyn M. Patton, June 1, 2011, in Montgomery, Alabama, Library of Congress, Civil Rights History Project Collection AFC 2010/039: 0020, https://www.loc.gov/ (accessed September 10, 2021), 40.

72. Mosnier, Gwendolyn M. Patton interview, 24, 40.

73. Mosnier, 26.

74. Mosnier, 29; for more details on Tuskegee student activism, see Brian Jones, "The Tuskegee Revolt: Student Activism, Black Power, and the Legacy of Booker T. Washington" (PhD diss., The Graduate Center, City University of New York, 2018).

75. Mosnier, Gwendolyn M. Patton interview, 23, 40.

76. Norrell, *Reaping the Whirlwind*, 137–43.

77. The plaintiffs sought the integration of the all-white Tuskegee High School in Macon County. The original lawsuit filed in 1963 was expanded to include all of Alabama's primary, secondary, and postsecondary educational institutions. See *Lee v. Macon County Board of Education* 231 F. Supp 743 (M. D. Ala. 1964), https://law.justia.com/.

78. Alabama State University, "History and Tradition," accessed September 10, 2021, https://www.alasu.edu/.

79. Kelsey Davis, "The Quiet History of How ASU Shaped the Civil Rights Movement," *Montgomery Advertiser*, February 17, 2017, accessed April 20, 2021, https://www.montgomeryadvertiser.com/, paras. 5 and 6.

80. Mary Fair Burks, "Trailblazers: Women in the Montgomery Bus Boycott," in *Women in the Civil Rights Movement: Trailblazers and Torchbearers 1941–1965*, Vicki L. Crawford, Jacqueline Anne Rouse, and Barbara Woods, eds. (Bloomington: Indiana University Press, 1990), 71. Tara Y. White, a former Alabama archivist and faculty member currently in the History

Department at the University of North Carolina Wilmington (https://uncw.edu/hst/facstaff/white.html), has chronicled and presented on the contributions of Black women to the Alabama civil rights movement, with some emphasis on the Women's Political Council; Tara Y. White, "The Role of Women in the Civil Rights Movement," presentation to the "Stony the Road We Trod . . . ," National Endowment for the Humanities Summer Teacher Institute, Wallace State Community College, Selma, Alabama, July 16, 2018.

81. Burks, 71.

82. Burks, 72.

83. Burks, 76.

84. Burks, 79.

85. Burks, 80.

86. Burks, 81.

87. Burks, 81.

88. Claudette Colvin was arrested at age fifteen on March 2, 1955, for refusing to give up her seat to a White woman on a segregated Montgomery bus, nine months before Rosa Parks took the same stand. She later challenged Montgomery's Jim Crow bus law in court, along with three other women plaintiffs, in Browder v. Gayle, which overturned these laws. When asked why she felt she was overlooked as an icon of the movement, she surmised that Rosa Parks was deemed more respectable than she was by the Black community because of Parks's middle-class status and lighter skin tone. Colvin became pregnant out of wedlock after the arrest, which, she acknowledged, was not viewed favorably by her community during that time. See NPR, "Before Rosa Parks, There was Claudette Colvin," March 15, 2009, accessed September 10, 2021, https://www.npr.org/.

89. Stefanie Decker, "Black Women in Alabama, 1954–1974," in Southern Black Women in the Modern Civil Rights Movement, Bruce A. Glasrud and Merline Pitre, eds. (College Station: Texas A & M University Press, 2013), 88.

90. Decker, "Black Women in Alabama," 89; Jo Ann Robinson, with a foreword by David J. Garrow, ed., The Montgomery Bus Boycott and the Women Who Started It: The Memoir of Jo Ann Gibson Robinson (Knoxville: University of Tennessee Press, 1987), 69–76.

91. Fred D. Gray, Bus Ride to Justice: The Life and Works of Fred D. Gray, rev. ed.

(Montgomery: New South Books, 2013), 36–37; Robinson, Montgomery Bus Boycott, 44–45.

92. Burks, "Trailblazers," 75; F. Gray, Bus Ride, 51; Robinson, Montgomery Bus Boycott, 45–46.

93. Robinson, Montgomery Bus Boycott, 47–50.

94. Robinson, 50.

95. Robinson, 50.

96. Robinson, 52.

97. Martin Luther King Jr. to Mary Fair Burks, April 5, 1960, The Martin Luther King, Jr. Research and Education Institute, Stanford University, accessed September 10, 2021, https://kinginstitute.stanford.edu/.

98. Jerome A. Gray et al., History of ASTA, 169–70.

99. Eddie R. Cole, The Campus Color Line: College Presidents and the Struggle for Black Freedom (Princeton, NJ: Princeton University Press, 2020), 63–64, 203.

100. Varel, The Scholar and the Struggle.

101. Varel, 126.

102. King, "Letter to Mary Fair Burks," para. 2.

103. Varel, The Scholar and the Struggle, 150.

104. Burks used the term firing, and Robinson used the term resignation, to describe ASU faculty departures. Burks, "Trailblazers," 75–76; Robinson, Montgomery Bus Boycott, 169.

105. The Martin Luther King, Jr. Research and Education Institute, Stanford University, accessed September 10, 2021 "Trenholm, Harper Councill," https://kinginstitute.stanford.edu/.

106. Favors, Shelter, 104.

107. Favors, Shelter, 105.

108. Jerome A. Gray et al., History of ASTA, 90–91; Favors, Shelter, 108–9; Givens, Fugitive Pedagogy, 180.

109. Favors, Shelter, 109.

110. Robinson, Montgomery Bus Boycott, 152.

111. Eskew, But for Birmingham, 264.

112. Tara Y. White, "Black Women in the Civil Rights Movement, 1954–1963. Women of the Alabama Christian Movement for Human Rights in Birmingham, AL" (MA thesis, SUNY-Oneonta, Cooperstown Graduate Program, 2002), 103–6; Loder-Jackson, Schoolhouse Activists, 58–61; Jerome A. Gray et al., History of ASTA, 186.

113. Horace Huntley and John W. McKerley, eds., "Carlton Reese" in Foot Soldiers for Democracy: The Men, Women, and Children of

the *Birmingham Civil Rights Movement* (Champaign: University of Illinois Press and Birmingham Civil Rights Institute, 2009), 103.

114. Huntley and McKerley, "Carlton Reese" in *Foot Soldiers*, 103.

115. W. Arnett Bryant, "Walter White Expected to Speak Here," *Birmingham Post-Herald*, September 20, 1951, Birmingham Public Library Digital Collection, Newspaper Clippings, Blacks in Birmingham #017.

116. Guzman, *Crusade*, 29.

117. Andrew M. Manis, *A Fire You Can't Put Out: The Civil Rights Life of Birmingham's Reverend Fred Shuttlesworth* (Tuscaloosa: University of Alabama Press, 2001).

118. Andrew Michael Manis, Interview with Reverend Fred L. Shuttlesworth, undated, Andrew M. Manis Oral History Interviews 1981–1990, Birmingham Public Library Digital Collections, http://www.bplonline.org/, 4.

119. Manis, "Interview with Shuttlesworth, 4; Loder-Jackson, *Schoolhouse Activists*, 45–46.

120. White, "Black Women in Civil Rights," 106.

121. Manis, "Interview with Shuttlesworth," 17–18.

122. Manis, 17–18.

123. Huntley and McKerley, "Annetta Streeter Gary" in *Foot Soldiers*, 118.

124. Willoughby Anderson, Interview with Lillie Fincher, October 29, 2004, Interview #U-0038, Program #4007, transcript, Southern Oral History Program Collection, University of North Carolina at Chapel Hill, 30.

125. Anderson, Interview with Lillie Fincher, 30.

126. White, "Black Women in Civil Rights," 106.

127. White, 106.

128. Loder-Jackson, *Schoolhouse Activists*, 67–71.

129. Miles College Student Body, "Join the Fight" Selective Buying Campaign Flier, Miles College Learning Center Archives.

130. *Stand!: Untold Stories from the Civil Rights Movement*, written and directed by Donna Dukes (2013; Birmingham, AL: Donna Dukes Production), documentary film; Jonathan McPherson with Nathan Hale Turner Jr., *A Drum Major for God and a Perfume Sprinkler to Man: The Life and Theology of Unsung Civil Rights Hero Rev. Dr. Jonathan McPherson, Sr.*

(Jonesboro, AR: Granthouse Publishers, 2013), 36.

131. Dukes, *Stand!*

132. Toni-Lee Capossela, *John U. Munro: Uncommon Educator* (Baton Rouge: Louisiana State University Press, 2012), 84; Miles College Centennial History Committee, *Miles College: The First One Hundred Years* (Charleston, SC: Arcadia, 2005), 70.

133. Barbara Thomas and Carol Nunnelley, "The Real L. H. Pitts: Uncle Tom or Radical?" *Dixieland* (May 2, 1971): 20. Available at Miles College Learning Center, Birmingham, AL. Originally archived at University of Alabama at Birmingham Archives, Series 3.3.1, Folder 6.20. Also available in *Birmingham News*, May 2, 1971.

134. Manis, "Interview with Shuttlesworth," 18–20.

135. Thomas and Nunnelley, "Real L. H. Pitts," 24.

136. Callie Crossley, Interview with Rev. Frederick Reese, December 5, 1985, gathered as part of *Eyes on the Prize: America's Civil Rights Years (1954–1965)*, produced by Blackside, Inc. Housed at the Washington University Film and Media Archive, Henry Hampton Collection, 6–9; George Littleton, "Teacher, Civil Rights Icon Frederick D. Reese Dies," April 10, 2018, Auburn University College of Education, last modified January 18, 2019; Andrew Michael Manis, Interview with Frederick D. Reese, August 1, 1989, Andrew M. Manis Oral History Interviews, Birmingham Public Library Digital Collections, http://www.bplonline.org/, 9–11; Frederick D. Reese and Kathy M. Walters, *Selma's Self-Sacrifice* (Sparta, GA: Reese Enterprise, 2019), 1–24; J. Mills Thornton III, *Dividing Lines: Municipal Politics and the Struggle for Civil Rights in Montgomery, Birmingham, and Selma* (Tuscaloosa: University of Alabama Press, 2002), 482–83.

137. There are various estimates of how many teachers actually participated. Reese, in his interview with Crossley, stated that over three hundred marched, whereas Thornton's *Dividing Lines* noted one hundred twenty-five teachers. A National Park Service bill titled "Teachers March through Selma, January 22, 1965," noted "a core group of 105 African-American teachers."

138. Crossley, "Interview with Frederick Reese," 7.

139. Crossley, 4.

140. Manis, "Interview with Frederick D. Reese," 15–16.

141. Manis, 15.

142. Reese and Walters, *Selma's Self-Sacrifice*, 21.

143. Sheriff Clark's command is quoted in Littleton, "Teacher, Civil Rights Icon"; Crossley, "Interview with Rev. Frederick D. Reese," 9.

144. Reese and Walters, *Selma's Self-Sacrifice*, 1–24, 117, 165–68.

145. Jerome A. Gray et al., *History of ASTA*, 196–97.

146. Littleton, "Teacher, Civil Rights Icon."

147. Manis, Interview with Frederick D. Reese, 11–15.

148. Reese and Walters, *Selma's Self-Sacrifice*, 87–89.

149. Reese and Walters, 107–11.

150. See iconic civil rights photographs of Reverend Frederick D. Reese taken by James "Spider" Martin, former staff writer of *The Birmingham News*, at spidermartin.com.

151. Reese and Walters, *Selma's Self-Sacrifice*, 93.

152. Jerome A. Gray et al., *History of ASTA*, 202–4, 206–11; Reese and Walters, *Selma's Self-Sacrifice*, 86–89.

153. Alabama A&M University, accessed September 15, 2021, https://www.aamu.edu/about/our-history/ and https://www.alasu.edu/about-asu/history-tradition; The HistoryMakers, interview with James Roberson, Tape 3, titled "James Roberson Recalls Organizing Sit-ins in Huntsville, Alabama," https://www.thehistorymakers.org/.

154. Vanessa Siddle Walker, *The Lost Education of Horace Tate: Uncovering the Hidden Heroes Who Fought for Justice in Schools* (New York: New Press, 2018); Sonya Yvette Ramsey, *Reading, Writing, and Segregation: A Century of Black Women Teachers in Nashville, Tennessee* (Champaign: University of Illinois Press, 2008).

155. Loder-Jackson, *Schoolhouse Activists* and "AATC Keynote"; John A. Kirk, "The NAACP Campaign for Teachers' Salary Equalization: African American Women Educators and the Early Civil Rights Struggle," *Journal of African American History* 94, no. 4 (Fall 2009), 529–552; Lee Sartain, *Invisible Activists: Women of the Louisiana NAACP and the Struggle for Civil Rights, 1915–1945* (Baton Rouge: Louisiana State University Press, 2007); Carol F. Karpinski, *"A Visible Company of Professionals": African Americans and the National Education Association during the Civil Rights Movement* (New York: Peter Lang, 2008).

GARRY AND ISAAC-SAVAGE: FROM JIM CROW TO THE CIVIL RIGHTS MOVEMENT

1. Gary R. Kremer and Antonio F. Holland, *Missouri's Black Heritage, Revised Edition* (Columbia: University of Missouri Press, 1993), 164.

2. United States Commission on Civil Rights, *Equal Protection of the Laws in Public Higher Education, 1960*, 85 Cong., August 25, 1961, 15. https://www.crmvet.org/.

3. James W. Endersby and William T. Horner, *Lloyd Gaines and the Fight to End Segregation* (Columbia: University of Missouri Press, 2016), 60–65; Larry Grothaus, "'The Inevitable Mr. Gaines': The Long Struggle to Desegregate the University of Missouri 1936–1950," *Arizona and the West* 26, no. 1 (Spring, 1984): 21–42; Gary R. Kremer, *Race & Meaning: The African American Experience in Missouri* (Columbia: University of Missouri Press, 2014), 164.

4. Colin Gordon, *Mapping Decline: St. Louis and the Fate of the American City* (Philadelphia: University of Pennsylvania Press, 2008), 69–82.

5. Muhammad Ahmad, "On the Black Student Movement—1960–1970," *The Black Scholar* 9, nos. 8/9 (1978): 2–11; Martha Biondi, *The Black Revolution on Campus* (Berkeley: University of California Press, 2014), 13–42; Joy A. Williamson, *Black Power on Campus: The University of Illinois, 1965–75* (Champaign: University of Illinois Press, 2013), 35–53; Mary Ann Wynkoop, *Dissent in the Heartland; The Sixties at Indian University* (Bloomington: Indiana University Press, 2002), 115–34.

6. Biondi, *The Black Revolution*, 13–42.

7. Stefan M. Bradley, *Upending the Ivory Tower: Civil Rights, Black Power, and the Ivy League* (New York: New York University Press, 2021), 167–96.

8. The BFSO Constitution, 1978, C1/29/1, Box 5, MU Black Faculty and Staff Organization, (University Archives, University of Missouri, Columbia, Missouri; hereinafter cited as University Archives).

9. Louise Cook, "No Sure Formula for Success, Student Demonstrations Prove," *Warren Times-Mirror and Observer*, June 12, 1969, 2.

10. Vanessa Garry, "'Ruth Harris: A Reticent Disrupter in St. Louis Public Schools' Stowe Teachers College during Jim Crow Era," *Journal of Urban History* 47, no. 6 (2021): 1348–62, https://doi.org/10.1177/0096144220917471.

11. Aldon Morris, "Birmingham Confrontation Reconsidered: An Analysis of the Dynamics and Tactics of Mobilization." *American Sociological Review* 58 (1993): 621–36.

12. Ibram X. Kendi, *The Black Campus Movement: Black Students and the Racial Reconstitution of Higher Education, 1965–1972* (New York: Palgrave Macmillan, 2012), 20–32. According to Kendi, the student movement activities in the 1960s were the culmination of the efforts of those who came before them in the 1930s, 1940s, and 1950s. Joshua M. Myers, *We Are Worth Fighting for: A History of the Howard University Student Protest of 1989* (New York: New York University Press, 2022), 15–22.

13. Jelani M. Favors, *Shelter in a Time of Storm: How Black Colleges Fostered Generations Leadership and Activism* (Chapel Hill: University of North Carolina Press, 2019), 70–100.

14. Muhammad Ahmad, "On the Black Student Movement—1960–1970, *The Black Scholar*, 9, nos. 8/9 (1978): 2–11; Joy A. Williamson, *Black Power on Campus: The University of Illinois, 1965–75* (Champaign: University of Illinois Press, 2013), 35–53.

15. "University Computer Center Sit-in," accessed September 27, 2021, https://pittarchives.tumblr.com/.

16. "History of AAFSA," accessed March 20, 2021, http://www.fullerton.edu/.

17. "Meeting the Challenge of Diversity 1968–1976: The Intensive Educational Development Program and Change at the University of Maryland," https://www.ugst.umd.edu/.

18. "History," accessed March 21, 2021, https://www.usf.edu/.

19. The BFSO Constitution, 1978, Box 5, University Archives.

20. BFSO Constitution, 1978, University Archives.

21. Black Faculty Meeting Notes, April 29, 1979, CA4995, Box 1, Folder 1 (Black Faculty and Students University of Missouri) Arvarh E. Strickland Papers (State Historical Society of Missouri, Columbia, Missouri; hereinafter cited as Strickland Papers).

22. Prentice Gautt's Letter to Strickland, March 1, 1979, Folder 1, Strickland Papers.

23. *Columbia Tribune* article, "Little Here to Lure Black Employees, Authorities Say," February 25, 1974, Folder 1, Strickland Papers.

24. William Wilson Elwang, "The Negroes of Columbia Missouri: A Concrete Study of the Race Problem," Master's thesis, University of Missouri, 1904, 1–69.

25. *Columbia Tribune* article, "Little Here to Lure Black Employees," February 25, 1974, Folder 1, Strickland Papers.

26. Letter to Arvarh Strickland from Dean Willard L. Eckhardt, April 1, 1972, Folder 1, Strickland Papers.

27. Letter to Dean Willard L. Eckhardt, April 21, 1972, Folder 1, Strickland Papers.

28. *Columbia Tribune* article, "Minority Hiring Problem in Columbia Feeds on Itself," February 24, 1974, Folder 1, Strickland Papers.

29. *Columbia Tribune* article, "Blacks Fight Definition of 'Qualified,'" February 24, 1974, Folder 1, Strickland Papers.

30. "The Saga of the Sharp End: CoMo's Lost Black Business District, Part 1," *Columbia Heartbeat*, http://www.columbiaheartbeat.com/.

31. "Urban Renewal Dismantled the Sharp End, a Black Business District in the 20th Century," accessed February 25, 2021, https://krcgtv.com/.

32. A History of Columbia's Black Churches, November 1, 1977, Folder 1 (UMOJO/UMOJA), University Archives.

33. Traci L. Hodges, Michael L. Rowland, and E. Paulette Isaac-Savage, "Black Males in Black Churches," *New Directions for Adult and Continuing Education* 150 (June 2016): 47–57.

34. A History of Columbia's Black Churches, November 1, 1977, Folder 1 (UMOJO/UMOJA), University Archives, 10.

35. A History of Columbia's Black Churches, November 1, 1977, Folder 1 (UMOJO/UMOJA), University Archives, 9.

36. *Columbia Missourian* article, "M.U. Policy on Blacks Criticized: First Black Professor Says Hiring Shows Little Progress," December 11, 1979, Folder 1, Strickland Papers.

37. *Columbia Missourian* article, "M.U. Policy on Blacks Criticized: First Black Professor Says Hiring Shows Little Progress," December 11, 1979, Folder 1, Strickland Papers.

38. *Columbia Missourian* article, "M.U.

Enrollment of Minorities Declines," July 14, 1977, Folder 1, Strickland Papers.

39. *Columbia Missourian* article, "M.U. Enrollment of Minorities Declines," July 14, 1977, Folder 1, Strickland Papers.

40. Joe L. Saupe and James R. Montgomery and Association for Institutional Research, "*The Nature and Role of Institutional Research . . . Memo to a College or University [microform] / Joe L. Saupe and James R. Montgomery* Distributed by ERIC Clearinghouse, Washington, DC, 1970, https://eric.ed.gov.

41. *Columbia Missourian* article, "M.U. Enrollment of Minorities Declines," July 14, 1977, Folder 1, Strickland Papers.

42. *Columbia Missourian* article, "M.U. Policy on Blacks Criticized: First Black Professor Says Hiring Shows Little Progress," December 11, 1979, Folder 1, Strickland Papers.

43. *Columbia Missourian* article, "M.U. Policy on Blacks Criticized: First Black Professor Says Hiring Shows Little Progress," December 11, 1979, Folder 1, Strickland Papers.

44. Associated Press, "Morris' Carbondale Office Damaged," *Edwardsville Intelligencer*, May 9, 1968, 1.

45. Cook, "No Sure Formula," 2.

46. Associated Press, "Black Students Occupy Office at University," *Daily Capital News*, April 29, 1969, 5.

47. Robert E. Weems Jr., "The Incorporation of Black Faculty at Predominantly White Institutions: A Historical and Contemporary Perspective," *Journal of Black Studies* 34, no. 1 (September 2003): 101–11, https://doi.org/10.1177/0021934703253663.

48. Delia Crutchfield Cook, "Shadow Across the Columns: The Bittersweet Legacy of African Americans at the University of Missouri," PhD diss., University of Missouri–Columbia, 1996, 99–100.

49. The Black Letter Newspapers, April–May 1974, Folder 1, Strickland Papers.

50. William J. Waugh, "Black Studies Making Their Way into Elementary, Secondary Schools," *The Park City Daily News*, August 9, 1970, 30.

51. Favors, *Shelter*, 237–52.

52. MU Black Faculty and Staff, Folder 5, University Archives, University of Missouri.

53. Patricia L. Roberts, *A Lynching in Little Dixie: The Life and Death of James T. Scott, ca.*

1885–1923 (Jefferson, NC: McFarland & Company, 2018).

54. MU Black Faculty and Staff, October 11, 1979, Folder 5 University Archives.

55. Erik Potter, "Brooks Scholarship Turns 30," accessed September 23, 2021, https://showme.missouri.edu/.

56. Randall D. Kennedy, "A Historical Study of the Development of the Total Person Program: The Evolution of Academic Support Services for Student-Athletes at the University of Missouri," PhD diss., University of Missouri–Columbia, 2007.

57. The Black Letter, Vol. II, Number 1, September/October 1973, Folder 1, University Archives.

58. The Black Letter, Vol. II, Number 1, September/October 1973, Folder 1, University Archives.

59. "Militants Take Over Meeting," *The Black Letter* 2, no. 7 (April–May, 1974) p. 2. Charles Nilon, interview with Vanessa Garry and E. Paulette Isaac-Savage, Virtual, September 27, 2021.

60. "Militants Take Over Meeting," p. 2.

61. [Charles Nilon, interview . . .]

62. The Black Letter, Volume I, Number 6, June/July 1973, Folder 1, University Archives.

63. The Black Letter, Volume I, Number 6, June/July 1973, Folder 1, University Archives.

64. Robert E. Weems Jr., interview with Vanessa Garry and E. Paulette Isaac-Savage, Virtual, September 3, 2021.

GANAWAY: W. E. B. DU BOIS AND THE UNIVERSITY OF BERLIN

1. W. E. B. Du Bois, *The Souls of Black Folk* (New York: Dover Thrift, 1994), 1.

2. It is pointless to list all of the recent scholarship on Du Bois, but what follows is a sample. David Levering Lewis, *W. E. B. Du Bois: Biography of a Race, 1868–1919* (New York: Henry Holt, 1993); Edward J. Blum, *W. E. B. Du Bois: American Prophet* (Philadelphia: University of Pennsylvania Press, 2007); Gerald Horne, *W. E. B. Du Bois: A Biography* (Oxford: Greenwood Press, 2010); Raymond Wolters, *Du Bois and His Rivals* (Columbia: University of Missouri Press, 2002); Daniel Agbeyebiawo, *The Life and Works of W. E. B. Du Bois* (Accra, Ghana: Stephil Print, 1998); Thomas Aiello, *The Battle for the Souls of Black Folk: W. E. B. Du Bois, Booker T. Washington, and the Debate*

that *Shaped the Course of Civil Rights* (Santa Barbara, CA: Praeger, 2016); Derrick Alridge, *The Educational Thought of W. E. B. Du Bois: An Intellectual History* (New York: Teachers College Press, 2008); Gary Dorrien, *The New Abolition: W. E. B. Du Bois and the Black Social Gospel* (New Haven, CT: Yale University Press, 2015); Booker T. Hae-Sung Hwang, *Washington and W. E. B. Du Bois: A Study in Race Leadership* (Seoul, Korea: Seoul National University, 1992); Manning Marable, *W. E. B. Du Bois: Black Radical Democrat* (Boulder, CO, Paradigm Publishers, 2005); Jacqueline Moore, *Booker T. Washington, W. E. B. Du Bois, and the Struggle for Racial Uplift* (Wilmington, DE: Scholarly Resources, 2003); Aldon Morris, *The Scholar Denied: W. E. B. Du Bois and the Birth of Modern Sociology* (Oakland: University of California Press, 2015). There are a number of very helpful bibliographies, including the following: Joan Nordquist, *W. E. B. Du Bois: A Bibliography* (Santa Cruz, CA: Reference and Research Services, 2002); Dan Green, "Bibliography of Writings about W. E. B. Du Bois," *College Language Association Journal* 20, no. 3 (March 1977): 410–21. Major articles from the past five years include the following: Derrick Alridge, "On the Education of Black Folk: W. E. B. Du Bois and the Paradox of Segregation," *Journal of African American History* 100, no. 3 (Summer 2015): 473–93; Patrick Anderson, "Pan-Africanism and Economic Nationalism: W. E. B. Du Bois's *Black Reconstruction* and the Failings of the 'Black Marxism' Thesis," *Journal of Black Studies* 48, no. 8 (November 2017): 732–57; Valethia Watkins, "Votes for Women, Race, Gender, and W. E. B. Du Bois's Advocacy of Woman Suffrage," *Phylon* 53, no. 2 (Winter 2016): 3–19; Andrew Zimmerman, "A German Alabama in Africa: The Tuskegee Expedition to German Togo and the Transnational Origins of West African Cotton Growers," *American Historical Review* 110, no. 5 (December 2005): 1362–98.

3. See, for example, Heinrich von Treitschke, *Ein Wort über unser Jüdenthum* (Berlin: G. Reimer, 1881). It reads, in part: "A cleft has always existed between Occidental and Semitic essences [. . .]; there will always be Jews who are nothing more than German-speaking Orientals. A specific Jewish civilization will also always flourish, as befits a historically cosmopolitan power. But the conflict will lessen when the Jews, who speak so much of tolerance, really become tolerant and show respect for the faith, customs, and feelings of the German people, who have atoned for the old injustice and bestowed upon them the rights of man and citizen. That this respect is wholly missing in a section of our commercial and literary Jewry is the ultimate basis for the passionate embitterment of today."

4. David Thelen, "The Nation and Beyond: Transnational Perspectives on the United States History," *Journal of American History*, 86, no. 3 (December 1999): 967–72, 974.

5. Thomas Bender, *A Nation among Nations: America's Place in World History* (New York: Hill and Wang, 2006), 3, 5.

6. Bender was committed to this project. He organized a series of conferences on global history from 1997 to 1999 that brought together a diverse group of leading scholars. Their presentations eventually resulted in a book, *Rethinking American History in a Global Age*, Thomas Bender, ed. (Berkeley: University of California Press, 2002). In particular, see the introduction by Bender and the article by Prasenjit Duara.

7. Shelley Fisher Fishkin, "Crossroads of Cultures: The Transnational Turn in American Studies–The Presidential Address to the American Studies Association, November 12, 2004," *American Quarterly* 57, no. 1 (March 2005): 18. See also footnote 10 on page 45.

8. Fishkin, "Crossroads of Cultures: The Transnational Turn in American Studies," *American Quarterly*, 57, no. 1 (March 2005): 19, 21–35.

9. W. E. B. Du Bois, *The Autobiography of W. E. B. Du Bois: A Soliloquy on Viewing My Life from the Last Decade of Its First Century* (New York: International Publishers, 102–6); W. E. B. Du Bois, *Dusk of Dawn: An Essay Toward an Autobiography of a Race Concept* (New York: Library of America, 1986), 577, 622–25; Lewis, *W. E. B. Du Bois: Biography of a Race*, 77.

10. Du Bois, *Autobiography*, p. 126.

11. Du Bois, *Autobiography*, 124, 133; Du Bois, *Dusk of Dawn*, 626; Bruce Kuklick, *The Rise of American Philosophy* (New Haven, CT: Yale University Press, 2009); H. S. Thayer, *Meaning and Action: A Critical History of Pragmatism* (Indianapolis: Bobbs-Merrill, 1968).

12. For examples. see John Connelly, "Catholic Racism and Its Opponents," *Journal of*

Modern History 79, no. 4 (2007): 813–47; Stephen Collins and Katherine Scott Sturdevant, "The History and Rhetoric of the NAACP: The Origins," *Black History Bulletin* 71, no. 2 (2008): 12–21; Andrew Sartori, "The British Empire and Its Liberal Mission." *Journal of Modern History* 78, no. 3 (2006): 623–42; Mary Dewhurst Lewis, "Geographies of Power: The Tunisian Civic Order, Jurisdictional Politics, and Imperial Rivalry in the Mediterranean, 1881–1935," *Journal of Modern History* 80, no. 4 (2008): 791–830; Aldon Morris, *The Scholar Denied: W. E. B. Du Bois and the Birth of Modern Sociology* (Oakland: University of California Press, 2015); Tukufu Zuberi and Eduardo Bonilla-Silva (eds.), *White Logic, White Methods: Racism and Methodology* (Lanham, MD: Rowman and Littlefield, 2008).

13. Asa Gray, *Darwiniana: Essays and Reviews Pertaining to Darwinism* (New York: D. Appleton, 1876), 10; Richard Hofstadter, *Social Darwinism in American Thought, 1860–1915* (Boston: Beacon Press, 1955); Robert C. Bannister, *Social Darwinism: Science and the Myth in Anglo-American Social Thought* (Philadelphia: Temple University Press, 1979); Audrey Smedley, *Race in North America: Origin and Evolution of a Worldview* (Boulder: Westview Press, 1993); Reginal Horsman, *Race and Manifest Destiny: The Origins of American Racial Anglo-Saxonism* (Cambridge, MA: Harvard University Press, 1986); George M. Fredrickson, *The Black Image in the White Mind: The Debate on Afro-American Character and Destiny, 1817–1914,* (Middleton, CT: Wesleyan University Press, 1987), 230–57; Francis Galton, *Inquiries into the Human Faculty and Its Development* (New York: E. P. Dutton, 1907); Daniel Kevles, *In the Name of Eugenics: Genetics and the Uses of Human Heredity* (New York: Knopf, 1985); Dorothy Ross, *The Origins of American Social Science,* (Cambridge, England: Cambridge University Press, 1991); William James, *Manuscript Lectures* (Cambridge, MA: Harvard University Press, 1988), 180–85.

14. Quoted in Barrington Steven Edwards, "W. E. B. Du Bois: Empirical Social Research and the Challenge to Race, 1868–1910" (PhD diss., Harvard University, 2001), 1.

15. Edwards, *W. E. B. Du Bois*, 59–62.

16. See David S. Landes, *The Unbound Prometheus: Technological Change and Industrial Development in Western Europe from 1750 to the Present* (New York: Cambridge University Press, 1969); Eric Hobsbawm, *Industry and Empire: The Birth of the Industrial Revolution* (New York: The New Press, 1968); Hans-Ulrich Wehler, *The German Empire, 1871–1918,* trans. Kim Traynor (New York: Berg Publishers, 1985); Jürgen Kocka, *Industrial Culture and Bourgeois Society: Business, Labor and Bureaucracy in Modern Germany* (New York: Berghahn, 1999); Eric Dorn Brose, *Technology and Science in the Industrializing Nations, 1500–1914* (Atlantic Highlands, NJ: Humanities Press, 1998); Abigail Greene, *State-Building and Nationhood in 19th Century Germany* (New York: Cambridge University Press, 2001); Konrad Jaurausch, *Students, Society and Politics in Imperial Germany: The Rise of Academic Illiberalism* (Princeton, NJ: Princeton University Press, 1982); Fritz Ringer, *The Decline of the German Mandarins: The German Academic Community, 1890–1933* (Lebanon, NH: University Press of New England, 1990).

17. See *Teach the Freeman: The Correspondence of Rutherford B. Hayes and the Slater Fund for Negro Education: 1888–1893,* Louis D. Rubin, Jr, ed. (Baton Rouge: Louisiana State University Press, 1959); W. E. B. Du Bois, "Darkwater," *Voices from the Within the Veil* (New York: Harcourt, Brace and Howe, 1921), 15; Du Bois, *Autobiography,* 150; Du Bois, W. E. B. (William Edward Burghardt), 1868–1963, Letter from W. E. B. Du Bois to Rutherford B. Hayes, November 4, 1890, W. E. B. Du Bois Papers (MS 312). Special Collections and University Archives, University of Massachusetts Amherst Libraries. For such a young man (he was twenty-two years old), Du Bois was not intimidated by Hayes, who did not believe that he was qualified to go to Berlin, writing "that you have been looking for men to liberally educate in the past may be but it certainly strange so few have heard of it." See Herbert Aptheker, *The Correspondence of W. E. B. Du Bois, Vol. 1, Selections, 1877–1934* (Amherst: University of Massachusetts, 1973), 13–14.

18. Friedrich Paulsen, *The German Universities and University Study,* trans. Frank Thilly (New York: Charles Scribner's Sons, 1906); Adolph Wagner, *Die Entwicklung der Universität Berlin, 1810–1896,* (Berlin: Julius Becker, 1896); J. Conrad, *The German Universities for the*

Last Fifty Years (Glasgow: David Bryce, 1885); Max Lenz, Geschichte der königlichen Friedrich-Wihlems-Universität zu Berlin (Halle, Germany: Verlag der Buchhandlung des Waisnehauses, 1910); Jurgen Herbst, The German Historical School in American Scholarship: A Study in the Transfer of Culture (New York: Cornell University Press, 1965); Charles Franklin Thwing, The American and German University: One Hundred Years of History (New York: MacMillan Company, 1928); Iggers, The German Conception of History.

19. See Anthony Oberschall, Empirical Social Research in Germany, 1848–1914 (Berlin: Walter de Gruyter, 1965); Woodruff Smith, Politics and the Sciences of Culture in Germany, 1840–1920 (Oxford, England: Oxford University Press, 1991); Ringer, Decline of the German Mandarins.

20. Quoted in Edwards, Du Bois, Empirical Social Research and the Challenge to Race, 1868–1910, 106–7.

21. See Emanuel Sax, Die Hausindustrie in Thüringen: I. Theil, Das Meininger Oberland (Jena, Germany: Gustav Fischer, 1882), 25; Paul Ehrenberg, "Hausindustrie und Heimarbeit in Deutschland und Österreich: Die Spielwarenhausindustrie des Kreises Sonneberg," Schriften des Vereins für Socialpolitik, LXXXVI, Band III (Leipzig: Verlag von Dunker & Humblot, 1899): 224, 237; Wilhelm Stiede, "Lieteratur, heutige Zustände und Entstehung der deutschen Hausindustrie," Schriften des Vereins für Socialpolitik, XXXIX, Band III (Leipzig, Germany: Verlag von Dunker & Humblot, 1889): 58, 64; Wilhelm Uhlfelder, "Hausindustrie und Heimarbeit in Deutschland und Österreich: Die Zinnmalerinnen in Nürnberg und Fürth," Schriften des Vereins für Socialpolitik, LXXXVI, Band III (Leipzig, Germany: Verlag von Dunker & Humblot, 1899): 165; Gertrud Meyer, Die Spielwarenindustrie im sächsischen Erzgebirge (Leipzig, Germany: A. Deichert'sche Verlagsbuchhandlung Nachf., 1911): 40, 57; Otto Senst, Die Metallspielwarenindustrie und der Spielwarenhandel von Nürnberg und Fürth, unpublished dissertation, Erlangen, Germany, 1901, 7–8; Reible, Die deutschen Spielwarenindustrie, 19–20; Ernst Rausch, Die Sonneberger Spielwaren-Industrie und die verwandten Industrien der Griffel- und Glasfabrikation unter besonderer Berücksichtigung der Verhältnisse in der Hausindustrie (Sonneberg, Germany: Druck und Verlag Gräbe & Hetzer, 1900), 19; Prof. Dr. Anschütz, Industrie, Handel und Verkehr im Herzogtum Sachsen-Meiningen, (Sonneberg, Germany: Gräbe & Hetzer, 1904), 47.

22. Du Bois, W. E. B. (William Edward Burghardt), 1868–1963. Lecture notebook, ca. 1896, W. E. B. Du Bois Papers (MS 312), Special Collections and University Archives, University of Massachusetts Amherst Libraries. The sections on Schmoller are on pp. 28–37.

23. For an idea about what a Treitschke lecture involved, see Andreas Dorpalen, Heinrich von Treitschke (New Haven, CT: Yale University Press), 227–29.

24. See Adolf Hausrath, Treitschke: His Life and Works (London: Jarrold & Sons, 1914); Adam L. Gowans, Selections from Treitschke's Lectures on Politics (New York: Frederick A. Stokes, 1914), 11, 21, 23, 34, 60, 103, 116; Heinrich von Treitschke, Auffsätze, Reden, und Briefe, Vols. I–IV, Karl Martin Schiller, ed. (Meersburg Germany: F. W. Hendel Verlag, 1929), (Vol. I) 672, (Vol. II), 768, (Vol. III), 24, 26, (Vol. VI), 483, 787.

25. Quoted in Heinrich von Treitschke, Politics, Vol. I, trans. Blance Dugdale and Torben de Bille (New York: Macmillan, 1916), 299–302.

26. Du Bois, Autobiography, 164. This can be translated as "mulattoes are inferior; they feel themselves to be substandard [in the face of racially pure nations]." Du Bois was almost certainly the only person of color in the lecture hall. He would have been twenty-four or twenty-five at the time.

27. See Alexander, Du Bois: An American Intellectual and Activist, 15–17; Wolters, Du Bois and His Rivals, 18–22; Francis L. Broderick, Du Bois: Negro Leader in a Time of Crisis (Stanford, CA: Stanford University Press, 1959), 26–30; Horne, W. E. B. Du Bois: A Biography, 12–15; Blum, W. E. B. Du Bois: American Prophet, 20–24.

28. Du Bois, Autobiography, p. 168.

29. See Sean Wilentz, "Hearts and Souls: The Strange Education of W. E. B. Du Bois," New Republic, April 4, 1994, 28–35; Kenneth Barkin, "W. E. B. Du Bois and the Kaiserreich," Central European History 31, no. 3 (September 1998): 155–70; Axel R. Schafer, "W. E. B. Du Bois, German Social Thought, and the Racial Divide in American Progressivism," Journal of

American History 88, no. 3 (December 2001): 925–49; Charles H. Wesley, "W. E. B. Du Bois–The Historian," *Journal of Negro History* 30, no. 3 (July 1965): 147–62; Richard Cullen Rath, "Echo and Narcissus: The Afrocentric Pragmatism of W. E. B. Du Bois," *Journal of American History* 84, no. 2 (September 1997): 461–95; L. D. Reddick, "A New Interpretation for Negro History," *Journal of Negro History*, 22, no. 1 (January 1937): 17–28; Ira Katznelson, "Du Bois's Century," *Social Science History* 23, no. 4 (Winter 1999): 459–74.

30. W. E. B. Du Bois, "The Present Condition of German Politics (1893)," republished in *Central European History* 31, no. 3 (1998), 172–73.

31. Ibid., 176. The full quote reads: "[They were] a typical Coney Island throng—perhaps a bit less independent and self-assertive, and a bit poorer, but with all the same good-natured, curious, happy, dirty and enthusiastic crowd of everyday working people. I asked a neatly dressed and harmless looking little maiden with whom I danced, 'Are you too a socialist?' 'O Yes!' she replied, 'And why?' She looked a bit puzzled and then answered half-timidly. 'Because my father is.' I danced with her again."

32. Barkin, "W. E. B. Du Bois and the Kaiserreich," *Central European History* 31, no. 3 (September 1998): 167.

33. Ingersoll, William T., oral history interview of W. E. B. Du Bois by William Ingersoll, ca. June 1960, W. E. B. Du Bois Papers (MS 312), Special Collections and University Archives, University of Massachusetts Amherst Libraries, 119. "At the time I could see what the Germans were thinking and feeling, and I could have a vicarious sympathy. I know how Negroes would feel, if, after a war, they had gained equality and indeed superiority in the world . . . I excused [German chauvinism] . . . it can't go on forever, but, after all, these people had been downtrodden."

34. Du Bois, *Autobiography*, 156–57.

35. Quoted in Lewis, *W. E. B. Du Bois: Biography of a Race*, 145.

36. W. E. B. Du Bois, *The Philadelphia Negro: A Social Study* (New York: Schocken Books, 1899): 1–9, 97–146, 385–99.

37. See Sheats, W. N. (William Nicholas), 1851–1922, Letter from W. N. Sheats to W. E. B. Du Bois, April 29, 1902, W. E. B. Du Bois Papers (MS 312), Special Collections and University Archives, University of Massachusetts Amherst Libraries; North Carolina Department of Public Instruction, Letter from State of North Carolina to W. E. B. Du Bois, April 30, 1902, W. E. B. Du Bois Papers (MS 312), Special Collections and University Archives, University of Massachusetts Amherst Libraries; South Carolina Department of Education, Letter from South Carolina Department of Education to W. E. B. Du Bois, April 28, 1902, W. E. B. Du Bois Papers (MS 312), Special Collections and University Archives, University of Massachusetts Amherst Libraries; West Virginia Department of Free Schools, Letter from the West Virginia Department of Free Schools to W. E. B. Du Bois, April 30, 1902, W. E. B. Du Bois Papers (MS 312), Special Collections and University Archives, University of Massachusetts Amherst Libraries.

38. Derrick P. Alridge, *The Educational Thought of W. E. B. Du Bois: An Intellectual History* (New York: Columbia University, 2008); *Du Bois on Education*, Eugene F. Provenzo Jr, ed. (New York: Altamira Press, 2002).

39. W. E. B. Du Bois, *The Souls of Black Folk* (New York: Dover Thrift, 1903), 40.

40. W. E. B. Du Bois, "Editorial," *The Crisis* 1, no. 1 (November 1910): 10.

ALRIDGE, HALE, AND
LODER-JACKSON: AFTERWORD

1. Katie Shepherd, "Texas Parents Accused a Black Principal of Promoting Critical Race Theory. The District Has Now Suspended Him," *Washington Post*, September 1, 2021; https://www.washingtonpost.com/, accessed September 27, 2021.

2. Charles M. Blow, "The War on 'Wokeness,'" *New York Times*, November 10, 2021, https://www.nytimes.com/.

3. Danya Hajjaji, "Anti-Critical Race Theory Activists Are Drowning Out Black Parents Fighting Racism," *Newsweek*, August 10, 2021, https://www.newsweek.com/; Tyler Kingkade and Mike Hixenbaugh, "Parents Protesting 'Critical Race Theory' Identify Another Target: Mental Health Programs," *NBC News*, November 15, 2021, https://www.nbcnews.com/.

4. Tyler Kingkade, Brandy Zadrozny, and Ben Collins, "Critical Race Theory Battle Invades School Boards - with Help from Conservative Groups," *NBC News*, June 15, 2021, https://www.nbcnews.com/

5. Sarah Schwartz, "Map: Where Critical Race Theory Is Under Attack [interactive map]" (Updated February 4, 2022), *Education Week*, accessed March 23, 2022, https://www.edweek.org/.

6. Zack Beauchamp, "Did Critical Race Theory Really Swing the Virginia Election?" *Vox*, November 4, 2021, https://www.vox.com/.

7. Alexander Bolton, "Cruz Presses Jackson on Critical Race Theory in Tense Questioning," *The Hill*, March 22, 2022, https://thehill.com/.

8. Hannah Natanson, "Schools Nationwide Are Quietly Removing Books From Their Libraries," *Washington Post*, March 22, 2022, https://www.washingtonpost.com/.

9. Valerie Strauss, "Teachers Across the Country Protest Laws Restricting Lessons on Racism," *Washington Post*, June 12, 2021, https://www.washingtonpost.com/; Annie Gowen, "'Blue' Suburban Moms Are Mobilizing to Counter Conservatives in Fights Over Masks, Book Bans, and Diversity Education," *Washington Post*, February 9, 2022, https://www.washingtonpost.com/; Nick Anderson and Susan Svrluga, "College Faculty Fight Back Against Critical Race Theory Bills," *Washington Post*, February 19, 2022, https://www.washingtonpost.com/education/2022/02/19/colleges-critical-race-theory-bills/; Tyler Kingkade, "As Parents Protest Critical Race Theory, Students Fight Racist Behavior in Schools," *NBC News*, December 16, 2021, accessed March 23, 2022, https://www.nbcnews.com/; Leslie Gray Streeter, "'A Dog Whistle and a Lie': Black Parents on the Critical Race Theory Debate," *Washington Post*, December 7, 2021, https://www.washingtonpost.com/.

10. Associated Press, "Black Mississippi Senators Walk Out in Protest Over Critical Race Theory Ban," *NPR*, January 22, 2022, https://www.npr.org/.

11. Emma Pettit, "'Cynical and Illegitimate': Higher-Ed Groups Assail Legislative Efforts to Restrict Teaching of Racism," *Chronicle of Higher Education*, June 16, 2021, https://www.chronicle.com/.

12. National Education Association, "We Need to Teach the Truth about Systemic Racism, Say Educators," https://www.nea.org/, accessed March 23, 2022; American Federation of Teachers, "American Federation of Teachers Passes Resolution Expanding Its Efforts to Combat Racism, Aligning Itself with the Movement for Black Lives," https://www.aft.org/.

13. James Anderson, "'A Tale of Two *Browns*': Constitutional Equality and Unequal Education," *Yearbook of the National Society for the Study of Education* 105, no. 2 (2006): 30–32; see also Michael Fultz, "The Displacement of Black Educators Post-*Brown*: An Overview and Analysis," *History of Education Quarterly* 44, no. 1 (2006): 11–45.

14. National Center for Education Statistics, US Department of Education, "Black or African American Teachers: Background and School Settings in 2017–18," (February 2022), https://nces.ed.gov/; National Center for Education Statistics, US Department of Education, "Racial/Ethnic Enrollment in Public Schools," May 2021, https://nces.ed.gov/ .

15. James Banks (ed.), *Multicultural Education, Transformative Knowledge and Action: Historical and Contemporary Perspectives* (New York: Teachers College Press, 1996); James Banks and Cherry Banks (eds.), *Handbook of Research on Multicultural Education* (New York: Macmillan, 1995).

16. Gloria Ladson-Billings, *Culturally Relevant Pedagogy: Asking a Different Question* (New York: Teachers College Press, 2021); Geneva Gay, *Culturally Responsive Teaching: Theory, Research, and Practice*, 2nd ed. (New York: Teachers College Press, 2010); Django Paris and H. Samy Alim (eds.), *Culturally Sustaining Pedagogies: Teaching and Learning for Justice in a Changing World* (New York: Teachers College Press, 2017).

17. Django Paris and H. Samy Alim (eds.), *Culturally Sustaining Pedagogies*; Gloria Ladson-Billings, "But That's Just Good Teaching! The Case for Culturally Relevant Teaching," *Theory into Practice* 34, no. 3 (1995): 159–65; Nikole Hannah-Jones and the *New York Times Magazine* (eds.), *The 1619 Project* (New York: One World, 2021).

18. Mark Lieberman, "Racist Bomb Threats and Post-Civil War School Burnings: A Scholar Connects the Dots," *Education Week*, March 9, 2022, https://www.edweek.org/; Campbell F. Scribner, "Surveying the Destruction of African American Schoolhouses in the South, 1864–1876," *Journal of the Civil War Era* 10, no. 4, (December 2020): 469–94.

19. Joe Heim and Lori Rozsa, "African

Americans Say the Teaching of Black History is Under Threat," *Washington Post*, February 23, 2022, https://www.washingtonpost.com/.

20. Kelli Goff, "Heather Heyer Is Our Viola Liuzzo–A Hero Who Will Help Save Lives," *Daily Beast*, August 15, 2017, https://www.the dailybeast.com/.

21. Dana R. Fisher, "The Diversity of the Recent Black Lives Matter Protest is a Good Sign for Racial Equity," Brookings, July 8, 2020, https://www.brookings.edu/; Kim Parker, Juliana Menasce Horowitz, and Monica Anderson, "Amid Protests, Majorities Across Racial and Ethnic Groups Express Support for the Black Lives Matter Movement," Pew Research Center, June 12, 2020, accessed March 27, 2022, https://www.pewresearch.org/.

SELECTED BIBLIOGRAPHY

ARCHIVES
Amherst, Massachusetts
University of Massachusetts–Amherst

Du Bois, W. E. B. The W. E. B. Du Bois Papers. Library, Robert S. Cox Special Collections and University Archives Research Center.

Augusta, Georgia
Paine College

Lucius Pitts Archives, Library.

Birmingham, Alabama
Birmingham Civil Rights Institute

Oral History Project.

Birmingham Public Library

Digital Collections.

Miles College

Learning Center Archives.

Chapel Hill, North Carolina
University of North Carolina

Southern Oral History Project.

Charleston, South Carolina
College of Charleston

Lois Simms, Papers, 1920–2003, Avery Research Center for African American History and Culture.

Charlottesville, Virginia
University of Virginia

Teachers in the Movement Oral History Collection, School of Education and Human Development.

Columbia, Missouri
State Historical Society of Missouri

Strickland, Arvarh E. April 29, 1979. Black Faculty Meeting Notes, CA4995, Box 1, Folder 1 (Black Faculty and Students University of Missouri) Arvarh E. Strickland Collection.

Durham, North Carolina
Duke University

John Hope Franklin Library's Behind the Veil Project. *SNCC Digital Gateway*, SNCC Legacy Project and Duke University.

New Orleans, Louisiana
Tulane University

Charles Hatfield Collection, Amistad Research Center.

Norfolk, Virginia
Norfolk State University

The Civil Rights History Project: Survey of Collections and Repositories, Norfolk State University, Harrison B. Wilson Archives and Art.

Old Dominion University

School Desegregation in Norfolk, Virginia, Old Dominion University Libraries Digital Collections.

Tuskegee, Alabama
Tuskegee University

Digital Collections, Library, Archives.

Washington, DC
Library of Congress

Civil Rights History Project Collection.

PUBLISHED PRIMARY SOURCES (INCLUDES MEMOIRS,
CIVIC AND EDUCATIONAL ORGANIZATION HISTORIES,
CLASSIC COMMENTARIES, AND GOVERNMENTAL REPORTS)

Bowman, Glen. *Elizabeth City State University, 1891–2016: The Continuity of a Historical Legacy of Excellence and Resilience.* Virginia Beach, VA: Donning, 2015.

Bryant, Florence C. *Memoirs of a Country Girl.* New York: Vantage Press, 1988.

Burks, Mary Fair. "Trailblazers: Women in the Montgomery Bus Boycott." In *Women in the Civil Rights Movement: Trailblazers and Torchbearers 1941–1965,* edited by Vicki L. Crawford, Jacqueline Anne Rouse, and Barbara Woods, 71–83. Bloomington: Indiana University Press, 1993 (first paperback edition).

Clark, Septima Poinsette, and Cynthia Stokes Brown, eds. *Ready from Within: Septima Clark and the Civil Rights Movement.* Navarro, CA: Wild Trees Press, 1986.

Crow, Jeffrey J., Paul D. Escott, and Flora J. Hatley, *A History of African Americans in North Carolina.* Raleigh: North Carolina Department of Cultural Resources, 2002.

DeVore, Donald, and Joseph Logsdon. *Crescent City Schools: Public Education in New Orleans, 1841–1991.* Lafayette: Center for Louisiana Studies, 1991.

Du Bois, W. E. B. *The Souls of Black Folk.* New York: Dover Thrift, 1994.

———. *The Philadelphia Negro: A Social Study.* New York: Schocken Books, 1899.

Gray, Jerome, Joe L. Reed, and Norman W. Walton. *History of the Alabama State Teachers Association (ASTA).* Washington, DC: National Education Association, 1987.

Guzman, Jessie Parkhurst. *Crusade for Civic Democracy: The Story of the Tuskegee Civic Association, 1941–1970.* New York: Vantage, 1984.

Huntley, Horace, and John W. McKerley, eds. *Foot Soldiers for Democracy: The Men, Women, and Children of the Birmingham Civil Rights Movement.* Champaign: University of Illinois Press and Birmingham Civil Rights Institute, 2009.

Jefferson County Memorial Project and Equal Justice Initiative, "Elizabeth Lawrence," *Lynching in America: A Community Remembrance Project.* Montgomery, AL: Equal Justice Initiative, 2019.

Jones, Thomas J. *A Study of the Private and Higher Institutions for Colored People in the United States.* Washington, DC: Government Printing Office, 1916.

Murray, Percy. *History of the North Carolina Teachers Association.* Washington, DC: National Education Association, 1984.

Perry, Thelma D. *History of the American Teachers Association.* Washington, DC: National Education Association, 1975.

Picott, J. Rupert. *History of the Virginia Teachers Association.* Washington, DC: National Education Association, 1975.

Potts, John F., Sr. *A History of the Palmetto Education Association.* Washington, DC: National Education Association, 1978.

Reese, Frederick D., and Kathy M. Walters. *Selma's Self-Sacrifice.* USA: Reese Enterprises, 2018.

Robinson, Jo Ann (edited with a foreword by David J. Garrow), *The Montgomery Bus Boycott and the Women Who Started It: The Memoir of Jo Ann Gibson Robinson.* Knoxville: University of Tennessee Press, 1987.

Simms, Lois Averetta. *A Chalk and Chalkboard Career in Carolina.* New York: Vantage Press, 1995.

Thompson, Cleopatra D. *The History of the Mississippi Teachers Association.* Washington, DC: National Education Association, 1973.

Woodson, Carter G. *Epigraphs–The Mis-Education of the Negro.* Washington, DC: Associated Publishers, 1933.

SECONDARY BOOKS AND ACADEMIC ARTICLES

Alridge, Derrick P. *The Educational Thought of W. E. B. Du Bois: An Intellectual History.* New York: Columbia University Press, 2008.

———. "HES Presidential Address Teachers in the Movement: Pedagogy, Activism, and Freedom." *History of Education Quarterly* 60, no. 1 (February 2020): 1–23.

Anderson, James A. *The Education of Blacks in the South, 1860–1935.* Chapel Hill: University of North Carolina, 1988.

Baker, R. Scott. *Paradoxes of Desegregation: African American Struggles for Educational Equity in Charleston, South Carolina, 1926–1972.* Columbia: University of South Carolina Press, 2007.

Barksdale, Marcellus. "The Indigenous Civil Rights Movement and Cultural Change in North Carolina: Weldon, Chapel Hill, and Monroe: 1946–1965." PhD diss., Duke University, 1977.

Bradley, Stefan M. *Upending the Ivory Tower: Civil Rights, Black Power, and the Ivy League* New York: New York University Press, 2021.

Brown, Karida L. *Gone Home: Race and Roots through Appalachia.* Chapel Hill: University of North Carolina Press, 2018.

Butchart, Ronald E. "Courage in the Classroom: When Teachers Faced Violence and Worse for their Activism and Advocacy on Behalf of Black Freedom." *The Georgia Social Studies Journal* 3, no. 1 (Winter 2013): 7–15.

Carson, Clayborne. *In Struggle: SNCC and the Black Awakening of the 1960s.* Cambridge, MA: Harvard University Press, 1981.

Cecelski, David S. *Along Freedom Road: Hyde County, North Carolina and the Fate of Black Schools in the South.* Chapel Hill: University of North Carolina Press, 1994.

Cecelski, David S., and Timothy B. Tyson, eds. *Democracy Betrayed: The Wilmington Race Riot of 1898 and Its Legacy.* Chapel Hill: University of North Carolina Press, 1998.

Chafe, William. *Civilities and Civil Rights: Greensboro, North Carolina, and the Black Struggle for Freedom.* New York: Oxford University Press, 1980.

Cha-Jua, Sundiata Keita, and Clarence Lang. "The 'Long Movement' as Vampire: Temporal and Spatial Fallacies in Recent Black Freedom Studies." *Journal of African American History* 92, no. 2 (Spring 2007): 265–88.

Charron, Katherine. *Freedom's Teacher: The Life of Septima Clark.* Chapel Hill: University of North Carolina Press, 2009.

Cole, Eddie R. *The Campus Color Line: College Presidents and the Struggle for Black Freedom.* Princeton, NJ: Princeton University Press, 2020.

Collins, Patricia Hill. *Black Feminist Thought: Knowledge, Consciousness, and the Politics of Empowerment*, 2nd ed. New York: Routledge, 2000.

Dagbovie, Pero. *The Early Black History Movement, Carter G. Woodson, and Lorenzo Johnston Greene*. Champaign: University of Illinois Press, 2007.

Daniels, Maurice C. *Horace T. Ward: Desegregation of the University of Georgia: Civil Rights Advocacy, and Jurisprudence*. Atlanta: Clark Atlanta University Press, 2001.

Danns, Dionne, Purdy, Michelle A., and Span, Christopher M., eds. *Using Past as Prologue: Contemporary Perspectives on African American Educational History*. Charlotte, NC: Information Age Publishing, 2015.

Dent, Tom. *Southern Journey: A Return to the Civil Rights Movement*. New York: William Morrow, 1997.

Dorrien, Gary, *The New Abolition: W. E. B. Du Bois and the Black Social Gospel*. New Haven, CT: Yale University Press, 2015.

Du Bois, W. E. B., ed. *The Negro Common School*. Atlanta: Atlanta University Press, 1901.

Edmonds, Helen G. *The Negro and Fusion Politics in North Carolina, 1894–1901*. Chapel Hill: University of North Carolina Press, 1951.

Fairclough, Adam. *Teaching Equality: Black Schools in the Age of Jim Crow*. Athens: University of Georgia Press, 2001.

———. *A Class of their Own: Black Teachers in the Segregated South*. Cambridge, MA: Harvard University Press, 2007.

Favors, Jelani M. *Shelter in a Time of Storm: How Black Colleges Fostered Generations of Leadership and Activism*. Chapel Hill: University of North Carolina Press, 2019.

Foster, Michele. *Black Teachers on Teaching*. New York: New Press, 1997.

Franklin, V. P. "Cultural Capital and African American Education." *Journal of African American History* 87, no. 2 (Spring 2002): 175–81.

Fultz, Michael. "The Displacement of Black Educators Post-*Brown*: An Overview and Analysis." *History of Education Quarterly* 44, no. 1 (March 2004): 11–45.

Garcia, David. *Strategies of Segregation: Race, Residence, and the Struggle for Educational Equality*. Berkeley: University of California Press, 2018.

Givens, Jarvis R. *Fugitive Pedagogy: Carter G. Woodson and the Art of Black Teaching*. Cambridge, MA: Harvard University Press, 2021.

Gordon, Colin. *Mapping Decline: St. Louis and the Fate of the American City*. Philadelphia: University of Pennsylvania Press, 2008.

Grothaus, Larry. "The Inevitable Mr. Gaines": The Long Struggle to Desegregate the University of Missouri 1936–1950." *Arizona and the West* 26, no. 1 (Spring 1984): 21–42.

Hale, Jon D. "'The Development of Power is the Main Business of the School': The Agency of Southern Black Teacher Associations from Jim Crow through Desegregation." *Journal of Negro Education* 87, no. 4 (Fall 2018): 444–59.

Hall, Jacquelyn Dowd. "The Long Civil Rights Movement and the Political Uses of the Past." *Journal of American History* 91, no. 4 (March 2005): 1233–63.

Hobson, Maurice J. *The Legend of the Black Mecca: Politics in the Making of Modern Atlanta*. Chapel Hill: University of North Carolina Press, 2017.

Hogan, Wesley. *Many Minds, One Heart: SNCC's Dream for a New America*. Chapel Hill: University of North Carolina Press, 2007.

hooks, bell. *Teaching to Transgress: Education as the Practice of Freedom*. New York: Routledge, 1994.

Johnson, Karen A., Abul Pitre, and Kenneth L. Johnson, eds. *African American Women Educators: A Critical Examination of Their Pedagogies, Educational Ideas, and Activism from the Nineteenth to the Mid-Twentieth Century*. Lanham, MD: Rowman and Littlefield Education, 2014.

Karpinski, Carol. *"A Visible Company of Professionals": African Americans and the National Education Association During the Civil Rights Movement*. New York: Peter Lang, 2008.

Kelley, Robin D. G., *Freedom Dreams: The Black Radical Imagination*. Boston: Beacon, 2002.

Kelly, Hilton. *Race, Remembering, and Jim Crow's Teachers*. New York: Routledge, 2010.

Kendi, Ibram X. *The Black Campus Movement: Black Students and the Racial Reconstitution of Higher Education, 1965–1972*. New York: Palgrave Macmillan, 2012.

King, Martin Luther, Jr. "The Role of the Behavioral Scientist in the Civil Rights Movement." *American Psychologist* 23, no. 3 (March 1968): 180–86. https://doi.org/10.1037/h0025715.

Kirk, John A. "The NAACP Campaign for Teachers' Salary Equalization: African American Women Educators and the Early Civil Rights Struggle," *Journal of African American History* 94, no. 4 (Fall 2009): 529–52.

Kousser, J. Morgan. "Progressivism—for middle-class whites only: North Carolina Education, 1880–1910. *Journal of Southern History* 46 (1980): 169–94.

Kremer, Gary R., and Antonio F. Holland. *Missouri's Black Heritage, Revised Edition*. Columbia: University of Missouri Press, 1993.

Ladson-Billings, Gloria. *Culturally Relevant Pedagogy: Asking a Different Question*. New York: Teachers College Press, 2021.

Leloudis, James. *Schooling the New South: Pedagogy, Self, and Society in North Carolina, 1880–1920*. Chapel Hill: University of North Carolina Press, 1996.

Lewis, Earl. *In Their Own Interests: Race, Class, and Power in Twentieth-Century Norfolk, Virginia*. Berkeley: University of California Press, 1991.

Loder-Jackson, Tondra L. *Schoolhouse Activists: African American Educators and the Long Birmingham Civil Rights Movement*. Albany: State University of New York Press, 2015.

Ludwa, Sandi. *Ashes to Incense: Emancipation from Jim Crow: The Story of the Rock Hill South Carolina Oratorians*. Bloomington, IN: Xlibris, 2017.

McCluskey, Audrey Thomas. *Forgotten Sisterhood: Pioneering Black Women Educators and Activists in the Jim Crow South*. Lanham, MD: Rowman and Littlefield, 2014.

Morris, Jerome E., and Carla R. Monroe. "Why Study the U.S. South? The Nexus of Race and Place in Investigating Black Student Achievement." *Educational Researcher* 38, no. 1 (January 2009): 21–36.

Moye, J. Todd. *Ella Baker: Community Organizer of the Civil Rights Movement*. Lanham, MD: Rowman and Littlefield Publishers, 2013.

Myers, Joshua M. *We Are Worth Fighting For: A History of the Howard University Student Protest of 1989*. New York: New York University Press, 2022.

Newbold, Nathan C., ed. *Five North Carolina Negro Educators*. Chapel Hill: University of North Carolina Press, 1939.

Perillo, Jonna. *Uncivil Rights: Teachers, Unions, and Race in the Battle of School Equity*. Chicago: University of Chicago Press, 2012.

Pierson, Sharon G. *Laboratory of Learning: HBCU Laboratory Schools and the Alabama State College Lab High in the Era of Jim Crow*. New York: Peter Lang, 2014.

Prather, H. Leon. *Resurgent Politics and Educational Progressivism in the New South, NC 1890–1913*. Rutherford, NJ: Fairleigh Dickinson University Press, 1979.

Pratt, Robert. *We Shall Not Be Moved: The Desegregation of the University of Georgia*. Athens: University of Georgia Press, 2005.

Preston-Grimes, Patrice. "Fulfilling the Promise: African American Educators Teach for Democracy in Jim Crow's South." *Teacher Education Quarterly* 37, no. 1 (Winter 2010): 35–52.

Rabinowitz, Howard N. "Half a Loaf: The Shift from White to Black Teachers in the Negro Schools of the Urban South, 1865–1890." *Journal of Southern History* 40, no. 4 (November 1974): 565–94.

Ramsey, Sonya Yvette. *Reading, Writing, and Segregation: A Century of Black Women Teachers in Nashville, Tennessee*. Champaign: University of Illinois Press, 2008.

Randolph, Adah Ward. "'It is Better to Light a Candle than to Curse the Darkness': Ethel Thompson Overby and Democratic Schooling in Richmond, Virginia, 1910–1958." *Educational Studies* 48, no. 3 (May 2012): 220–43.

Ransby, Barbara. *Ella Baker and the Black Freedom Movement: A Radical Democratic Vision*. Chapel Hill: University of North Carolina Press, 2003.

Sartain, Lee. *Invisible Activists: Women of the Louisiana NAACP and the Struggle for Civil Rights, 1915–1945*. Baton Rouge: Louisiana State University Press.

Savage, Carter J. "'Because We Did More With Less': The Agency of African-American Teachers in Franklin, Tennessee: 1890–1967." *Peabody Journal of Education* 76, no. 2 (2001): 170–203.

———. "Cultural Capital and African American Agency: The Economic Struggle for Effective Education for African Americans in Franklin, Tennessee, 1890–1967." *The Journal of African American History* 87, no. 2 (2002): 206–35.

Scribner, Campbell F. "Surveying the Destruction of African American Schoolhouses in the South, 1864–1876." *Journal of the Civil War Era* 10, no. 4, (December 2020): 469–94.

Shircliffe, Barbara J. *Desegregating Teachers: Contesting the Meaning of Equality of Educational Opportunity in the South post Brown*. New York: Peter Lang, 2012.

Stewart, Alison. *First Class: The Legacy of Dunbar, America's First Black Public High School*. Chicago: Lawrence Hill Books, 2013.

Urban, Wayne. *Why Teachers Organized*. Detroit, MI: Wayne State University Press, 1982.

Vansina, Jan. *Oral Tradition as History*. Madison: University of Wisconsin Press, 1985.

Varel, David A. *The Scholar and the Struggle: Lawrence Reddick's Crusade for Black History and Black Power*. Chapel Hill: University of North Carolina Press, 2020.

Walker, Vanessa Siddle. *Their Highest Potential: An African American School Community in the Segregated South*. Chapel Hill: University of North Carolina Press, 1996.

———. "Organized Resistance and Black Educators' Quest for School Equality, 1878–1938." *Teachers College Record* 107, no. 3 (March 2005): 355–88.

———. *Hello Professor: A Black Principal and Professional Leadership in the Segregated South*. Chapel Hill: University of North Carolina Press, 2009.

———. "Ninth Annual *Brown* Lecture in Education Research: Black Educators as Educational Advocates in the Decades Before *Brown v. Board of Education*." *Educational Researcher* 42, no. 4 (May 2013): 207–22.

———. *The Lost Education of Horace Tate: Uncovering the Hidden Heroes Who Fought for Justice in Schools*. New York: New Press, 2018.

Zimmerman, Andrew. "A German Alabama in Africa: The Tuskegee Expedition to German Togo and the Origins of West African Cotton Growers." *American Historical Review* 110, no. 5 (December 2005): 1362–98.

Zinn, Howard. *SNCC: The New Abolitionists*. Cambridge, MA: South End, 1964.

DISSERTATIONS AND THESES

Cook, Delia Crutchfield. "Shadow Across the Columns: The Bittersweet Legacy of African Americans at the University of Missouri." PhD diss., University of Missouri-Columbia, 1996.

Jones, Brian. "The Tuskegee Revolt: Student Activism, Black Power, and the Legacy of Booker T. Washington." PhD diss., The Graduate Center, City University of New York, 2018.

Westin, Richard B. "The State and Segregated Schools: Negro Public Education in North Carolina, 1863–1923." PhD diss., Duke University, 1966.

White, Tara Y. "Black Women in the Civil Rights Movement, 1954–1963. Women of the Alabama Christian Movement for Human Rights in Birmingham, AL." Master's thesis. SUNY-Oneonta, Cooperstown Graduate Program, 2002. Available at the Birmingham (AL) Public Library Department of Manuscripts and Archives.

CONTRIBUTORS

DERRICK P. ALRIDGE, a former middle school and high school social studies and history teacher, is the Philip J. Gibson Professor of Education and an affiliate faculty member in the Carter G. Woodson Institute for African-American and African Studies at the University of Virginia (UVA). An educational and intellectual historian, Alridge's work examines American education, with foci in Black education and the civil rights movement. He is author of *The Educational Thought of W. E. B. Du Bois: An Intellectual History* (2008), and coeditor, with James B. Stewart and V. P. Franklin, of *Message in the Music: Hip-Hop, History, and Pedagogy* (2011). Alridge is also coeditor, with Cornelius Bynum and James B. Stewart, of *The Black Intellectual Tradition in the United States in the Twentieth Century* (University of Illinois Press, 2021). He has published numerous articles in journals such as *History of Education Quarterly, Journal of African American History, Teachers College Record, Educational Researcher*, and *Journal of Negro Education*. Alridge serves as principal investigator of the Teachers in the Movement oral history project and director of the Center for Race and Public Education in the South at UVA. Alridge is a 2021 recipient of the Carter Godwin Woodson Scholars Medallion from the Association for the Study of African American Life and History.

GLEN BOWMAN is professor of history at Elizabeth City State University, an HBCU that is also a constituent institution of the University of North Carolina. In honor of the university's long-time archivist, in 2005 Bowman established the Leonard Ballou Memorial Fund, which helps fund student scholarships. He wrote *Elizabeth City State University, 1891–2016: The Continuity of a Historical Legacy of Excellence and Resilience* (Donning, 2016) as a part of the university's 125th anniversary celebration. In 2022, he received the Robert D.W. Connor award from the Historical Society of North Carolina in recognition of research published in the North Carolina Historical Review.

KRISTEN L. BURAS is associate professor of educational policy studies at Georgia State University. She is the author of *Charter Schools, Race, and Urban Space: Where the Market Meets Grassroots Resistance* (Routledge, 2014). Additionally, Buras is coauthor of *Pedagogy, Policy, and the Privatized City: Stories of Dispossession and Defiance from New Orleans* (Teachers College Press, 2010). She has spent almost two decades studying Black education in New Orleans. Buras is the director of the Urban South Grassroots Research Collective for Public Education and was granted the Distinguished Scholar-Activist Award by Critical Educators for Social Justice of the American Educational Research Association. Her research has been published in *Harvard Educational Review, Peabody Journal of Education, Race Ethnicity and Education*, and other publications. Likewise, Buras has spoken by invitation at universities such as Columbia, Dillard, Fordham, Loyola, Harvard, and Tulane and as part of community-based forums in New Orleans, Nashville, Milwaukee, and other cities. Her forthcoming book, *The World Was Ours: Black Teachers and the Culture They Created*, chronicles the legacy of an historic Black high school in New Orleans.

BRYAN GANAWAY received a PhD in modern European history from the University of Illinois in 2003. He received Fulbright and DAAD research grants to support publication of *Toys, Consumption, and Middle Class Childhood in Imperial Germany, 1871–1918* (Peter Lang, 2010). He was managing editor of H-German from 2011 to 2013 and is a member of the steering committee for the Southeastern German Studies Workshop. Ganaway currently serves as the associate dean of the Honors College, College of Charleston, where he directs the International Scholars Program.

VANESSA GARRY received her PhD in Educational Leadership and Policy Studies from the University of Missouri–St. Louis (UMSL) where she is currently serving as an associate professor in the Department of Educator Preparation & Leadership in the College of Education. Garry is an active member of the Black Faculty/Staff Association at UMSL. Garry trains aspiring principals and superintendents. Using a historical lens, her research involves the examination of urban education in the St. Louis region with an emphasis on African American leaders' influence on the development of the education of children of color during the Jim Crow era. In addition, Garry examines and presents research on teachers' data-use training and their implementation of the practice in schools as a vehicle to improve students' learning.

JARVIS R. GIVENS is associate professor of education and African & African American studies at Harvard University. He specializes in the history of education, African American history, and theories of race and power in education. Givens's first book, *Fugitive Pedagogy: Carter G. Woodson and the Art of Black Teaching* (Harvard University Press, 2021), won the 2022 Book Prize from the Association for the Study of African American Life and History, the 2022 Outstanding Book Award from the American Educational Research Association, the 2022 Lois P. Rudnick Book Prize from the New England American Studies Association, the 2022 Frederic W. Ness Book Award from the American Association of Colleges & Universities, and it was recognized as a finalist for the Museum of African American History's 2022 Stone Book Award. He has published his second book, *School Clothes: A Collective Memoir of Black Student Witness* (Beacon Press, 2023), and is currently building The Black Teacher Archive, an online portal that will house digitized records documenting the more than one-hundred-year history of "Colored Teachers Associations." Givens is originally from Compton, California, and currently resides in Roxbury, Massachusetts.

JON N. HALE is associate professor of education at the University of Illinois at Urbana–Champaign. His research focuses on the history of student and teacher activism, civil rights–based education programs, and the intersection of race and educational policy. Hale has published *The Freedom Schools: A History of Student Activists on the Frontlines of the Mississippi Civil Rights Movement* (Columbia University Press, 2016), which was awarded the 2017 New Scholars Book Award (American Educational Research Association) and the 2018 Critics Choice Book Award (American Educational Studies Association); and *The Choice We Face: How Segregation, Race, and Power Have Shaped America's Most Controversial Education Reform Movement* (Beacon Press, 2021). His book, *A New Kind of Youth* (University of North Carolina Press, 2022) examines the history of southern Black high school activism. Hale's research has been published in history and education journals, including *Journal of African American History, History of Education Quarterly, Journal of Southern History*, and *Journal of Negro Education*. His work has also been featured in outlets such as *Atlantic, C-SPAN, American Scholar, Chicago Tribune, CNN*, and *Washington Post*.

HUNTER HOLT is a doctoral candidate in the Social Foundations of Education program at the University of Virginia's (UVA's) School of Education and Human Development. He studies the history of education, educational policy, and metropolitan development. He is a graduate research assistant with UVA's Center for Race and Public Education in the South and the Teachers in the Movement oral history project. Before starting his doctoral program, he worked as the program coordinator for the Mississippi Teacher Corps and taught high school science.

ALEXANDER HYRES is assistant professor of History of US Education in the Education, Culture, and Society Department at the University of Utah. He is a 2022 NAEd/Spencer Foundation Postdoctoral Fellow and a Research Affiliate of the Teachers in the Movement Oral History Project at the University of Virginia. He earned a BA in history and an MIT in secondary social studies education at the University of Washington. Hyres taught English and social studies to middle and high school students in the San Francisco Bay Area before earning a PhD in the Social Foundations of Education at the University of Virginia. His research focuses on the history of Black education, teacher and student activism, curriculum and pedagogy, and the American high school. Hyres's writing has appeared in *Black Perspectives, Journal of African American History, History of Education Journal,*

Teachers College Record, and *Washington Post*. Currently, he is finishing a book, *Protest and Pedagogy: Black Resistance and the American High School, 1890–1990*, in which he examines how and in what ways high school teachers and students propelled and sustained the Black freedom struggle in Charlottesville, Virginia.

E. PAULETTE ISAAC-SAVAGE received her EdD in adult education from the University of Georgia. She is a professor of adult education at the University of Missouri–St. Louis, and her research interests include adult religious education with a focus on the Black church and Black adult learners. Isaac-Savage serves on the editorial review board for *Education and Urban Society*, *Adult Learning*, and *Adult Education Quarterly*. She is president-elect of the American Association for Adult and Continuing Education and a member of the International Adult and Continuing Education Hall of Fame.

ALEXIS M. JOHNSON is a PhD candidate in the Social Foundations of Education program at the University of Virginia School of Education and Human Development. Specializing in the history of education, she serves as an associate director of the Teachers in the Movement oral history project; a coprincipal investigator with the National Park Service's Carter G. Woodson Home National Historic Site Ethnographic Resource Study; and an intern with the School of Education's Office of Diversity, Equity, and Inclusion. Her research interests include the histories of Black education and higher education, student activism, and the relationship between social movements and education reform. Johnson worked as a writing center coordinator and an academic advising director in two minority-serving institutions of higher education before beginning her doctoral studies.

TONDRA L. LODER-JACKSON holds a primary appointment as professor of educational foundations in the School of Education and secondary appointments as professor of African American studies and professor of history in the College of Arts and Sciences at the University of Alabama at Birmingham (UAB). She is also a senior faculty associate with the UAB Institute for Human Rights. Her scholarship bridges historical and contemporary perspectives on Black education in the US South, with an emphasis on educators' contributions to civil and human rights movements in Alabama. Loder-Jackson is author of *Schoolhouse Activists: African American Educators and the Long Birmingham Civil Rights Movement* (State University of New York Press, 2015). Her historiography scholarship and commentary have also been published in *History of Education Quarterly*, *Journal of Negro Education*, *Urban Education*, *Journal of the American Educational Studies Association*, *Peabody Journal of Education*, *Journal of Southern History*, and *Journal of African American History*. In addition, her 2019 American Association of Teaching and Curriculum (AATC) Marcella Kysilka Keynote Address appears in AATC's journal, *Curriculum and Dialogue*. Loder-Jackson also conducts teacher training on civil rights and Black educational history through collaborations with the National Endowment for the Humanities (in partnership with the Alabama Humanities Alliance and the Birmingham Civil Rights Institute), The University of Virginia's Teachers in the Movement oral history project, The Coalition for True History, and The Morgan Project in Birmingham, Alabama. She recently established and funded the Schoolhouse Activist Endowed Award in Education at UAB.

KRISTAN L. MCCULLUM is a doctoral candidate in the Social Foundations of Education program at the University of Virginia's (UVA's) School of Education and Human Development and a Provost's dissertation fellow in the College of Liberal Arts, Education and Human Development at the University of New Orleans. Her research is at the nexus of twentieth-century cultural and social history with a focus on race, education, community, and memory in Appalachia and the US South. McCullum is assistant program director of the Eastside Project, an oral history project that documents the long history of a historically Black school in the Mississippi Delta, and she serves as a graduate research assistant with UVA's Center for Race and Public Education in the South and the Teachers in the Movement oral history project. Her work has been published in *History of Education Quarterly* and *Black Perspectives*.

CRYSTAL R. SANDERS is an award-winning historian of the United States in the twentieth century. Her research and teaching interests include African American history, Black women's history, and the history of Black education. She received her BA (cum laude) in history and public policy from Duke University and a PhD in history from Northwestern University. She is an acting associate professor of African American studies at Emory University and the former director of the Africana Research Center at Pennsylvania State University. Sanders is author of *A Chance for Change: Head Start and Mississippi's Black Freedom Struggle* (University of North Carolina Press, 2016), part of the John Hope Franklin Series in African American History and Culture. The book won the 2017 Critics Choice Award from the American Educational Research Association and the 2017 New Scholar's Book Award from Division F of the American Educational Research Association. The book was also a finalist for the 2016 Hooks National Book Award. Sanders is recipient of a host of fellowships and prizes, including the C. Vann Woodward Prize (Southern Historical Association), the Huggins-Quarles Award (Organization of American Historians), an Andrew Mellon Graduate Fellowship in Humanistic Studies, a Ford Foundation Dissertation Fellowship, a National Academy of Education/Spencer Foundation Dissertation Fellowship, a National Academy of Education/Spencer Foundation Postdoctoral Fellowship, and a Visiting Scholars Fellowship at the American Academy of Arts and Sciences.

DANIELLE WINGFIELD is assistant professor of law at the University of Richmond School of Law. Prior to joining Richmond Law, she served as a fellow and visiting assistant professor at Gonzaga University School of Law's Center for Civil and Human Rights. Wingfield serves as a faculty affiliate of the University of Virginia's Center for Race and Public Education in the South in the school of education. She is associate director of national oral history projects, Teachers in the Movement, and the Carter G. Woodson Home National Historic Site Study. Her primary areas of teaching and scholarship include legal history of education, constitutional law, family law, race and the law, family law, and education law and policy. Wingfield earned her PhD in education from the University of Virginia, her JD from the University of Richmond, and her BA in sociology and philosophy from the College of William & Mary. Her latest article, "Movement Lawyers: Henry Marsh's Long Struggle for Educational Justice," examines the strategies and approaches of lawyers in their struggle to overcome discriminatory laws, systems, and policies related to education.

INDEX

1619 Project, 1, 221

Alabama State College, 170, 175, 177
Alabama State University, 170, 185, 256n13
Alridge, Derrick P., ix, 1–11, 39–56, 216, 219–22, 277; and University of Virginia Teachers in the Movement Project, 41–42
American Missionary Association, 61, 95, 236n37, 237n52
American Teachers Association, 35, 182. *See also* National Association of Teachers in Colored Schools
Anderson, James A., 3, 40, 121; and *Education of Blacks in the South,* 121
Antiblackness (anti-blackness, anti-Blackness), 2, 22–23; and curricula, 8, 15–17, 19, 31; curricular violence, 17–18, 21, 25; fugitive pedagogy, 38; physical violence, 30; predominantly Black schools, 2, 93
Association for the Study of Negro Life and History, 29–30, 32–35, 63, 66; and Hilda Grayson, 35; Dwight O. W. Holmes, 35
Atlanta University, 47. *See also* Clark Atlanta University
Attucks, Crispus, 24, 28, 95
Aycock, Charles, B., 117, 119

Baker, Ella J., 3, 46, 76, 103, 182
Baker, R. Scott, 3, 40; and pedagogies of protest, 3; educational strategies of John Dewey, 41
Bender, Thomas H., 206–7, 217–18, 265n6
Bethune, Mary M., 43, 58, 69–70, 141; and Association for the Study of Negro Life and History, 33–34; civil rights-based activism, 4; Mary McLeod Bethune Future Teachers of America Club, 69; National Association of Teachers in Colored Schools, 34; race as a central focus of discourse, 62; as public intellectual, 164
Bismarck, Otto von, 208, 211–13
Black faculty and staff associations, or organizations, 10–11, 187, 191
Black freedom struggle, 1, 8–10, 40; and

Florence C. Bryant, 148, 165; Willa C. Johnson, 91; North Carolina, 93, 243n11; Lois A. Simms, 57–75, 93, 97–98, 105; valued segregated space, 78; Virginia, 149, 165
Black intellectualism, 18–20, 22, 24, 28, 32, 223–24n5; and *The Black Intellectual Tradition in the United States in the Twentieth Century* (Alridge, Bynum, Stewart), 277; William E. B. (W. E. B.) Du Bois as exemplar, 206, 218; Tuskegee Institute, 176
Black Lives Matter, 2, 175
Black Reconstruction: Toward a History of the Part Which Black Folk Played in the Attempt to Reconstruct Democracy in America, 1860–1880 (Du Bois), 32, 33
Bowman, Glen, 111–25, 277; on Negro national anthem, 248n74; Henry L. (H. Leon) Prather Sr., 246n25; school consolidation in North Carolina, 117–23, 125, 246n34, 247n44; Wilmington massacre (insurrection, coup), 115–16, 246nn25, 27; Yale University language requirement, 247n51
Briggs v. Elliott, 65, 92
Brown, John, 19–20, 23, 73
Brown, Roscoe C., 25, 29; and National Association of Colored Women, 25
Brown v. Board of Education of Topeka (1954), 65, 72, 128, 175, 186, 219, 221; and American Federation of Teachers, 220–21; Florence C. Bryant, 149, 155–56, 162, 164; Mary F. Burks, 177; Kenneth B. Clark, 167; Mamie P. Clark, 167; Lenora Condoll, 144; inherent inferiority, 59–60; intellectual activism, 5; job security among Black teachers, 6, 91–92, 149; Louisiana, 126–29; North Carolina, 52, 54, 92, 105; Lois A. Simms, 70, 75; Ernest Thompson, 70; Virginia, 53, 149, 156–57
Brown v. Board of Education of Topeka (1955), 65, 220
Bryant, Florence C., 10, 148–65, 252n2; awards and recognitions, 153; Black History Week, 159; *Brown v. Board of Education of Topeka,* 149, 156, 157, 164; Buford Junior High School, 157; Charlottesville High School, 148, 160–63;

Bryant, Florence C. (*continued*)
  Louise B. Carter, 152–53; church affiliation,
  150–51; Delta Sigma Theta Sorority, Incorporated, 153; desegregation, 149–50, 155, 157–60,
  162–64; educational philosophies and pedagogical techniques, 153–57, 159–60; family,
  150, 159–60, 163; Maude Gamble, 154; Mary
  L. Hunter, 157; Virginia S. Jackson, 152; Jack-
  son P. Burley High School, 148–49, 155–56;
  Jefferson School, or Jefferson Elementary
  School, 148, 153–54, 157, 164; Jefferson High
  School, 148, 153–55; Lane High School, 157,
  159–60, 165; Chester A. Lindsay, 150–51;
  Douglas MacArthur, 156–57; *Memoirs of
  a Country Girl*, 162; *A Nation at Risk*, 148;
  Negro History Week, 154; *One Story About
  School Desegregation*, 164; "The People's
  Pulpit," 153; *Rebecca Fuller McGinness, A
  Lifetime*, 163; resegregation, 163; Walter
  Ridley, 157; *The Road to Brown*, 162; Alexan-
  dria Searls, 164; St. John Elementary School,
  151; Gregory Swanson, 157; Union High
  School, 148, 151–53; University of Virginia,
  149, 156–57, 160; Venable Elementary School,
  157, 159; Virginia State College, 153; *Virginia
  Statesman*, 153; Virginia State University,
  148, 154; Virginia Way, 149; Walker Junior
  High School, 157–58; as public intellectual,
  162, 164
Buras, Kristen L., 10, 126–47, 277–78; and oral
  history, 249n6
Burks, Mary F., 170, 177–80, 185, 260n104
Busch, Yvonne, 126, 127, 129, 139–42, *141*,
  146, 147; and Albert Wicker School, 139;
  awards, 140; Booker T. Washington High
  School, 140; Craig Elementary School, 140;
  T. LeRoy Davis, 139; George Washington
  Carver Senior High School, 139, 140–42;
  Gilbert Academy, 139; Joseph Clark Senior
  High School, 140; Joseph Craig Elementary
  School, 139; *A Legend in the Classroom*, 141;
  Louisiana Weekly, 140; McDonogh No. 41
  Junior High School, 140; notable students,
  140; Piney Woods Country Life School, 139;
  James C. Polite, 139; Herlin Riley on, 140–41;
  Leonard Smith on, 141; Southern University,
  139–40; Tristate Music Festival, 139; upbring-
  ing, 139; VanderCook College of Music, 140

Cale, Hugh, 112, *113*
Carmichael, Stokely S. C., 83, 85–86, 198, 200
Cheyney Institute, 27, 29

Civil War, 21, 207; and Black educational
  opportunities in prewar and postwar Missouri, 188; Black postwar advancements and
  school-building processes, 1, 3, 23, 253n9;
  Black Unionism, 130, 188; Black wartime
  schooling in Virginia, 151, 153; Henry
  Cofield, 94; competing textbook ideologies
  during wartime, 21; curricular violence, 37;
  Charlotte L. B. F. Grimké, 19–21; Charles
  Hatfield, 130; Montgomery, Alabama, as
  Confederate capital, 170; prewar population
  in Charleston, South Carolina, 57; prewar
  population in Columbia, Missouri, 192;
  postwar Black prosperity in Columbia, 195;
  postwar population in North Carolina, 42
Clark, Kenneth B., 5, 65, 167
Clark, Mamie P., 5, 65, 167
Clark, Septima P., 3–4, 57–58, 62; and civil
  rights-based activism, 4
Clemson University, 48, 50; and desegregation,
  48, 50; Harvey B. Gantt, 48, 50
Cofield, Mae, 94–95
Cofield, Thomas, 94–95, 103
Congress of Racial Equality (CORE), 190–91;
  and Freedom Rides, 43
Crisis, The, 26, 28, 95, 172, 217
Critical race theory, 1, 220; and Ketanji B. Jack-
  son, 220; Glenn Youngkin, 220
Cromwell, John W., 29, 30; and *The Negro in
  American History*, 30
Culturally relevant education (pedagogy, teach-
  ing), 5, 40, 55, 59, 221
Curricular violence, 7–8, 15–38; and Woodson,
  Carter G., 17. *See also* Givens, Jarvis R.; Jim
  Crow

Davis, Angela Y., 85, 199–200
Davis, Joe, 201, 203
Desegregation, 2, 7, 57–58, 74–75, 162–63, 191;
  and Alabama, 41, 51, 182; American Federa-
  tion of Teachers, 220–21; Ross R. Barnett,
  49–50; *Boynton v. Virginia*, 189–90; *Brown v.
  Board of Education of Topeka* (1954), 91–92,
  126, 128, 149, 157, 167; *Brown v. Board of
  Education of Topeka* (1955), 149, 157, 220–21;
  CORE, 43; James Farmer Jr., 43; Harvey
  B. Gantt, 50; Georgia, 41; *Green v. County
  School Board of New Kent County*, 53; John F.
  Kennedy, 49; Louisiana, 10, 126, 128–29, 138;
  James Meredith, 49–50; Mississippi, 59–50,
  72; Missouri, 11, 194–95; National Education
  Association, 220–21; North Carolina, 9, 39,

52–56, 93, 97–102, 105, 108; resegregation,
163; Sonya Ramsey, 41; South Carolina, 8,
41–42, 47–51, 56, 72–73; Southern Conference Educational Fund, 102–3; *Swann v. the
Charlotte-Mecklenburg Board of Education,* 52–54; Virginia, 10, 72, 148–51, 153–57,
159–60, 162–65; and George C. Wallace Jr., 51
Dewey, John, 40, 61, 63–62, 63, 226n20
Douglass, Frederick, A. W. B., Sr., 19; and birth-
day commemoration, 29; Peter W. Moore,
121; reverence for, 35; struggle as a precursor
of progress, 111; use of photography and
literature, 21; as hero, 24
Du Bois, William E. B., 3–4, 30, 44–45, 205–18;
and American Negro Academy, 28; antisemi-
tism, 213, 215; autonomous Black communities in North Carolina and Virginia, 44;
Thomas H. Bender on, 206–7, 217; Otto von
Bismarck, 208; *Black Reconstruction,* 32; civil
rights-based activism, 4; *Crisis* editorship,
28, 217; familial background, 208; federal
model of government, 206; Fisk University,
208; Charles G. Gomillion, 172; Harvard
University, 208, 210, 211, 213, 214; Albert B.
Hart, 208, 214; Rutherford B. Hayes, 210,
266n17; Humboldt University in Berlin,
Germany, 205, 210, 211; William Ingersoll,
215, 268n33; intellectual genesis, 3, 206, 213,
218; John F. Slater Fund, 210; Kaiserreich,
213–15; Marxism, 205, 214–15; National Association for the Advancement of Colored
People (NAACP), 205, 206, 215, 217; Niagara
movement, 217; pedagogical activism, 206;
The Philadelphia Negro, 211, 216, 218; "The
Present Condition of German Politics," 213,
218; race as a central focus of discourse,
62, 205–6, 208–9, 211–13, 215; Gustav F.
Schmoller, 210; significance of Black history,
45; Social Democratic Party, 214; *The Souls of
Black Folk,* 205, 211, 217, 218; talented tenth,
61, 217; transnationalism, 205–18; Heinrich
von Treitschke, 206, 210, 211–13, 216–18;
University of Berlin, 11, 205–18; University of
Pennsylvania, 215–16; *Verein für Sozialpolitik*
(German Economic Association), 211, 213;
Booker T. Washington, 125, 172, 176, 209,
215; as pan-Africanist, 205; public intellectual, 62, 164, 205–6, 218; sociologist, 205–6,
208, 209, 215, 217–18. *See also* Ganaway,
Bryan
Dunbar, Paul L., 24, 68, 70; and eponymous
school in Washington, DC, 30–31

East Carolina University, 111, 117; as East
Carolina Teacher Training School, 117, 125
Education of Blacks in the South, 1860–1935, The
(Anderson), 121
Elizabeth City State Colored Normal School, 9,
111–14, 118–25; and Hugh Cale, 112; consoli-
dation crises, 118–19, 120–24; distinguished
alumni, 125; W. E. B. Du Bois, 125; Freed-
men's Bureau, 122; funding disparities,
111–12; House Bill 691, 114; John B. (J. Bryan)
Grimes, 120; industrial education, 112, 117,
119–21, 124; Peter W. Moore, 112; Populist-
Republican fusion, 114–15; Ella Y. Preyer, 122;
Robert Preyer, 122; Negro History Week, 125;
Tuskegee Institute, 119; Booker T. Washington, 119, 125; White supremacy movement,
115–18, 124; Mary Yost, 122; William Yost, 122.
See also Elizabeth City State University
Elizabeth City State University, 111, 113, 245n1,
246n25, 247n43. *See also* Elizabeth City State
Colored Normal School
Emancipation, 18–19; and W. E. B. Du Bois on,
32; fiftieth anniversary of, 29; permanent
proclamation of Abraham Lincoln, 168; post-
emancipation narrative condemnation, 21;
pre-emancipation revolutionaries, 23; White
resistance to, 38; Richard R. Wright, 23

Fairclough, Adam, 6, 62, 149, 168, 235n20
Farmer, Genevieve, M., 8, 76–81, 83–84, 87–90;
and Carroll Junior High School, 77; Carnage
Junior High School, 77; Daniels Junior High
School, 77; Garner Senior High School, 77;
Hampton Institute, 77, 80, 83, 87; indirect
student activism, 87; integration, 80; intel-
lectual activism, or resistance, 88; Kingstree,
South Carolina, 79, 81; music as educational
tool, 83–84; North Carolina Central College,
77; parental influences, 81–82; Tomlinson
School, 79; Washington School, 77
Farmer, James L., Jr., 43; and CORE, 43
Fauset, Jessie R., 26, 27, 29, 30
Favors, Jelani M., 45, 180, 204
Fisk University, 11, 62, 172, 208
Franklin, John H., 5, 34, 65
Franklin, Vincent P., 3, 40; and young
crusaders, 40
Frazier, Edward F. (E. Franklin), 166, 167
Fultz, Michael, 3, 149

Gaines, Lloyd L., 188, 189, 204. *See also*
Missouri ex rel. Gaines v. Canada

Ganaway, Bryan, 11, 278; on Derrick P. Alridge, 216; American studies, 206–7; Thomas H. Bender, 206–7; Otto von Bismarck, 208, 211–13; Ludwig J. (Lujo) Brentano, 210; George W. Bush, 207; Charles R. Darwin, 209, 211; W. E. B. Du Bois, 205–18; eugenics, 209; Shelley F. Fishkin, 207; Frances Galton, 209; German imperialism, 206, 210, 212, 217–18, 278; *Hausarbeiter* (piece workers), 211; Hohenzollern dynasty, 210; Iraq, 207; William James, 208, 216; *Leitkultur* (dominant culture), 212; nationalism, or nationhood, 206, 208, 210–17; Aihwa Ong, 206; Eugene F. Provenzo Jr., 216; Prussian military, 210; Gustav F. Schmoller, 210, 213; 215; September 11, 2001, 207; social Darwinism, 209; Social Democratic Party, 210, 214; Werner Sombart, 210–11; David Thelen, 206–7; transnationalism, 205–18; Heinrich von Treitschke, 206, 210, 211–13, 215–17, 265n3; Frederick J. Turner, 207; *Verein für Sozialpolitik* (German Economic Association), 210–11, 213, 217; Booker T. Washington, 209, 215–17; Maximilian K. E. (Max) Weber, 210; Wilhelm, or William, II (né Friedrich W. V. Albert), 213

Gantt, Harvey B., 48, 50

Garry, Vanessa, 10, 187–204, 278

Gautt, Prentice, 192, 201–2

George Washington Carver Senior High School, 10, 126–30, 132–34, 136–43, 145–47, 249n6; and Black power, 127; Yvonne Busch, 126–27, 129, 139–42, 141, 146–47; civic, political, and social consciousness, 127, 130, 134, 142–43, 146; Desire Housing Project, 129; Lenora C. Gray, 127, 142; Charles J. Hatfield, 126–27, 129–34, 137, 139–40, 146; Enos Hicks, Sr., 126–27, 129, 136–40, 136, 146; intergenerational networking, 130; self-determination, 10, 126–27, 130, 135, 143; Lamar Smith Sr., 127, 129, 133–37, 137, 140, 146; Leonard Smith, 126, 141; as Negro school, 128

Givens, Jarvis R., 7–8, 15–38, 112–13; and anti-Black curricular violence, 17–18; Black intellectualism, 18–20, 22, 24, 28, 32; William W. Brown, 227n13; chattel principle, 18, 19, 227n11; Walter Johnson, 227n7; James W. C. Pennington, 18–19, 227n14; Benjamin A. Quarles, 20; scripts of knowledge, 16, 19, 25–26, 28, 34, 37; on Paul Gilroy, 22n7; Stuart M. P. Hall, 227n7

Gomillion, Charles G., 170, 171–74, 175–76, 185, 259n63; and Ralph D. Abernathy Sr., 175; Alabama State College, 175; boycotting, 174; civic democracy, 173–74; Crusade for Citizenship, 174; Alonzo J. Davis Sr., 173; W. E. B. Du Bois, 172; Samuel M. Engelhardt Jr., 174–75; family, 171–72; Federal Bureau of Investigation, 175–76; Fisk University, 172; *Gomillion v. Lightfoot*, 171, 174–75; Jessie P. Guzman, 174; Howard University, 175; Charles S. Johnson, 172; James A. Johnson, 173; Lewis W. Jones, 175; *Journal of Negro Education*, 173; Martin L. King Jr., 171, 175, 185, 259n63; Morehouse College, 175; Negro History Week, 174; James H. Owens, 175; Paine College, 171–72; Frederick D. Patterson, 176; Hollis F. Price, 173; purported communist ties, 175; selective buying, 174; Frederick L. Shuttlesworth, 175; Frank J. Toland Sr., 174; Tuskegee Civic Association, 173–75, 183; Tuskegee Institute, 172–73; Tuskegee Institute Federal Credit Union, 173; Tuskegee Men's Club, 172–73; voting, 173–75; Monroe N. Work, 172; on Booker T. Washington, 172

Gray, Fred D., Sr., 177, 178

Gray, Lenora C., 127, 142–45, 145, 146; and awards and recognitions, 143–44; Close Up program, 143–44; educational philosophy and pedagogy, 142–44; family, 142; fundraising, 143; George Washington Carver Senior High School, 142–43; McDonogh No. 35, 142; Southern University, 142

Greene, Lorenzo J., 34–35

Grimké, Angelina W., 74

Grimké, Charlotte L. B. F., 19–21; and John Brown, 19–20

Hale, Jon N., ix, 1–11, 57–75, 219–22, 278–79; on Jonna Perillo, 234n8; Southern White state lawmakers subsidizing the out-of-state graduate and professional learning of non-White students, 235n20; Clinton I. Young, 235n20

Hampton Institute (later University), 76, 81, 83, 87, 96–97, 151, 242n46

Hart, Albert H., 208, 214, 216, 218

Hatfield, Charles J., 126, 127, 129, 130–34, 137, 139–40, 146; and Alpha Kappa Delta National Honor Sociology Fraternity, 132; American Federation of Teachers Local 527 (later United Teachers of New Orleans),

132–33; Atlanta University, 132; collective bargaining, 132–33; familial history, 130; George Washington Carver Senior High School, 126, 127, 129–30, 132; Gilbert Academy, 130, 132; Louis Berry, 131; Great Depression, 130; Joseph Clark Senior High School, 132; Lafitte Housing Project, 130; Lake Pontchartrain, 130; Louisiana State University, 130–31; Thurgood Marshall, 131; NAACP Legal Defense and Educational Fund, 131; Marilyn Pierre on, 133; Pioneer Award, 133; Pythian Temple, 131; Southern University, 131, 133; Spelman College, 132; Alexander P. (A. P.) Tureaud Sr., 131, 132; Works Progress Administration, 130, 131; Xavier University, 131, 132

Hicks, Enos, Jr., 136, 137, 138; and McNeese State University, 138

Hicks, Enos, Sr., 126, 127, 129, 136–40, 136, 146; and athleticism, 136; awards, 136; George Washington Carver Senior High School, 136–39; Ernest Charles on, 138–39; biological family, 136, 137, 138; Herman Gray on, 138; Joseph Clark Senior High School, 136; Xavier University, 136

Historically Black colleges and universities, 7–9, 62, 76–77, 85, 88, 160, 170, 222; and Alabama, 170, 177, 185–86; Atlanta University, 47; Benedict College, 47; Cheyney Institute, 27; Chicago State University, 204; Elizabeth City State University, 111; faculty recruitment to predominantly White institutions, 191, 200; Howard University, 62, 143, 175; Johnson C. Smith University, 45; Kittrell College, 231n34; Morehouse College, 62, 175; North Carolina, 46; Paine College, 171; South Carolina, 45, 47, 69; South Carolina State College, 69; South Carolina State University, 232n64; student demonstrations, 190; Tougaloo College, 62; Virginia, 151; Xavier University, 131

Hollings, Ernest F. (Fritz) Hollings, 49–50; and Edgar Brown, 50; desegregation of Clemson University, 50; Robert C. Edwards, 50; Marion Gressette, 50; Robert F. Kennedy, 50

Holt, Hunter, 8, 76–90, 279; and educators as civil rights activists, 241n35; experienced freedom, 240n12; freedom spaces, 240nn5, 12; Robin D. G. Kelley, 240n12; Teachers in the Movement, 240n7, 279; on David G. Garcia, 240n5; Carter J. Savage, 240n5

Hurt, Delores J., 48, 52

Hyres, Alexander, 10, 148–65, 279; on Black activism, organizing, and Jim Crow in Virginia, 253n7; Black high schools in the South, 254n11; Black public intellectuals and progressivism, 255n44; bigotry, Thomas Jefferson, and the University of Virginia, 252n3; equalization in the South, 254n18; heritages of Black educators, 255n44; high schools as mass institutions, 254n15

Industrial education, 121, 124, 237n51; and Alabama, 129; W. E. B. Du Bois, 216; North Carolina, 9, 112, 117, 119–21, 124

Intellectual activism, 2, 4–5, 7, 9–11, 65, 88, 220. See also pedagogical activism

Isaac-Savage, E. Paulette, 10, 187–204, 279

Jim Crow, 10–11, 43, 65–67, 84, 220, 222; and Alabama, 171–72, 176–77, 181, 183; Carter G. Woodson, 16–17; curricular violence and race, 17–18, 37, 222; historically Black colleges and universities, 45; legal challenges, 64–65; Louisiana, 127–28; Missouri, 187–91, 195, 201; NAACP, 64; nadir, 3; participatory democracy, 3; religiosity, 44; socioeconomic class, 168–69; South Carolina, 39–40, 42–43; teaching demands, 16, 25–26, 57–58, 63, 67, 75–78, 127–28; Tennessee, 208; Virginia, 148, 150–51, 162

Johnson, Alexis M., 8, 39–56, 279–80; and University of Virginia Teachers in the Movement Project, 41–42

Johnson C. Smith University, 39, 43, 45–47, 69, 75

Johnson, Reed, 97, 99, 100, 103. See also Johnson, Willa C.

Johnson, Willa C., 91, 93; and American Missionary Association, 95; Black Women's History Conference and Women in Conversation, 107; Brick Rural Life School, 97; The Brick School Legacy, 107; Brick Tri-County High School, 95–96; Wade Bruton, 105; civil rights activity, 91, 93–94, 97–109; civil rights education, 97–100; Eva M. Clayton, 108–9; collective action, 96; Eastman High School, 96, 97, 101; Enfield Colored Graded School, 95; familial background and influence, 94–95, 97–98, 103–4, 106; flower cultivation, 94, 97, 102; Halifax Voters Movement, 102–6; Hampton Institute, 96, 97; Phillip Hirschkop,

Johnson, Willa C. (*continued*)
105; housing campaign, 107; Inborden
Elementary School, 97; insubordination,
91, 104–5; Esther M. Jackson, 96; Reed
Johnson, 97, 99, 100, 103; Joseph Keasby
Brick Agricultural, Industrial, and Normal
School (later Brick Junior College), 95–96;
Ku Klux Klan, 105–6; William Kunstler, 104,
105; John D. Larkins Jr., 104, 106; Louise
Lassiter, 98; March on Washington for Jobs
and Freedom, 100; Floyd B. McKissick,
99; Dan Moore, 105; Macon Moore, 106;
National Education Association, 106;
National Honor Society, 91; National Seeking
Educational Equity and Diversity (SEED)
Project, 107; New Jersey Department of
Education, 107; *The Nine O'Clock Whistle*,
107; North Carolina College, 98; North
Carolina Fund, 107; William Overman, 102;
pedagogical activism and system, 93, 95,
96–100; Phillips High School, 96; Jay S. (J.
Saunders) Redding, 96; Rutgers University,
107; John R. Salter Jr., 102–3, 105; Lillie C.
Smith, 101–2; Southern Christian Leadership
Conference, 106; Southern Conference
Educational Fund, 102–3; student activism,
91, 96, 98–101; F. C. Sykes, 101; T. S. Inborden
High School, 91, 96, 97, 98–99, 103–5; voting,
97–98, 102–5; Luther Williams, 91, 97, 99,
101–2, 104, 106
Joseph Clark Senior High School, 132–33, 136,
138, 140, 144
Journal of African American History, 57, 277,
279, 280
Journal of Negro History, 30, 33
Joyner, James Y., 119, 120, 121, 122, 123–24,
247n45

Kennedy, John F., 49–50, 54, 103
King, Coretta S., 88, 185
King, Martin L., Jr., 83, 85, 169, 185, 221, 257–
58n28; and American Psychological Associa-
tion address (1967), 10, 166–67; Birmingham,
Alabama, selective buying campaign, 182–83;
Mary F. Burks, 177, 179, 185; Kenneth B.
Clark, 167; Mamie P. Clark, 167; Charles G.
Gomillion, 171, 175, 185, 259n63; militant-
middle strategy, 166, 185; Montgomery
Improvement Association, 178; Bishop L. H.
(Lucius) Pitts Sr., 182; Lawrence D. Reddick,
185; Frederick D. Reese, 184–85; Jo Ann G.

Robinson, 179, 185; Fred L. Shuttlesworth,
182–83; threefold social scientist foci, 166–67,
171; Harper C. Trenholm Sr., 178–80, 185; as
civil rights pioneer versus torchbearer, 177
Kunstler, William M., 104, 105; and Center for
Constitutional Rights, 105; Halifax Voters
Movement, 104–5; Phillip Hirschkop, 105

Larkins, John D., Jr., 104, 106
Lewis, John R., 43, 46
Loder-Jackson, Tondra L., 1–11, 40, 65, 166–86,
219–22, 280; on 1965 Voting Rights Act,
171; Ralph D. Abernathy Sr., 175; Alabama
Christian Movement for Human Rights, 181;
Alabama State College (later University),
170, 175, 177; Alabama State Teachers Association, 170, 179, 180, 184; James Baldwin,
167; Birmingham, Alabama, 166, 169–70;
Black mayors, 170; Bloody Sunday (March 7,
1965), 184; *Browder v. Gayle*, 260n88; *Brown
v. Board of Education of Topeka*, 167, 175, 177,
186; Mary F. Burks, 170, 177–80, 260n104;
George W. Carver, 176; Children's March
(1963), 166, 180; civic democracy, 173–74;
James G. (Jim) Clark, 184; Kenneth B. Clark,
167; Mamie P. Clark, 167; Patricia H. Collins,
257n26; Claudette Colvin (née Austin), 178,
260n88; Theophilus E. (Bull) Connor, 168,
183; Crusade for Citizenship, 174; Alonzo J.
Davis Sr., 173; Evelyn Dilworth-Williams,
167; John Dittmer, 168; W. E. B. Du Bois,
172, 176; educators as civil rights activists,
166–86; Samuel M. Engelhardt Jr., 174–75;
Equal Justice Initiative Legacy Museum, 168;
Glen Eskew, 168; Federal Bureau of Investigation, 175–76; fear narratives, 168, 180; Lillie
Fincher, 182; Fisk University, 172; Luther H.
Foster, 176; Edward F. (E. Franklin) Frazier,
166, 167; Annetta S. Gary, 181; Frank Dukes,
183; Charles G. Gomillion, 170–76; *Gomillion
v. Lightfoot*, 171, 174–75; Fred D. Gray Sr., 177,
178; Jessie P. Guzman, 174; Lola Hendricks,
182; Howard University, 175; Lawrence Huggins, 184; interdisciplinarity, 256n10; Kelly
Ingram Park, 168, 183; Vernon Johns, 177;
Charles S. Johnson, 172; James A. Johnson,
173; Robert C. Johnson, 180; Lewis W. Jones,
175; *Journal of Negro Education*, 173; Coretta
S. King, 185; Martin L. King Jr., 166–67,
169, 171, 177, 179–80, 182–83, 184; Elizabeth
Lawrence, 168, *169*; Detroit Lee, 176; *Lee*

v. Macon County Board of Education, 176, 259n77; Malcolm X (Malik el-Shabazz [né Malcolm Little]), 167; Miles College, 170, 182–83; Montgomery, Alabama, 166, 167, 169–70, 184; Montgomery bus boycott, 177, 178; Montgomery Improvement Association, 178, 179; Harriette V. S. Moore, 169, 257n24; Harry T. Moore, 169, 257n24; Morehouse College, 175; Negro History Week, 174; Negro Youth City, 178; Idus A. Newby, 168; Nichelle Nichols, 257–58n28; James H. Owens, 175; Paine College, 171–72; Rosa M. Parks, 170–71, 177; Frederick D. Patterson, 176; John M. Patterson, 179–80; Gwendolyn M. Patton, 176; Bishop L. H. (Lucius) Pitts Sr., 170, 182–83; *Plessy v. Ferguson,* 177; Hollis F. Price, 173; National Education Association, 184; Project Confrontation, 183; Lawrence D. Reddick, 170, 179; Carlton Reese, 181; Frederick D. Reese, 170, 177, 183–85; Bruce B. Robey, 181; Lucinda B. Robey, 170, 180–82; Jo Ann G. Robinson, 170, 177, 178–80, 260n104; selective buying, 174, 182; Selma, Alabama, 166, 167, 169–70, 184–85; Selma-to-Montgomery march, 184, (Bloody Sunday), 185; Selma Teachers march, 184, 185, 261n137; Selma University, 170; schoolhouse activism, ix, 8, 40; Frederick L. Shuttlesworth, 175, 181–82, 183, 184; social history, 256n10; Southern Christian Leadership Conference, 175, 181, 182–83; Frank J. Toland Sr., 174; Harper C. Trenholm Sr., 178–80; Portia L. Trenholm, 178; Tuskegee, Alabama, 167, 169–70, 258n34; Tuskegee Civic Association, 173–76; Tuskegee Institute (later University), 170–76; Tuskegee Institute Advancement League, 176; Tuskegee Institute Federal Credit Union, 173; Tuskegee Men's Club, 172–73; Veterans Administration Hospital, 171, 175; Norman W. Walton, 179; Booker T. Washington, 171, 172, 176; Tara Y. White, 259–60n80; Women's Human Relations Council, 178; Women's Political Council, 177–78, 180, 259–60n80; Monroe N. Work, 172; Samuel L. Younge Jr., 176. *See also* Schoolhouse Activists: African American Educators and the Long Birmingham Civil Rights Movement (Loder-Jackson)

Louverture (or L'Ouverture), Toussaint (né François Dominique Toussaint), 20, 21, 27

Long civil rights movement, ix, 1–3

Mackey, Arnetta G., 48, 52
Malcolm X (Malik el-Shabazz [né Malcolm Little]), 83, 85, 167
March on Washington for Jobs and Freedom, 100, 101
Mays, Benjamin E., 3–4, 24–25, 62, 228n32; and civil rights-based activism, 4; Benjamin R. Tillman, 24
McCullum, Kristan, 8, 76–90, 240n12, 280; and educators as civil rights activists, 241n35; freedom spaces, 240nn5, 12; Robin D. G. Kelley, 240n12; Teachers in the Movement, 240n7, 280; on David G. Garcia, 240n5; Carter J. Savage, 240n5
Miles College, 7, 170, 182–83, 256n13
Mis-Education of the Negro, The (Woodson), 15, 113
Missouri ex rel. Gaines v. Canada, 11, 188–89. *See also* Gaines, Lloyd L.
Moore, Peter W., 112–15, *114, 116,* 119, 121–25; and administrative building honoring Moore, 249n74; Edward A. Johnson, 112–13; general educational philosophy, 112–13; legal woes, 248n65; Ku Klux Klan violence, 112; *A School History of the Negro Race in America,* 112; Shaw University, 112; Slater School, 115; Booker T. Washington, 119, 121, 124; George H. White, 113; White people's praise, 247n45

Nadir, 3, 23
National Association for the Advancement of Colored People (NAACP), 3, 4; and desegregation, 6; W. E. B. Du Bois, 11, 205
National Association of Teachers in Colored Schools, 34, 35, 66; and American Teachers Association, 35, 182
Negro History Bulletin, 34, 37, 180; and Albert N. D. Brooks's advocacy, 37
Negro History Week, 5, 29, 31, 33, 125; and Florence C. Bryant, 154, 165; W. E. B. Du Bois, 32, 125; Tuskegee Civic Association, 174
North Carolina Agricultural and Technical College, or North Carolina Agricultural and Technical State College, 44, 46; and 1960 student sit-in campaign, 76, 85, 190; as Agricultural and Mechanical College for the Colored Race, 114

North Carolina Central College (later University), 77, 85

Orality, 2–3, 41, 223n4

Parks, Rosa M., 170–71, 177–78, 221, 260n88
Paul, Muriel, 201, 203
Pedagogical activism, ix, 2, 4–5, 7–11, 39–41, 221; and Florence C. Bryant, 165; W. E. B. Du Bois, 206; Willa C. Johnson, 93; Lois A. Simms, 57–75; Arvarh E. Strickland, 187, 193–94, 196–98, 203. *See also* intellectual activism
Pendleton, Leila A., 26–27, 29; and *A Narrative of the Negro*, 26; Harriet Tubman, 27; Sojourner Truth, 27; Denmark Vesey, 27
Pennington, James W. C., 18–19, 227n14; and African Free School, 19; chattel principle, 18, 19; Frederick A. W. B. Douglass Sr., 19; Harriet Jacobs, 19; on Noah Webster, 19; *A Text Book on the Origins and History of the Colored People*, 19
Philadelphia Negro: A Social Study, The (Du Bois), 211, 216, 218
Pitts, Bishop L. H. (Lucius), 170, 182–83, 185
Pope, Oliver, 23, 24, 25
Practice of freedom, 8, 78, 84, 88–89; and bell hooks, 78, 88–89
Pratt, Robert A., 41, 149; and *We Shall Not Be Moved*
Predominantly White educational institutions, 11, 190–91, 202–3; and Missouri, 187, 189, 198, 200, 204

Ramsey, Sonya Y., 3, 41, 149; and *Reading, Writing, and Segregation*, 41
Reconstruction, 2–3; and James D. Anderson on, 40; Black professional networks, 4–5; *Black Reconstruction* (Du Bois), 32–33; Roscoe C. Bruce, 25; as curricular problem, 23; W. E. B. Du Bois on, 32; William A. Dunning on, 23; education policy, 68; equality, 23; intellectual and pedagogical activism, 4–5, 7; Ku Klux Klan, 42; legislative bills, 42; Benjamin E. Mays on, 24; North Carolina, 107; Oliver Pope, 23–24; post-Reconstruction nadir, 23; school-building, 3; Virginia, 153
Reese, Frederick D., 170, 177; and Alabama State Teachers Association, 184; Bloody Sunday (March 7, 1965), 184, 185; James G. (Jim) Clark, 184; Clark Elementary School, 183; Courageous Eight, 185; Dallas County

Voters League, 183; Lawrence Huggins, 184; Coretta S. King, 185; Martin L. King Jr., 184, 185; Montgomery, Alabama, bus boycott, 183; National Education Association, 184; R. B. Hudson High School, 184; Selma City Teachers Association, 183, 184; Selma Teachers march, 184, 185; Selma-to-Montgomery march, 184 (Bloody Sunday), 185; voting, 183–85; on Martin L. King Jr., 184
Revis, Delores, 8, 76–81, 83–84, 87–90; and Brentwood Elementary School, 77; Crosby Sixth Grade Center, 77; Duke University, 77; integration, 80; intellectual activism, or resistance, 88; J. W. Ligon Jr.-Sr. High School, 77; J. W. York Elementary School, 77; Jesse L. Jackson Sr., 88; Coretta S. King, 88; Kingswood Middle School, 77; M. E. Phillips High School, 77; Needham B. Broughton High School, 77; rearing community, 78–79; Saint Augustine's College, 77, 79; student activism, 87–88; W. B. Wicker High School, 77
Riley, Herlin, 140–41, 145
Robertson, William E. (Gene), 201, 203
Robey, Lucinda B., 170, 180–82, 185
Robinson, Jo Ann G., 170, 177–80, 185, 260n104
Rock Hill, South Carolina, 8, 56, 231n16; and civil rights, 42, 44, 231n16; Cecil Ivory, 42; CORE, 43; Freedom Rides, 43; Friendship Junior College Nine, 42–43; Jim and Jane Crowism, 39, 42; John R. Lewis, 43; William Massey, 43; NAACP, 42; Plair family heritage, 43–44, 51; as progressive Southern town, 39, 230n2; Reconstruction population changes, 42; Cynthia P. Roddey, 8, 39; student activism, 42–43; Student Nonviolent Coordinating Committee, 43; Winthrop College (and later University), 39, 48
Roddey, Cynthia P., 4, 8, 39–56; and Atlanta University, 47; Benedict College, 47; Black power movement, 54; Black studies, or campus, submovement, 54–55; Charlotte-Mecklenburg, North Carolina, public school system, 52, 53; Clinton College, 56; culturally relevant pedagogy, 55; Delta Sigma Theta Sorority, Incorporated, 56; Ebony Forum, 55; Emmett Scott High School, 47, 231n20; Arnetta Gladden, 52; Greensboro, North Carolina, educational opportunities, 44–45; educational philosophies, 44–45, 53–56; Delores Johnson, 52; Fritz Hollings, 49; Delores Johnson Hurt, 48; Johnson C.

Smith University, 45–46; Lancaster, South Carolina, 53; Sue F. Meriwether, 52; Arnetta G. Mackey, 48; Mid-Atlantic Theological Seminary, 56; music, 43, 44; Olympic High School, 53–54; Plair family heritage, 43–44, 51; Pentecostalism, 44; Louise Reinhart, 48; John T. Roddey, 48–49; Sue F. M. Steed, 48; teaching tolerance, 54; William Witherspoon, 47; Winthrop College, 39, 41, 47–52, 56

Sanders, Crystal R., 9, 91–110, 280; and Black activist educator terminations, 242–43n2; Black newspaper subscriptions, 243n18; ethnic terminology, 243n3; North Carolina Black Belt, 243n15; North Carolina and civil rights scholarship, 243n11; North Carolina Fund, 107, 244–45n77; Southern Conference Educational Fund, 102–3, 244n55; Voter Education Project, 103, 244n59

Schmoller, Gustav F., 210–11, 213, 215, 217, 218, 267n22

Schomburg, Arturo A., 27–29; and American Negro Academy, 28; Black Renaissance, 27; on Crispus Attucks, 28; "Racial Integrity," 27, 28, 29

Schoolhouse Activists: African American Educators and the Long Birmingham Civil Rights Movement (Loder-Jackson), ix, 40

Segregation, 2–3, 5–6, 57–59, 66, 220, 222; and Alabama, 171, 174, 176–77, 182–84; Black professional women, 61; corrective curricula, 65–66; W. E. B. Du Bois, 44; Harvey B. Gantt, 50; historically Black colleges and universities, 85, 88; legal system, 17–18; Louisiana, 129–30; Missouri, 188; North Carolina, 8–9, 44, 76–77, 91; resegregation, 163; social policy, 18; South Carolina, 8, 43, 50, 60, 70–71; Larry Talbot, 69; teacher education and Black progressivism, 63; teacher salary equalization, 65; Tennessee, 11; Virginia, 44, 160, 162, 165. *See also* Valued segregated space

Shaw University, 46, 76, 88, 112

Shuttlesworth, Frederick L., 175, 181–82, 183, 184, 185

Simms, Lois A., 4, 8, 57–75; and 1868 South Carolina Constitution, 61; 1969 hospital strike in Charleston, South Carolina, 71; *Alexander v. Holmes County Board of Education*, 72; American Missionary Association, 61; Avery Normal Institute,

60–61, 64, 67–68, 75, 236n37, 237n52; Association for the Study of African American Life and History, 75; Avery Research Center for African American History and Culture, 75; *Bantam* student newspaper, 73; Barber-Scotia Junior College, 61, 69, 75; Black Lives Matter, 75; *Brown v. Board of Education of Topeka*, 70; Burke High School, 58, 60, 65, 67–72, 237n50; *A Chalk and Chalkboard Career in Carolina*, 70, 75; Charleston High School, 58, 73; community engagement, 66; Frank A. DeCosta, 64–65; John Dewey, 61; *Duvall v. J. F. Seignous et al.*, 58, 65, 233n2; educational progressivism, 61–63; ethnic equality, 63–64; feminization of teaching, 58; *Green v. County School Board*, 72; Angelina W. Grimké, 74–75; *Growing Up Presbyterian*, 60, 75; Howard University, 54, 61, 63–64, 75; indirect civil rights activity, 66, 71, 72; Johnson C. Smith University, 61, 75; *Journal of Negro History*, 64; lifelong learning, 73; long freedom struggle, 59; John Milton, 52, 73; National Education Association, 62; National Teacher Examination, 73; Palmetto Education Association, 62; pedagogy and philosophy, 59, 68–69; Presbyterianism, ix, 4, 60, 75; *Profiles of African-American Females in the Low Country of South Carolina*, 75; salary equalization, 65; Syracuse University, 61; Young Women's Christian Association, 61

Smith, Lamar, Sr., 127, 129, 133–37, 137, 140, 146; and awards and recognitions, 135; family, 135; George Washington Carver Senior High School, 133–34; G. W. Carver Community School, 134; Douglass Haywood on, 135; Joseph Clark Senior High School, 133; Theron Lewis on, 134; military service, 133; NAACP, 135; religiosity, 135; Samuel Green Junior High School 133; Lamar Smith Jr. on, 135; socially conscious educating, 134; Southern Organization for Unified Leadership, 135; St. David's Holy Name Society, 135; unionism, 134; University of New Orleans, 133; Xavier University, 133

Smith, Leonard, 126, 141

Souls of Black Folk: Essays and Sketches, The (Du Bois), 205, 211, 217, 218

South Carolina State College, 25, 43, 45, 60, 69

South Carolina State University, 45, 232n64

Southern Christian Leadership Conference, 46, 76, 106, 175, 181–83, 185

Steed, Sue F. M., 48, 52

Strickland, Arvarh E., 189, 192, 193–94, 196–201, 203–4

Student Nonviolent Coordinating Committee, 43, 46, 76, 190–91, 198

Talented tenth, 61. *See also* Du Bois, William E. B.

Teacher activism, 4, 7, 9, 11, 85, 226n17, 234n7; and Alabama, 185; Florence C. Bryant, 149, 165; Willa C. Johnson, 108; Lois A. Simms, 75; South Carolina, 40

Teacher associations, 5, 66, 221, 225n12, 226nn17, 18, 234n7; and the NAACP, 65; parents, 103; professional networks, 225n12

Teacher tenure laws, 9, 92–93, 169; and Alabama, 185; continuing contracts, 92–93; desegregation, 92; Florida, 191; Missouri, 197, 199–201; NAACP, 92; New Jersey, 92; North Carolina, 92, 105; yearly employment contracts, 92

Thompson, Dorothy, 8, 76–87, 89–90; and art as educational tool, 84; Atkins Senior High School, 77, 86; Black History Week, 83; Black Parents Association (later Concerned Citizens for Education Advocacy), 82–83; Stokely S. C. Carmichael, 83, 85–86; Enloe Senior High School, 77; historically Black colleges and universities, 85, 88; intellectual activism, or resistance, 88; J. W. Ligon Jr.-Sr. High School, 77; Martin L. King Jr., 83, 85; Malcolm X (Malik el-Shabazz [né Malcolm Little]), 83, 85; National Teacher Examination and Scholastic Aptitude Test, 86–87; North Carolina Central College, 77, 85; parental influences, 82, 83, 85; student activism, 85

Trenholm, Harper C., Sr., 178–80, 185

Tubman, Harriet, 27, 35, 141

University of Missouri, 10–11, 187–204; and Black Faculty and Staff Organization, 10–11, 187, 189, 192, 196–97, 200, 202–4; Black Culture Center (later Gaines/Oldham Black Culture Center), 197, 199–200, 203, 204; Black faculty, 187–89, 191, 192–94, 196, 199–204; *Black Letter*, 189; Black staff, 187–89, 192, 197, 201–4; Black students, 187–189, 191–92, 196, 198–200, 202–4; Black studies, 189, 199; Lucile H. Bluford, 189; Horace J. (Julian) Bond, 199; George Brooks, 201; Stokely S. C. Carmichael, 200; civil rights

movement, 188–89; Walter Daniel, 201; Joe Davis, 202; Angela Y. Davis, 200; Lloyd L. Gaines, 188; Prentice Gautt, 192, 201–2; Sandra W. Gautt, 201; Jennifer Hill, 201; Barbra A. Horrell, 201; Ellis Ingram, 203; Donald Johnson, 201; *LBC Newspaper*, 189; Legion of Black Collegians, 190, 196, 197–200, 202–3; Lincoln University, 188, 190; *Missouri ex rel. Gaines v. Canada*, 188; Missouri Students Association, 200, 202; James R. Montgomery, 197; Muriel Paul, 201, 203; Office of Equal Opportunity, 192; Charles B. Ratchford, 194; William E. (Gene) Robertson, 201, 203; Joseph L. (Joe) Saupe, 196–97; John T. Scott, 201; Araminta Smith, 201; Harold Sims Jr., 201; state education laws and policies, 187–88, 195, 204; Arvarh E. Strickland, 189, 192, 193–94, 196–201, 203–4; Keener Tippin, 201; *UMOJO*, 189, 195; University of Missouri–Kansas City, 196; University of Missouri–Rolla (later Missouri University of Science and Technology), 196; University of Missouri–St. Louis, 196, 198, 278, 279; Clarence Wine, 201

University of Virginia Teachers in the Movement Project, ix–x, 8, 12, 231n12, 240n7, 277, 279–81; and experienced freedom, 240n12; primary goal, 7, 41–42; oral histories, 41

Valued segregated space, 8–9, 76–79, 90, 94

Vesey, Denmark (né Telemaque), 27, 57

Walker, Vanessa S., 3, 40, 62, 77, 95, 149–50; and valued segregated schooling, 77

Waring, Julius W., 58, 65

Washington, Booker T., 24, 176; and accommodationism, 172, 216–17; Cotton States and International Exposition address in Atlanta, Georgia, 215; W. E. B. Du Bois, 125, 172, 209, 215–17; eponymous school in New Orleans, Louisiana, 128, 140; Charles G. Gomillion on, 171–72, 176; Charles S. Johnson, 172; Benjamin E. Mays's reverence, 24; Peter W. Moore, 121, 124; Gwendolyn Patton on, 176; Emmett J. Scott, 47; Tuskegee Institute, 119, 171; as idealist, 125; old Negro, 176

Wheatley, Phillis, 20, 29, 141

White supremacy, 4, 26, 36, 168–69; and *The Birth of a Nation* (Griffith); 29–30; Willa C. Johnson, 91, 93, 105; Louisiana, 142; North Carolina, 9, 46, 92, 94, 104, 111–25; Virginia, 149, 154

Williams, Luther, 91, 97, 99, 101–2, 104, 106. *See also* Johnson, Willa C.

Wingfield, Danielle, 8, 39–56, 281; and University of Virginia Teachers in the Movement Project, 42

Winthrop College, 8, 39, 41, 47–52, 56; and desegregation, 47–52, 56. *See also* Winthrop University

Winthrop University, 4, 7, 48, 56. *See also* Winthrop College

Woodson, Carter G., 16–17, 31–32, 35–37, 66; and American Negro Academy, 28–29; Association for the Study of Negro Life and History, 29, 30, 33–35; *The Education of the Negro Prior to 1861*, 30; Jessie R. Fauset, 30; fugitive pedagogy, 40; Georgia Teachers and Education Association, 36; Lorenzo J. Greene, 34–35; William B. Hartgrove, 30; *Journal of Negro History*, 30; lynching, 17; *The Mis-Education of the Negro*, 15, 113; Missouri State Association of Negro Teachers, 34; Negro History Week, 5, 154; Thelma Perry on, 35; Pearl Schwartz, 34; significance of Black history, 45; Mary C. Terrell, 30; Harper C. Trenholm Sr., 180; as public intellectual, 62, 164

Wright, Richard R., 22–23, 28, 35–36; and American Negro Academy, 28; "The Possibilities of the Negro Teacher," 22

Wynter, Sylvia, 15, 16, 17; and anti-Black curricular violence, 17; narratively condemned status of Black people, 16; "No Humans Involved," 15; psycho-social responses, 16; Carter G. Woodson, 16, 17